INSIDERS' GUIDE® TO

ANCHORAGE AND SOUTHCENTRAL ALASKA

INCLUDING THE KENAI PENINSULA, PRINCE WILLIAM SOUND, AND DENALI NATIONAL PARK

SECOND EDITION

DEB VANASSE

INSIDERS' GUIDE®

GUILFORD, CONNECTICUT
AN IMPRINT OF THE GLOBE PEQUOT PRESS

All the information in this guidebook is subject to change. We recommend that you call ahead to obtain current information before traveling.

INSIDERS' GUIDE®

Copyright © 2007, 2009 Morris Book Publishing, LLC

Text design: Sheryl Kober
Maps: XNR Productions, Inc. © Morris Book Publishing, LLC
Layout artist: Maggie Peterson

Library of Congress Cataloging-in-Publication Data is available on file.
ISBN 978-0-7627-5071-9

Printed in the United States of America
10 9 8 7 6 5 4 3 2 1

CONTENTS

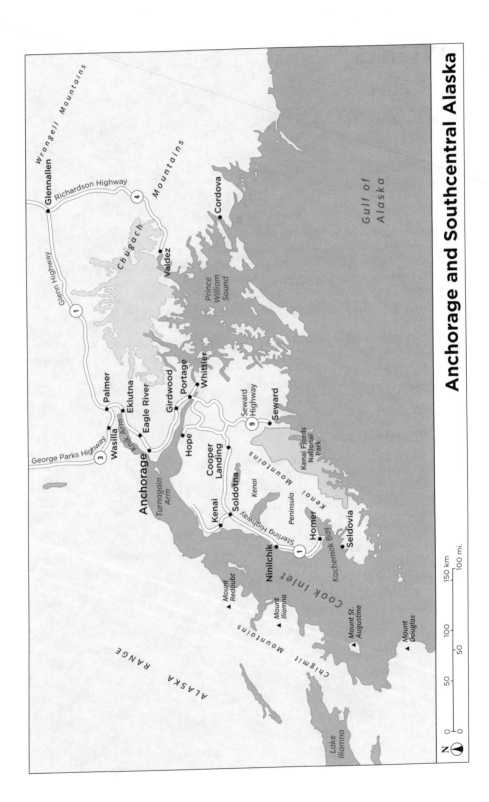

Anchorage and Southcentral Alaska

Anchorage

Downtown Anchorage

Matanuska-Susitna Valley

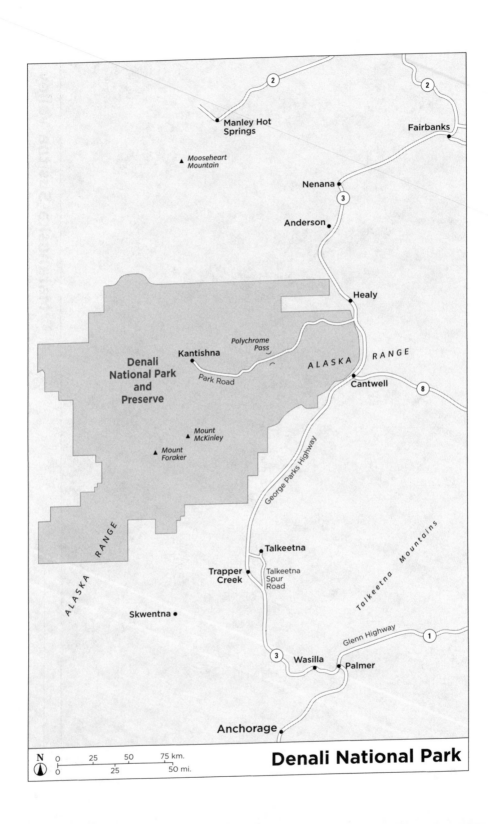

Denali National Park

PREFACE

It was nearly midnight. Sun streamed through the windows of the Hotel Captain Cook in downtown Anchorage, illuminating the cafe table where I sat with my companions. Energized by the long June day, we were in the midst of a lively discussion about Alaska's economy when one friend leapt to his feet. "Have to say hi to the governor," he announced, making his way to the door, where former governor Wally Hickel was on his way out.

That's how it is in Anchorage. Alaska's largest city is also in many ways a small town, where pretenses dissolve and people are drawn together by their love of the outdoors and the spectacular beauty of the place. Mountains rise up behind the skyline and the waters of Cook Inlet stretch along the western edge of town while lakes and creeks dot the city landscape. Head east to Prince William Sound, north to Denali National Park, or south to the Kenai Peninsula, and you'll encounter mile after mile of pristine wilderness that makes this country like no other.

It's a place that attracts rugged individualists, yet it's also a place where folks go out of their way to help each other. Native Alaskans, commercial fishermen, miners, oil company executives, construction workers, or white-collar professionals—it doesn't so much matter who you are. It's all about an independence of spirit, a sense of community, and a love of the land. It takes a certain something to call yourself an Alaskan, to know when you've moved from being a wet-behind-the ears cheechako to a real sourdough.

Expect to be delighted. Expect to be charmed. Most of all, expect the unexpected, because Anchorage and Southcentral Alaska are full of surprises, from the double rainbows that span the expansive sky after a summer shower to the blanket of snow that glitters on a moonlit night to the northern lights that dance across a December sky. There's the surprise of finding world-class entertainment at the performing arts center in downtown Anchorage, of enjoying jazz in the park on a summer evening, of strolling a top-notch museum to admire the stunning landscapes painted by artists such as Sydney Laurence. There's the delight of watching your kids grin as they encounter their first moose, reel in a big salmon, or climb aboard a dogsled for a quick ride. And there's the sense of finding yourself all over again as you hike a wilderness trail into the mountains for an unforgettable view of the ocean and valleys below.

It's not easy to pack a place so vast into the pages of a book, but we've done our best to show you all of the best that this region has to offer. We hope you'll return again and again.

ACKNOWLEDGMENTS

Alaska is a big and humbling place. I couldn't have begun to do justice to such a vast region without a lot of help. Countless shopkeepers, bartenders, waiters, and business owners took the time to give me their insiders' perspective on their hometowns and their places of business. Of particular assistance were Bryan Zak, Jeff Huffman, Leeanne Mercier, Dorothy Johnson, Dr. Karen French, Jacqui Johansen, Jill Reese, Glenda Feeken, and Sharon Minsch. Sincere thanks go also to Kirsten Dixon and Janet Shafsky, two amazing Alaskan women who graciously shared a bit of their lives with me, and to Amy Murrell and the Haunold family for all their help with the Kenai section.

To my friends, colleagues, and family goes much appreciation for putting up with my long hours, my obsession with deadlines, and my enthusiasm about all the great things I discovered along the way. A special thanks to my longtime friend Karla Gleason, who checked, double-checked, and made lots of suggestions for the Anchorage portion of the book, and to Guy (Mike) Ferency, who spent a whole lot of time driving me all over Anchorage and the Valley looking for just the right spots. You all made it good.

HOW TO USE THIS BOOK

You can experience Alaska from the comfort of a cruise ship deck or a luxurious domed railroad car, or you can grab a pack and your hiking boots and head out into the wilderness. We've made every attempt to include information that will be helpful to all sorts of travelers with plans as diverse as the state itself. Almost all area chapters include sections on how to get there, how to get around, accommodations, restaurants, shopping, attractions, hiking, camping, fishing, parks, recreation, and tours. Where applicable, chapters also include information on nightlife, kidstuff, annual events, and the arts. Throughout the book we've included Insiders' Tips, indicated by an **i** icon, which give you the sort of perspectives that come with sourdough status, the Alaskan measure of proving yourself in a place where it takes a certain degree of hardiness to get by. Our Close-up sections put you in touch with some of the fascinating people, places, events, and phenomena that make this place truly special.

If you dream of calling Alaska home, you're not alone. Never mind the long, cold winters and the top-of-the-world remoteness. There's a certain allure that draws folks here and won't let go. If your heart is calling you north, you'll want to check out our relocation section, with lots of useful information on real estate, education, child care, health care, worship, and even retirement. Our chapter on media will point you toward newspapers, magazines, and other resources to keep you in touch with all that's happening in the 49th state.

So dive in where you like, using the table of contents and the index as a guide. Use the book to plan and dream, bring it on your travels, and keep it as a handy reference on your shelf should you fall in love and decide to stay.

Welcome to the Last Great Place.

AREA OVERVIEW

Maybe you're arriving in Alaska independently or as part of a tour group. You could be traveling by plane, cruise ship, car, or RV. You might have plans to stay for a few days or for a lifetime. In any case, this book is designed to help you get your bearings and get to know this region the way those of us who love it well do. The vast landscape, the seemingly endless miles of wilderness, and the rich beauty of the Last Frontier can seem overwhelming at times. Many visitors leave feeling like they've only begun to discover all that Alaska has to offer. It's our hope that this guide will make your Alaskan experience richer, deeper, and more memorable than it would have been otherwise.

We've begun by giving you an overview of the region, followed by tips on how to get here and how to get around. From there, the book is organized geographically, beginning with Anchorage, Alaska's largest city. Subsequent chapters spin out from Anchorage the way our road system does—south to the Kenai Peninsula, north and east to Prince William Sound, and north and west to the Matanuska-Susitna (Mat-Su) Valley and Denali National Park. Though Denali is technically beyond what most folks consider to be Southcentral Alaska, it is such a key part of the Alaskan experience that we've given it full coverage in this guide. For the most part, we've focused on communities that are accessible by road or ferry, though we've also featured a number of fly-out adventures for those looking to truly get away from it all.

CLIMATE AND SEASONS

No one comes to Alaska to bask in the heat, but you may be surprised to find that Anchorage and Southcentral Alaska are quite temperate considering their proximity to the Arctic Circle. The average high temperature in January is 21 degrees Fahrenheit, which is downright balmy compared to places farther north. July is typically the warmest month, with an average high of 65 degrees Fahrenheit. Summer temperatures generally climb as you travel north toward Fairbanks, but with those higher temperatures and drier conditions come the risk of forest fires that sometimes blanket Alaska's interior with smoke. For the most part, Anchorage and Southcentral Alaska still enjoy smoke-free summers, and their maritime setting means winter temperatures stay mostly above zero. Snowfall in Anchorage is typically heaviest in December, with an average of nearly 14 inches falling during that month.

Valdez gets pummeled with an average of 27 feet of snow every winter, and Denali has its share as well, but in most of Southcentral Alaska, snowfall is about average for a northern climate.

While Alaska technically has four seasons, our spring and fall can be downright skimpy. On the highway between Anchorage and Denali, leaves will begin to turn in August, and a brief blaze of gold can be followed quickly by the first snowfall come September. Anchorage doesn't usually see significant amounts of the white stuff until late October or early November, with breakup arriving about six months later. Snow might fall in May or September, but it probably won't stick. June, July, and August are typically snow-free, except in Denali Park, where snow has fallen in every month of the year. Annual precipitation in Anchorage is close to 16 inches per year, while annual snowfall is just short of 70 inches per year.

Though Anchorage is well to the south of the Arctic Circle, the city still enjoys 24 hours of functional daylight on the summer solstice, meaning that though the sun has set, there is enough light to get by without artificial illumination. It's the tilt of the earth on its axis that creates this phenomenon, with the Northern Hemisphere tipped toward the sun in the summer and away from the sun in the winter, so that Anchorage has approximately five and a half hours of daylight on the winter solstice. In the winter, some Alaskans suffer from Seasonal Affective Disorder, or SAD, which may be the result of higher melatonin levels in the blood as daylight decreases. Indoor light boxes that mimic natural sunlight can help those who suffer from this disorder; experts also recommend supplementing vitamin D to replace what you're not getting from the sun.

i Remember your sunglasses, especially in the winter, when the sun's proximity to the horizon means it's shining right in your eyes. If you're out on the snow, shades are extra-imporant for avoiding a condition called "snow blindness."

NATURAL WONDERS

Describing natural wonders in a place that's almost synonymous with the term is tough. No matter what you read or hear about the incredible natural phenomena of Alaska, it ends up seeming like understatement when you cruise next to a calving glacier, gaze up at the northern lights leaping in the winter sky, or marvel at the beauty of mountains that press up against the sea.

When you look out across Cook Inlet, you'll see a string of volcanoes that are part of the Ring of Fire, where the Pacific tectonic plate is sliding beneath the North American plate. Approximately 10 percent of the world's active volcanoes are in Alaska. Occasionally eruptions disrupt air travel, as has been the case in recent years with Mount St. Augustine and Mount Redoubt.

The Alaska Range and the Chugach Mountains are integral to the landscape of Southcentral Alaska. The Alaska Range stretches 600 miles from the Canadian border into Southwest Alaska, creating a natural northern boundary of sorts for the Southcentral region. Mount McKinley, also called Denali, is the highest peak in the Alaska Range as well as in all of North America. The Chugach Mountains form a natural backdrop for the city of Anchorage, offering abundant recreational opportunities and spectacular vistas. Along with the Wrangell and Aleutian Ranges, these mountains cause air to dry as it rises and moves north.

With northern mountains come glaciers, and Alaska has thousands of them. As snow accumulates beyond the amount that can melt in a summer season, it crystallizes into solid ice that may build for thousands of years. The most accessible glaciers are tidewater glaciers that extend into the sea, such as Columbia Glacier in Valdez, and valley glaciers such as Portage Glacier, south of Anchorage.

Some of the forests in Southcentral Alaska, particularly those of the Kenai Peninsula, are boreal forests, which include aspen, birch, poplar, cottonwood, and white spruce. Around Cook Inlet and Prince William Sound, you'll find coastal forests, including some temperate rainforest, featuring primarily Sitka spruce. Where you see wet, treeless areas or stunted black spruce, you're probably looking at permafrost, where subsoils are frozen for two or more years. Farther north, there's continuous permafrost, while in Southcentral, the permafrost is discontinuous, meaning that it's found sporadically.

Beetle-killed spruce trees have turned parts of the Kenai Peninsula into kindling for wildfires that periodically plague the state. The year 2004 brought a record fire season as 6.4 million acres burned, though most of the activity was in Alaska's interior. Despite the annoyance of smoke and occasional road closures, most of Alaska's wildfires are allowed to burn, as they provide a natural renewal for the landscape by removing organic material that would otherwise keep soils from warming.

The northern lights, or aurora borealis, are the most famous phenomenon associated with

Alaska's skies. You won't see them in the summer when the skies stay light, but from September to March, particularly between 10 p.m. and 2 a.m., you may be lucky enough to witness one of the most spectacular light shows in all of nature. Far away on the surface of the sun, solar flares create winds that blow a stream of particles toward earth. As these winds hit the earth's magnetic shield, they create charged electrons that discharge electricity when they encounter gas particles. The result is a brilliant, dancing display of light. The most common color is green, but you also may see red when oxygen is struck at elevations of 150 miles or more, and blue or purple if nitrogen molecules are involved.

Aurora activity is most typical at 67 degrees magnetic latitude. Anchorage is at 60 degrees. So when activity is low, you'll have better luck driving north toward Denali or Fairbanks. When activity is high, you can see the aurora throughout Southcentral Alaska, although you'll need to get away from artifical lights.

Less exciting but still unique is Alaska's airglow effect, an atmospheric condition that makes our skies a little brighter and our stars a little dimmer than in most other places. During the day, you may also see sun dogs—little rainbows flanking the sun, caused by ice crystals in the air.

i **Many Alaskan newspapers feature aurora forecasts on their weather pages. You'll also find aurora forecasts at the University of Alaska-Fairbanks Geophysical Insitute Web site (www.gedds .alaska.edu/AuroraForecast/), where you can sign up for e-mail alerts. Some hotels even offer a wake-up call service when the northern lights are active.**

WILDLIFE

Uniquely adapted for life in the Far North, wildlife has free reign over Alaska's mostly uninhabited lands. Moose, with long legs that help them forge through deep snow, are among the mammals you're most likely to see. They're not shy about coming into town or crossing roadways, so you'll want to be alert for them when you're driving. Though moose are normally docile creatures, they will charge and stomp when threatened, and a cow will do just about anything to protect her calves.

Bears also frequent urban areas, so you'll want to exercise caution even when hiking on trails close to town, keeping trash in bear-proof containers and away from human habitation. In Anchorage, you can be fined from April through October for leaving out trash, pet food, or bird feeders that attract bears. Bear–human incidents have been on the rise in Anchorage in recent years due to a growing grizzly population near the Chugach Mountains, on the east side of town.

Wolves, fox, lynx, marmot, and a host of other smaller mammals are among those you may be lucky enough to see while you're here. Remember, though, that we've got a lot of land for these critters to call home. Some folks have been here for decades without spotting a wolf or a lynx in the wild. For the most predictable wildlife-viewing opportunities, try the Alaska Zoo, the Wildlife Conservation Center, or the bus ride into Denali National Park. If you'd love to see such marine mammals as sea lions, dolphins, seals, and otters, take a cruise from the coastal towns of Valdez or Seward.

i **Be wildlife savvy. Give moose a wide berth, and don't get between a cow and a calf. If a moose charges, get behind or into a tree. Bears don't like surprises, and most will go out of their way to avoid confrontations with humans. Make noise when you're in the woods, and stay away from salmon streams where bears are likely feed. Unlike moose, bears can climb and run faster than humans.**

HUMAN INHABITANTS

It's thought that the first humans came to Alaska tens of thousands of years ago via the Bering Land Bridge, following the retreating ice, though recent evidence also points to migrations across the Pacific. Eventually three distinct groups emerged. The Aleuts and Eskimos (Yupik, Cupik, and Inupiat) formed primarily coastal cultures, while several tribes of Indians settled in the Interior and Southcentral regions. The Athabascans, who are linguistically related to the Navaho and Apache of the Southwestern United States, were at one time the predominant people in Southcentral Alaska. They lived a migratory subsistence lifestyle, following food sources with spring, fall, winter, and summer fish camps. Today Alaskan Natives work hard to preserve their traditional cultures while meeting the challenges of surviving in a money-based economy.

GETTING HERE, GETTING AROUND

Part of the allure of Alaska is that it's so far from the rest of the country, a vast expanse of mostly wilderness set off by itself at the top of the world. But getting here need not be a struggle, and there are lots of ways to do it. Once you're here, there are all sorts of ways to get around. Some options, such as horseback riding, trolley tours, ATV rides, snowmobiling, and bicycle riding, are more about having fun than getting from point A to point B, so we'll discuss those in the Recreation and Attractions sections of each chapter.

BY AIR

There are plenty of nonstop flights offered by major air carriers from such cities as Seattle, Los Angeles, Minneapolis, Denver, Chicago, and Salt Lake City, especially in the summer when tourists come and go in droves. Thanks to a major renovation, the Ted Stevens International Airport in Anchorage now offers a stunning point of entry for visitors, with gleaming marble floors and walls of windows opening up to striking views. Most flights go in and out of the renovated portion of the airport, which includes a museum-quality exhibit of Alaskan native artifacts and a display of planes from bygone days. Some of the smaller carriers still use two of the older concourses (a renovated B concourse is expected to reopen in the fall of 2009), but the airport is small enough that you'll never be far from a nice assortment of shops and restaurants. A shuttle ride away is a second terminal used primarily by international carriers and Delta Airlines.

Once you're here, the flying doesn't have to end. You can hop on small commuter planes to get from Anchorage to some of the more popular destinations in Southcentral Alaska, or you can get a bird's-eye view of the state's expansive beauty by taking a flight-seeing tour with one of the air services listed here. Most smaller flying services in Anchorage depart from either Lake Hood or Lake Spenard (just east of the airport) or Merrill Field east of downtown on Fifth Avenue. Prices,

of course, are subject to change. Alaskan bush pilots are a legendary species unto themselves, so expect the guy (or gal) at the controls to be part of your memorable experience.

ALASKA FLIGHT TOURS/VERNAIR
1704 East Fifth Ave., Anchorage
(907) 258-7822
www.alaska.net/~vernair/
For $195 per seat, you can opt for one of three two-and-a-half-hour tours. The Mount McKinley trip will take you up the Matanuska Valley, where you'll see active gold claims and hopefully some impressive wildlife. From there you'll fly over Mount McKinley's Tokositna and Kahiltna Glaciers, and then you'll see the stunning peaks of the Ruth Glacier Gorge. On the Columbia Glacier tour, you'll see your first glacier within 15 minutes, with up to 33 more glaciers to follow. Dall sheep and sea lions are commonly spotted on this tour, and you'll pass over Whittier, Portage, and Cook Inlet on your way back. The volcano tour will take you over two active volcanoes as well as offshore oil platforms in Cook Inlet, fish camps, commercial fishing boats, and the native village of Tyonek. Other tour options include Knik Glacier, Kenai Fjords, Prince William Sound, and a wildlife tour. Custom tours to more remote locations, such as Lake Clark, Lake Iliamna, Katmai National Park, and the Brooks Range, also can be arranged.

ELLISON AIR SEAPLANE TOURS

4520 Wisconsin Dr., Anchorage
(907) 243-1959
www.ellisonair.com

From Lake Spenard, this family-owned and family-operated business can send you off on a variety of airborne adventures. If you want just a glimpse of what's up there, opt for a $50, 30-minute local seaplane ride over the Anchorage Bowl, four mountain ranges, and the Susitna River drainage. If you have more time, you can take in a lot more wildlife and scenery on the Chugach State Park or Prince William Sound Tours, with prices ranging from $135 to $400, depending on the length of your flight. Ellison's most popular tour is the Wildlife Glacier Tour, with two hours of flight time for viewing massive ice fields and glaciers. Moose, bear, sheep, goats, caribou, and beluga whales are among the wildlife you may see. The tour includes a landing on a remote wilderness lake. Ellison Air pilots boast more than two decades of Alaskan flying experience. There are passenger minimums on all tours, with group and family discounts available.

SOUND AVIATION

Merrill Field and Reeve Boulevard, Anchorage
(907) 229-2462
www.soundaviation.com

Family owned and operated, Sound Aviation's Bill Marsan has more than 9,000 hours of Alaska flying experience. Starting at $49 per person, you can take the Anchorage Scenic Tour, or you can opt for more expensive tours of Eagle, Knik, Blackstone, or Columbia Glacier. Tours of Mount McKinley, Kenai Fjords, and Prince William Sound are offered. All tours include music and pilot narration as well as wildlife viewing. There's also the option of 360-degree trips around Denali, weather permitting. Sound Aviation offers personalized custom tours as well as statewide charter and air taxi service. Tour rates are based on a minimum of three passengers.

TAKE FLIGHT ALASKA

1740 East Fifth Ave., Anchorage
(907) 274-9943
www.takeflightalaska.com

Specializing in "earth and sky" experiences, Take Flight offers several excursion packages to maximize your flight-seeing adventure. Take a flight through the Alaska Range to Denali, or splurge on a full-day Mount McKinley-Columbia Combo tour, where you'll see 30 tidal glaciers through Prince William Sound. Another option is to head south on a scenic Kenai Fjords Tour, with a pass through Gold Gulch on the way home. Another popular option is the two-hour Extended Knik Glacier Tour, where for a slight additional charge you can land for a picnic. There's a two-person minimum on all tours; call for current prices.

RUSTS FLYING SERVICE, ANCHORAGE

(907) 243-1595, (800) 544-2299
www.flyrusts.com

Among the most trusted flying services in the state, Rusts was voted the best flightseeing service by readers of the *Anchorage Daily News*. Family-owned and -operated since 1963, Rusts offers every passenger a window seat with two-way headset for full pilot interaction during flights. In addition to a half-hour Anchorage flight-seeing safari ($100), there's Discover McKinley and Denali National Park ($365), a Glacier and Wildlife Tour ($225–$275), and the Prince William Sound Glacier Tour (summers only; $325–$365). Rusts also offers Bear Viewing and Fly-In Fishing and Lodge packages. Hotel and airport transfers and custom tours are available as well.

i For road conditions, closures, construction, urgent reports, ferry information, weather, and other travel advisories in Alaska, dial 511, or go to 511.alaska.gov. From out of state, call (866) 282-7577.

BY WATER

Cruise ships are another popular way of getting to Alaska. Cook Inlet is not suitable for cruise ship docking, so the luxury boats arrive at Whittier or Seward, with transfer service by bus or train to and from Anchorage. The cruise companies offer a dizzying array of air, land, and sea packages, so you can arrive by one means of transportation and leave by another, with land tours by bus or rail in between. Alaska also has a state-operated ferry system that can get you to Southcentral Alaska from ports in Southeast.

The Alaska Marine Highway System (AMHS), also known as the Alaska State Ferry system, offers three ferry service routes. Most popular is the Inside Passage route from Seattle north to Haines and Yakutat, with stops at Ketchikan, Petersburg, Sitka, Juneau, and several smaller towns along the way. You can fly from any of the larger Southeast Alaskan towns to Anchorage, or you can drive to Anchorage from Skagway or Haines, though both trips require a minimum of two days.

The AMHS also provides summer Cross-Gulf service from the Inside Passage to the Gulf of Alaska, where passengers disembarking at Whittier or Seward can catch ground transportation to Anchorage. Southwest Alaska service runs west from Cordova through the Gulf of Alaska and around the Kenai Peninsula to Kodiak Island; the truly adventurous with plenty of time can even go on to the Aleutian Islands. A great benefit of the ferry is that you can get off at any stop and hang around till the next boat comes through. For those in a hurry, the AMHS offers fast-ferry service between major ports. The Alaska Marine Highway is about practical transport, not luxury, and like everything else it gets crowded in the summer, so make sure to plan ahead, especially if you want to book a stateroom or bring a vehicle.

BY CAR

For lots of people, driving the Alaska Highway, commonly known as the Al-Can, is part of the big Alaskan Adventure. Back in the day when the road was mostly gravel, driving up was a lot more "exciting" than it is today. People still display "I survived the Al-Can" bumper stickers with a sense of pride and accomplishment, but now that the road is mostly paved, the main challenges are the long distances between services, prices that get higher as you go north, winding mountain roads, lots of road construction during the short summer season, and the overall length of the trip. Diehards have been known to get from the northern United States to the Alaskan border by driving nonstop for a couple of days, but most folks allow five to seven days so they can take their time, enjoy the scenery, and sleep once in a while.

RV traffic, including caravans, used to be thick during the summer, but with the rising cost of fuel, it has waned somewhat. RVers will still find Anchorage and Southcentral Alaska well-suited for accommodating their needs. Whether you're driving an RV, car, or motorcycle, you'd be foolish not to bring a copy of the *Alaska Milepost*, a detailed driving guide published each year by Alaska Northwest Books. Organized by highway name, the *Milepost* can be a bit cumbersome to use, but it's really the best way to navigate the state's roadways. By the way, you'll get some blank looks from locals if you ask for help finding a highway by number. No one knows who slapped those numbers on the highways a few decades ago, and no one cares. Alaskans refer to their highways by name—the Seward, the Glenn, the Richardson, and so on.

i **Alaska has an impeding-traffic law. If you're on a two-lane highway outside an urban area where passing is unsafe and you're driving under the speed limit, you must pull over and allow vehicles to pass if five or more are backed up behind you.**

Soils in many parts of Alaska are wet, fine-grained clay or silt, letting in lots of water that expands when it freezes. Add some groundwater into the mix, and you get frost heaves, those jarring dips and humps in Alaska's roadways that can eat axles and take out shock absorbers. Road authorities mark and repair these damaged roads in due time, but not all are marked right away, so beware. Watch for dips and valleys in the roads, and slow down before you encounter them. One advantage to gravel over asphalt is that frost heaves aren't an issue. Major thoroughfares around Anchorage, especially the Glenn Highway stretching north to the Matanuska-Susitna Valley, are plagued with hazardous tire ruts that can cause serious accidents if you change lanes too fast, especially when the roads are icy or wet.

Some Alaskan highway corridors have been identified by the state as high-accident zones. Obey the posted speed limits of 55 miles per hour in these areas, which include portions of the Glenn Highways going north to the Matanuska-Susitna Valley as well as most of the Seward Highway between Anchorage and Girdwood. Throughout Alaska in the winter, be especially wary of black ice. Tough to see and very hazardous, it's especially prevalent when temperatures warm after a cold spell.

Finally, Alaska's construction season is short, so expect a lot of it during the summer. Double fines are levied for traffic violations in construction zones. Lots of daylight means road crew can work all night, so be advised that some roads may be closed completely during the wee hours to maximize this opportunity. If you're planning an all-nighter, call 511 for construction updates.

i There are huge distances between services along most portions of Alaska's highways, so in addition to the usual flares, toolkit, jumper cables, and spare tire you keep in your vehicle, you should also have a first-aid kit, tow cable, flashlight, matches, drinking water and food, rope, and insect repellant. Try to keep your vehicle's gas tank at least half full at all times. In winter, make sure you have chains, a shovel, an ice scraper, a bag of sand or kitty litter, a blanket or sleeping bag, and extra warm clothing.

i From mid-May to mid-September, you can ride one of America's last flag stop trains, the Hurricane Turn, on a route used by locals to reach their remote cabins since 1923. Starting in Talkeetna, you can get on and off where you please along 55 miles on the 115-mile route. To flag the train, stand 25 feet from the rail and wave a large white cloth until the engineer sounds the whistle to let you know he saw you. Now that's an Alaskan experience.

BY TRAIN

You can't get to Alaska by train, but you can get around using the state's top-notch Alaska Railroad system once you're here. From Anchorage, you can head out to Girdwood, Portage, Seward, Wasilla, Talkeetna, Denali, and Fairbanks, with special wilderness adventure stops at Spencer Lake and Grandview. All the scenery is spectacular, but arguably the best is on the Anchorage–Seward run. Alaska Railroad cars have large picture windows, forward-facing reclining seats, and dining service. Passengers also receive historical route maps and a complimentary *Alaska Railroad* magazine. From June through August, local high school students are trained to offer professional commentary and assistance on board.

If you're looking for luxury, upgrade to Gold-Star Service on the Denali Star Train that runs from Anchorage to Fairbanks with stops at Wasilla, Talkeenta, and Denali. This first-class service includes seats in the railroad's new double-deck dome cars with custom-designed interiors and original Alaskan art, complimentary appetizers, and access to a private, one-of-a-kind outdoor viewing platform. There's even a spacious dining room and bar with big picture windows so you don't miss anything along the way. In addition to regular service, the Alaska Railroad offers several tour packages. Some service is seasonal. Locals enjoy special interest train packages, like the Blues Train featuring music, drinks, and an overnight jam in Seward, or the Beer Train, where sampling is encouraged. To get details on all your options, contact the Alaska Railroad at (907) 265-2300, (800) 321-6518, or www.alaskarailroad.com.

BY BUS

If you don't want the hassles of driving and the train's not your thing, you can get around Southcentral Alaska by bus. Grayline of Alaska (888-452-1717, www.graylineofalaska.com) offers all sorts of tour packages in and around the region. The Alaska Park Connection (800-266-8625, www.alaskacoach.com) offers daily service between Seward, Anchorage, and Denali in highway-quality motor coaches with onboard restrooms and informative narration by the driver/guide. Combination bus/rail trips are available, and most tours include admission to the Anchorage Museum. Another option is the Alaska Transportation Group (907-952-1249; 866-425-8687, www.alaskatransportation.net), with scheduled and chartered service between Anchorage, Wasilla, Talkeetna, Cantwell, Denali, Fairbanks, Seward, and many points en route via shuttle bus, private van, or limousine.

ANCHORAGE

Surrounded by six mountain ranges and the waters of Cook Inlet, Anchorage is awash in scenic beauty year-round. The maritime climate makes temperatures quite tolerable by Alaskan standards, and as the city has grown into itself, it offers plenty to do, whether you're looking for nightlife, culture, sporting events, shopping, or outdoor recreation. Like every city, it has its problems. Traffic bogs down at rush hour, and the city is just about out of raw land for residential development. But the inconveniences are small, and the quality of life is large. In fact, Anchorage has been recognized four times as an All-American city.

Living in what's far and away the largest city in Alaska, Anchorage residents catch a lot of grief from Alaskans in smaller towns and more remote areas, who call the city "Los Anchorage" and joke that there's Alaska, and then there's Anchorage. But the truth is that Anchorage has an energy you won't find elsewhere in the state. Politically engaged, active in the arts, eagerly partaking of the city's amazing parks and trails, Anchorage residents live with enthusiasm and gusto. A bit less than half of the state's residents, 279,000 people, live within the boundaries of the municipality, stretching from Eagle River to Girdwood. While the pace is less hectic than in many other cities its size, Anchorage still supports thriving retail and business sectors that serve Alaskans from the far-flung corners of the state. The Ted Stevens International Airport is uniquely positioned for top-of-the-world routing between Europe, Asia, and North America. On the northeast end of town, Elmendorf Air Force Base and Fort Richardson take similar advantage of the city's strategic location.

For visitors, Anchorage is a great place to get your bearings and launch into Alaskan-style adventures. Here you'll find everything from world-class restaurants and hotels to down-home cafes and bed-and-breakfasts, from downtown shopping malls to quirky secondhand shops, and from sprawling nightclubs to eclectic coffeehouses. No matter what your style, budget, or interests, Anchorage has plenty to offer.

GETTING AROUND

Anchorage is a small city, and while there's public transportation, the system is not extensive, so most people get around by private car or taxi. If you're visiting for just a few days and are content with limiting yourself to downtown destinations, you can take a taxi or a limo from the airport to your hotel and walk pretty much everywhere else. Otherwise, a car will be your best bet, though motorcycles are also available for rent for those with a yearning for the open road.

ℹ Downtown at the corner of Fourth Avenue and F Street is a log cabin bustling with activity. Under the sod roof of the Anchorage Convention and Visitors Bureau Visitor Information Center (907-274-3531) are all sorts of great resources. It's open daily, with abbreviated hours in the winter. Both airport terminals have visitor information centers as well. Their Web site, www.anchorage.net, is another helpful planning resource. A special feature is the "Ask a Local" contact form, where you can get answers to questions about the Anchorage area.

By Car

Finding your way around Anchorage isn't all that tough if you have a good map. First big tip: The mountains are east, the ocean is west. Numbered downtown streets run from east to west, beginning with Second Avenue, a short street close to the water. Fourth, Fifth, and Sixth Avenues are the main downtown streets, and of course they're one-ways. Cross streets running north and south are named by letter, with A Street being farthest to the east and closest to the mountains, while L Street is farthest west, closest to Cook Inlet. East–west numbering spans out from A Street, where to the east streets fan out by place name, more or less alphabetically: Barrow, Cordova, Denali, Eagle, and so on. Several downtown blocks are fused together with the Egan Center, the Town Square Park, the Alaska Center for the Performing Arts, and the Fifth Avenue Mall, so you can't count on all of the lettered streets to run the distance to Second Avenue. A Street, C Street, and L Street are your best bets for multiple lanes with minimal stops running the full span from north to south.

Anchorage streets have a bad habit of ending and picking up again a few blocks away, sometime to allow for greenbelts and creeks, and sometimes just because that's how the town grew. They also suffer from multiple identities. The big ones to know: Minnesota turns into I Street going north (and L Street turns into Minnesota going south), and it also turns into O'Malley going south and east. Tudor turns into Muldoon going east and north, while one-ways Gambell and Ingra become the Seward Highway going south and Fifth and Sixth merge into the Glenn Highway going east.

i There are more than 5,700 parking spots in downtown Anchorage. Twenty-five cents buys you a whopping 12 minutes, with monthly permits available for lots and garages. Street-side parking is free after 6 p.m. on weekends and on municipal holidays. For more information on parking in Anchorage, call (907) 276-PARK or go to www.anchorageparking.com.

Many businesses are also located on the Old Seward Highway, which runs parallel to the New Seward Highway through most, but not all, of town. Annoyingly, International Airport Road does not connect with the Seward Highway; if that's where you're headed, veer north to Tudor instead. Northern Lights and Benson Boulevards are important one-ways for making your way from east to west in midtown Anchorage, while Minnesota Drive is the major north–south artery moving traffic from the airport north to downtown and south to the busy Dimond shopping area. Spenard Road cuts through older neighborhoods on a diagonal between the airport and downtown.

For a smaller city, the major thoroughfares can get surprisingly busy during rush hours, but you won't find many of those freeway standstills suffered in major urban areas. The intersection at Lake Otis and Tudor as well as the Merrill Field corridor of the Glenn Highway are notoriously bad. Still, even during peak traffic, it shouldn't take more than an hour to get from one end of town to the other.

As you might expect, there's ample parking at retail outlets, restaurants, and hotels beyond the downtown area. Anchorage retail stores tend to be fairly lenient about free overnight parking for RVs, but policies get tighter every year, so don't assume anything without checking out the particular retailer. Downtown parking is another story. There's metered parking along most streets, but it's tough to find a spot unless you're there early or late, or you're willing to walk. Pay lots and parking garages are your best bets; just plan on walking a few blocks to your destination. The Fifth Avenue, Sixth, and Seventh Avenue Parking Garages, along with the JCPenney Parking Garages, offer good opportunities. If parking at the JCPenney garage, be sure to take your ticket with you, as some stores will validate it for two free hours with a purchase. There are plenty of side-street lots in between these larger garages.

Icy roads pose plenty of driving hazards from October all the way through April. If you're used to winter driving conditions, you'll be able to manage with front-wheel drive, but if you're at all hesitant or you're going to venture up into the hillside, a four-wheel-drive or all-wheel-drive vehicle is your best bet. Keep a safe distance between yourself and the vehicle in front of you, don't be in a hurry, and drive defensively when the roads are slick. And don't count on locals to model good winter driving skills—Alaska is a transient state, and some of them won't be doing much better than you are, especially in the fall when everyone's making the transition to the challenges of ice and snow.

Public Transportation

The Anchorage People Mover is the local public transit system. It's a bus-only option, with no subway or commuter train service. One-way fares are $1.75, or you can opt for a $4 day pass. Senior and disabled one-way fares are 50 cents, and university students ride free. Bus Route 7 offers hourly service from the airport to the Downtown Transit Center, Spenard Road, and the Dimond Center. Many buses have bike racks on the front. Check out www.peoplemover.org for more details on bus service, including shared-ride options and van service for senior citizens and the wheelchair bound.

Taxis and Limousines

You might be able to hail a taxi near one of the big downtown hotels, but for the most part you'll need to phone ahead, allowing approximately 20 minutes for pickups unless traffic is extra-heavy or bad weather is keeping people from driving themselves. Recent rates for taxis are $2 for the pickup and $2 per mile. Try Anchorage Yellow Cab (907-272-2422), which has a taxi equipped with a wheelchair lift, Anchorage Checker Cab (907-276-1234), or Alaska Yellow Cab (907-222-2222). Most taxi services can deal with a phone call the night before if you need to set up an early morning pickup.

You'll find some fun options if you want to treat yourself to a limousine ride, including popular Hummer and SUV limos that offer a real Alaskan take on the typical fare.

BAC LIMOUSINE AND BUS SERVICES
(907) 222-2600, (866) 589-5466
www.baclimoandbus.com
With a large line of vehicles and 24-hour phone reservations, BAC is one of the bigger players in the Anchorage limo market. They've got limos and mini-coaches to accommodate up to 20 passengers, with drivers well-versed in service and local knowledge. A nonrefundable deposit of 50 percent is required at the time of booking, and major credit cards are accepted. They offer Hummer and Lincoln Navigator limos as well as mini-coach service and traditional Lincoln Town-car limousines.

LIMOUSINE OF ALASKA
(907) 350-9428, (866) 907-2005
www.limousineofalaska.com
Impress your friends and enjoy some great Alaskan photo ops with an airport or cruise ship

Shuttle Service

Several attractions offer free or low-cost daytime shuttle service. Take "Lolly the Trolley" along Fourth and Fifth Avenues, compliments of the Ulu Factory. You can flag down the trolley or pick it up at one of the marked stops. The Ship Creek shuttle runs year-round, Monday through Saturday, from several downtown locations to Ship Creek for a nominal charge. The Alaska Native Heritage Center Shuttle, a free service during the summer, picks up at five downtown locations, including the Anchorage Museum and the Anchorage Convention and Visitors Bureau Log Cabin. The Alaska Zoo runs periodic shuttle service; for times, cost, and pickup locations, call (907) 346-1285.

transfer in the Monster SUV limo, which holds up to 40 pieces of luggage and comes equipped with a full assortment of luxury features, including flat screen television, air-conditioning, and complimentary champagne. Anchorage's Limousine of Alaska guarantees your satisfaction. For alternate rides, choose from the Monster SUV or coach bus service.

Rental Cars and Shuttles

Anchorage has the usual airport-based rental car companies, and thanks to the recent airport expansion, you most likely won't have to take a shuttle to pick up your car, though it is a bit of a hike across the uncovered lot. You may get better prices at some of the off-site rental outfits, but they're generally not as close to the airport as you might think, so allow some extra time for pickups and returns.

Don't count on landing at the airport during the busy summer season and just grabbing a car at the counter. Advance reservations are essential during peak travel months. As with hotels, you'll be paying top dollar in the summer but can get some great deals on cars in the winter. Most companies will have you sign an affidavit stating that you won't take the car on any gravel roads. Virtually all the roads in Anchorage proper are paved, but if you're staying at a bed-and-breakfast on the outskirts of town or planning on some adventure driving, you may end up taking your chances. Gravel roads are hard on cars and especially on windshields.

Avis, Budget, Dollar, Enterprise, Hertz, and Thrifty all have counters at the Ted Stevens International Airport. Alaska Car and Van Rentals (907-243-4444, www.alaskacarandvan.com) is 15 minutes from the airport and also has a downtown office in the Hilton Hotel; they can pick you up as well. Denali Car Rental (907-276-1230, www.denalicarrentalak.com) is another local company that advertises rates close to half of what the big boys charge on used vehicles. They offer pick-up service and winterized vehicles with studded tires.

Feeling adventurous? You can rent a motorcycle at Alaska Rider Tours (907-272-2777, 800-756-1990, www.akrider.com), where both guided and self-guided tours on three different makes of cycles are available. They provide complimentary airport pickups as well as space to store your gear and change your oil. Along with information on road conditions, they offer free camping, showers, and coffee. If you get attached to your Harley, you can purchase one at the House of Harley right next door and drive it home. In fact, House of Harley (907-248-5300; 800-248-5305, www.harleyalaska.com) has an adventure planner who'll set you up with a Fly-Buy-Ride package so you can fly up and ride home.

There are a few shuttle services in Anchorage, but for the most part they offer transfer service to and from such tourist destinations as the Alaska Railroad, the Seward and Whittier Cruise Ports, and Alyeska Ski Resort. Some shuttle companies also offer service between the airport and private residences, including bed-and-breakfasts, but depending on the location, a taxi may be cheaper. Try the Alaska Transportation Group (907-952-1249, 866-425-8687, www.alaskatransportation.net), Alaska Shuttle (907-694-8888, www.akshuttle.com), or the ever-fun Magic Bus (907-230-6773, www.themagicbus.com). Alaska Shuttle offers rides to Eagle River, Peter's Creek, and Eklutna, plus they'll go up to the Matanuska Valley upon request.

HISTORY

Human history in the Anchorage area doesn't go back as far as it does in some other places, but it has been a wild ride nonetheless. Evidence of the first indigenous people in the area dates from only 3000 B.C., when the first wave of Native Alaskans left artifacts discovered at the Beluga Point Site, not far from where downtown Anchorage stands today. Two additional waves of people of a similar background came through, one in 2000 B.C. and the other close to the turn of the millennium. Sometime between A.D. 500 and 1650, the Athabaskan Dena'ina people displaced the original inhabitants.

More displacement was to follow. Russians explored the general region in 1784, but it was famed explorer James Cook who reached the place now known as Anchorage and misnamed its flagship body of water "Turnagain River." Later, explorer George Vancouver corrected the error by renaming it Turnagain Arm.

After the Russians sold Alaska to the United States for 7.2 million dollars in the famed "Seward's Folly" transaction of 1867, the Alaska Commercial Company moved in, setting up posts along Cook Inlet to outfit gold miners conducting explorations along Turnagain Arm and in the Kenai Peninsula. Though large fortunes eluded miners in the Anchorage area, President Wilson created a boom when in 1915 he sanctioned the Alaska Railroad with the Ship Creek landing as its headquarters. A tent city sprang up, and on July 9 of the same year, 600 town-site lots were sold at auction, with a total of $150,000 put up in exchange for the land. Today those lots are valued at upwards of $150,000 apiece. The U.S. Postal Service recognized Anchorage as the official name of the burgeoning community, and on November 23, 1920, the town was incorporated.

Eight years after it was begun, the Alaska Railroad project was finished, becoming a mainstay of both transportation and the Anchorage economy until Merrill Field opened in the 1930s. The airfield quickly became one of the busiest crossroads for civilian aircraft in the world, a distinction that continues today. The federal government gave another boost to the Anchorage area by sending colonists to the Matanuska-Susitna Valley under the authority of the Depression-era Federal Relief Agency.

The threat of Japanese aggression, followed by the cold war, made Anchorage a strategic military site. The population of Anchorage soared from 3,000 in 1940 to 47,000 in 1951. With the influx of people and military spending, Anchorage experienced one of several bouts with growing pains as both the cost of living and crime rates skyrocketed.

In 1951 the Anchorage International Airport opened, connecting the city with the outside world, albeit on a slow and sometimes delayed basis. The Seward Highway connected Anchorage with the Kenai Peninsula at about the same time. On January 3, 1959, Alaska was admitted as the 49th state in the Union, causing inevitable changes that old-timers continue to lament.

But nothing changed Anchorage like the Good Friday Earthquake on March 27, 1964. The epicenter of this 9.2 trembler was only 75 miles from Anchorage. Streets buckled, buildings collapsed, homes slid down hillsides, and lives were lost. It took the rest of the decade for Anchorage and its sister cities of Seward and Valdez to rebuild.

In 1968, rumbling of a different sort began. Oil was discovered on Alaska's North Slope, and while the ramifications were slow in coming, the discovery changed the area forever. First was the Alaska Native Claims Settlement Act, commonly known as ANCSA, which settled land-rights issues with the formation of 12 regional Native corporations, plus one additional organization for Natives living outside the state. It's still too soon to judge the long-term success of this grand experiment imposing a corporate structure on local Native groups, but most of the corporations are now turning a profit and creating economic opportunities for their shareholders.

In 1974, one year after the first modern Iditarod Sled Dog Race left from Anchorage, construction began on the trans-Alaska oil pipeline. Having served as a supply center when the Swanson River oil fields opened up in 1957, Anchorage was poised to be the hub of this huge project. Money flowed as freely as the oil did when the pipeline was completed in 1977, and you'll still hear folks talking about pipeline wages that were so extravagant they make even the tallest gold rush tales pale in comparison. "Please, God, send us another pipeline," reads a well-loved Alaskan bumper sticker.

The boom continued well into the 1980s. Alaskans would love another pipeline, with surplus North Slope natural gas as the new target fuel, but no matter what you heard during the 2008 presidential campaign, the project's still in the planning stages. If a gas pipeline is eventually built, we're promising not to waste it this time around. At least that's what the bumper sticker says.

Close-up

Oil to Cash: Alaska's Permanent Fund Dividend Program

PFD. It might stand for Personal Flotation Device in some circles, but Alaskans know it as an acronym for another sort of lifesaver: the Permanent Fund Dividend.

Each October since 1980, every eligible Alaskan man, woman, and child has received a check, courtesy of the Alaska Permanent Fund Dividend Corporation. The highest payout so far was more than $2,000 per person in 2008. Even though most years the payouts are considerably less, Alaskans look forward to their annual October checks the way kids look forward to a visit from Santa.

Considering that most states collect money from their residents in the form of state income taxes, state sales taxes, and state property taxes (Alaska has none of these), it's quite the reversal to have the state pay us. Don't even think about questioning the logic. Alaskans fiercely defend their PFDs.

That's exactly what former governor Jay Hammond had in mind when he came up with the concept as a way to get Alaskans on board with saving rather than squandering the state's windfall from North Slope oil production. The first $900 million in oil money the state received back in 1970 disappeared in three short years. Based on a program he developed as mayor of Bristol Bay, Governor Hammond pushed through a constitutional amendment mandating that at least 25 percent of the state's oil royalties be set aside in a permanent savings account. Though investments suffered in the economic downturn of 2009, as of February 2009, the unaudited value of the Permanent Fund account was nearly $29 billion.

A large portion of the earnings on the Permanent Fund principal is distributed annually to the state's residents, who must prove that they've lived in the state for the required number of days each year and that they intend to continue living here indefinitely. With the distribution of PFD checks each fall, retailers offer all sorts of enticements to get Alaskans to spend them, from airline ticket deals to "double your dividend" specials on big-ticket items such as cars and snowmachines.

Certainly the free-flowing cash is good for the state's economy, but the bigger impact comes in the form of the voters' almost religious commitment to the state's savings plan. You can propose almost anything as a politician, but start talking about tinkering with the Permanent Fund, and you'll have a bunch of angry Alaskans on your tail.

That's not to say some haven't tried. Whenever the state's budget turns red, the healthy Permanent Fund is a natural place to look for extra cash. And some worry that the program draws freeloaders to the state and encourages families to have more children than they otherwise would, since each means another check. Fighting dividend fraud becomes a bigger task every year. But it seems whenever talk of ditching or changing Permanent Fund payouts heats up, sky-rocketing oil prices infuse the fund with cash, and the checks keep pumping money into Alaska's economy by way of its people.

By then the population of Anchorage, at 184,775, was more than half that of the entire state, and the city and borough had merged into the municipality of Anchorage, covering an area from Eagle River to Portage that encompassed 1,955 square miles. From 1980 to 1987, almost $1 billion of capital project money flowed into Anchorage, and the city came of age. Oil prices plunged in 1987, and a bust followed on the heels of the big boom, but by the mid 1990s, the state's economy was flourishing again, with tourism playing no small part in the diversification and recovery. Thanks to relatively strong employment in non-industrial sectors, Anchorage tends to fare rather well even during times of economic struggles elsewhere—that is, as long as oil keeps flowing and prices are high. The cost of living in Anchorage isn't significantly higher than the national average now, but transportation costs to the Lower 48 must be factored into personal budgets. And despite millions of gallons of crude oil flowing from Prudhoe Bay, our gasoline prices are among the highest in the nation.

ACCOMMODATIONS

Like everything else in Anchorage, the options for overnight accommodation get better and better every year. From luxury hotels to budget motels to home-style bed-and-breakfasts and bare-bones hostels, there's an option to fit every traveler, as long as you plan ahead during the summer season. While the hotel industry is doing a good job of keeping up with demand, reservations should be made well in advance for visits from May through mid-September. Availability increases dramatically, with a corresponding decrease in rates, during the winter, except during such special events as the Alaska Federation of Natives convention in October, Fur Rondy in February, and the Iditarod in early March.

You won't find luxury inns or resorts in Anchorage, but we have included some exceptional fly-out options if you're looking for an all-inclusive wilderness resort experience. Likewise, keep in mind that bed-and-breakfasts in Alaska are not usually the specialty inns you'll find in the Lower 48. Most are run by friendly hosts renting out a few rooms in rather ordinary homes, where in many cases you'll share a bath. It's the chance to chat with longtime Alaskans to learn all about living in the 49th state that makes this option attractive to most visitors, not to mention the fact that prices tend to be significantly lower than at hotels during the peak tourist season. At hostels, you'll be bunking in rooms with strangers, but at bargain prices.

Most downtown hotels and motels do not offer airport shuttle service, but it's only a 10- or 15-minute drive from the airport to downtown,

depending on traffic, so taxi fares are reasonable.

You might not be thinking about air-conditioning when you visit Alaska, but it's not a bad feature to have if you're bothered by the heat—they may be few and far between, but there are some warm days in Anchorage in the summer. A few of the larger hotels offer air-conditioned rooms. A unique Alaskan amenity at some accommodations is freezer space for storing fish and game.

Price codes indicate the cost of a room for two during the peak season—generally May through mid-September—excluding the 12 percent bed tax. Some establishments offer attractive shoulder-season rates before Memorial Day and after Labor Day. You can assume that major credit cards are accepted and that the place is open year-round unless we note otherwise. Count on bringing the kids but not the pets unless the listing says differently. While hotels and motels generally have rooms with wheelchair access and rooms for smokers, we'll make a special note if these are available at B&Bs, hostels, guesthouses, and inns.

Price Codes

$	Less than $150
$$	$150–$200
$$$	$201–250
$$$$	More than $250

Hotels and Motels

THE ANCHORAGE DOWNTOWN HOTEL $$
826 K St.
(907) 258-7669
www.anchoragedowntownhotel.com
Here's a small family-operated hotel, almost like a B&B, right in the heart of the city. All 16 rooms have been freshly remodeled, and suites are available as well. Rooms come with coffeemaker, microwave, minifridge, hair dryer, iron, ironing board, and free continental breakfast. The Anchorage Downtown boasts a quiet location just 5 blocks from the city center, right across the street from a midtown park. Enjoy the ambience of an inn with the comforts of a hotel, including

Anchorage Vital Statistics

Most of these facts and figures pertaining to Anchorage and Alaska are covered in much greater detail in the following pages of this guide. However, here's an at-a-glance overview of the area for first-timers and international visitors—plus a quick reference for those in a big hurry.

Anchorage mayor: Matt Claman

Alaska governor: Sarah Palin (R)

Population: Municipality of Anchorage: 279,671 (in 2007); Alaska: 686,293 (in 2008)

Anchorage Median Age: 32.4

Area (square miles): Municipality of Anchorage: 1955 square miles; Alaska: 570,373 square miles

Anchorage mascot and slogan: Seymour the Moose; Big Wild Life

Anchorage average temperatures: January: 20°F; July: 65°F

Anchorage average rainfall: 15.71 inches per year

Anchorage daylight: Averages 19 hours, 21 minutes in summer; 5 hours, 28 minutes in winter

Alaska Time zone: Alaska Standard Time (AST), 1 hour earlier than Pacific Standard Time

City/state founded: Alaska Purchase from Russia ("Seward's Folly"): 1867

City of Anchorage incorporated: 1920

Alaska statehood: 1959

Alaska's major cities: Juneau (state capital), Anchorage, Fairbanks

Major colleges/universities in Anchorage: University of Alaska Anchorage, Alaska Pacific University

Important dates in Alaska history:
1898   Klondike Gold Rush
1915   Construction of Alaska Railroad began

---

cable television, high-speed Internet access, free continental breakfast, free local calls, and free downtown parking.

ANCHORAGE GRAND HOTEL $$$
505 West Second Ave.
(907) 929-8888, (888) 800-0640
www.anchoragegrand.com
The Anchorage Grand combines the charm of the original 1950s building with the luxury of modern amenities and custom furnishings, thanks to a complete renovation in 2001. Known for its friendly service, this private boutique hotel is just off the Second Avenue entrance to the Tony Knowles Coastal Trail, 1 block from the train depot and 3 blocks from the convention center and the Fifth Avenue Mall. Their 500-square-foot suites

come with queen- or king-size bed, fully equipped kitchen, iron, ironing board, free morning paper, free continental breakfast, free high-speed Internet, two-line business phone, hair dryer, and same-day laundry service or in-house coin-op laundry. Their Winter Special includes a one-night stay, a bottle of wine, dinner for two at Orso (see listing under Fine Dining in the Restaurants section), and late checkout. They've got great inlet and city views plus a business center for guest use. Two of the suites are wheelchair accessible.

ANCHORAGE HAWTHORN SUITES $$$
1100 West Eighth Ave.
(907) 222-5005, (888) 469-6575
www.hawthorn.com
A great option for comfort and style on the west

1923	Alaska Railroad completed
1942	Alaska-Canadian Highway (ALCAN) completed
1959	Alaska statehood
1964	Alaska earthquake
1977	Trans-Alaska Pipeline completed
1989	Exxon Valdez oil spill

Major Alaska private employers: Providence Health and Services, Carrs/Safeway, Trident Seafoods, BP Exploration, Alaska Airlines, FedEx

Famous sons and daughters: Susan Butcher, Iditarod musher; Joe Reddington Sr., "father of the Iditarod"; Tommy Moe, Alpine Olympic skier; Jewel, singer/songwriter; Scott Gomez, NHL hockey player; Irene Bedard, actress; Trajan Langdon, NBA basketball player; Sarah Palin, Alaska governor and Republican vice-presidential candidate; Wally Hickel, former Alaska governor and Secretary of the Interior; Jay Hammond, former Alaska governor and initiator of the Alaska Permanent Fund.

Major airports/interstates: Ted Stevens International Airport, Glenn Highway, Seward Highway, Parks Highway, Dalton Highway

Anchorage trails: More than 200 miles of summer trails; 130 miles plowed walkways in winter; 100 miles groomed ski trails; 36 miles of dog mushing trails

Military bases: Fort Richardson, U.S. Army home of the Arctic Warriors; Elmendorf Air Force Base, home of the Alaska Command, Alaska NORAD Eleventh Air Force, and the Third Wing

Driving laws: Right turn on red permitted. Seatbelts must be worn at all times in moving vehicle. Speed limit on state highways is 55 mph on high-accident corridors, 65 mph on other highways.

Alcohol laws: Legal drinking age is 21 years; blood-alcohol content of .08 percent or higher is DUI in Alaska.

Daily newspaper: *Anchorage Daily News*, daily circulation 71,711; Sunday circulation 89,423

Sales tax: No sales tax; 12 percent bed tax

end of downtown, within several blocks of most attractions. Enjoy a deluxe, hot complimentary breakfast buffet, high-speed wireless Internet, in-room efficiency kitchens and living space, two televisions per suite, and guest laundry services. To top it all off, there's a heated indoor pool and spa. Free airport shuttle, free weekday newspaper, exercise room, and a 24-hour business center add to the conveniences here. Pets allowed with additional fee.

COAST INTERNATIONAL INN $$$
3333 West International Airport Rd.
(907) 243-2233, (800) 663-1144
www.coasthotels.com
Next to Lake Hood and minutes from the Ted Stevens International Airport, the Coast Interna-

tional has 141 newly refurbished rooms with lake or mountain views. Rooms come with spacious desks, dual-line speakerphones, in-room movies and Nintendo, irons, ironing boards, coffeemakers, and hair dryers. Guests can access the fitness center, sauna, fax machine, copier, high-speed wireless Internet, business center, and walk-in freezer for storing fish and game. There's round-the-clock airport shuttle service, too. Piper's Restaurant and Lounge offers a full menu of Alaskan fare and an open-air deck overlooking the lake.

COMFORT INN SHIP CREEK $$
111 Ship Creek Ave.
(907) 277-6887
www.comfortinn.com
Affordable digs close to downtown are the big

plus at the Comfort Inn. The Ship Creek location is not exactly in the midst of the action (unless you're fishing), but it's within walking distance if you don't mind taking the stairs up a steep hill. You may also wake to the sound of railroad trains pulling in and out of the nearby station. But what other hotel supplies free fishing gear along with a free weekday newspaper, free deluxe continental breakfast, and free 24-hour coffee service? The Comfort Inn is a pet-friendly hotel, with extra charges for your four-legged friends and a limit of three animals per room. It's also unique among downtown hotels in providing 24-hour airport shuttle service in the summer, subject to demand in the winter.

COURTYARD ANCHORAGE AIRPORT　　$$$
4901 Spenard Rd.
(907) 245-0322
www.marriott.com/hotels/travel/
anccy-courtyard-anchorage-airport/
Conveniently located just 2 miles from the Anchorage International Airport, the Courtyard offers plush beds, free high-speed Internet access, inviting outdoor spaces, and the Marriott reputation for quality and service. Rooms feature a desk with ergonomic chair and two phones, complimentary weekday newspaper, microwave, and refrigerator. To relax, enjoy the hotel's swimming pool, whirlpool, and exercise room. A breakfast buffet is available for an additional fee.

DAYS INN　　$
321 East Fifth Ave.
(907) 276-7226, (800) 329-7466
www.daysinnalaska.com
Offering moderately priced accommodations in the heart of downtown Anchorage, the Days Inn has many of the amenities you'd expect from a larger hotel. They have 130 rooms with coffeemakers, irons, ironing boards, in-room movies, and Internet access. They also offer courtesy parking, banquet and meeting facilities, and a restaurant right across the street. As an added perk, they provide courtesy shuttles to and from the airport and the train station. They have both smoking and wheelchair-accessible rooms, and pets are allowed.

DIMOND CENTER HOTEL　　$$$$
700 East Dimond Center Boulevard
(907) 770-5000, (866) 750-5002
www.dimondcenterhotel.com
The Seldovia Native Association operates this modern hotel next to the largest shopping area in Alaska. The spacious rooms include plush beds, oversize soaking tubs with separate shower areas, televisions, microwaves, refrigerators, coffeemakers, and deluxe continental breakfast featuring Belgian waffles. There's also high-speed and wireless Internet access, an exercise area, coin-op laundry facilities, free airport shuttle, and seasonal downtown shuttle service. At the adjacent Dimond Center Mall, you'll find dining, shopping, bowling, ice skating, movie theaters, and a complete athletic club. Both wheelchair-accessible and smoking rooms are available. Ask about special rates for AAA, AARP, and Alaska residents.

EMBASSY SUITES ANCHORAGE　　$$$$
600 East Benson Blvd.
(907) 332-7000
embassysuites1.hilton.com
A popular midtown choice, this hotel greets guests with soaring timbered ceilings in the lobby. Suites include a well-lit work area with high-speed Internet access and kitchen with refrigerator, microwave, and coffeemaker. No need to cook in the morning—made-to-order breakfast comes free with the room. Two televisions with premium cable channels round out the in-room amenities. There's also a pool, fitness room, business center, and coin-op laundry.

FAIRFIELD INN AND SUITES　　$$
5060 A St.
(907) 222-9000
www.marriott.com
Near the intersection of International Airport Road and A Street, the Fairfield has become a favorite for affordability, comfort, and convenience. There's free shuttle service from the airport, complimentary on-site parking, high-speed Internet access, and free cable TV with HBO. Complimentary breakfast includes waffles,

hot breakfast sandwiches, and an assortment of breads, cereals, and fruit. Rooms include a desk with two phones, iron and ironing board, and hair dryer. The Fairfield is a Marriott property.

HILTON GARDEN INN $$$$
100 West Tudor Rd.
(907) 729-7000, (877) 782-9444
http://hiltongardeninn1.hilton.com

The Hilton Garden Inn is a newer hotel in Anchorage's midtown area, within walking distance of several dining and entertainment options. Rooms include coffeemakers, microwaves, minifridges, irons, ironing boards, free morning papers, and free high-speed and wireless Internet access. Opt for either a king-size bed or two queen-size beds. The Hilton offers free airport transportation, fitness and business centers, a heated pool, and a whirlpool. The enthusiastic staff will help with your travel plans in the state, and there's a restaurant on-site. Renovations completed in the spring of 2009 should make this an especially nice choice. Smoking rooms are available.

HISTORIC ANCHORAGE HOTEL $$$–$$$$
330 E St.
(907) 272-4553, (800) 554-0998
www.historicanchoragehotel.com

This elegantly restored boutique hotel, established in 1916, offers 26 charming rooms and suites in the heart of Anchorage. Just 1 block from the Egan Convention Center and within walking distance of just about everything downtown, the Historic Anchorage Hotel features European ambience with a friendly yet professional atmosphere. This is the only hotel in Anchorage that's on the National Register of Historic Places, with celebrities from Walt Disney to John Denver among those who've stayed there over the years. The hotel's comfortable, spacious, and well-appointed rooms include coffeemaker, microwave, minifridge, iron, ironing board, free morning paper, free continental breakfast, discounts at local attractions, and Wi-Fi Internet access. Book directly with the hotel and enjoy late-check-out privileges, too. Ask about their

romantic "Night to Remember," which includes a tour by horse-drawn carriage and dinner for two at Orso (see listing under Fine Dining in the Restaurants section). It's also a favorite spot for locals to watch the ceremonial start of the Iditarod Sled Dog Race during the first weekend in March.

HOMEWOOD SUITES ANCHORAGE $$$$
140 West Tudor Rd.
(907) 762-7000, (800) 225-4663
www.anchorage.homewoodsuites.com

Operated by the same folks that run the Hilton Garden, the Homewood offers another new upscale option in midtown Anchorage. The hotel has 122 suites, most with a king-size bed plus a pull-out sofa bed. Each suite has a full kitchen plus separate living and sleeping areas. Irons, ironing boards, free morning papers, and free high-speed and wireless Internet come with the suites. Guests enjoy a full breakfast buffet every morning, with light dinners offered Monday through Thursday. There's also a swimming pool and whirlpool for guest use. Free area transportation is provided, and smoking rooms are available, as are rooms with wheelchair access.

THE HOTEL CAPTAIN COOK $$$$
939 West Fifth Ave.
(907) 276-6000, (800) 843-1950
www.captaincook.com

The Hotel Captain Cook, an Anchorage landmark, is the only Alaskan property in the Preferred Hotels and Resorts Worldwide, a worldwide network of independent luxury hotels that sets high

i Every night during the summer and on Fridays and Saturdays during the off-season, you can grab a horse-drawn carriage in front of the Hotel Captain Cook (939 West Fifth Avenue; see hotel's listing) and treat yourself to a chauffeured ride through downtown Anchorage. Choose from quarter- to half- and full-hour rides and enjoy the sights of town in style. For details, contact the Horse-Drawn Carriage Company (907-688-6005, www.alaska.net/~carriage).

Close-up

Within the Wild

Wisps of fog rise from the glassy waters of Lake Hood, backlit by a brilliant sun rising over the Chugach Mountains. The hour may be early, but the folks at Rust's Flying Service are already multitasking, checking with remote weather stations, doling out fishing licenses, and herding passengers toward seaplanes that will transport them to their wilderness destinations.

"McKinley is out like a sore thumb," announces Warren, the bush pilot flying us to Winterlake Lodge. After we taxi around the lake and take off, we see exactly what he means. Some 250 miles to the north, the Great One dominates the skyline. We're lucky. Due to cloud cover, there's only a one in ten chance of seeing North America's tallest mountain on any given day.

Warren is as skilled an entertainer as he is pilot. Scooting our Beaver DeHavailland around Mount Susitna, he recounts the legend of the Sleeping Lady for whom the mountain is named. Spotting a lone black bear galloping across the alpine tundra, he circles again and again until everyone onboard has had a look.

After an hour in flight, we touch down on Finger Lake, exhilarated by our journey, awestruck by the spot where we've landed. It's immediately apparent that Winterlake Lodge is a special place, an outpost of adventure nurtured by a family in love with the wilderness.

In the mid-1980s, Carl and Kirsten Dixon traded their city jobs for a remote lifestyle, starting a business from scratch and raising their two daughters where it's easy to remember what really matters. "We never once thought about failing," says Kirsten. "We were very naive, but we never looked back. We've been able to create our own lives here, and our own vision of what we want people who visit Alaska to experience."

It's a vision that's easy to embrace. With soaring ceilings and open spaces, the lodge is the kind of place that inhabits the dreams of those who love the outdoors. It's comfortable but elegant, brimming with big windows and replete with cozy nooks. Pretty much by himself, Carl built not just Winterlake but also two other remote lodges for the couple's Within the Wild Adventure Company—no small feat, since all supplies must arrive by small plane, as we did.

But don't look for either Carl or Kirsten, a renowned chef, to dwell on their accomplishments. For them, it's all about the guests. "People are coming here for a broader experience, a life-style experience, exploring a little of this and a little of that," Kirsten says. "We befriend our guests. We have a rich relationship with them."

Today's experience begins with a hike down the famed Iditarod Trail, led by the Dixons' daughter Carly. We encounter beaver dams and bear scat, flush out grouse, and admire blazing fireweed. If we'd been ambitious enough to trek to the top of the ridge, we would have been treated to a panoramic view of the valley and Mount McKinley. After a gourmet lunch featuring glazed country ham and red lentils, there's time to check out the dog team, canoe among the loons, practice a few casts, ponder a game of chess, or catch a nap. Other options include rafting, kayaking, massage therapy, and yoga. In Kirsten's words, it's all about offering "more of the best of what Alaska really is."

standards for detail and service. Relax on down duvets and pillows, lounge in a plush robe, and enjoy twice-daily maid service, including an evening turndown. The theme of exploration and discovery carries throughout the hotel, with solid teakwood decor and rich colors. Opt for a room on the private Captain's Deck in Tower II, and you'll enjoy a panoramic view, complimentary newspapers, continental breakfast, evening hors d'oeuvres, and a juice and soft drink bar. On-site you'll find four restaurants, 12 boutique shops, an athletic club with swimming pool, and wireless Internet access. On cruise ship days in the summer, the hotel is packed with people, but the

A lodge favorite is the open invitation to the kitchen, where we learn to make Gruyère puffs and fill them with cardamom salmon spread. "It's very rewarding for us to have people in the kitchen learning something," Kirsten says, speaking of the exhilaration she gets from sharing her love of cooking. Years ago, Kirsten made the leap from country cook to gourmet chef when some regular guests invited her to Paris to attend the famed Cordon Bleu cooking school. Many trips to France and a master's degree in gastronomy later, Kirsten has acquired a stellar reputation among her peers.

Like Carl with his building projects, Kirsten makes turning out gourmet meals with ingredients that must be grown on-site or shipped in by plane look easy, calling her kitchen "my playhouse all day long." Every dish that comes from Winterlake's massive kitchen features fresh, quality food, reflecting Kirsten's passion and that of her chefs. The author of two full-color cookbooks, Kirsten also conducts cooking weekends at the lodge with instructors from around the world.

Winterlake is one of a handful of Alaskan lodges that is open year-round, except during breakup and freeze-up, when planes can't land on the lake. "It's really fun for us in the winter," Kirsten says. More Alaskans visit then, foodies as well as skiing and mushing enthusiasts. From mid-February to mid-March, there's a flurry of activity as the Iditarod Trail Committee sets up a race checkpoint at the lodge. In June, there's heli-skiing with world-class athletes such as Olympic champion Tommy Moe. Carl also puts the chopper to good use transporting ordinary mortals on glacier trekking, rafting, wildlife viewing, and sport-fishing adventures.

Catering to the high-end crowd in the wilderness has its challenges. "Alaska is different," Kirsten explains. "It's more elusive to travelers. Some people don't get it." The "aha" moments come at special times. A guest relaxing on the deck spies first a moose, then a bear, then an eagle flying overhead. A visitor with a passion for mushrooms turns a 10-minute hike into a two-hour foraging expedition, delighting his hosts by spotting more than 200 species. The edible finds make their way to the dinner table, of course.

It's this sort of intimate sharing of lifestyles, forged with outstanding service, that keeps Winterlake's guests returning year after year. Winterlake and the other Within the Wild lodges don't advertise much; word of mouth and a few good agents keep them full. Kirsten admits that for the average traveler, finding a wilderness experience like the kind they offer can be something of a crapshoot. "One of the challenges of tourism in Alaska is a real gradient of quality in terms of backcountry standards," she says, suggesting that travelers connect with top agents who do site inspections and check references.

After sampling our crescent-shaped Gruyères, hot from the oven, we retire to the massive deck overlooking the lake, rocking and sipping tea as we watch the clouds roll in. The air turns cool, a reminder that fall is on the way, even though the gardens still abound with edible flowers and plants. Content in body and soul, we wish for clouds that bring a storm strong enough to strand us here another day, away from the worries of the world, in the heart of Alaska's wilderness.

courteous staff manages to keep everything running smoothly even on the busiest days.

INLET TOWER HOTEL AND SUITES $$$$
1200 L St.
(907) 276-0110, (800) 544-0786
www.inlettower.com

This apartment-complex-turned-hotel offers spectacular views of Mount Susitna, Cook Inlet, and the Chugach Mountains at a convenient location between the airport and downtown. Amenities include ample free parking, free local calls, luxury linens, in-room movies, speakerphones with voice mail, on-site laundry facilities, and free shuttle service to the airport and the train station. Rooms have coffeemakers, refrigerators, microwaves, cable televisions, and free high-speed Internet access. It's a bit of a walk to shopping and restaurants, but the Mixx Grill offers fine cuisine on-site (see listing under Fine Dining in the Restaurant section).

LONG HOUSE ALASKAN HOTEL $$
4335 Wisconsin St.
(907) 243-2133, (888) 243-2133
www.longhousehotel.com

With design and decor reflective of the Native heritage of Southeast Alaska, the Long House offers a convenient location near the airport with 54 spacious, comfortable rooms. Choose from a deluxe room, grand room, or personal suite. Opt for either a king-size bed or two queen-size beds with cable television, in-room movies, refrigerator, microwave, and telephone with voice mail and free local calling. Guests enjoy the use of the convenient laundry room, walk-in freezer space, and 24-hour courtesy airport shuttle. Enjoy an evening walk along the shore of Lake Hood, watching the floatplanes and waterfowl come and go. Pets are allowed, and smoking rooms are available.

MILLENNIUM ALASKAN HOTEL $$$$
4800 Spenard Rd.
(907) 243-2300, (800) 544-0553
www.millenniumhotels.com

There's a warm Alaskan ambience at this lakeside retreat, with decor featuring animal mounts and Native artifacts. Spacious rooms and suites, colorfully decorated, include refrigerators, coffeemakers, televisions with in-room movies, telephones with voice mail, modems, and 24-hour room service. There's a health club with whirlpool, steam bath, and sauna, or you can jog the path around Lake Spenard. The hotel is only a mile from the airport, with complimentary airport and downtown transportation. Gleaming wood and polished brass form the backdrop for casual dining at the Fancy Moose Lounge, or enjoy a meal at the Flying Machine Restaurant, with a

great view of the floatplane base right out front and patio seating in the summer. In March, the Millennium bustles with activity, serving as headquarters for the world-famous Iditarod Sled Dog Race. Smoking and wheelchair-accessible rooms are available.

PARKWOOD INN $$
4455 Juneau St.
(907) 563-3590, (800) 478-3590
www.parkwoodinn.net

Tucked 1 block off International Airport Road is a lodging option that's especially affordable for extended stays. Fifty 450-square-foot studio suites come with your choice of queen- or king-size beds, full kitchen, work area, private balcony, and cable television. The business center offers Internet access, and there's a barbecue on the landscaped grounds for guest use. The Parkwood is a short drive from the hospital and university, but it's not within walking distance of the usual tourist attractions and there's no shuttle service, so guests would do well to have their own transportation. Pet and smoking rooms are available. Ask about discounts for seniors, government employees, and long-term guests. There's a limit of five persons per room.

PUFFIN INN $$
4400 Spenard Rd.
(907) 243-4044, (800) 478-3346
www.puffininn.net

The Puffin Inn has been an affordable favorite of Alaskan travelers for years. They've expanded and remodeled to offer 86 deluxe, boutique, moderate, and economy rooms to travelers. Rooms include refrigerators, microwaves, hair dryers, irons, coffeemakers, free local calls, free daily newspaper, and complimentary continental breakfasts. Guests also have access to the business center, fitness facility, guest laundry, freezer space, and 24-hour complimentary airport shuttle. Puffin guests also may reserve rooms at the nearby Chandler Inn, a classy 14-room boutique hotel just half a block away. Wheelchair-accessible rooms are available, as are pet-friendly, hiking, and fishing packages. Ask about early bird discounts for booking summer rooms before March 31. Contrary to what some might make of its name, the Puffin Inn is a nonsmoking facility.

VOYAGER HOTEL $$$
501 K St.
(907) 277-9501, (800) 247-9070
www.voyagerhotel.com

Another favorite with Alaskans, the Voyager mixes the friendliness and ambience of a small hotel with service, style, and a fabulous location in the heart of downtown Anchorage. They have 40 nicely appointed guest rooms with hair dryers, makeup mirrors, microwaves, coffeemakers, refrigerators, filtered water taps, air-conditioning, and cable televisions. For business travelers, rooms have voice mail, broadband Internet, and dial-up modem ports. Guests have access to free overnight parking, same-day valet service, guest fax services, a health club, and complimentary continental breakfast. On the lower level, the Voyager's Corsair Restaurant (see lisiting under Fine Dining in the Restaurant section) is another local favorite.

Fly-out Lodges

RIVERSONG LODGE $$$$
P.O. Box 191029, Anchorage, AK 99519
(907) 350-2392
www.riversonglodge.com

Seventy air miles northwest of Anchorage along the southern bank of the Yentna River, you'll find the peace and tranquility of Riversong Lodge. They offer 10 cabins that accommodate a total of 44 guests, with a variety of all-inclusive packages that include transportation from Anchorage, meals, accommodations, fishing guide, and fishing equipment. The rustic lodge with its spacious decks, inviting living room, and tasteful decor serves as a gathering place for meals, activities, and relaxation. The grounds are lush with herbs, flowers, and gardens that contribute to the lodge's award-winning cuisine.

WINTERLAKE LODGE $$$$
Within the Wild Adventure Company
2463 Cottonwood St.
(907) 274-2710
www.withinthewild.com

Pristine wilderness and warm Alaskan hospitality grace this lakeside lodge 198 miles from Anchorage on the historic Iditarod Trail. All-inclusive rates include accommodations, genuine gourmet meals, and a wide variety of activities, from hiking to fly-out fishing to cooking classes and bear watching at the sister property, Redoubt Lodge. Winterlake is a stunning hand-crafted lodge with soaring ceilings, large windows, and spacious decks for taking in the spectacular wilderness view. Hosts Carl and Kirsten Dixon cater to an upscale clientele with some of the most gracious hospitality you'll find anywhere. They also own and operate Redoubt Bay Lodge, a great bear-watching location at the entrance to Lake Clark Pass, and Tutka Bay Lodge along Katchemak Bay outside of Homer.

Bed-and-Breakfasts

AAWESOME RETREAT B&B $$
16528 Kings Way Dr.
(907) 338-8873, (877) 226-9645
www.aawesomeworld.com

Surround yourself with original artwork in this stunning mountain retreat just 20 minutes from the Ted Stevens International Airport. You can walk the path to the meadow pond or simply enjoy the beauty of the 13-acre grounds with mountain and inlet views from your private deck. This unique B&B has three spacious suites with king-size beds and either one or two twin beds, marble tub surrounds, satellite television, microwaves, and refrigerators. Guests have full use of the guest kitchen and the Vortex Lounge, which has sunset views. The kitchen is stocked with continental fare for self-serve breakfasts. A full-view open room, the Penthouse, can be rented for group events. Two suites are wheelchair accessible, and pets may be accepted on approval. Rate discounts are available for consecutive-night stays.

ALASKA FRONTIER GARDENS BED AND BREAKFAST $–$$
7440 Alatna Ave.
(907) 345-6556
www.alaskafrontiergardens.com

Not only has host Rita Gittins won an award for outstanding service in the tourism industry, she's also won a Best of Gardens award. You'll enjoy both the exceptional service and the lush gardens when you stay at this custom cedar home in the hills just 1 mile from Chugach State Park, near Flattop Mountain. Gorgeous views, outdoor spa, sauna, and decks hung with more than 50 flowering baskets are among the luxuries that await. In your room, you'll enjoy luxury linens, plush pillows, and European goose down comforters. Wireless Internet, cable TV, and refrigerators add to in-room amenities. Full breakfasts feature Amaretto French toast, Alaskan blueberry pancakes, reindeer sausage, gourmet coffee, and seasonal fruits. Laundry facilities, copier, and fax are available for your use, and children are welcome. Therapeutic spa and massage available by appointment.

ALL THE COMFORTS OF HOME $
12531 Turk's Turn
(907) 345-4279
www.alaska.net/~comforts/

Relaxation is the watchword at this custom-built cedar home on a mountainside just 20 minutes from downtown Anchorage. Soak in the outdoor hot tub surrounded by towering spruce trees, bask in the sauna, or curl up by the fireplace. Lodgings are furnished with antiques, Alaskan memorabilia commonly known as Alaskana, local art, and an extensive book and video collection. From your vantage point on the west veranda, at an elevation of 1,100 feet, you'll be able to see all of Anchorage with its surrounding mountains and spectacular sunsets, plus Mount McKinley if the weather is cooperative. The Victorian and Sunset Rooms share a bath, but each room has its own sink and vanity. The Sourdough Suite is a romantic retreat with private bath, sitting alcove, television, VCR, refrigerator, and whirlpool

tub. Your hostess, a lifelong Alaskan, serves a full breakfast including fresh brown eggs and reindeer sausage, or you may opt for a continental spread if it's more to your liking. Well-behaved children older than age 12 may accompany guests, and four-wheel drive is recommended if you're visiting after the snow flies.

ANCHORAGE LAKESIDE JEWEL B&B $$
8840 Gloralee St.
(907) 242-2126, (866) 539-3555
www.anchoragelakesidejewel.com

Only 4 miles from the Ted Stevens International Airport, you can enjoy lakeside serenity with fishing, swimming, hiking, and skiing right out this bed-and-breakfast's back door. Alaskan themes prevail, with rooms like the Fishin' Hole and the Loon's Nest, which include robes, television, queen-size bed, and shared bath with whirlpool tub. The Top of the World Suite sleeps four and includes private deck, sunroom with lake view, walk-in closet, washer/dryer, television, fireplace, and private bath with whirlpool tub. Household amenities include wireless Internet, guest telephone with private voice mail, video library, games, lakeside gardens, and full breakfast or buffet. The friendly hosts are longtime Alaskans who've lived and worked in Bush Alaska as well as in Anchorage. Boat rentals and free concierge service are nice extras.

BIG BEAR B&B $
3401 Richmond Ave.
(907) 277-8189
www.alaskabigbearbb.com

Specializing in full breakfasts, comfortable rooms decorated with Alaskan art, and affordable rates, the Big Bear offers several accommodation options, all with private baths. Choose from the Glacier Room, decorated in blues with a polar bear theme, the yellow-hued Toklat Room, the elegant Grizzly Room, or the family-size Denali Room with whirlpool tub. The guest living room features Native crafts, a polar bear rug, and antique furniture, and here guests may use the cable television, a minifridge stocked with soda, and a microwave. Complimentary coffee, tea, and microwave popcorn are provided. The owner, a lifelong Alaskan and certified tour guide, cooks up breakfasts featuring a variety of Alaskan treats, including sourdough waffles, blueberry coffee cake, and salmon quiche. Ask about discounts for seniors and weeklong stays.

CAMAI BED AND BREAKFAST $
3838 Westminster Way
(907) 333-2219, (800) 659-8763
www.camaibnb.com
Camai (pronounced chah-my) means "welcome" in Yupik, the native language of Southwestern Alaska. This award-winning B&B, the longest-operating one in Anchorage, offers three spacious suites in a quiet residential neighborhood with gardens bordering the Chester Creek greenbelt. Each has a private bath, queen-size bed, and separate sitting room or second bedroom. Some suites have private entrances, and guests share an office area with computer and Internet access. Rooms come with coffeemakers, microwaves, minifridges, telephones, balconies, irons, and ironing boards. Full breakfasts are served in the summer, with continental breakfasts offered during the winter. Discounts are offered for consecutive-night stays.

COPPER WHALE INN $$$
440 L St.
(907) 258-7999, (866) 258-7999
www.copperwhale.com
Anchorage Daily News readers voted the Copper Whale Inn the best B&B in Alaska, and it's easy to see why. The inn is something of an Anchorage icon, perched atop a downtown hill overlooking Bootlegger's Cove. Gardens grace the property, where 14 rooms in the 1939 home await guests. Wireless Internet and continental breakfast are free. From downtown's west end, you can walk to dozens of shops and restaurants, or hop over to the 11-mile coastal trail. In fact, you can rent a bicycle right from the inn. A dozen rooms have private baths, and the entire inn is nonsmoking. Parking at nearby city lots is $12 and up.

DONNA'S BED & BREAKFAST $
11335 Via Balboa
(907) 522-6025, (888) 421-6025
www.anchoragedonnasbandb.com
Families are welcome at this home away from home, approximately 10 minutes from the airport and downtown. The Forget-Me-Not, Iditarod, and Mount McKinley Rooms come with cable televisions, VCRs, telephones, and refrigerators. Guests share kitchen and laundry privileges as well as use of the backyard barbeque and the family room, which includes books, magazines, microwave, and Internet access. Each evening, guests select a main course and a time for the next day's breakfast. In addition, bagels, toast, and a variety of cereals and juices are served each morning. Pets are allowed, and there are cats on the premises.

FRENCHY'S ADVENTURE BED AND BREAKFAST $
3807 West Northern Lights Boulevard
(907) 344-4846, (800) 939-4846
www.adventurebnb.com
You'd be hard-pressed to find a friendlier or more accommodating hostess than Frenchy, a long-time Alaskan teacher and author who loves to help guests plan their Alaskan adventures. Conveniently located midway between the airport and downtown, Frenchy's serves a full breakfast with reservations, or a continental breakfast if guests prefer. There's cable television, telephone, iron, ironing board, free morning paper, free Wi-Fi, and airport transportation upon request. The Musher's Retreat, Loon's Nest, and Tranquility Rooms are tastefully decorated with shared baths. Children are accommodated on a case-by-case basis.

LAKE HOOD INN $$
4702 Lake Spenard Dr.
(907) 258-9321, (866) 663-9322
www.lakehoodinn.com
Watch the seaplanes come and go from this four-room inn on the shores of Lake Hood, the world's largest floatplane lake. The decor naturally includes aviation displays and other Alaskana, with

sunsets over Mount Susitna and local waterfowl providing more outdoor ambience. Located just minutes from the Ted Stevens International Airport, the inn provides coffeemakers, minifridges, in-room safes, hair dryers, televisions with VCRs, microwaves, irons, and ironing boards for guest use. Continental breakfast and airport transportation are also provided.

MAHOGANY MANOR BED AND
BREAKFAST INN $$$-$$$$
204 East 15th Ave.
(907) 278-1111, (888) 777-0346
www.mahoganymanor.com

Casual elegance is the watchword at the Mahogany Manor, which caters to discriminating guests with a combination of historical charm, hotel amenities, and Alaskan hospitality, re-creating the feel of a secluded lodge in downtown Anchorage. Huge fireplaces and a floor-to-ceiling waterfall grace the well-appointed lounge, while a private collection of museum-quality Alaskan art plus mountain and city views provide a feast for the eyes. There's free on-site parking, high-speed Internet, and cable television along with heated whirlpool swim-spa facilities. A hearty continental breakfast is available anytime. The Governor's Suite includes two private bedrooms, private bath with double sink, a large sitting area, and a spacious private deck. Three smaller guest rooms are also available. Minimum stays may apply during the high season. The Mahogany also offers budget accommodations.

NORTHERN B&B $-$$
9431 Emerald St.
(907) 336-4248
www.northernbandb.com

Tucked away in a quiet neighborhood not far from the airport, Northern B&B offers comfortable accommodations with a full breakfast of eggs cooked to order, your choice of breakfast meats, potatoes, toast, juice, and coffee or tea. Guests share a spacious living room with large windows, vaulted ceiling, fireplace, and television. This property has a three-bedroom family suite,

a room that shares a bath with the owner, and a sumptuous suite decorated in rich burgundy hues with a large private bath and whirlpool tub plus a private living room with fireplace. The owner is a longtime Alaskan who cooked at Land's End Resort (see the Kenai Peninsula chapter) back when it was just a fisherman's hangout. Airport transportation is available, and guests have access to the kitchen and a free morning paper. Small pets are welcome.

PARKSIDE GUEST HOUSE $$
1302 West Tenth Ave.
(907) 683-2290
www.campdenali.com

Owned and operated by the Cole family of Camp Denali and North Face Lodge (see the Denali National Park chapter), the Parkside makes a convenient Anchorage add-on to your Denali adventures. Distinctively designed in the Arts and Crafts tradition, this downtown home features a spacious second-story living room with sweeping views of the inlet, mountains, and city. Laundry facilities are available, and continental breakfast comes with the room. Credit cards are not accepted.

RABBIT CREEK BED & BREAKFAST $-$$
P.O. Box 112842, Anchorage, AK 99511
(907) 345-0733, (866) 345-0733
www.arabbitcreekbandb.com

Nine miles from the airport, you can enjoy a panoramic view and the gentle sounds of the creek in this 3,000-square-foot home. Follow the hiking trails along the creek, relax in the outdoor hot tub, or browse the art and antiques, including some that are for sale. Choose from the Honeymoon Hideaway, Asian, Safari, and Antique Rooms, all with private baths and wireless Internet access. Morning brings a deluxe complimentary breakfast featuring fresh fruit, juices, cereals, bagels, coffee, and tea. Ask about discounts for seniors, ministers, and Alaska residents. There's an additional $20 charge for one-night stays. They also have a downtown location, Rabbit Creek North, with rentals by the week.

size bed, sleeper sofa, master bath, private deck, and fireplace. The home is decorated with a mix of contemporary and traditional furnishings peppered with antiques.

Guesthouses

26 STREET HOSTEL $
1037 West 26th St.
(907) 274-1252
www.26streethostel.com
Simple, no-frills accommodations await the budget traveler at this hostel that's close to trails and accessible by bus from the Ted Stevens International Airport. Guests enjoy free Internet access, 24-hour check-in, use of cooking facilities, coin-op laundry, and access to television with video and DVD. Outside there's a barbeque and garden area. Bike rentals are available, and breakfast is included with your stay. Rent by the bed or by the room; either way, the rates are happily affordable.

ANCHORAGE GUESTHOUSE $
2001 Hillcrest Dr.
(907) 274-0408
www.akhouse.com
Clean and comfortable rooms at bargain prices are available here, as long as you don't mind sharing your space with other travelers. The nearby Coastal Trail offers convenient access to downtown, especially if you rent one of the guesthouse mountain bikes. There's an Alaska library to help you plan your adventures, and you can stay in touch with friends back home with on-site Internet and fax services. There's no curfew, and laundry and storage facilities are available. Choose from shared or private rooms; three bathrooms are shared by all guests.

ANCHORAGE INTERNATIONAL HOSTEL $
700 H St.
(907) 276-3635
www.anchorageinternationalhostel.org
Located in a no-nonsense building in the heart of downtown Anchorage, this is the granddaddy of the local hostels. There are separate dormitory

---

Reservations

A reservations service can be a big help when you want to book private lodging. The Anchorage Bed and Breakfast Association (907-272-5909, 888-584-5147, www.anchorage-bnb .com) inspects facilities with a wide range of amenities and prices. Anchorage Vacation Rentals, which is also known as 49th State Vacation Rentals, Lodging and Tours (907-242-6708, 877-888-6867, www.49thstatelodging. com), offers free concierge service and custom travel planning in addition to booking accommodations at B&Bs and vacation rental cabins, apartments, condos, and houses in Anchorage, Denali, Fairbanks, Homer, Kenai, Seward, and other cities upon request. Spanish and German language service is also available. At Alaska Vacation Rentals (907-278-1111, 888-766-2667, www.alaska-bnb-rentals.com), they book everything from budget rooms with shared baths to studios with minikitchens and larger units with full kitchens in downtown and midtown Anchorage.

SUSITNA PLACE $
727 N St.
(907) 274-3344
www.susitnaplace.com
Fabulous views of the ocean and mountains await you at this 4,000-square-foot bed-and-breakfast in a quiet spot near downtown Anchorage. Guests in each of the nine rooms enjoy cable television with HBO, a generous continental breakfast, unlimited local calling, free Wi-Fi, and covered parking. Two of the rooms have private baths, and there's a luxury suite with king-

rooms for men and women with three to six beds in each, though mixed-gender groups may be accommodated by special request. Small lockers are available in every room, but you must bring your own padlock. The hostel also has a limited number of private rooms and a second-floor common area with kitchen. There's no on-site parking, but if you're traveling without a car, you're well-situated here, just 1 block from the bus station and 6 blocks from the train station, with shuttles to outlying areas that stop right at the hostel. Guests enjoy use of the Internet, courtesy phone, and rented bicycles. Wheelchair access is available.

DUBEN PLACE, A GUEST HOUSE $
8307 Duben Ave.
(907) 351-2004
www.dubenplace.com

Duben Place offers private guesthouse accommodations in a fully furnished two-bedroom duplex in a quiet eastside neighborhood. In addition to the queen-size beds in the bedrooms, there are two full-size futons in the living room, making this a great option for families or groups of travelers. Guests enjoy the feather beds, fully equipped kitchen, and fresh vegetables and berries from the garden, in season. Pets are accepted on approval.

OFF THE TRACKS WOMEN'S GUEST HOUSE $
342 West 11th Ave.
(907) 272-6537
www.offthetracks.com

Here's a great downtown location providing a safe, convenient lodging option for women and children. The self-contained guest area has a private entrance, and the common area includes a kitchenette, shared bath, and private phone line. Breakfast foods are provided for a fix-it-yourself meal, and off-street parking is available.

RESTAURANTS

Decades ago the dining options in Anchorage were rather limited, but today you can satisfy just about any palate, whether it be for fresh sushi, eclectic vegetarian, a hearty steak, or home-style Alaskan fare. Fresh seafood is on nearly every fine dining menu, so you don't have to make a special effort to find it.

Don't be put off by the fact that many of the best Anchorage restaurants are in strip malls. It's just the way the city grew. The good news is that Anchorage is just the right size for satisfying whatever cravings you have for lunch or dinner. No one thinks twice about driving across town to their favorite steak house or brewpub, and in fact folks head out to Girdwood in droves to partake at the popular Double Musky restaurant, even though they don't take reservations. With that in mind, we've organized restaurants here by specialty rather than by location.

Compared to many other cities, Anchorage is a rather casual town when it comes to dress. Even in fine dining spots, you may see folks in casual shirts and baseball hats. While it's not exactly anything goes, you're less likely to feel uncomfortable about what you're wearing here than you might somewhere else.

Unlike restaurants in smaller, more remote Alaskan towns, the eateries in Anchorage are generally open year-round. We'll note any that say they're open fewer than seven days a week, but of course those policies are subject to change. Assume major credit cards are accepted and wheelchair access is available unless we say otherwise.

The price codes indicate the average cost of a meal for two, excluding cocktails, wine, appetizers, desserts, tax, and tips. Most establishments that serve dinner have a license for beer and wine, and many also serve cocktails.

Price Codes

$	Less than $30
$$	$30–$44
$$$	$45–$60
$$$$	More than $60

All-American/All-Alaskan

ARCTIC ROADRUNNER $
2477 Arctic Blvd.
(907) 279-7311

5300 Old Seward Hwy
(907) 361-1245

Classic burgers are the mainstay at this longtime Anchorage favorite. The walls are covered with photos of longtime patrons and historical trivia dating from the restaurant's beginning in the 1960s. In addition to hearty beef burgers, they offer salmon and halibut patties. Expect large portions, and don't forget the fries and milk shakes if you want the full experience. The place is not fancy (counter service only), but the service is good, and it has plenty of character at both locations, one on Arctic Boulevard and the other at the intersection of International Airport and the Old Seward Highway. The Arctic Roadrunner is closed on Sunday.

CLUB PARIS $$$
417 West Fifth Ave.
(907) 272-6332
www.clubparisrestaurant.com

Serving up some of the best steaks in Anchorage since 1957, Club Paris is a perennial favorite with locals. Among its claims to fame are surviving the 1964 earthquake (many downtown structures didn't) and a Rogues Gallery of famous and infamous clientele. Beyond the decidedly unassuming decor, you'll find a menu full of thick steaks individually cut and aged on-site as well as fresh Alaskan seafood. The four-inch thick filet mignon is a dinner favorite, as are the Australian lobster tail served steamed with lemon and drawn butter and the hearty clam chowder. Fresh ground filet mignon burgers top the lunch menu along with a nice assortment of sandwiches, homemade soups, salads, and lunch specialties. For a special treat, ask the chef to stuff your steak with bleu cheese. Desserts are also made from scratch, with Stan's Key Lime Pie, Crème Caramel, and New York Style Cheesecake topping the list of choices.

Club Paris is open daily for lunch and dinner, and dinner reservations are recommended. Parking is available in the lot behind the restaurant.

GWENNIE'S OLD ALASKA RESTAURANT $$
4333 Spenard Rd.
(907) 243–2090
www.gwenniesrestaurant.com

Gwennie's is a perennial Alaskan favorite, famous especially for breakfasts so large that even the hungriest sourdough will be hard-pressed to clean his plate. They have gigantic omelets filled with all sorts of goodies, as well as whopping pancakes and towers of French toast. This is a fun all-Alaskan spot that's not a tourist trap; in fact, you'll find a whole lot of locals stuffing themselves on Gwennie's ample portions. It's always busy, especially on weekends, but even if you have to wait, you'll enjoy checking out all the Alaskan memorabilia that makes the place special. Even though Gwennie's is renowned for its breakfast fare, they're open for hearty Alaskan-style lunches and dinners as well. Located in the lower Spenard area, Gwennie's is a short drive from the Ted Stevens International Airport.

HENRY'S GREAT ALASKAN RESTAURANT $$
8001 Old Seward Highway
(907) 770-0500
www.henrysanchorage.com

Henry's is another of those big, eclectic Alaskan eateries reminiscent of the pipeline days, when people were looking for food and lots of it. Known for comfort food and homemade desserts, they now have one of the most expansive menus in town, including a nice selection of fresh salads and soups. Beyond the food, you'll find something for pretty much everyone here, from Alaskan artifacts to Aces hockey in the bar to Tuesday Night Magic for the family. This is a fine place to get Alaskan salmon, scallops, and halibut. Not so Alaskan, another Henry's staple is the "take and bake" crawfish pie.

JACKIE'S PLACE $

2636 Spenard Rd.

(907) 274-3211

www.jackiesplacerestaurant.com

If you're looking for breakfast or lunch cooked the way you want it and served with a smile, Jackie's is the place. A perennial favorite with locals, Jackie's typically ranks among the top three breakfast spots in Anchorage. The decor may remind you of Grandma's living room (complete with grizzled old-timers), but the menu is large and flexible. On a health kick? Order your omelet with egg whites. Choose from four kinds of cheeses. Have brown rice on the side instead of potatoes. Substitutions and special orders are commonplace here. No wonder it's a bodybuilders' favorite. Look for Jackie's at the corner of 26th and Spenard, across from the Bear Tooth Theatre Pub. They're open till 3:40 p.m. daily (no one seems to remember why).

LUCKY WISHBONE $

1033 East Fifth Ave.

(907) 272-3454

No one will accuse it of being either fancy or healthy, but if you're looking for great fried chicken, the Lucky Wishbone is your place. A lot of Anchorage residents grew up on family dinners at the Wishbone, which also features tasty burgers and some of the best milkshakes around. Located across from Merrill Field in East Anchorage, with shades of the pipeline era, the Wishbone has been an Anchorage icon for more than 50 years. It's open daily (except Sunday) from 10 a.m. to 11 p.m. in the summer, closing an hour earlier in the winter.

WINGS 'N THINGS $

701 West 36th Ave. (Olympic Center)

(907) 277-9464 (WING)

Quite a few people in Anchorage feared the prophecy of Joni Mitchell's "Big Yellow Taxi" had come true when the original Wings 'n Things location was paved into a parking lot in 2007. Smiles returned 18 months later when the eatery reopened at the corner of Arctic Boulevard and 36th Avenue, with a new owner but the original recipes. Wings come with five sauces ranging from mild through "nuke." There's talk of growing the business into a franchise, but for now, Anchorage residents are just glad to have their wings back.

Brewhouses and Pubs

BEAR'S TOOTH THEATRE PUB AND GRILL $–$$

1230 West 27th Ave.

(907) 976-4200

www.beartooththeatre.net

Brought to you by the same folks who run the popular Moose's Tooth Pub and Pizzeria (see the listing in this section), the Bear's Tooth offers two dining options in the Spenard area of midtown, one with a movie theater and one with traditional casual dining. You can catch an affordable movie in the 400-seat theater while enjoying food and beverages (including great on-tap microbrews) from their extensive menu, and there's a non-drinking, all-ages section for those younger than age 21. You'll get a whole lot more than the popcorn-and-candy fare that is served up at most theaters—the burritos and quesadillas are especially good. Beyond the theatre, you can indulge in favorites such as Southwest Steamer Clams, Chicken Bomber Burrito, Habanero Chicken Skewers, Setting Sun Halibut, Lemon Beurre Blanc Salmon, and Seafood Enchiladas. It's a popular spot, with a large parking lot and street-side parking for the spillover. Don't park in tow-away zones belonging to nearby business—it makes

i Looking for alternatives to the usual movie experience? Check out the Movies for Your Mind series at the Anchorage Museum, featuring great classic and contemporary films from around the world. Show times are at 6 p.m. every Saturday and Sunday, and admission is just $6, with discounts for seniors and museum members. Go to www.anchoragemuseum.org for a list of what's showing each month. And don't forget about the watch-and-dine fun at the Bear's Tooth Theatre Pub and Grill.

the tab for your outing a little too pricey. First-tap Thursdays feature live entertainment, and the Bear Tooth also hosts topical film festivals.

GLACIER BREWHOUSE $$$
737 West Fifth Ave.
(907) 274-2739
www.glacierbrewhouse.com

A great selection of microbrews, weekly menus with distinctive entrees, and a warm, inviting atmosphere complete with a huge 360-degree fireplace make this a favorite downtown eatery, evidenced by a pile of reader's choice awards from the local paper. The lunch menu features such specialty sandwiches as the Chicken Thai Chile as well as pizzas, entree salads such as the Cajun Duck and Spinach, and several seafood options. The dinner menu includes meats roasted over an Alderwood-fired rotisserie and pastas such as the Jambalaya Fettucine. Top it all off with a signature dessert such as the World-Famous Bread Pudding, a classic apple and currant treat roasted in the wood oven and topped with caramelized pecans and Yukon Jack sauce. Chefs work a gleaming kitchen in full view of diners, while copper-colored vats of beer, including cask-conditioned real ale and specialty taps, are brewed in an adjacent, glass-fronted room (look for the basking iguana). Brewery tours can be arranged through your server. Besides the great beers, there's a nice selection of wines and infused cocktails. All food, beverages, and service are unconditionally guaranteed, and substitutions are welcome. This place is always hopping, so reservations are a good idea.

HUMPY'S GREAT ALASKAN ALEHOUSE $$
610 West Sixth Ave.
(907) 276-2337 (that's 276-BEER)
www.humpys.com

Humpy's lives up to its claim of being the ultimate watering hole in town with draft beers, 20 Belgian ales, lots of live music, and an expansive menu of seafood, burgers, and pasta. The casual alehouse atmosphere makes everybody feel at home, and while it may not be the best choice if you're look-

ing for quiet conversation, it's guaranteed to be a whole lot of fun. The food's great, especially considering that Humpy's is known first and foremost for its good-time bar fun. The smoked salmon scallops and halibut tacos are especially good. Check out the weekend breakfast menu (not for early birds—they start serving at 9 a.m.) and the outdoor patio in the summer.

MOOSE'S TOOTH PUB AND PIZZERIA $
3300 Old Seward Highway
(907) 258-2537
www.moosestooth.net

If you're looking for great pizza, locals will without hesitation point you toward the Moose's Tooth, an eclectic pub and eatery just off the Old Seward Highway in midtown Anchorage. In a casual atmosphere with warm, artsy Alaskan decor, they serve up such an amazing variety of pizzas along with hefty sandwiches (word is that they can transform any combination of pizza toppings into a sandwich) and meal-size salads. You'll see lots of people ordering more than they could eat so they can indulge in the pleasure of taking some home. Moose's Tooth brews their own signature ales, including Fairweather IPA, Pipeline Stout, Klondike Golden, and—when you can get it—the deliciously decadent (and rather high in alcohol) Darth Delerium. Moose's Tooth servers are trained to help you find a favorite—or for the truly indecisive, to suggest the beer sampler. Rotating pizza-by-the-slice specials make Moose's Tooth a popular hit with the lunch crowd. Open since 1996, the Moose's Tooth attracts a diverse clientele, including families, adventurers, and professionals. There's on-site parking, but there's almost always a crowd and they don't take reservations, so come early if you can.

SNOW GOOSE RESTAURANT $$$
717 West Third Ave.
(907) 277-7727
www.alaskabeers.com

From a three-story building overlooking Ship Creek and Cook Inlet, one of Anchorage's first brewpubs serves up pub food and unique beers from their own on-site Sleeping Lady Brewery. The menu offers some great options, including Borealis Blackened Mango Rockfish, Sitka Salmon Cheese Pizza with garlic cream pesto sauce, Old-English Prime Rib of Beef, and the Wasabi-Lime Halibut Cove Sandwich. If your timing's right, you can catch a concert at their theater, or book the whole thing for a private event. There's live music to celebrate the release of a new specialty brew on the first Friday of every month, plus local acoustic musicians every Saturday night. Handcrafted root beer plus top-quality wines and cocktails are also on the menu. In the summer, you'll want to get there early to grab a seat on the popular double-decker outdoor deck (limited drinks and no food on the top level).

Cafes and Bistros

ALASKA BAGEL RESTAURANT $

113 West Northern Lights Boulevard, Suite L
(907) 276-3900
www.alaskabagel.com

Though the setting is nothing fancy, this is a great place to grab a bagel, salad, or sandwich from an extensive menu. Bagels are baked fresh daily, with more than two dozen varieties to choose from. With an equally extensive variety of schmears, it would take years to try all the possible combinations. Bagel sandwiches include The Pipeline, with roast beef, turkey, lox, cheddar, Swiss, cream cheese, olives, pickle, and tomato on two bagels, and The Cook Inlet, with shrimp, avocado, and cheddar. They're open until 3:30 p.m. daily, with breakfast served until 1 p.m. on weekdays and until 3 p.m. on weekends. Call ahead for orders of six dozen bagels or more. Delivery and shipping are available.

CAFE AMSTERDAM $$$

520 East Benson #3
(907) 274-0077
www.cafe-amsterdam.com

Located in the Metro Mall, this European-style cafe has a loyal following. Though the portions aren't overly hearty, they've got a nice menu for breakfast, lunch, and dinner, not to mention a lovely selection of beers, meads, and ales. Start off with pierogies or an olive and goat cheese platter, and move on to a choice of entrees that includes German schnitzel, Spanish paella, vegetable stir-fry, and a tasty assortment of Alaskan seafood.

CAFE CROISSANT $$$

3002 Spenard Rd.
(907) 677-2577

The building's a bit odd—as if a converted car wash or garage—but the quasi-European ambience is lovely, and the menu, though not extensive, is satisfying. Weekend breakfasts feature include eggs benedict and five-egg omelets with asiago potatoes and fresh croissants. There's a bakery on-site, and this relatively new eatery has expanded to serve both lunch and dinner.

MIDDLE WAY CAFE AND COFFEE HOUSE $

1200 West Northern Lights Boulevard
(907) 272-6433

Its shopping-center setting may not provide much ambience, but there's plenty of parking plus a lot of great menu items at this midtown cafe, located next to REI. The Middle Way specializes in creative vegetarian fare, but they serve nonveggie items as well. Try a fresh gourmet sandwich, such as the Southwestern Turkey with low-fat turkey and cream cheese blended with jalapeño, sun-dried tomato and herbs, leaf lettuce, sprouts, onion, tomato, and avocado. The menu also features organic wraps, such as the Quantum, which is stuffed with organic pinto beans and brown rice, cheddar cheese, sprouts, red cabbage, scallions, carrots, avocado, and homemade salsa. As you might expect from a place that emphasizes fresh food, they also have great salads, such as the Italian Bruschetta Plate, with toasted sourdough, pesto, fresh tomato, provolone, and a hefty salad blend. Baked goods, such as the marion berry scones, come fresh from the oven daily. There's an espresso bar, organic juice bar, and a selection of no-fat smoothies to complement your meal. They're open daily for breakfast, lunch, and dinner.

MUMBO GUMBO CAFE $$
2446 Tudor Rd.
(907) 770-1919

You'll think you've dropped about 3,000 miles south and landed in the savory kitchen of somebody's grandma when you step inside this quaint cafe serving up good food with lots of love and affection. There are three items on the lunch menu, and there's a different dinner entree each night of the week, with fried chicken and Gullah Gullah gumbo served daily, along with a choice of five sides. Owner and chef Patricia Dakota Grant brings patience to her kitchen, and it shows in dishes that Anchorage-ites, especially displaced Southerners, come back for again and again. The Mumbo Gumbo is open for breakfast on Saturday only, and they're closed on Sunday.

ORGANIC OASIS RESTAURANT AND JUICE BAR $
2610 Spenard Rd.
(907) 277-7882
www.organicoasis.com

This is a fun little place with lots of plants, about 20 wooden tables, and artwork on the walls. Organic Oasis often hosts live entertainment, including regular open-microphone and talent show fare. As the name implies, everything's organic here, right down to the beer and wine selections. Look for a large selection of delicious soups, salads, sandwiches, entrees, and desserts. Vegetarian and non-veggie fare is available, and you'll find health and nutrition information on everything they serve.

SNOW CITY CAFE $
Fourth Ave. and L St.
(907) 272-2489
www.snowcitycafe.com

One of the most popular breakfast and lunch spots in Anchorage is the Snow City Cafe, conveniently located downtown. Local art decorates the walls, and the place hums with a diverse clientele. There's a huge selection of egg dishes, including the Snow City Scramble with Black Forest ham, cheddar, sun-dried tomatoes, mushrooms, and onions; the Heart Attack on a Plate, featuring hash browns topped with bacon crumbles, sautéed onions and mushrooms, cheddar, and sour cream; made-to-order omelets; and great eggs benedict. For another breakfast treat, try the Stuffed French Toast, packed with mandarin orange cream cheese and toasted walnuts. Among the sandwich choices are the Salmon Cake Hero and the Grilled Italian Classic. There's also a nice selection of fruit smoothies to go with your meal, along with beer and wine after 10 a.m. The Snow City Cafe is open from 7 a.m. to 3 p.m. weekdays, and until 4 p.m. on weekends. This popular spot doesn't take reservations, but calling ahead to put your name on the wait list will get you in faster than if you just show up.

SOUTHSIDE BISTRO $$$
1320 Huffman Park Rd.
(907) 348-0088
www.southsidebistro.com

Enjoy lively European ambience with open kitchen, wine bar, gas fireplace, and French vintage posters in this popular American bistro serving fresh, fun food. You can opt for formal dining on the restaurant side or a more casual meal in the bistro area. An award-winning wine list, attentive waitstaff, and professional chefs keep their clientele, mostly a mix of local professionals and visitors, coming back. Try the roast rack of lamb with cilantro pesto, the fresh mussels in saffron cream, or the peach-raspberry cobbler with vanilla ice cream. Flat breads and unique pizzas are baked in the wood-fired brick oven, and desserts come with signature handpainted designs. In business since 1995, they've got ample parking in a South Anchorage location off Huffman Road and are open for lunch and dinner Tuesday through Saturday.

Ethnic

ALADDIN'S $$
4240 Old Seward Highway, Suite 20
(907) 561-2373
www.aladdinsak.com

One of the best-kept secrets in town, this family-owned restaurant offers fine dining that won't break the budget. Here you can experience authentic Mediterranean cuisine—a full menu of meats, seafood, and vegetarian fare—cooked by mom and served with professional flair by dad and the kids. Try their Vegetarian Mousaka with eggplant, mushrooms, zucchini, and tofu, or their Fesanjan Persian Style, featuring chicken breast cooked in walnut, pomegranate, and pistachio sauce. Meat dishes include Lamb Shiskabob and the Kefta Sandwich with grilled beef sauce in a pita served with mint yogurt. Desserts include favorites such as baklava, Chocolate Decadence, and Bread of Tunisia. Not to be missed is the bottomless mint-honey tea, elegantly poured from silver pots and served in glass mugs. The cozy restaurant is upbeat and personable, with the chefs going out of their way to cater to vegan or other special dietary requests.

DAMI JAPANESE RESTAURANT $$
642 East Fifth Ave.
(907) 274-5211
www.damirestaurant.com

With affordable sushi, special rolls and appetizers, and a varied lunch and dinner menu, Dami is the premier Japanese restaurant in Anchorage. Specials include Don Buri, Dami Maki, Crunch and Best Friend Rolls, Sunomono, and three varieties of the popular California Roll. For a midday treat, choose from sushi, sashimi, and teriyaki lunch specials. With an almost unlimited number of combinations, your meal at Dami is guaranteed to be anything but boring.

GUIDO'S $
549 W. International Airport Rd.
(907) 563-2222
www.guidospizza.net

One of the original pizzerias in Anchorage, Guido's offers ample seating and some big tasty salads as well as pizza and standard Italian fare. Any pizza can be made Greek style, and there's baklava on the dessert menu as well as a scrumptious Greek salad that's a challenge for two. Strombolis, Vegibolis, and meatball sandwiches round out the menu.

LA MEX $
2550 Spenard Rd.
(907) 274-7511

8330 King St.
(907) 344-6399

La Mex has been an Anchorage favorite for great Mexican food since 1969, when they opened in a log cabin that had seating for 12. They now have seating for more than 600, and they're serving their second generation of loyal Alaskan clientele, who appreciate the comfortable atmosphere, colorful Mexican decor, tasty food, and generous portions. While the menu emphasizes such Mexican favorites as tostaditos, the Queen Tostado, chips and dips, and fajitas, there's standard American fare as well. Their famous Margarita Grandes are a great accompaniment to just about anything on the menu. They're the only Mexican restaurant in town that makes their own chips and tortillas fresh daily, and their salsa is so well-loved that they sell it by the gallon. Family owned and operated, La Mex welcomes families and longtime Alaskans as well as visitors looking for a well-prepared, affordable meal along with great service. They've got a second location at 8330 King Street, near the Dimond Center Mall, with high ceilings, a more hip decor, a fascinating tortilla machine, and patio dining in the summer. Both locations offer a full bar menu and ample free parking.

PIZZA OLYMPIA $$
2809 Spenard Rd.
(907) 561-5264

Fresh, healthy European-style cooking is the trademark here. This popular family-run restaurant features authentic, homemade Greek and Italian fare, with free delivery and bookings for large parties. There's an extensive pizza menu, with dough made from scratch and homemade sauce. A favorite is Athina's Delight, with fresh garlic, feta cheese, onions, green peppers, fresh tomatoes, and artichoke hearts. Greek dinners include Olympia Roast Leg of Lamb served with oreganato potatoes and spaghetti, and mousaka, featuring layers of potatoes, eggplant, zucchini, and seasoned ground beef topped with béchamel sauce. For dessert, you can't go wrong with baklava.

SORRENTO'S $$
610 East Fireweed Lane
(907) 278-3439

One of the best Italian places in town, Sorrento's has a comfortable decor accented in reds and greens to complement a full menu of pastas, pizzas, seafood, and other Italian dishes. Among the specialties are Tournedos Siciliano, featuring medallions of beef served with sautéed peppers, mushrooms, and fresh tomatoes, and the Taste of Sorrento's, a plate of lasagna, chicken a la Sorrento, and fettuccine. Seafood options include several tempting halibut entrees, including Halibut al Vino Blanco and Halibut Almondine. All dinners are served with garlic bread and your choice of soup or salad. The longtime waitstaff is friendly and professional. Conveniently located across from the Fireweed Theaters, Sorrento's makes a great before- or after-the-movie stop.

THAI ORCHID $
219 East Dimond Boulevard
(907) 770-7936

At the corner of King Street and Dimond Boulevard, this cozy restaurant makes up in food what it lacks in seating. You'll find consistently tasty curries, pad thai, and other Thai specialities served by prompt and friendly waitstaff. Don't look for anything fancy here—just good food at reasonable prices.

THE THREE AMIGOS $
360 Boniface Parkway
(907) 770-5656

The location is nothing spectacular, but if you're after Mexican fare from scratch, The Three Amigos is the place. What do you get with Mexican from scratch? Tasty (though hardly low-cal) Queso Fundido—melted cheese baked with tomatoes, green chiles, onions, and chorizo. Enchiladas Acapulco, with shrimp and veggies. Not to mention a vast selection of Mexican soups, burritos, gorditas, quesadillas, and of course combination dinners. Open from 10 a.m. to 10 p.m. seven days a week, they even serve Mexican breakfasts. There's free delivery on orders over $20, too.

YAK AND YETI HIMALAYAN $
3301 Spenard Rd.
(907) 743-8078

This hugely popular family-owned eatery serves authentic, homecooked Tibetan, Indian, and Nepalese fare. The menu features a nice balance of vegetarian and nonvegetarian options, including several types of curry, masala, and spicy lentil bhatt, all at very reasonable prices. Naan, classic Indian flat bread cooked in a tandoor oven, is a must with any meal, as is the Darjeeling Chai tea, served warm or iced. Like many favorite restaurants in Anchorage, they don't take reservations, so come early or be prepared to wait. Seating is cozy and limited, and the waiting area is pretty much nonexistent. Hours are limited as well: They're open weekdays for lunch from 11 a.m. to 2:30 p.m., and Thursday through Saturday only for dinner (5 to 8:30 p.m.).

Fine Dining

CORSAIR RESTAURANT AND LOUNGE $$$$
944 West Fifth Ave.
(907) 278-4502
www.corsairrestaurant.com

Tucked in the lower level of the Voyager Hotel at the corner of K and Fifth Avenues, this Anchorage gem replicates the onboard feel of a well-furbished ship. From high-backed booth seating, you'll sample French haute cuisine mingled with New World fare. Many favorites are prepared with tableside flair, including the Flaming Spinach Salad and the famed Cafe Diable. There's also a cozy, quiet bar featuring original cocktails along with a selection of 800 wines. An Anchorage favorite since 1979, the Corsair is open only for dinner except for once-monthly upscale Friday luncheons. Closed Sunday. Reservations recommended.

THE CROW'S NEST $$$$
Hotel Captain Cook
Fourth Ave. at K St.
(907) 276-6000, (800) 843-1950
www.captaincook.com

Atop Tower Three of the luxurious Hotel Captain Cook in downtown Anchorage (see the listing earlier in this chapter under Hotels and Motels), you can experience some of Alaska's finest dining while taking in panoramic views of the city, mountains, and ocean. Decorated in rich wood tones and featuring alcove seating, the award-winning Crow's Nest serves New American cuisine with French overtones. The menu changes often, but sample fare includes nori-wrapped Hawaiian ahi, lightly breaded and served with Asian slaw and spicy ginger butter sauce, or try the seared foie gras with cinnamon sugar brioche, caramelized granny smith apples, sweet Alaskan onions, balsamic reduction, and apple syrup. Dinner favorites include the potato herb–crusted Alaskan halibut, the Crow's Nest surf and turf, and the herb-crusted New Zealand rack of lamb. Desserts prepared at the table top off your meal. If you like, you can order from the monthly Chef's Tasting Menu, which features special starters, entrees, and desserts, each paired with a wine. The Crow's Nest has the largest wine selection in the state, with 10,000 bottles in its cellar and a sommelier on staff to assist with your selections. The service is impeccable, and if you're lucky, you might catch a glimpse of Alaska's well-known former governor Wally Hickel, a hotel owner and frequent guest.

DOUBLE MUSKY INN $$$$
Mile 0.3 Crow Creek Rd., Girdwood
(907) 783-2822
www.doublemuskyinn.com

The Double Musky is more than a great restaurant, it's a phenomenon. Press coverage from around the world has lauded the quirky decor and stunning food as among the finest in not only Alaska but in the nation. No one thinks twice about driving from Anchorage to Girdwood in hopes of getting a table—the Double Musky doesn't take reservations, and that's part of its charm. Nestled at the foot of the Chugach Mountains, the restaurant serves fabulous steaks and Alaskan seafood with New Orleans–style seasonings in a quaint, intimate atmosphere that showcases mirror art, stained glass, and "a million doodads." Pepper steak, jambalaya, étouffée, and gumbo are among the house favorites. Appetizers are hefty enough to pass as entrees if you're not in the mood for a huge meal. The place is packed with tourists and locals in the summer and with fun-loving ski bums in the winter. Your fellow diners might be bush pilots, movie stars, governors, senators, or just plain old Alaskans and wannabe Alaskans looking for a truly memorable dining experience. In business since 1961, the Double Musky is open for dinner only. A tip: show up when they open (5 p.m. weekdays, 4:30 p.m. weekends) and if a line has already formed outside, slip around to the side entrance and sit in the bar. They're closed on Monday and from late October through early December.

GINGER $$$
425 West Fifth Ave.
(907) 929-3680
www.gingeralaska.com

A relative newcomer to the downtown dining scene, Ginger is gaining a following with Pacific Rim and classic Asian cuisine served in a contemporary, urbanesque setting. Alongside Panong Beef Curry and classic pad thai, you'll find filet mignon served with wasabi mashed potatoes and a raspberry demi-port glace. Select wines, sakes, and microbrews may be enjoyed with your meal or in the cozy lounge.

JENS' RESTAURANT $$$
Olympic Center
701 West 36th Ave.
(907) 561-5367
www.jensrestaurant.com

At the corner of Arctic Boulevard and 36th Avenue, Jens' serves new American cuisine with a French twist along with a lunch menu of Danish specialties in an elegant, light dining room enhanced by museum-quality art and a classy wine bar. The strip mall location may put off some visitors, but locals know that with Jens at the helm, there's great food to be had here, with a menu that changes daily to optimize the use of fresh ingredients. Favorite items on the lunch menu include Danish meatballs and chicken-fried steak. For dinner, try the Halibut Meuniere with wild mushrooms in garlic and herb sauce, or the popular pepper steak. Chef Jens Hansen is acclaimed for his ways with seafood, but everything here is tastefully prepared and served with style. Choose from more than 160 wine selections as well as beers from Alaska and around the world. In addition to the regular seating, there's a private dining room that can accommodate up to 20 guests. The wine bar serves appetizers from 4 p.m. to midnight Tuesday through Saturday. Jens' is closed on Sunday.

KINCAID GRILL $$$$
6700 Jewel Lake Rd.
(907) 243-0507
www.kincaidgrill.com

"Fine dining without the attitude" is the mantra at the Kincaid Grill, where you'll find fresh seafood, specialty meats and game, Alaskan regional cuisine, and handcrafted desserts in an unpretentious setting just a few miles from the Ted Stevens International Airport. Everything is made in-house, from sauces and reductions to homemade dressings and accompaniments. Even the meats are carved on-site. Locals come back again and again for such favorites as the Seafood Fusion Soup, crab cakes, shrimp gumbo, and filet of beef served with fresh creamed spinach. The restaurant has a chic neighborhood feel, an extensive wine list, a friendly waitstaff, and ample on-site parking. Chef and owner Al Levinsohn, with an impressive resume featuring some of the most well-known restaurants in the area, hosts a weekly cooking show on a local television station—and recently authored a cookbook. The Kincaid is open for dinner only Tuesday through Saturday. Reservations are recommended.

MARX BROS. CAFE $$$$
624 West Third Ave.
(907) 278-2133
www.marxcafe.com

Unlike most cafes, this place comes to life at night with an imaginative menu of contemporary cuisine featuring fresh Alaskan seafood, game meats, and other unique ingredients. Don't be fooled by this unassuming little 1916 house-turned-restaurant. Inside you'll find tasteful furnishings, a collection of original Alaska art, stained glass, and classic table settings to complement the innovative Northwest cuisine that's been drawing locals and visitors alike since 1979. Among the favorite dishes are the deviled crab cakes with Dungeness crab, chili aioli, and jicama-orange slaw; tableside Caesar salad; halibut baked in macadamia nut crust; and grilled Kodiak scallops coated with poppy and sesame seeds and served with salmon polenta, proscuitto, and mustard-shallot vinaigrette. Enjoy a selection from the extensive wine list, and top off your meal with a dessert specialty, such as the warm berry crisp or the chocolate truffle tart. The Marx Bros. serves dinner only, and it is closed on Sunday and Monday. You'll enjoy an intimate dining atmosphere, with seating for only 60, so reservations are highly recommended. To sample the acclaimed Marx Brothers fare in a more casual setting, stop by their second location inside the Anchorage Museum.

MIXX GRILL STEAK AND SEAFOOD $$$
1200 L St.
(907) 222-8787
www.inlettower.com

With an emphasis on fine-quality ingredients and creative presentation, the Mixx (formerly Mick's at the Inlet) offers fresh Alaskan seafood, North American game meats, and homemade pastas and pastries from its location in the lobby of the Inlet Tower Hotel on the south end of downtown Anchorage. The atmosphere is casual and relaxed, with polished black stone tables, brightly colored walls, and well-appointed lighting. Enjoy menu favorites prepared with local ingredients such as the Blackened Alaskan Prawns and Chorizo or the Savory Mushroom Cheesecake, an appetizer served with bleu cheese, red wine syrup, and fried leeks. They also offer a unique pastaless Spaghetti Provençale with squash noodles, yellow and grape tomatoes, fresh basil, and bleu cheese. There's a full bar menu featuring wines, local brews, and specialty cocktails. Ample parking is another plus. Mixx is open for breakfast, lunch, and dinner seven days a week.

ORSO $$$
737 West Fifth Ave.
(907) 222-3232
www.orsoalaska.com

Sharing owners with the nearby Glacier Brewhouse, Orso is downtown favorite with its upscale Italian atmosphere and emphasis on global flavors with an Alaskan twist. Decorated in warm colors, seating includes an intimate loft level with fireside dining. The menu features fresh wild Alaskan seafood, seasonal Alaskan-grown herbs and vegetables, and locally made pasta. Popular dishes include the fennel-roasted clams in lemon-herb broth; the cashew-crusted halibut in golden raisin-caper sauce with spinach and roasted pepper couscous; the braised lamb Osso Buco with sweet and sour onions, kalamata olives, plum tomatoes, and creamy polenta; and the Molten Chocolate Cake, a dark chocolate flourless cake served with rich chocolate sauce and ice cream. Specialty cocktails, Glacier Brewhouse beers, and a selection of fine wines are available with your meal. Orso is open Monday through Friday for lunch and nightly for dinner. Validated parking is available, and reservations are recommended (you can even make them online).

SACK'S CAFE AND RESTAURANT $$$
328 G St.
(907) 274-4022
www.sackscafe.com

A warm art deco atmosphere showcasing original creations provides the perfect setting for Sack's innovative cuisine. Locals and visitors alike enjoy Sack's extensive, eclectic menu that is new every day. Typical lunch fare includes a tiger prawn and avocado sandwich with herb cream cheese and Dijon mustard, or a Panzanella Bread Salad with buffalo mozzarella, capers, oven-roasted tomatoes, minced olives, and toasted pine nuts. For dinner you're likely to find fabulous seafood choices, such as oven-roasted halibut with chorizo drunken goat cheese, marinated artichoke hearts, and proscuitto-wrapped asparagus, along with pasta, Thai favorites, and such meat dishes as the organic free-range chicken stuffed with proscuitto, spinach, caramelized onions, and manchego cheese. There's a huge wine list as well as draft and bottled beer to accompany your meal. Sack's is open Monday through Friday for lunch, with a brunch menu on weekends. The folks at Sack's will even graciously share some of their best recipes with you.

SIMON AND SEAFORTS $$$$
420 L St.
(907) 274-3502
www.simonandseaforts.com

Stunning views of Cook Inlet and an upscale saloon atmosphere provide the perfect backdrop for the fabulous food that keeps this non-smoking restaurant on the list of Anchorage favorites. The friendly, professional waitstaff will help you choose from weekly specials that highlight fresh fish and seafood but also include original entrees, such as Grilled Elk Chops with Frangelico-Hazelnut Hollandaise and Smoked Reindeer Tenderloin with Blackberry Sage Sauce. The clientele include professionals, tourists, old-time Alaskans with their hallmark baseball hats, and families. The wine list and bar menu are extensive, and all the beer is draft. This place is so well-loved that they hardly need to advertise; in fact, the sign out front of the boxy building that houses the restaurant is so small you'll miss it if you're not looking closely. The bar is a popular Anchorage rendezvous, with half-price appetizers during "happy hour" (4 to 6 p.m. and after 9 p.m.). Reservations for the dining room are advised.

SULLIVAN'S STEAKHOUSE $$$$
320 West Fifth Ave.
(907) 258-2882
www.sullivansteakhouse.com

Sullivan's sleek 1940s-style decor makes this a popular spot for the local business crowd. They often have live jazz music in the bar plus a variety of appetizers and bar menu specials. For lunch, choose from a selection of salads, seafood, steaks, chops, and burgers, with the 10-ounce charbroiled burger a perennial favorite. There's also a business lunch with choice of salad, entree, and side dish. Dinner entrees include the 20-ounce house special Bone-In Kansas City Strip, along with a wide selection of chops, seafood, and steaks. Steaks and chops can be ordered Oscar-style, stuffed with crabmeat. Entrees are served with a wedge of iceberg lettuce and blue cheese dressing; other side dishes are extra. Lunch is served Monday through Friday, with dinner offered seven days a week.

NIGHTLIFE

There's an upside to our long Alaskan winters: The nights go on and on, so there's plenty of time to get out and explore the nightlife. And summer nights? Truly magical. Even at midnight the day's still young and the party has just begun, with lots of open decks and patios available for revelers who want to soak up the light. Don't even think about sleeping.

Since the pipeline days, bars have been the mainstay of Anchorage nightlife. By law, there is one liquor license per 3,000 people, but some 70 establishments were grandfathered in when the municipality came into being, so there's really an abundance of options. In variety and quality, these places have come a long way. Fourth Avenue downtown used to be a red-light district, with one seedy bar after another. That has all been cleaned up. Now there are lots of fun, upscale downtown night spots.

By municipal ordinance, establishments serving alcohol must be closed from 2:30 to 10 a.m. on weekdays, and from 3 to 10 a.m. on weekends and holidays. By municipal ordinance, all Anchorage bars are nonsmoking. Some provide outdoor smoking areas at a designated distance from buildings, but keep in mind that of course it's chilly in winter, especially downtown where wind funnels up from Cook Inlet.

If your blood alcohol level is .08 percent or higher, you're risking a DUI conviction in the state of Alaska. As in most states, this is a serious offense, resulting in confiscation of your license at the time of your arrest followed by a minimum of three days in jail, a $1,500 fine, and a three-month license suspension if you're convicted. And that's just for the first offense. It's best to play it safe and grab a taxi if you need it. Also, be advised that it is illegal to have an open container of alcohol in any vehicle except a chauffeured limousine.

Pubs and Clubs

AL'S ALASKAN INN
7830 Old Seward Highway
(907) 344-6223
www.alsalaskaninn.com

Classy isn't the first word that comes to mind at Al's, but there's a lot happening here, with five bars, three levels, and a Plexiglas dance floor. The South Main Bar is packed with abstract iron art, with bicycle rims, mirrors, and signs protruding from the walls. To top off the unique atmosphere, the walkways, walls, and dance floors are diamond plated. For a more intimate setting, check out the North Cozy Bar or the New Orleans–style Voodoo lounge. Textured aluminum walls, a stainless-steel bar embedded with crop circles and life-size aliens—you can't expect anything much more unusual than Area 51. Head to the North Hollywood Bar if you'd rather have a life-size Marilyn Monroe watching you drink. And if you've had too much to drink, there's a motel conveniently located on the premises—no guarantees that you'll sleep through the nightclub noise.

THE ANCHOR
712 West Fourth Ave.
(907) 677-7979

One of the newer after-hours spots in downtown

Anchorage, the Anchor features a classy interior graced with stainless and polished wood. On Fridays there's live jazz with no cover, and a full dinner menu makes this a quiet place to meet for drinks in the early evening. Later on, expect more activity.

BERNIE'S BUNGALOW
626 D St.
(907) 276-8808
www.berniesbungalowlounge.com
A fun, friendly, relaxed martini lounge at the corner of Seventh Avenue and D Street in downtown Anchorage, Bernie's features more than a dozen martinis plus a dozen beers on tap. Comfy sofas, art on the walls, bright colors—this place will lift your spirits even before you have a drink. There's occasional local music, and Tuesday is karaoke night. Bernie's now offers lunch and dinner menus loaded with tasty appetizers and salads as well as entrees such as Seared Salmon and Seafood, shrimp pad thai, and New York steak and fries.

i For the latest on the Anchorage arts and entertainment scene, pick up a free copy of the *Anchorage Press*. Printed every Thursday, the *Press* is jam-packed with information on theater, live music, restaurants, and everything that's happening in the area. You can also access the *Press* online at www.anchoragepress.com. Another option for staying in the know is the Friday Play section in the *Anchorage Daily News*, with great tips on what's happening over the weekend.

BLUES CENTRAL
825 West Northern Lights Boulevard
(907) 272-1341
Voted the best blues joint in Anchorage, Blues Central brings in musicians from around the area as well as outside for live performances pretty much every night. It's just the sort of dark, funky place where you'd expect a good crowd and

great music, including Blues Jam Sessions and Jazz Jams. Pick up a free Blues Central music calendar for all the entertainment details. Food is served from 11 a.m. to 11 p.m. daily, with French dips on fresh-baked bread a house specialty.

CHILKOOT CHARLIE'S
2435 Spenard Rd.
(907) 272-1010
www.koots.com
Without question the most famous nightspot in Anchorage, Chilkoot Charlie's, better known as Koot's, is pretty much always rocking with a wild and crazy crowd. Ten bars, four dance floors, a big long bar, padded tree-stump seats, sawdust floors—the character of this place just goes on and on. No wonder it made the list of *Playboy*'s top bars in America. DJs play top dance music on the bar's South Stage, while the North Stage spotlights house bands and acts from across the country. Try a custom martini to a backdrop of smooth music in the Swing Bar, or check out the famed Bird House, transplanted from Bird Creek—the panties hanging from the ceiling are your clue that you're in the right place. The windmill in the parking lot will let you know you've found the place. Expect a cover charge and a one-drink minimum to get in on the fun, and if you don't like crowds, you're in the wrong place. The clientele is mostly young, but there's enough action that old-timers won't feel out of place. Koot's motto: "We cheat the other guy and pass the savings on to you."

DARWIN'S THEORY
426 G St.
(907) 277-5322
www.alaska.net/~thndrths
Young, old, regulars, the curious—you'll meet all sorts of people at this hole-in-the-wall bar with an upbeat reputation. Grab some free popcorn and a drink, edge your way to a seat, and do some people watching. It's eclectic, energetic, and interesting, but don't expect live music or anything really upscale here. Cinnamon schnapps is their signature drink, but they've got all the usual

stuff, too. There's wheelchair access, and in fine Alaskan tradition, they serve drinks from 10 a.m. to 2 a.m., 3 a.m. on weekends.

F STREET STATION
325 F St.
(907) 272-9196

The 40-pound block of cheese at the bar is one of the legends about this fun little bar and restaurant. Supposedly the health department complained, so the HELP YOURSELF sign had to come down. The cheese remains, with a FOR DISPLAY ONLY warning that everyone ignores. It's all in the Alaskan spirit of fun, as is the bar's aviator theme. In fact, the bar is a favorite after-hours hangout for pilots. There's a full menu of salads and sandwiches, along with a daily seafood special. The calamari and the eggs benedict (not necessarily together) are especially tasty. Food is served from 11 a.m. to 1 a.m. seven days a week, but don't expect live entertainment here—it's mainly a great spot to wind down and relax with friends.

HUMPY'S GREAT ALASKAN ALEHOUSE
610 West Sixth Ave.
(907) 276-2337
www.humpys.com

Already featured in this chapter's Restaurant listings, Humpy's also earns a spot among the top places to have fun in Anchorage. There's live entertainment every night—Pub Quiz night is legendary—with a casual, quirky, upbeat atmosphere with humpies, also known as pink or dog salmon, represented just about everywhere you turn. Great food, a big bar, and a reputation for being a happening place make this a gathering spot for all sorts of people looking for a good time. There's something for just about everyone here, from live music to the four big-screen plasma TVs. Humpy's is also a favorite watering hole for the after-theater crowd coming from the nearby performing arts center.

MAD MYRNA'S
530 East Fifth Ave.
(907) 276-9762
www.alaska.net/~madmyrna

The premier gay bar in Anchorage, there's always something happening at Mad Myrna's. Dancing, drinks, fashion shows, comedy nights, and Sunday matinees—it's all going on. The Friday Divas Variety Show is a hoot.

MCGINLEY'S PUB
645 G St.
(907) 279-1782
www.mcginleyspub.com

One of the classiest downtown meeting spots is McGinley's, at the corner of Seventh Avenue and G Street, across from the Dena'ina Convention Center. Billed as a touch of old Ireland in downtown Anchorage, McGinley's features a gorgeous bar with lots of mirrors and wood, plus comfortable, upscale seating. Weekends generally bring live music with no cover, though without a stage it sometimes gets swallowed up in the conversation. There's typically a good crowd and lots going on, with Irish beers among those on tap and a wicked Irish coffee. Irish pub food hits the spot for those with a wee bit of hunger. McGinley's celebrates First Fridays with First Taste, with special prices on specialty beers.

PEANUT FARM
5227 Old Seward Highway
(907) 563-2383
www.wemustbenuts.com

This sprawling sports bar at the corner of Interational Airport Road and the Old Seward Highway has something for everyone. Old-timers still flock to the original Peanut Farm, a dark cabin-style bar with peanut shells on the floor and plenty of Alaskan character. If you prefer light and space, move on down to the 20,000-square-foot addition, where lots of big-screen and tabletop TVs feature your favorite sporting events. In the summer there's outdoor seating overlooking Campbell Creek. Besides the sports, the stage, and the dance floor, food is a big draw here. They serve big burgers, including a buffalo burger with pepper jack and barbeque sauce. Fresh-shucked oysters, oyster shooters, or hot-hot-hot oysters are other bar menu favorites. From 6 a.m. to noon during football season, you can grab breakfast along with your game—remember, those East Coast games hit Alaskan screens pretty early. There's plenty of parking and plenty of room inside for you and all of your friends.

PIONEER BAR
739 W. Fourth Ave.
(907) 276-7996
www.pioneerbaralaska.com

Every town has its go-figure bar, the one that's been around forever and suddenly becomes absolutely the place to be, especially if you're young and happening. In Anchorage, that's the Pioneer, which advertises "new life in the old Pioneer" and "home of the almost-perfect bartender." This place first opened its downtown doors in 1916, and while it has doubtless seen its share of rowdy adventure over the last almost-century, it's hard to imagine they've packed in more of a crowd than they do now. Drinks, pool, and a whole lot of shoulder-rubbing—that's what keeps them coming.

PLATINUM JAXX
901 West Sixth Ave.
(907) 278-5299
www.platinumjaxx.com

One of the newer clubs in town, Platinum Jaxx capitalizes on a prime location and spacious building formerly occupied by the popular La Mex restaurant, which relocated south of downtown. Decorated in silver, blue, and gray, this upbeat club offers music, dancing, food, and a low-key dress code (jeans are okay, but hats and

i During the winter, you'll find club-style boxing, complete with bikini-clad ring girls, every Thursday night at the Egan Convention Center. For more information, check out the listing in this chapter's Recreation section, or visit www.thursday nightfights.com. Anchorage plays to Ultimate Fighting fans, too, drawing crowds of more than 3,000 to the Sullivan Arena for fights paired with heavy metal concerts.

grunge gear aren't). Downstairs you'll find a bar that has more than 40 beers on tap and the usual assortment of drinks, seating at booths and tall tables, plasma TVs, a couple of pool tables, and a generally busy dance floor. Upstairs in the VIP lounge there's a smaller bar with leather chairs and walkways that look down into the main bar. The crowd is on the younger side. On the menu, there's chicken, burgers, ribs, and salads.

RUMRUNNER'S OLD TOWNE BAR AND GRILL
Fourth Ave. and E St.
(907) 278-4493
www.rumrunnersak.com

One of the newer, larger downtown hangouts, Rumrunner's recently reopened under new ownership, with a big menu, a lighted dance floor, and a lineup of fun almost every night of the week. Fuel up on your choice of burgers, sandwiches, ribs, or a full seafood dinner, with Rumrunner's own draft beers to go with your meal. Look for DJ music, lots of dancing, and a young crowd Thursday through Saturday nights. There's also a new VIP hangout, the Black Pearl, with black lights and splashes of neon.

SUBZERO MICROLOUNGE
612 F St.
(907) 276-2337

No sense lamenting Alaska's wicked cold—Subzero celebrates the Arctic in style with an iced stainless-steel bar to keep your drinks nicely chilled. And if you like Belgian ales, this is definitely the place to be, with more than 100 Belgian brews to choose from, many of which are on tap. Owned by the same folks who operate Humpy's, Subzero offers a quiet alternative to all the excitement around the corner. They open at 7 p.m. Wednesday through Saturday.

Coffeehouses

CAFE DEL MUNDO
341 East Benson Boulevard
(907) 274-0026

The first coffee roaster in Anchorage, Cafe del Mundo set up shop in a converted greenhouse in 1975. Today they roast coffee for distribution throughout Alaska and to mail-order customers in the Lower 48 and even as far away as Antarctica. In addition to serving a full menu of specialty coffees, Cafe del Mundo offers fine teas and chai, specialty hot chocolate, fresh pastries, Italian gelato, and free Wi-Fi. They also have a south-side coffee shop at 2278 Abbott Road in the Fred Meyer shopping center.

KALADI BROTHERS
6921 Brayton Dr.
(907) 344-6510
www.kaladi.com

The premier coffee roaster in Anchorage, Kaladi's Brayton Drive location is where the whole thing began back in 1986, and it's their roasting and wholesale distribution headquarters, as you'll smell as soon as you pull up. They've now got nine popular locations in Anchorage, including one next to Title Wave Books. All are comfy locations to meet up and relax with a cup of your favorite java roasted the Kaladi way, with fresh hot air. Free Wi-Fi is available at all except the New Sagaya and City Market locations.

MODERN DWELLERS CHOCOLATE LOUNGE
751 East 36th Ave., Suite 105
(907) 677-9985
www.moderndwellers.com

Why settle for coffee when you could have chocolate? At Alaska's only chocolate lounge, you can sample two warm drinking chocolates, one dark and one spicy, and then have your choice mixed with milk or espresso—unless you're a hard-core chocolatier, in which case you'll order it straight. As if that's not tempting enough, there's a large assortment of handcrafted artisan truffles and a full espresso bar. It's a comfortable urban-chic setting to meet with friends and indulge together.

SNOW GOOSE RESTAURANT
717 West Third Ave.
(907) 277-7727
www.alaskabeers.com

What better place than this popular downtown

brewery to host live entertainment on Friday and Saturday nights? Enjoy a view of the inlet, sample some great house brews, and order from a full menu while listening to local musicians. See the full listing in this chapter's Restaurants section.

i When you're looking for weekend activities, don't forget the First Friday Art Walk. Grab a map from the free *Anchorage Press* or the Play section of the Friday edition of the *Anchorage Daily News* and head to the downtown galleries for a host of receptions and art shows. For more about First Fridays, see this chapter's The Arts section.

SHOPPING

When you live in the Alaskan Bush, those regions inaccessible by road, Anchorage seems like a shoppers' paradise. Outsiders will undoubtedly have a different take on the Anchorage shopping scene. Anchorage might not be a true shopping mecca, but between the big franchise stores and the eclectic shops that cater to both tourists and residents you can find pretty much everything you need and a lot of what you want. And Anchorage is small enough that you don't have to think twice about driving across town to that specialty store you love.

Anchorage residents do most of their shopping at the Dimond Center Mall on the south side of town just off the Old Seward Highway, the Northway Mall on the northeast end of town just off the Glenn Highway, and the Fifth Avenue Mall downtown. The Fifth Avenue Mall, anchored by Nordstrom and JCPenney, is the most upscale of the three. Nordstroms, by the way, is such a big landmark that many shops identify their location as "SoNo," meaning south of Nordstroms.

The Dimond Center Mall has seen some lean times, but with a flood of such big box stores as Borders and the Sportsman's Warehouse popping up nearby, the mall has experienced a lot more activity in recent years. A new shopping area, Tikahtnu Commons, is under construction on the east side of town, at the corner of Muldoon Road and the Glenn Highway. Anchored by several box stores, including Target and Lowes, Tikahtnu will be the largest shopping center in Alaska, no doubt siphoning what little traffic remains at the Northway Mall.

Many of the small shops in Anchorage specialize in uniquely Alaskan merchandise. Beads, gold, ivory, furs—these are treasures for tourists and visitors alike. We've given these Alaskan specialty shops their own category, but be sure to check the listings under Boutiques/Gift Shops, Specialty Food Shops, and Souvenir Shops for other places to buy Alaskan gifts and souvenirs.

Alaskan Specialty Shops

ALASKA BEAD COMPANY
2217 East Tudor Rd., Suite 7
(907) 563-2323, (888) 946-2323
www.alaskabead.com
If you'd like to try your hand at creating some of the gorgeous handiwork that Alaska's Native beaders produce, here's a great place to get started. Alaska Bead has beading supplies, tools, books, and wire, along with all sorts of beads. Check out their Japanese seed beads, Austrian crystals, cabochons, Czech seed beads, and, of course, their uniquely Alaskan beads. Located at the corner of Lake Otis Parkway and Tudor Road, the shop offers more than 70 on-site classes featuring local and visiting instructors.

ALASKA FUR EXCHANGE
4417 Old Seward Highway
(907) 563-3877
www.alaskafurexchange.com
Not only is Alaska Fur the state's largest pelt dealer, they also feature a huge collection of museum-quality gifts, including masks, horn carvings, dolls, ivory, whalebone, jade, soapstone, and other Native arts and crafts. They've got a free wildlife exhibit (think taxidermy), and they ship products anywhere. Located at the corner of the Old Seward Highway and Tudor Road, they're closed on Sunday during the winter.

ALASKA IVORY EXCHANGE
700 West Fourth Ave.
(907) 272-3662
www.alaskaivoryexchange.com
A favorite with tourists, Alaska Ivory Exchange showcases all sorts of collectible ivory pieces in a small but inviting retail venue. They have pieces carved from ancient mammoth ivory, some of it 10,000 years old. In addition, you'll find walrus ivory carvings, whalebone carvings, scrimshaw, and soapstone carvings. If you want to whet your appetite before visiting the store, check out their online virtual gallery.

i Due to the Marine Mammals Act, contemporary ivory and baleen must be crafted into art of some type by Alaskan Natives before it can be sold. Scrimshaw and carving are two common art forms for these marine mammal products, though sometimes the work is as simple as the scratching of initials on a piece of baleen.

ALASKA MILL FEED AND GARDEN CENTER
1501 East First Ave.
(907) 276-6016
www.alaskamillandfeed.com
It's neither trendy nor chic, but Alaska Mill and Feed is where Anchorage-ites stock up on bird feed and satisfy their four-legged friends. There's a huge supply of dog food and pet supplies as well as garden stuff and a gift section. You'll know you're in Alaska when you spot the kick sleds and musher's specials.

ALASKA MINT
429 West Fourth Ave.
(907) 278-8414
www.alaskamint.com
There's so much to see at this retail outlet that it's as much a local attraction as it is a store. On display are the largest gold scales in the state along with Alaskan Native and gold-mining artifacts. You can also watch as the mint's craftspeople make medal-

lions with unique Alaskan designs. The Alaska Mint is the official manufacturer of the state medallion and boasts longtime relationships with some of Alaska's oldest sourdough miners. Holiday medallions, Alaskan medallions, natural nugget jewelry, gold quartz jewelry, coin jewelry, and charms are all part of their extensive inventory.

i Those huge black crescents with feathery tufts along the bottom edge? That's baleen, from inside the mouth of a plankton-eating whale. Baleen hangs from the upper jaw of a whale's mouth, with the hairy tendrils used to filter krill. Before modern plastics were invented, baleen was used in women's corsets. It's also called whalebone. Sometimes you'll see it for sale on street corners in the summer.

BELL'S NURSERY
13700 Specking Ave.
(907) 345-4476
www.bellsnurseryak.com
One way Alaskans survive the long winters is by hanging out at Bell's Nursery, where dreams of the next summer's garden are just around the corner. Since 1972, Bell's has been growing quality plants and flowers for the Anchorage market, specializing in the hardy varieties that do well here. Although Bell's has three Anchorage locations, the Specking Road store (just off the exit ramp from the Seward Highway south to DeArmond) is the largest, with a large gift shop and a cozy coffeeshop in addition to all the plants. Bell's is a great place to get fresh Christmas trees, too.

DAVID GREEN, MASTER FURRIER
130 West Fourth Ave.
(907) 277-9595
www.davidgreenfurs.com
Furs aren't for everyone, but they're a mainstay of Alaskan retail, and if you want a coat, David Green has a great reputation around town. Lynx, mink, fox, and beaver are all represented here, with a total inventory of more than 3,000 pieces. The

store is a combination factory and retail outlet. The original David Green started it all in 1922, and his grandson carries on the tradition today.

FIFTH AVENUE JEWELERS
345 West Fifth Ave.
(907) 258-3635, (888) 983-2052
www.productsofalaska.com
The state's leading maker of jewelry crafted from gold quartz, the rarest of natural gold products, Fifth Avenue jewelers sells hundreds of uniquely Alaskan designs. If you don't find what you're looking for, the jewelers can create a custom piece. You'll also find good values on diamonds, Alaska mint coins, watch bands, and a variety of Alaskan-made products. In fact, Fifth Avenue Jewelers promises to beat competitors' prices. They're conveniently located across from the Fifth Avenue Mall.

i If you want a real Alaskan creation, look for the "Made in Alaska" label. Products with the polar bear label have been manufactured or crafted in Alaska, using materials from Alaska whenever possible. The "Silver Hand" label authenticates original handiwork by Alaskan Natives, while the "Alaska Grown" emblem showcases products made with Alaskan raw materials.

OOMINGMAK
604 H St.
(907) 272-9225, (888) 360-9665
www.oomingmak.com
In business since 1969, this Alaskan Native–owned cooperative is a great place to get handknit products made from qiviut (pronounced ki-vee-ute), an extraordinarily warm, soft fiber made from the underwool of the domestic musk ox. Eight times warmer than sheep wool, quiviut isn't scratchy and won't shrink when washed. Knitters in more than 250 isolated villages throughout Alaska create signature designs on scarves, hats, tunics, stoles, and the popular pullover scarf called a

"smoke-ring." Qiviut products are not cheap, but the unique grayish-brown yarn is coveted by Alaskans for its style and warmth.

ULU FACTORY
211 West Ship Creek Ave.
(907) 276-3119, (800) 488-5592
www.theulufactory.com
Originally made of naturally curved slate, the traditional Native knife known as the ulu (pronounced oo-loo) is now formed from steel, but it's still as functional as ever for skinning, filleting, and sewing. You might not get the hang of using this clever tool for cleaning and cutting fish, but you can take one home to chop nuts, slice meats, and do other kitchen tasks. At the Ulu Factory, you can watch the knives being made or catch one of the weekly Native performances in addition to shopping for your own personal ulu. Of course, there are plenty of other Alaskan products and souvenirs for sale here, too.

i There's a great gift shop filled with craft items made by Alaskan Natives at the Alaska Native Medical Center (4315 Diplomacy Dr. Anchorage, AK 99508; 907-563–2662).

Antiques
ANTIQUE GALLERY
1001 West Fourth Ave., Suite B
(907) 276-8986
In one of those "only in Alaska" combinations, you'll find both fine art and rare firearms at this downtown shop. American and European oils, watercolors, bronzes, and prints meet up with the work of such famed Alaskan painters as Sydney Lawrence and Fred Machetanz. There are also Russian icons, Fabergé, estate jewelry, and Indian art and basketry—in short, a little of everything, all upscale.

PACK RAT MALL
5911 Old Seward Highway
(907) 522-5272, (907) 276-8551

Enjoy a complimentary cup of coffee and browse 23,000 square feet of antiques, gifts, and collectibles between this location and the northside shop at 1036 East Seventh Avenue. Among the goodies you'll find are Alaskana, Fenton Art Glass, Fiestaware, and Tiffany lamps. With more than 75 dealers and 1,850 consignors, you can count on doing a whole lot of shopping here. Make sure you plan plenty of time and ask one of the helpful clerks if you're looking for something special.

SANDY'S FAB FINDS
430 C St., Suite 320
(907) 333-4637
This little hideaway, tucked upstairs on a downtown side street, is jam-packed with fun vintage clothing and accessories. Costume jewelry, purses of all shapes and sizes, shoes, and hats can all be found here. Be sure to give yourself plenty of time to shop, because there are literally thousands of things to look at. Owner Sandy Gottstein, from one of Alaska's pioneering retail families, shares her enthusiastic love of all things fun and eclectic, and her black lab gives customers a warm welcome. The shop is closed on Monday.

Bookstores
A NOVEL VIEW
335 E St.
(907) 278-0084
www.homestead.com/anovelview
At a new location between Third and Fourth Avenues downtown, this charming shop is packed with used books. Active in the arts, A Novel View hosts Interactive Novel Dinners, "Saturdays at 2" events showcasing the talents of local performers, and First Friday art receptions. And where else will your quarter buy either a used paperback or a cup of coffee? Ask also about trading credit for your used books.

TITLE WAVE BOOKS
1360 West Northern Lights Boulevard
(907) 278-9283, (888) 598-9283
www.wavebooks.com
Book lovers won't want to miss Alaska's largest

bookstore, with more than 33,000 square feet packed with more than a quarter of a million books. Despite its size, Title Wave is a friendly, relaxed place, and the staff is always at the ready to assist you in finding what you want. They offer a huge selection of used books and a great exchange program. They carry a wide range of Alaskan titles along with large print and audio books. With a great midtown location at the corner of Minnesota and Spenard Avenues, not far from Barnes & Noble, Title Wave hosts author events and musical performances. When Cook Inlet Books went out of business, Title Wave picked up a second location at 415 West Fifth Avenue, across from the Fifth Avenue Mall.

Boutiques/Gift Shops

ALASKA GLASS GALLERY
423 G St.
(907) 279-4527
www.alaskaglassgallery.com
Fluid lines and translucent colors abound in this shop's collection of handblown and sculptured glass art. Gallery director Cynthia England has been working glass since 1980 and has studied with some of the best glass artists in the world, amassing what is arguably the country's finest collection of glass art right here in Anchorage. The colors and detail you'll find here are nothing short of amazing.

ANCHORAGE MUSEUM SHOP
121 West Seventh Ave.
(907) 343-6163
www.anchoragemuseum.org
This attractive shop is one of the best places in the state to get Native art, because they guarantee its authenticity. They also carry fine jewelry by Alaskan craftspeople, distinctive apparel with the crests of North Coast cultures, and books about our state and its history. Besides picking up some quality merchandise, you'll have the added feel-good of knowing that you've supported the museum's exhibits and programs.

Native Arts

The Alaska Museum of Natural History offers pointers on selecting authentic Native arts and crafts. One is to check for quality work. Baskets should have a tight weave and symmetrical shape, while stitching on beadwork and skin products should be neat and regular. Check for authenticity by asking the artist's name and location as well as finding out about the raw materials used. In particular, the use of eagle and duck feathers is not in compliance with the Migratory Bird Act. Buy what you love, and make special note of traditions or innovations that reflect the cultural heritage of the artist.

CABIN FEVER
650 West Fourth Ave.
(907) 278-3522
www.cabinfeveralaska.com
Like its sister shop The Raven, Cabin Fever is one of the most tasteful Alaskan gift shops in town. Supporting more than 400 Alaskan artists, they offer everything from traditional Native dolls and baskets to fun jewelry, handblown glass, ivory ulus, scrimshaw knives, and Alaskan books, all artfully displayed in a way that makes shopping a pleasure. Look for the purple banners at the corner of Fourth Avenue and G Street.

CELTIC TREASURES
4240 Old Seward Highway, Suite 2
(907) 333-2358 (CELT)
www.celtictreasures.us
A favorite with the Anchorage Irish and Scottish crowd, Celtic Treasures offers a charming atmosphere and friendly service from the corner

of Tudor Avenue and the Old Seward Highway. A cup of tea is offered while you browse the unique imports from Ireland, Scotland, and Wales, displayed creatively for your shopping pleasure. The shop offers the state's largest variety of Celtic jewelry and gifts.

CIRCULAR
320 West Fifth Ave.
(907) 274-2472
www.circularstore.com
Relatively new on the Anchorage shopping scene is Circular, an eco-friendly chic boutique across from Nordstroms. Specializing in organic and free-trade products, Circular features an eclectic inventory of clothing, accessories, home decor, bath and body, furniture, and jewelry. Brands include Artechica, Vy & Elle, Del Forte, and Little Earth.

DOWNTOWN CO-OP
320 West Fifth Ave.
(907) 277-5620
Owned and operated by a cooperative of local craftspeople, the Downtown Co-op has a large selection of arts, crafts, and collectibles. Whether you're looking for country or Victorian, stained glass or sweatshirts, rubber stamps or ornaments, there's a good chance you'll find a handcrafted item to take home. The Downtown Co-op is on the first floor of the Fifth Avenue Mall, near the Sixth Avenue entrance.

STYLE OF RUSSIA
333 West Fourth Ave.
(907) 276-5906
www.styleofrussia.com
The Russian influence in Alaska runs deep, and this little shop shows off some of the best of our sister country's art and giftware. Whether you're drawn to Lomonosov porcelain, Siberian shawls, hand-etched crystal eggs, miniature lacquers, Siberian birch bark crafts, Russian Baltic amber, or traditional Russian nesting dolls, they'll not only have something to show you but will also give you a card explaining the item's history, significance, and artistic highlights.

TULIQI
410 G St.
(907) 272-4070, (866) 442-8854 (TULI)
www.tuliqi.com
Tuliqi (pronounced tooly-key) is a bed and bath boutique with a focus on organics. Located in the oldest concrete building in Anchorage, Tuliqi blends natural wood and corrugated roof tin for a truly unique and artistic ambience, creating a tranquil place to shop for earth-friendly linens, sleepwear, and skin-care products. Beauty, wilderness, and home come together in this peaceful, spa-like setting featuring the earth's finest materials, including organic cotton, bamboo, wool, and silk.

Outfitters/Sports Shops

6TH AVENUE OUTFITTERS
520 West Sixth Ave.
(907) 276-0233, (800) 276-0233
www.6thavenueoutfitters.com
When Alaskans are looking for sturdy, practical outdoor gear, they head downtown to 6th Avenue Outfitters and its friendly competition nearby, the Army/Navy Store (see next listing). The clerks at 6th Avenue will be happy to help with your selection of fishing tackle, arctic wear, rain gear, snowshoes, hip boots, camping gear, rods and reels, and pretty much anything else you need to enjoy the great outdoors.

ARMY/NAVY STORE
320 West Fourth Ave.
(888) 836–3535
www.army-navy-store.com
Since 1947, Alaskans have looked to the Army/Navy Store as a great source for government surplus and all types of outdoor gear. They offer a huge selection of Carhartt and Columbia sportswear along with a whole lot of other work wear and boots. Fishing licenses, gloves, rain gear, parkas—you name it, and Army/Navy probably has it. Located right downtown on the corner of Fourth Avenue and C Street, they also do in-house embroidery. BP Exploration, Conoco

Phillips, and Alyeska Pipeline Service Company all send their employees here for gear.

MOUNTAIN VIEW SPORTS CENTER
3838 Old Seward Highway
(907) 563-8600
www.mtviewsports.com

Fishing, camping, hunting, clothing—these are what Mountain View Sports Center is all about. With a long-standing reputation as Alaskan outfitters, the store has taken an upscale turn, featuring brands like Filson, Tibor, and Patagonia. Anglers appreciate the large collection of fly rods and reels, fly-tying materials, and casting and spinning gear. You'll also find a large selection of knives, guns, and ammunition. Pick up a cup of free coffee and browse. You can get licenses and tags for hunting and fishing here, too.

SKINNY RAVEN SPORTS
800 H St.
(907) 274-7222
www.skinnyraven.com

Specializing in running and casual shoes, the Skinny Raven offers such brands as Ibex, Kenneth Cole, Nike, and Patagonia. Try on a new pair of shoes and hop on the Gait Analysis Machine for a computerized opinion on how they're working for you. With the help of this technology, the Skinny Raven's friendly staff will compute the angle of impact and offer advice on how to

i Don't miss Alaska's largest outdoor market, the Downtown Saturday Market, held on summer weekends at the corner of Third Avenue and E Street. Look for the white tents housing more than 300 vendors, who offer everything from fresh seafood to Alaskan-grown produce to arts, crafts, and collectibles. There's also nonstop, live entertainment featuring local acts and groups from across the country, and great food to eat there or take home. Saturday and Sunday markets are open from 10 a.m. to 6 p.m.

improve your running gait. Across the street, the Skinny Raven's sister store, Her Tern, specializes in fine women's shoes and accessories.

Souvenir Shops

ONCE IN A BLUE MOOSE
547 West Fourth Ave.
(907) 276-2141, (888) 490-1898
www.onceinabluemoose.com

Besides the fun name, this sprawling gift shop carries just about everything you could want when it comes to souvenirs. T-shirts, sweatshirts, jackets, hats, gloves, books, videos, dolls, housewares, ulus, and gourmet food are all part of the big selection here. Products from more than a thousand vendors are featured here, with high-quality goods in addition to more affordable souvenirs. Free gifts are offered for purchases above $30 and $100, and there's free gift wrapping, too. They have a second location at the Fifth Avenue Mall, and the same friendly, lifelong Alaskan owners operate several Remember Alaska gift shops. Their free email newsletter is a great way to stay informed on what's happening.

POLAR BEAR GIFTS
442 West Fifth Ave.
(907) 274-4387
www.polarbeargifts.net

There's a lot of fun kitsch here, right down to the player piano plunking away in the background. Polar Bear is the largest souvenir shop in Anchorage, and they specialize in low-end pricing, so if your distant cousins are clamoring for Alaskan souvenirs, this is the place to find them. It's a huge shop with plenty of opportunities for browsing.

TRAPPER JACK'S TRADING POST
701 West Fifth Ave.
(907) 272-6110, (866) 272-6110

With more than 7,000 feet devoted to souvenirs and gifts, Trapper Jack's has the potential to be your one-stop-shop for Alaskan stuff. It's a fun place with a lodge-style interior befitting the woodsy Alaskan items they sell. Don't miss the photo ops with the big stuffed moose and bear. Shop here for jewelry, jade, ulus, Native crafts, apparel, Russian gifts, soapstone, ivory, gold, totems, videos, hats, mugs, throws, and plush animals. There's a large kids' department, and they have all sorts of collectibles, including the popular Snowbabies and wildlife carvings by Big Sky Carvers. If you find you've over-shopped, ask about their shipping services.

i Like to pick your own produce? Head north from Anchorage to Pyrah's Pioneer Peak U-Pick Vegetable Farm on Bodenburg Loop Road in the Matanuska-Susitna Valley, where you'll find prices that are about half of what you'd pay at the grocery store. Pyrah's is closed on Sunday. For more information, call (907) 745-4511. There are also several you-pick strawberry farms in the Mat-Su Valley.

Specialty Food Shops

ALASKA MAX GOURMET
737 West Fifth Ave.
(907) 274-0238
www.alaskamaxgourmet.com
Featuring gourmet foods with a good selection of Alaskan specialties, Alaska Max is a great place to treat yourself and your friends. Birch syrup, truffle oil, hot sauce, smoked salmon, chocolates, honey, and salsa are among the goodies you'll find here. The Made-in-Alaska baskets stocked with treats make great gifts. This is the perfect place to browse while you're waiting for a table at the nearby Glacier Brewhouse restaurant.

ALASKA SAUSAGE AND SEAFOOD
2914 Arctic Boulevard
(907) 562-3636, (800) 798-3636
www.alaskasausage.com
Since 1963, Alaska Sausage and Seafood has been making gourmet treats out of local fish and game. Bring in your own catch to be processed, or sample some of their prepackaged

fare. Salmon can be kipper smoked, smoked in strips, or cured into lox. They'll also cut, fillet, and vacuum pack fresh fish. Reindeer meat products are another specialty.

ALASKA WILD BERRY PRODUCTS
5225 Juneau St.
(907) 562-8858, (800) 280-2927
www.alaskawildberryproducts.com
It's easy to see why this massive candy company and retail outlet has been a favorite with Alaskans and their guests since 1946. Who could resist the world's largest chocolate "waterfall," the chance to see candies, jams, and jellies being made, or complementary samples of chocolates and truffles? Take a free kitchen tour and leave yourself plenty of time to shop, because they offer just about every Alaskan souvenir you can imagine. For added tourist fun, there's a Wild Berry Park and Village, complete with Holly the Reindeer. The main store is just past the corner of International Airport Road and the Old Seward Highway, behind the Peanut Farm and the Sourdough Mining Company. Other retail outlets are found in the Fifth Avenue Mall, in Wasilla, and in Homer.

FLYING DUTCHMAN EUROPEAN PASTRY
2101 Abbott Rd., #9
(907) 274-1072
www.ravenchocolates.com
Famous for luscious pastries and hand-dipped chocolates, the original Dutchman Ben Koper opened his first shop in 1982, the same year he got his private pilot's license. The success of his bakery proved that Anchorage residents did indeed appreciate his commitment to using only the finest and freshest ingredients. Ben's gone now, but daughter Frieda continues crafting chocolates, tortes, cakes, flans, and cheesecakes to satisfy Anchorage's collective sweet tooth.

KOBUK COFFEE AND TEA COMPANY
504 West Fifth Ave.
(907) 272-3626
www.kobukcoffee.com
Kobuk Coffee retains the 1915 charm of the original Kimball Dry Goods Store, with old-fashioned

candy on display in glass jars and the smell of their spicy Samovar tea greeting shoppers as they come through the door. Sample a cup of tea while browsing the gift and coffee selections. The living quarters in the back of the store have been converted into a bakery with all sorts of treats to eat in or take out.

NEW SAGAYA MARKETS
900 West 13th Ave.
(907) 274-6173, (907) 561-5173
www.newsagaya.com

With lots of trendy, upscale organics, the New Sagaya Markets are Anchorage's answer to Trader Joe's. Locally owned for more than 30 years, New Sagaya specializes in gourmet products, fresh produce, Alaskan seafood, and Asian groceries. Supplying local restaurants with top-notch ingredients, New Sagaya has its own great deli where you can pick up a tasty, healthy salad, sandwich, or entree to eat in or take home. In addition to the city market location at the corner of L Street and 15th Avenue, there's a New Sagaya Midtown Market at 3700 Old Seward Highway.

SUMMIT TEA AND SPICE
1120 Huffman Rd., #4
(907) 348-3585
www.summitspiceandtea.com

It's worth a stop at this family-owned specialty tea, spice, and chocolate shop just to take in the smells. Among more than 100 varieties of premium tea are special Alaskan blends like the Alyeska Spice and Denali breakfast blends. Most of the teas and spices are sold by the ounce, but there are packaged versions of many blends, including rubs and seasonings perfect for your Alaskan salmon and halibut. Cooks will delight in a variety of chiles, specialty foods, and kitchen goodies.

Women's and Children's Clothing

BLUSH
720 D St.
(907) 677-8967
www.boutiqueblush.com

Celebrating the individual in the trendy So-No (south of Nordstrom) district, this boutique owned and operated by a longtime Anchorage resident offers hand-picked contemporary collections from New York and Los Angeles. They carry BCBG, Free People, Hudson, Trovata, Burning Torch, LaMade, Velvet, Puella, True Religion, and Meli Melo brands. Bringing chic urban style to Alaska, Blush offers the largest premium denim selection in the state.

PIA'S SCANDANAVIAN WOOLENS
445 West Fourth Ave.
(907) 277-7964, (888) 274-9665
www.piasweaters.com

High-quality Nordic sweaters are the perfect apparel for Alaska's long cold winters, and Pia's is the place to get them. In this tasteful boutique, you'll find cardigans and sweaters for men and women, Icelandic jackets, children's woolens, lambskin slippers, and bulky but-oh-so-warm-and-comfy Loebben boots.

ROSITA'S BOUTIQUE
939 West Fifth Ave., Suite Q
(907) 274-7143

Tucked among the shops in the Hotel Captain Cook, Rosita's is a stand-out boutique with a fabulous assortment of women's clothing and accessories. Artful without being trendy, at Rosita's you can count on finding something unique and well-cut for all sorts of occasions, from unique European fashions to wearable art accessories. And a thank-you note from your sales clerk? That's just another reason to feel pleased with your purchase. Ask about their discounts for Alaskan residents—they really mean it.

SECOND RUN
720 D St.
(907) 277-6119
www.outoftheclosetalaska.com

Featuring "upscale resale" in sizes 0 to 16, this store made national news when it was reported that Alaska's governor and vice-presidential candidate Sarah Palin had shopped there. With the national attention came word that the store's original

Close-up

Lasting Impressions

Birch, forget-me-not, yarrow, black currant, wild chive, rose hips, and chickweed. To Janet Shafsky, these are not just wild Alaskan plants, they're the foundation of a unique line of skin-care products and cosmetics made in Anchorage and distributed throughout the world.

It would be hard to find a more committed and energetic entrepreneur than the founder of Impressions by Janet. When she first moved to Alaska from Southern California in 1979, Shafsky says she cried all the way here. Formerly a makeup artist for Hollywood celebrities, she found herself in a place where she couldn't even get television newscasters interested in professional makeup services because they had no budget for it. Her friends placed bets on how quickly she'd move back, but she drew on her Alaskan heritage—her mother was born here and her grandfather was a territorial judge—and settled happily into a homestead off O'Malley Road in Anchorage. "It's a pretty awesome place to live," Shafsky says now.

As hard as she works at fine-tuning her products, people are Janet's top priority. In fact, it was meeting the special needs of her clients and friends that got her to start using natural botanicals to counter the effects of the harsh Alaskan climate. The previous owner of their property, a master gardener who served on the Board of Directors for the University of Alaska Cooperative Extension program, had planted wildflowers and herbs across the homestead. Shafsky, a certified skin-care specialist, studied the medicinal properties of the plants growing in her own yard and began incorporating them into the products she used while giving facials. Her customers kept bringing back empty jars and asking for more, prompting Shafsky to start her own line of cosmetics and skin-care products using Alaskan ingredients.

"You think of Alaska, and Alaska is pure. It's the most natural place left on earth," Shafsky says. "We boil a lot of extracts, and we tap our trees. It's a lot of hard work." Now that the homestead has been subdivided, the company also acquires ingredients from suppliers around the state, always with an eye to quality and purity.

Shafsky tinkers with her products until she gets them right. She went back and forth with Iditarod veteran DeeDee Jonrowe for six months in order to perfect her Ididacreme, designed to protect skin from extreme conditions like those on the Iditarod Sled Dog Race. "It acts

name, Out of the Closet, had been spoken for, so the store became Second Run in February 2009. In addition to a famous customer, Second Run features designer labels that are tough to find in Anchorage. Sure, they're gently used, but that's a small sacrifice if you're out to impress. Located in Anchorage's SoNo district, Second Run's staff is fun, personable, and chic—and it even includes a couple of trend-setting canines.

SPOILED
1140 W. Dimond Boulevard, Suite A
(907) 743-3095
www.spoiledboutique.com

A sister store to Blush, Spoiled specializes in luxuries for little ones, with beautiful children's clothing for newborns to six year olds. They also carry imported nursery furniture, BumbleRide strollers, Dwell bedding, and unique baby gifts. Moms are pampered here as well, with beautiful maternity clothes you won't want to part with.

WOOLIES
1200 West Northern Lights Boulevard
(907) 563-1008, (907) 276-1008
Woolies imports colorful sweaters and hats— mostly from South and Central America—to warm Alaskans chilled by winter. Especially popular are

like a little glove," Shafsky says of the creme, which has proven very helpful and soothing to clients with extra-dry skin and eczema. Given the severe lack of humidity in Alaska as well as in much of the Lower 48, Ididacreme is one of Shafsky's most popular products, along with Sleeping Lady Night Creme, Aurora Orange Cleansing Sensation, Gold Rush Toner, and the Forget-Me-Not Daily Exfoliator.

A distribution stint with a big-name box store robbed Shafsky of the satisfaction she gets from customer contact, so she has returned to distributing her products primarily through online orders. "Customer service is the most important thing in the world to me," she says. "I love working with the Internet so I can still have the customer connection. It is so fun to get orders from all over the world. I feel like my wildflowers have blown to places in the world that I have only dreamed of." How many other cosmetic manufacturers have photos of their customers on the walls of their shop or send personal thank-yous with each purchase they ship?

Shafsky also provides professional makeup services. "I have been doing makeup non-stop on politicians, movie stars, films, print and video," she says. "I have been all over Alaska doing makeup—on top of glaciers, mountains, floating rivers, under the pipeline."

But even with all that activity, including providing products to more than 5,000 customers, Shafsky achieves a sense of balance in her life. Perhaps it's due to the tranquil setting in which she works. The lower level of her 4,800-square-foot log home is replete with rock walls, candles, and waterfalls, making it a soothing place for her to give facials and do makeovers. Shafsky claims giving facials is almost as relaxing for her as it is for her clients. "A lot of times, that's when I think of new ideas," she says. More proof of the balance in this entrepreneur's life is that she has never let her business override her commitment to her family. Her husband, with a degree in biology and field chemistry, has been an invaluable resource in product development, and her three daughters have grown up testing and modeling her cosmetics.

In Anchorage, you can find Impressions by Janet skin-care products by appointment only at First and Lasting Impressions, Inc. (907-522-4506). Better yet, order Janet's products online at www.impressionsbyjanet.com, or by calling toll-free (888) 522-4507.

their flap hats lined with fleece. Geared up from Woolies, winter seems almost fun. Woolies makes the rounds at Alaskan fairs each summer, selling gauzy dresses and skirts along with their woolens. You'll find them at two year-round locations in Anchorage, near REI in the Northern Lights Center and downtown at the Fifth Avenue Mall.

ATTRACTIONS

A number of Anchorage attractions celebrate the rich cultural diversity, the colorful history, and the abundant wildlife of Alaska. As an added bonus, most admission charges are minimal, and you're guaranteed to walk away knowing

a lot more about the 49th state than you knew going in. A note on museums: With the exception of the sprawling Anchorage Museum, the museums listed here are small and specialized. If you're looking for something on the order of the NASA Aerospace Museum, for instance, the Alaska Aviation Museum will disappoint. But for an insiders' look at what makes Alaska tick, many of these little places, assembled and sustained by dedicated volunteers, can't be beat.

Many attractions operate on abbreviated schedules or are closed completely in the winter, so be sure to pay attention to notes about winter hours in the listings below. The price codes show what you can expect to pay for one adult admission. Most offer discounts for children and seniors, and some offer military discounts as well. Attractions with free admission will have no price code.

Price Codes

$.................Less than $5
$$ ....$5–$10
$$$ ....$11–$15
$$$$ .... More than $15

ALASKA AVIATION HERITAGE MUSEUM $$
4721 Aircraft Dr.
(907) 248-5325
www.alaskaairmuseum.org
Alaska has always been on the cutting edge of what's happening in aviation, so it's not surprising that we have an entire museum devoted to aviation history. At the museum you'll see 25 rare bush planes plus photographs and memorabilia from some of the state's legendary bush pilots. You'll also get to see aircraft in the process of being restored. There's a theater where you can watch pioneer film footage and an observation deck where you can watch seaplanes taking off from and landing on Lake Hood. This is a great place to get a better appreciation for the incredible courage and pluck that put Alaskan bush pilots in a class by themselves. The Alaska Aviation Heritage Museum is just a short drive from the Ted Stevens International Airport, and shuttle service is available.

ALASKA BOTANICAL GARDEN $$
4601 Campbell Airstrip Rd.
(907) 770-3692
www.alaskabg.org
Alaskan summers are short by some standards, but our extensive daylight makes the growing season intense. The Alaska Botanical Garden is a great place to check out the beauty and diversity of the hardy plants, shrubs, herbs, and wildflowers that flourish in spite of the long, cold winters and the rather rushed summers. Nestled among the spruce and birch in this 110-acre sanctuary, you'll find more than 1,100 species of perennials and 150 native plants. Hike the self-guided, 1.1 mile Lowenfels Family Nature Trail down to Campbell Creek, where you may be treated to a glimpse of the king salmon run. The Alaska Botanical Garden hosts many special events throughout the year, and they offer free parking. Open year-round (the greenhouses make a lovely mid-winter retreat), the Alaska Botanical Garden offers guided tours at 1 p.m. daily during the summer.

ALASKA EXPERIENCE CENTER $$
333 W. Fourth Ave.
(907) 276-3730, (877) 276-3730
www.alaskaexperiencetheatre.com
In a new location in the Fourth Avenue Marketplace at the corner of Fourth Avenue and C Street, the Alaska Experience Center captures the highlights of our state with two virtual film experiences. Digital surround sound, breathtaking photography, and the domed screen create

Alaska's Native Cultures

Alaska's Native peoples enjoy a cultural diversity unmatched by any other state, with each group well-adapted to its own unique ecological and geographical landscapes. Eskimo groups include the Inupiat in the north and the Yup'ik/Cup'ik cultures in Southwestern Alaska. Athabascan Indians traditionally inhabited the interior regions of the state, while the Alutiiq are native to the Aleutian Islands. The Eyak, Haida, Tlingit, and Tsimshian are peoples of the southeastern coastal region. Unlike American Indians, Alaska's Native peoples do not live on reservations. Under provisions of the Alaska Native Claims Settlement Act, they own land and are shareholders in one of 13 Native corporations.

an illusion of reality, transporting you to places you'd love to go if only you had the time and the resources. After your 40-minute tour of the greatland, you can go back in time and relive Alaska's famous 1964 earthquake, which registered 9.2 on the Richter scale.

ALASKA MUSEUM OF NATURAL HISTORY $$

201 North Bragaw St.
(907) 274-2400
www.alaskamuseum.org

Two University of Alaska professors with a commitment to science education spearheaded an organizational effort that started in 1989 and culminated with the opening of this educational facility in 1994. In recent years the fledgling museum has acquired a 12,000-square-foot building to house exhibits featuring the geological, ecological, and cultural history of Alaska. The annual tally of 4,000 visitors is a drop in the bucket compared to what the larger, plusher Anchorage Museum takes in, but if you don't need a lot of fancy bells and whistles to pique your interest, you'll learn about Alaska's wildlife, rocks, minerals, dinosaurs, and artifacts here. Featured exhibits include the Broken Mammoth Dig Site and Ice Age Mammals.

ALASKA NATIVE HERITAGE CENTER $$$$

8800 Heritage Center Dr.
(907) 330-8000, (800) 315-6608
www.alaskanative.net

Alaska is so big that it's almost impossible to see it all. Visitors rarely get to the remote parts of the state where Alaskan Natives live a modified but still traditional lifestyle. To promote and share these traditions, the Alaska Federation of Natives established the nonprofit Alaska Native Heritage Center in 1989. Spread across 26 acres, the center includes a Welcome House plus five traditional outdoor village sites surrounding Lake Tiulana. The center hosts demonstrations by artists and dance groups, films and exhibits, story-telling, and classes in art, dance, and Alaska Native languages. After enjoying the day's program, you can take self-guided tours of the outdoor villages, where local Native students will answer your questions about the cultures represented.

At the Welcome House, you'll find a time-line of significant historical and legendary events, as well as video monitors showing clips of contemporary Native life. An 18-minute film, *Stories Given, Stories Shared,* introduces the diverse cultures of the Alaska Native people and the unique places where they live. In the Hall of Cultures, you'll find exhibits and demonstrations featuring Athabascan, Yup'ik, Cup'ik, Inupiaq, Alutiiq, Tlingit, Eyak, Haida, and Tsimshian cultures and lifestyles. At the Gathering Place, you can watch traditional dancers or listen to stories that have been passed from one generation to the next.

The center hosts an Institute of Alaska Native Artists, youth programs, school visits, and adult education classes and workshops, with class schedules changing every four weeks. Two Heritage Gift Stores, one in the Welcome House and one downtown at 333 West Fourth Avenue, support the ongoing work of the center. During the winter the center is open on Saturday only, featuring special Celebrating Culture Saturday programs.

ALASKA PUBLIC LANDS INFORMATION CENTER

605 West Fourth Ave.
(907) 644-3661
www.alaskacenters.gov

The Public Lands Information Center is a great place to orient yourself to the state and to plan your Alaskan adventures. They offer free natural history and cultural exhibits along with information on wildlife, camping, and recreational cabins on federal land. In the summer you can participate in a free special event almost every hour, whether it's a movie about the big earthquake or Alaskan wildlife, a Captain Cook Walking Tour, or a live animal program. You'll find the Public Lands Information Center downtown at the corner of Fourth Avenue and F Street, across from the Hilton Hotel. There's no admission charge, but because it's in the Federal Building, security screening is required.

ℹ **If you work up an appetite exploring downtown attractions, stop by the reindeer sausage stand in front of the Federal Building at 605 West Fourth Avenue. It's an Anchorage icon—just follow your nose.**

ALASKA STATE TROOPER MUSEUM
245 West Fifth Ave.
(907) 279-5050
www.alaskatroopermuseum.com

In a place known as the Last Frontier, you'd expect some hefty law enforcement challenges, and Alaska doesn't disappoint. At the Alaska State Trooper Museum, you'll get a free glimpse into the colorful history and excitement that are part of laying down the law in one of the most far-flung jurisdictions in the country. Exhibits include photographs, memorabilia, and historic police equipment, including a restored 1952 Hudson patrol vehicle. Located downtown off Fifth Avenue between B and C Streets, the State Trooper Museum includes a gift shop, with proceeds going to fund the activities of the Fraternal Order of Alaska State Troopers. There's no charge for admission.

THE ALASKA ZOO $$$
4731 O'Malley Rd.
(907) 346-3242
www.alaskazoo.org

Most newcomers to Alaska are anxious to see some wildlife, and even the most seasoned sourdoughs thrill at the sight of a grizzly, a moose, or an elusive lynx. But even though the wildlife is abundant, Alaska's huge wilderness provides plenty of room for animals to roam, so you may not see as many critters as you'd hoped. At the Alaska Zoo, guaranteed wildlife viewing attracts both locals and guests. The zoo is only 15 minutes from downtown Anchorage, and seasonal shuttle service is available. Founded in 1968, the Alaska Zoo is a private nonprofit that houses arctic and subarctic wildlife for the joint purposes of education and enjoyment. The zoo has a gift shop, coffee shop, and education center, and it's open year-round. Check the online calendar for special events.

ALYESKA TRAMWAY $$$$
Alyeska Resort
(907) 754-1111
www.alyeskaresort.com

The Alyeska Tramway whisks you from 306 feet above sea level to 2,334 feet above sea level in a matter of minutes. You'll have a spectacular view of mountains, glaciers, and streams en route, and when you reach the observation deck, you can hike, explore, pick berries, or even try some paragliding. The Swiss-built tram runs slower in the summer so you can soak up the view, and there are telescopes up top if you want to get a closer look. To catch the tram, take the Seward Highway south to Girdwood and follow the signs to Alyeska Resort.

Aurora Borealis

What causes the aurora borealis, or northern lights? Solar winds from eruptions on the sun are drawn into the earth's magnetic field, where they show up as dancing fingers of green, red, and purple light. Legends about the northern lights abound. Some Alaskan Native children are taught to whistle when they see the lights so they won't be snatched into the sky, while in some Asian cultures it's believed that a child conceived under the northern lights will be especially gifted. The *Anchorage Daily News* includes daily aurora forecasts, and many hotels provide aurora wake-up calls for those who want them. You'll see the lights best on dark, clear nights, away from the light pollution of the city.

ANCHORAGE MUSEUM OF
HISTORY AND ART $$
121 West Seventh Ave.
(907) 343-4326
www.anchoragemuseum.org

It's the largest museum in Alaska, it's one of the 10 most visited attractions in the state, and it hosts more than 150,000 guests each year. And that's just as it sits now. After a major expansion project slated for completion in early 2010, the Anchorage Museum will add 70,000 square feet to its current 93,000 square feet of interior space, including a fourth-floor library and a Smithsonian Arctic Studies Center. The expansion also includes development of a two-acre urban forest and incorporation of the Imaginarium for children, currently at a separate downtown location (see listing in our Kid Stuff section).

Making the museum bigger means more of what's already a very good thing for Anchorage. The Alaska Gallery, exploring 10,000 years of Alaskan history, is a great place to orientate yourself to the state. There you'll see Alaskan Native artifacts, life-size renditions of pioneer and Native dwellings, and a slice of the Alaska Pipeline. The six galleries in the Art of the North section display sculpture and paintings from the days of early exploration through modern times, while three additional galleries house special exhibits on art, archaeology, and history. There's also a Children's Gallery and adjacent Art Activity Room for hands-on family activities.

If all this exploring makes you hungry, don't despair. Anchorage's well-loved Marx Bros. Cafe operates a museum cafe that serves up dishes that rival museum fare from anywhere in the world. On top of that, the museum's gift shop has one of the best collections of authentic Alaskan Native art you'll find; see the complete listing on the gift shop in this chapter's Shopping section. In addition, the museum maintains a full slate of activities, including Historical Society lectures, First Friday "Singles After Hours," Sunday stories for children, book signings, workshops, and weekend Movies for Your Mind, featuring classic and contemporary global cinema.

The parking garage is open for handicap parking during the week and for public parking on weekends. During the winter the museum is closed on Monday.

AURORA: ALASKA'S GREAT
NORTHERN LIGHTS $$
Sydney Laurence Theatre Alaska Center
for the Performing Arts
Sixth Ave. and F St.
(907) 263-2993
www.thealaskacollection.com

When do they turn on the northern lights? Not in the summer, when almost endless daylight prevents us from seeing any heavenly attractions. But summer visitors can watch stunning digital images of this incredible phenomenon in the Sydney Laurence Theatre at the Alaska Center for the Performing Arts. Anchorage photographer Dave Parkhurst has been chasing and photographing rare auroral displays since 1981. You'll get to sit back and enjoy the fruits of his cold, midnight labors in comfort, complete with a background of original digital music. Shows run about 40 minutes, and reservations are not required. This attraction is open only in the summer, so if you're here in the offseason, you'll have to try your luck at seeing the real thing. If you'd like some help planning your aurora expeditions, the folks at the Alaska Collection offer winter Aurora Watch tours; for more information, check out the Web site.

CROW CREEK MINE $$$
P.O. Box 113, Girdwood, AK 99587
(907) 229-3105
www.akmining.com/mine/crow.htm

Just a few miles past Alyeska Resort, Crow Creek Mine is a great place to try finding your own gold nugget to take home. Over the years the mine has produced more than 45,000 ounces of gold, and there's an estimated one million yards left to be tried. Locals stop by to try their hand at a creek that yields more gold to metal detectors than any other in the state. First-timers are given a bag of gold-bearing dirt from the creek to help them get started. Even if you don't get lucky, you'll enjoy the wilderness setting. Crow Creek Mine is on the Register of National Historic Places, with old mining buildings and artifacts scattered throughout. This area can be damper than Anchorage, so be sure to bring rain gear. There's no food for sale on-site, so you'll want to bring your own. You can camp overnight for a fee.

EAGLE RIVER NATURE CENTER $
32750 Eagle River Rd., Eagle River
(907) 694-2108
www.ernc.org

In response to drastic cuts in the budget for Chugach State Park, park administrators linked avid nature lovers with corporate sponsors to create a gateway destination. Open year-round, the center provides great opportunities for wildlife viewing along with weekly interpretive programs and daily guided walks in the summer. If you want to spend the night, an easy 2-mile hike will take you to one of the center's yurts or cabins. The center maintains several trails and operates a gift shop. To get there, take the Eagle River Loop Road exit off the Glenn Highway, turn right at the third light, and continue 12 miles to the road's end, where you'll find the facility. No admission is charged, but there is a parking fee.

HERITAGE LIBRARY MUSEUM
301 West Northern Lights Boulevard
(907) 265-2834

For a museum experience with no admission charge, you can't beat the Heritage Library Museum, located on the first floor of the Wells Fargo Bank Building at the corner of C Street and Northern Lights Boulevard. Established in 1968, this is one of the largest privately owned displays of Alaskan culture and history that you'll find anywhere. The collection of Alaskan Native artifacts includes baskets, ivory carvings, household utensils, clothing, and hunting implements. The fine arts collection includes impressive landscapes by well-known Alaska painters Sydney Laurence, Eustace Ziegler, Magnus Heurlin, and James Belcher. The museum also maintains a

2,600-volume reference library on Alaska, along with photo archives featuring pictures from the gold rush era and beyond. The museum is open on weekday afternoons only. There is no admission charge, and parking is free.

i For fantastic views of Cook Inlet and downtown Anchorage, make your way into the Chugach Mountains via the Glen Alps Trailhead parking area (parking is $5). A short walking loop takes you to a prime photo spot. If you're feeling ambitious, venture down the Powerline Trail or the steeper Flattop Trail. For details and directions, see the listing for Chugach State Park under "Parks, Recreation, and Tours" later in this chapter.

INDIAN VALLEY MINE $
Mile 104 Seward Highway, Indian
(907) 653-1120
www.indianvalleymine.com

Though the address is out of town, this family-run mining attraction is only about 20 minutes south of Anchorage. For a nominal admission charge, you'll get to see two of the oldest structures on Turnagain Arm and browse a small museum. If you want to buy a bucket of pay dirt, you can learn to pan for gold and find out about other places to try your luck. While you're here, the Cowles family will tell you the story of Peter Strong, the original prospector who did some small-time mining and built the assay office here. Even if you're not into gold, you can relax at the picnic tables, enjoy the gardens, and take in some

i Catch a glimpse of local history at Historic City Hall at the corner of Fourth Avenue and E Street, where there's a free exhibit on Anchorage's pioneer days on the main floor. Or check out the Fourth Avenue Theatre, an art deco–style building dating from 1947. At the Ship Creek Center downtown, you might be lucky enough to catch one of two free daily summer performances of Alaskan Native dancing.

fabulous views of Turnagain Arm. This isn't a big, showy attraction, but sometimes it's a relief to go where you don't have to fight your way past busloads of tourists to try something new. The mine is open only during the summer.

OSCAR ANDERSON HOUSE MUSEUM $
420 M St.
(907) 274-2336
Back in 1915 when Anchorage was still a tent city, Swedish immigrant Oscar Anderson built the first frame house. Restored with period detail and many of the original fixtures, this is now the only house museum in town. Guided tours take approximately 45 minutes. You also can opt for a combined ticket that includes a 2-mile walking tour of historic downtown Anchorage with a volunteer guide. The museum is open afternoons in the summer only, and it is closed on Sunday and Monday. For the first two weekends in December, the house re-opens for Swedish Christmas Tours.

i For a fabulous picnic spot with great views of Knik Arm and, on clear days, Mount McKinely and Mount Foraker far to the north, stop by Point Woronzoff, at the end of Postmark Drive off the west end of International Airport Road. It's a romantic place to watch the sunset, too—right around midnight in the summer months.

WILDRIDE SLED DOG RODEO $$$$
185 E. Ship Creek Rd.
(888) 221-MUSH (6874) or
(907) 561-MUSH (6874)
www.ididaride.com/tours/anchorage/
wildride.htm
Can't make it to Alaska in March for the Iditarod? Iditarod veteran Mitch Seavey and family will give you a taste of the fun just north of downtown Anchorage. A cast of 20 sled dogs and four mushers will treat you to a rollicking tour of mushing history and demonstrations of the dogs' power and stamina. Adorable husky pups round out the show.

KIDSTUFF

Kids, like their parents, will have a lot of fun getting outside and enjoying all the outdoor recreation opportunities in Anchorage. But there's lots of indoor fun to be had as well. From science explorations to rollicking waterslides, kids in Anchorage will find plenty to do even on those cold winter days that don't lend themselves well to the great outdoors.

Be sure to check the listings under this chapter's Parks, Recreation, and Tours section for additional kid-friendly adventures, but keep in mind that Alaska is more wild and rugged than what some folks are used to. If you're biking, hiking, or skiing with kids, be extra-sure to prepare for the unexpected, whether it might be a change in weather, a lack of facilities, or rougher trail conditions than anticipated. If you're participating in an organized activity such as river rafting or horseback riding, ask about suitability for young adventurers.

Some of these kid-friendly spots are also discussed in this chapter's Attractions section. Many of them operate on an abbreviated schedule or are closed completely in the winter, so be sure to pay attention to notes about winter hours. The price codes show what you can expect to pay for one adult admission. Those geared to both adults and children tend to offer reduced admission for kids. Attractions with free admission have no price code.

Price Codes

$	Less than $5
$$	$5–$10
$$$	$11–$15
$$$$	More than $15

ALASKA BOTANICAL GARDEN $$
(907) 770-3692
www.alaskabg.org
The self-guided, 1.1-mile Lowenfels Family Nature Trail down to Campbell Creek makes a great family outing. The reward at the end of the trail, in season, is the salmon run. On Wednesdays dur-

ing the summer, there's a free storytime for kids at the garden. The garden is open from May 15 through September 15, with guided tours available for a nominal charge. See the complete listing in this chapter's Attractions section.

ℹ️ For fun storytime activities, check schedules at Borders Books, Title Wave Books, the Loussac Library, and the Anchorage Museum. Local bookstores also feature several Alaskan books for children.

ALASKA EXPERIENCE CENTER $$
333 West Fourth Ave.
(907) 276-3730, (877) 276-3730
www.alaskaexperiencetheatre.com
What kid doesn't like to rock and roll? The moving and shaking of this simulated seismic experience, based on the tremors of Alaska's famous Good Friday Earthquake of 1964, is sure to be a hit with youngsters. Even the tremor-free companion film, *Alaska the Greatland*, will awe viewers with its digital sound and three-story-high screen. For more information, check the complete listing in this chapter's Attractions section.

ℹ️ Make the most of Anchorage winter by zipping down one of the city's many sledding hills. At www.anchorage.net, you'll find a list of nine great sledding hills around town.

ALASKA WILD BERRY PRODUCTS
5225 Juneau St.
(907) 561-9498
www.alaskawildberryproducts.com
A chocolate waterfall and a huge candy store are great ways to distract the kids while you're busy hand-picking souvenirs for the folks back home. Kids can watch their favorite candies, jams, and jellies being made and even indulge in some free samples. Don't miss Holly the Reindeer in the adjacent Wild Berry Park and Village. See the full listing in this chapter's Shopping section under Specialty Food Shops.

ALASKA WILDLIFE CONSERVATION CENTER $$
Mile 79 Seward Highway, Portage Glacier
(907) 783-2025
awcc.org/home.html
Kids will love getting a close look at wildlife in its natural habitat at this drive-through wildlife park 48 miles south of Anchorage. They'll see dozens of species, from big game to smaller mammals and birds. All the animals here are rescued in a nonprofit effort to rehabilitate injured or orphaned animals while educating visitors on Alaskan wildlife. Admission fees are reasonable, and proceeds go toward supporting the continued efforts on behalf of the animals. The center is open daily throughout the year, from 8 a.m. to 8 p.m. during the summer season, from 10 a.m. to 6 p.m. from April to mid-May, and from 10 a.m. to 5 p.m. September through March. See the complete listing in the Portage/Whittier section of the Prince William Sound chapter.

THE ALASKA ZOO $$
4731 O'Malley Rd.
(907) 346-3242
www.alaskazoo.org
Sure, most kids have been to the zoo, but the Alaska Zoo is unique in presenting almost 50 native Alaskan mammals and birds in a natural setting about 15 minutes from downtown Anchorage. None of these animals was simply snatched from the wild; all were either orphaned, abandoned, endangered, or injured before being brought here. Among the kids' favorites is Apuhn the polar bear. In the summer, Tuesday is family night at the zoo, and there are also Summer Naturalist Tours. Ask for the zoo's *Unguided Tour Supplement*, which provides lots of fun facts for kids. Children must stay with adults during their visits to the zoo. For more details, check the complete listing in this chapter's Attractions section.

ALYESKA TRAMWAY $$$$
Alyeska Resort
(907) 754-2275
Short attention spans are welcome here, where the ride from 306 feet above sea level to 2,334

feet above sea level happens in about eight minutes during the summer. It's about twice as fast in the winter. At the top, kids can hike, explore, or pick berries. See our complete listing under this chapter's Attractions section.

i While downtown, take time for a short history lesson by viewing the Alaska Statehood Monument, a plaque and bust of President Eisenhower commemorating the Alaska Statehood Act. Nearby, the life-size Captain Cook Monument stands at the corner of Third Avenue and L Street, where you'll also find great views of Cook Inlet and Mount Susitna.

ANCHORAGE MUSEUM OF HISTORY AND ART CHILDREN'S GALLERY $$
121 West Seventh Ave.
(907) 343-4326
www.anchoragemuseum.org

With an emphasis on art, the Children's Gallery features yearlong special exhibits designed for kids. Past displays involved such fun themes as Dogs in Art, Toys and Games in Art, and an exhibition of art made from found objects. Other kid-friendly events at the Children's Gallery include art classes for children and adults, Saturday Artventure Workshops, and Sunday Family Art with a local artist-guide. In the main galleries of the museum, kids will enjoy seeing Alaskan Native artifacts, life-size renditions of pioneer and Native dwellings, and a slice of the Alaska Pipeline. The parking garage is open for handicap parking during the week and for public parking on weekends. During the winter, the museum is closed on Monday. See the full listing on the Anchorage Museum in this chapter's Attractions section.

DIMOND ICE CHALET $$
Dimond Center Mall
800 East Dimond Boulevard, #3–30
(907) 344-7788, (907) 522-6790
www.dimondicechalet.com

This indoor rink on the bottom level of the Dimond Center Mall is perfect for beginning skaters or for families who want to take a break from shopping. You can rent either hockey or figure skates and set off around the rink. The atmosphere is generally more recreational than competitive, making it perfect for kids. If your youngster has a special event to celebrate, the Ice Chalet offers party packages. There's food-court seating around the rink, and skating lessons are also available. See the listing within this chapter's Recreation section. Also, there's a bowling alley nearby if you're looking for another family-friendly recreational option.

i Looking for playgrounds? The Anchorage Department of Parks and Recreation Web site (www.muni.org/parks) includes a map of 72 parks with playgrounds, color-coded to direct you to age-appropriate playground equipment.

H2OASIS INDOOR WATERPARK $$$$
1520 O'Malley Rd.
(907) 522-4420
www.h2oasiswaterpark.com

Winters were a lot longer and colder for Alaskan kids before the H2Oasis came to town. No matter what it's like outside, you can count on 84-degree water and a whole lot of fun at this indoor water park. They've got a slew of kid-friendly water thrills, including the four-story Master Blaster Water Coaster, the Never Ending River, the wave pool, the Mushroom Water Drop, the Beached Boat Slide, the Enclosed Body Slide, the Children's Lagoon, and the Sea Dragon Pirate Ship. On the upper level, there's a food court and game arcade, too. If you're looking for structured activities, H2Oasis offers swim lessons, kayak lessons, water aerobics, and parent-toddler sessions. If you just go to play, parents may want to bring their ear plugs, as the screams of delight get a bit intense in the enclosed space.

IMAGINARIUM SCIENCE DISCOVERY CENTER $$
737 West Fifth Ave.
(907) 276-3179
www.imaginarium.org

With more than 50,000 visitors every year, Alaska's only hands-on science center must be doing something right. Here's a place where kids can touch exotic reptiles, fondle sea creatures, pet a life-size dinosaur, create giant bubbles, check out the aurora, and learn about physics by playing with specialized toys. In addition to providing fun science-based experiences for family, the Imaginarium runs workshops, school visits, and summer science camps. Monthly special events, including regular preschool science hours, make this a place that kids will want to return to again and again. The Imaginarium is located in the Glacier Brewhouse Mall, with parking available at nearby public lots, but it will be moving to the Anchorage Museum in 2010. It's open daily, with shortened hours on Sunday, and there's a science store on-site so kids can take some of their enthusiasm home.

> **i** Education, fun, and exercise come together in the Anchorage Lightspeed Planet Walk. Begin at the Sun Station at Fifth Avenue and G Streets, then stroll at a scale approximating the speed of light as you head west and south along the Coastal Trail until you reach Pluto, approximately five and half hours away. For details, visit www.anchorageplanetwalk.org.

INDIAN VALLEY MINE $
Mile 104 Seward Highway, Indian
(907) 653-1120
www.indianvalleymine.com

Perfect for a child-size attention span, this little mine 20 minutes south of Anchorage will give kids a taste of history and gold rush excitement without boring them to tears. Buy a bucket of pay dirt, and kids can try their hand at finding their own gold. Bring a picnic lunch and enjoy the views of Turnagain Arm. The mine is open only during the summer. For details, see the complete lisiting in this chapter's Attractions section.

SOUTHCENTRAL REGION ANNUAL FESTIVALS AND EVENTS

Alaskans are famous for their go-out-and-get-it approach to life, so if there's any cause to get together and celebrate something, someone has probably organized an event to do just that. In particular, the months of late winter and early spring are chock-full of activities designed to break the cabin-fever syndrome and get people out having a good time. Likewise, there are quite a few running, skiing, and dog-mushing events that capitalize on what Alaska does best—the outdoors.

Whether it's outdoors or indoors, you can expect a fun, low-key ambience at most of these affairs. Where else can you find a Duct Tape Ball or a Wilderness Women Contest and Bachelor Auction among the highlights for the year?

Anchorageites think nothing of driving a couple of hours to fun events across Southcentral Alaska, so we've collected all the events here, organized by the month, rather than separating them by location. Wherever possible, we've given general indications about cost and dates for these events, but keep in mind that it's all subject to change, so your best bet is to check directly with organizers for specifics.

January

ANCHORAGE FOLK FESTIVAL
(907) 566-2334
www.anchoragefolkfestival.org

More than 120 acts from across Alaska and around the world grace the stage at the annual Anchorage Folk Festival, spread over two weekends. The festival features performances by dancers, singers, storytellers, and groups with both traditional and original compositions in bluegrass, jazz, folk,

Celtic, and other musical styles. Concerts and workshops are free, and dance admission fees go toward funding future events. Most events are held at the University of Alaska Anchorage (UAA) Wendy Williamson Auditorium.

GREAT ALASKA BEER AND BARLEYWINE FESTIVAL
(907) 562-9911
auroraproductions.net/beer-barley.html
Alaska's coldest, darkest month has proved itself perfect for sampling beers and strong, complex ales known as barleywines. Head to the Egan Convention Center, where you'll find more than 175 beers to try. The admission fee includes a souvenir glass and 30 beer sample tickets, so you can hunker down and make a night of it. There's a detailed program and a good crowd, from twentysomethings to families and older couples. Any festival that draws celebrities this far north to join locals in a celebration of beer in mid-January must be doing something right.

POLAR BEAR PLUNGE
Seward
(907) 224-8051
www.seward.ak.org
On the third weekend in January, people flock to Seward from all over Southcentral Alaska to take the plunge—a dip in chilly Resurrection Bay, while dressed in costume. It all began in 1986 as a fundraiser for the American Cancer Society, and as word spread, the event garnered international attention, with coverage from faraway places such as Korea and Australia. Even if you're not feeling hardy (or foolhardy) enough to take the plunge, it's a whole lot of fun to watch the highlight of Seward's Winter Fun Festival.

i Within two downtown Anchorage blocks are three premier event venues: The Anchorage Performing Arts Center (PAC), the Egan Convention Center, and the brand new 215,000-square-foot Dena'ina Convention Center.

February
ALASKA SKI FOR WOMEN
Kincaid Park
www.anchoragenordicski.com
Each year on Superbowl Sunday, Anchorage hosts the largest women-only ski event in North America. Thousands of women turn out, many in costume, schussing in groups of 100 every five minutes on a 2.4-mile loop. The atmosphere is festive and fun, a little like Halloween on a ski-only freeway. Women of all ages and abilities participate. Awards are given to top teams categorized by relationship: Friends, Relatives, and Mother/Daughter. No partner? No worries. Event organizers will match you with another skier. Refreshments, door prizes, and a silent auction are all part of the fun. A race fee is charged.

ANCHORAGE FUR RENDEZVOUS (FUR RONDY)
(907) 274-1177
www.furrondy.net
This classic event got its start back in 1935, when Anchorage was a little town of 3,000 people. It didn't take long for folks to figure out that everyone could use some fun to break up the winter months, and with that in mind, a three-day festival was coordinated, featuring basketball, skiing, hockey, and a children's sled dog race. A big bonfire and torchlight parade capped off the festivities. Over the years, Fur Rondy got bigger and bigger, and in recent years it has undergone something of a revival.

Rondy typically starts in mid-February and continues through the first Saturday in March, when the Iditarod Sled Dog Race has its ceremonial start in downtown Anchorage. These days, Fur Rondy is jam-packed with just about every form of fun you can imagine: fireworks, a parade, blanket toss, a carnival, outhouse races, a Native crafts market, sled dog races, and snow sculpture competition. A new feature that has garnered tons of interest is Running with the Reindeer, modeled after Spain's Running with the Bulls. And if you've never seen softball played in snowshoes, you're missing out on a very good laugh. Even if you can sample only a few activities, you'll be glad you did. Many events are free.

MINERS AND TRAPPERS BALL
Egan Convention Center
555 West Fifth Ave.
(907) 349-2255
www.minersandtrappersball.org
As one of the mainstay Fur Rondy events, this flamboyant ball is big enough to get its own billing. From its roots in the drafty ACS warehouse, the Miners and Trappers Ball has moved into plush digs at the Egan Convention Center. The atmosphere is wacky and fun, with a costume contest drawing revelers dressed in all sorts of outrageous attire, especially those competing in the newsmakers category. The charity fund-raiser includes live music, alcohol, and a big-beard contest.

SUSITNA 100
14424 Canyon Rd.
(907) 345-2282
www.susitna100.com
Want a taste of the Iditarod trail without the dogs? The Susitna 100 and the Little Su 50K provide an opportunity for you to ski, bike, or run a portion of the challenging Iditarod route. It's not an undertaking for those uninitiated to the harsh winter conditions you're likely to encounter along the way. If the chances of frostbite, hypothermia, unpredictable weather, navigational challenges, and river overflow don't scare you away, you'll enjoy the rewards of traveling one of the world's most famous trails framed by winter landscapes of striking beauty. The race organizers provide a wealth of information on their Web site. A standard fee is charged to enter.

TESORO IRON DOG
Wasilla
(907) 563-4414
www.irondog.org
Head to Wasilla to watch the start of one of the world's most grueling snowmobile races, a 2,000-mile trek from Wasilla to Nome and back to either

Wasilla or Fairbanks. Interest in the race spiked when Alaska's governor and vice-presidential candidate publicized the fact that her husband Todd Palin was a regular participant. Temperatures down to 60 degrees below zero, speeds in excess of 100 mph, unpredictable trail conditions—it's all part of the fun. The race kicks off with a parade, followed by a fevered start the next day. There's no charge to watch the parade or the start of the race.

WINTER TRAILS DAY
Campbell Creek Science Center
(907) 267-1247
www.blm.gov/ak/st/en/prog/sciencecenter/
special_events/winter_trails_day.html#
Nearly 1,000 people turn out each year for a free chance to try Nordic skiing, skate skiing, and snowshoeing. Sponsored by the Bureau of Land Management (BLM) and REI, this event gets families out on the trails. Workshops, educational booths, and refreshments are all part of the fun. Learn about GPS navigation, snow shelter construction, skijoring with dogs, winter biking, and ski waxing, among other topics.

i If you're driving around downtown, take a look inside the fenced yard at the corner of 10th Avenue and I Street, and you just might see a reindeer. Back in 1960, Oro Stewart, wife of the founder of Stewart's photography, asked her husband for an Alaskan pet. He presented her with the first Star, a reindeer from breeder Larry Davis in Nome, so named because of the distinctive white patch on her forehead. There have been several Stars since, and they've all been a big hit with Anchorage children, who enjoy seeing her on weekly walks along the Park Strip as well as at Fur Rondy and in Christmas parades.

March
BEAN'S CAFE EMPTY BOWL PROJECT
(907) 274-9595
www.beanscafe.org

ANCHORAGE

Thousands of Anchorage residents line up at the Eagan Convention Center to choose their favorite handcrafted pottery bowls, then fill them with savory soups from local restaurants. People return year after year to collect pots by their favorite craftspersons. Proceeds benefit Beans Cafe, where the homeless find food and day shelter.

IDITAROD SLED DOG RACE
(907) 376-5155
www.iditarod.com
On the first weekend in March, Alaska comes into the international spotlight with the start of the 1,500-mile Iditarod Sled Dog Race. On Saturday, more than 1,300 sled dogs along with their owners and handlers line up on Fourth Avenue downtown for the ceremonial start of this popular event. Expect lots of barking and tail wagging along with big crowds along a 1-mile stretch of Fourth Avenue. Crowds spill over into the side streets to watch the frenzied teams shoot out.

After a quick 11-mile run, the mushers pack up their teams and head north to Willow for the real start of the race on Sunday. Some years the dogs must be trucked to Fairbanks, where snow is more plentiful. The race commemorates the famous 1925 diphtheria serum run from Nenana to Nome. The current trail takes mushers over the Alaska Range, across frozen tundra and rivers, and along the windswept coast of the Bering Sea, past 24 checkpoints at villages and wilderness cabins, to the finish line at Nome. The stakes are high in this grueling event: The first 30 finishers split a prize pot worth almost $800,000. But talk to these mushers, and you'll soon learn it's not about the money. These are folks who love their dogs, love their sport, and love the wilderness where they live and train. There's no charge to watch the start of the race—and folks come from all over the world to see it.

NORDIC SKIING ASSOCIATION OF ANCHORAGE SKI TRAIN
(907) 276-7609
www.anchoragenordicski.com

Hop aboard for a three-hour ride south to Grandview or a four-hour ride north to Curry, and enjoy backcountry skiing, touring, snowshoeing and snowboarding. Curry is the preferred destination for families and beginning to intermediate outdoor enthusiasts, while Grandview is more appropriate for intermediate to advanced wilderness sojourns. At both destinations, warming facilities are provided, either in the form of bonfires or on the train itself. These popular events sell out early, so be sure to get your tickets well in advance. The trips are on different weekends, with one typically in February and one typically in March, so you can do both if you like. Riding the train isn't cheap, but it's a fun, all-day adventure.

TOUR OF ANCHORAGE
Nordic Skiing Association of Anchorage
(907) 276-7609
www.tourofanchorage.com
A premier ski marathon event that's part of the American Ski Marathon Series, this is actually a collection of four races: a 50K, 40K, or 25K freestyle, or a 25K classical race. The longer races go from one side of Anchorage to the other, following bike trails, while the shorter races start in the middle of town. The finish line is at Kincaid Park, where you can catch transportation back to the start. An informal banquet follows. An entrance fee is charged.

April
ALASKA WOMEN'S SHOW
GEORGE M. SULLIVAN SPORTS ARENA
1600 Gambell St.
(907) 562-9911
auroraproductions.net/women.html
Billed as the only trade show in Alaska for women, this event typically follows a week or two after the Sportsman's Show at the Sullivan Arena. More than 200 vendors display all sorts of products, including cosmetics, crafts, apparel, and outdoor gear. Typically more than 12,000 people attend. Wheelchair access is available.

Close-up

Iditarod Sled Dog Race

In many parts of the country, March brings daffodils. In Anchorage, it brings dogs, lots of dogs, more than a thousand of them lined up along downtown streets on the first Saturday of the month for the ceremonial start of the internationally renowned Iditarod Sled Dog Race. You can feel the excitement as you walk the streets, looking for the best place to watch the teams take off. Dogs bark, mushers pose for pictures and sign autographs, and journalists from around the world jockey for position.

First run in 1973, the Iditarod was the brainchild of Joe Reddington Sr., known as the "Father of the Iditarod." The race commemorates the 1925 serum run to Nome, when a series of heroic mushers, including Gunner Kaasen and his lead dog Balto, rushed diphtheria vaccine from Nenana to Nome in a relay effort that managed to deliver the life-saving serum in only one week.

Mushers now follow either the northern or southern route of the Iditarod National Historic Trail for approximately 1,150 miles, through mountain passes, across frozen rivers, and over windswept tundra to reach their final destination in Nome. After the ceremonial start in Anchorage, they pack up their teams and head north for the official start of the race the following day, from Willow if trail conditions permit. The shortest finish time is just shy of nine days, while the longest, acknowledged by the annual Red Lantern Award, was nearly 33 days.

The mushing life is hard for most of us to fathom. There's so much to consider: the science of breeding, the commitment to training, and the strategy of how to outmaneuver your competitors in a grueling long-distance race when factors like weather and trail conditions can change without warning. There's a big purse for the winner: more than $72,000 and a brand-new pickup truck, but as mushers will be quick to admit, there's no purse big enough to truly compensate for the dedication of time and money that they put into their obsession. More than anything, they agree it's about the dogs. And these are dogs that love to run.

ARCTIC MAN SKI AND SNO-GO CLASSIC
Summit Lake
(907) 456-2626
www.arcticman.com

Eagerly anticipated by snowmachine enthusiasts, this annual shindig turns Mile 195 of the Richardson Highway into a recreational vehicle bonanza each April. In what's billed as one of the world's most extreme winter races, skiers descend 1,700 feet into a canyon, then hang on for a wild ride to the top, towed by snowmachine, before plunging 1,200 feet to the finish. It all makes for one big party, with 10,000 to 15,000 spectators to watch the daring feats.

GREAT ALASKA SPORTSMAN SHOW
George M. Sullivan Sports Arena
1600 Gambell St.
(907) 562-9911
www.greatalaskasportsmanshow.com

Alaska has no shortage of outdoor enthusiasts, and most of them love their outdoor toys, so it's no surprise that this annual event draws crowds topping 20,000. More than 300 booths cater to the whims and wishes of anglers, hunters, snowmobilers, rock climbers, and golfers. Look for lots of equipment demonstrations, seminars, and plenty of ways to spend your money. Past favorites have included a bird-treatment learning center, an interactive shooting range, and an archery range. This trade-show event has been an Anchorage tradition since 1984. Wheelchair access is available.

In Alaska, many of the Iditarod contenders are household names. Lance Mackey? He's the one who won the two big races (Yukon Quest and Iditarod) back to back, two years in a row. Rick Swenson? He's the one who's entered 20 Iditarods and never has finished out of the top 10; in fact, he's the only five-time winner. Libby Riddles? She broke the gender barrier by becoming the first woman to win the Iditarod in 1985. Following on her heels was Susan Butcher, winner of four Iditarods until she retired in 1993 to raise a family of the two-legged kind; she's remembered as well for her courageous battle against the cancer that took her life in 2006. And then there's Norman Vaughn, who ran the race at age 88 and was planning a comeback when he died at the age of 100.

The excitement of the race's beginning carries right on through to the finish. Folks from around the world follow the progress of the mushers as they travel through checkpoints from the mountains of Finger Lake and Rainy Pass, then along the Kuskokwim and Yukon Rivers and through coastal villages to No Man's Land, the final stretch to the finish, where no one has to give up trail to their competitors. Everyone's still talking about the photo finish in 1978, when Dick Mackey came in one second ahead of Rick Swenson, leading literally by the nose of his lead dog.

Conditions along the way can be brutal. Temperatures dip far below zero in many spots, and winds can whip up snow into total whiteout conditions. Teams and drivers can get soaked by overflow along the rivers, creating an almost instant danger of hypothermia. Mushers lose their way or lose their teams. Encounters with belligerent moose or ill-placed trees have caused them to withdraw. It's not a race for the faint of heart.

Still, 80 mushers, give or take a few, return year after year to test their mettle. And though much of the world's attention turns on the top 10 contenders, the rest of the pack have their own stories to tell. From Rachael Scdoris, the first legally blind musher to compete, to the drivers testing out puppy teams for some of the more prominent contenders, they all share a love of the wilderness and a spirit of adventure that embodies the spirit of the Iditarod.

HEART RUN
(907) 263-2013
www.heartrun.com
The largest footrace in Alaska unites serious competitors and casual strollers in a 5K course as a fundraiser to fight heart disease and stroke. Families and students are especially encouraged to participate. There's even a 3K Heart Lite course for those who don't want to overdo.

NATIVE YOUTH OLYMPICS (NYO)
(907) 793-3267
www.anchorage.net
More than 400 finalists from around the state travel to Anchorage each year to show their stuff in skills related to traditional hunting and subsistence activities. The one-hand reach and the arm pull, for instance, traditionally strengthened arm muscles for seal hunting, while the high kick was a means of communicating across the tundra. Other popular events include the stick pull, the scissor broad jump, and the toe kick. The NYO is a three-day event sponsored by the Cook Inlet Tribal Council.

May

ALASKA WOMEN'S GOLD NUGGET TRIATHLON
(907) 868-3630
www.goldnuggettriathlon.com
Billed as a fitness event for women of all abilities and ages, the Gold Nugget includes a 500-yard swim at Bartlett Pool, a 10-mile bicycle ride, and

a 4.1-mile run. Organizers recommend that you familiarize yourself with the course to enhance your chances of success. The event has been a fun fitness challenge for Alaskans since 1984. There's a standard entrance fee.

BEAR VALLEY 5K CHALLENGE
(907) 345-0434
www.bearvalleycommunityassoc.org
A favorite with families, the Bear Valley 5K course takes maximum advantage of the terrain of the Chugach foothills south of Anchorage. The race begins at the soccer field of Bear Valley Elementary, then winds into the mountains, through the woods, and over a creek before finishing at the school's hockey rink. The Bear Valley Challenge is a great way for kids and their parents to welcome spring.

KACHEMAK BAY SHOREBIRD FESTIVAL
Homer
(907) 235-7740
www.homeralaska.org
Spring brings flocks of shorebirds, and birders, to the beaches of Homer's Kachemak Bay. From the ornithological novice to the pro, the Shorebird Festival features dozens of events, including workshops, field trips, art events, and children's activities. The guests of honor: more than 25 species migrating from distant shores to feed at Kachemak Bay en route to their summer breeding grounds on the Alaskan tundra. Birders also delight in an additional 200 or so species that make their way through Homer in the spring.

VISITOR INDUSTRY CHARITY WALK
(907) 334-3550
www.alaskacharitywalk.org
You'll get some exercise, but don't expect to lose any weight on this 5K walk. Also known as "Graze to Raise," this annual event includes food villas along the route, with a grand finale at the new Dena'ina Convention Center, where you'll find a beer and wine garden, desserts, jugglers, clowns, face painting, door prizes, and carnival games. Individuals and teams walk to raise money in support of charities throughout Alaska.

June
ALASKA OCEANS FESTIVAL
(907) 274-3647
www.alaskaoceansfestival.org
In a favorite event to welcome summer, Anchorage residents and guests converge on the West Delaney Park Strip, where musicians, speakers, vendors, conservationists, and fisherman celebrate the wonders of Alaska's oceans. Among the highlights are films, a Seafood Olympics, a 5K Run for the Waves race, and a Moose's Tooth beer garden.

ALASKAN SCOTTISH HIGHLAND GAMES
Eagle River Lion's Park, Eagle River
(907) 243-7255
www.alaskascottish.org
Since 1981, the Alaskan Scottish Club has been hosting this two-day event, which begins on a Friday night with bagpipe competitions at the Loussac Library. From there the festivities move out to Eagle River's Lion's Park, where on Saturday you'll find athletic events, more pipe and dance competitions, historic reenactments, storytelling, fencing demonstrations, wandering minstrels, and vendors of all things Celtic. Enjoy food, world-class Celtic music, and dancing.

KENAI RIVER FESTIVAL
Soldotna
www.kenaiwatershed.org/kenairiverfestival.html
Celebrating the unique recreational, educational, and economic opportunities afforded by the Kenai River, this free event features more than 30 hands-on environmental activities such as Live Raptor and Build Your Own Birdhouse workshops. Food and artisan booths round out the fun. Run for the River, a 5K and 10-mile walk/run event, is another River Fest function.

MAYOR'S MARATHON AND HALF-MARATHON
(907) 786-1325
www.mayorsmarathon.com
In a summer solstice tradition, 4,500 runners from

around the state and around the world converge on Anchorage to compete in one of five simultaneous races. There's a 26.2-mile marathon, a 13.1-mile half-marathon, a recreational 5-mile event, a marathon relay, and a Youth Cup. The course spans from the Chugach Mountains on the east end of Anchorage to Cook Inlet on the west side. Shuttles run from major hotels to the start and finish lines. The race is a National Leukemia and Lymphoma Society "Team in Training" marathon, and the course is certified so runners may use their results as part of the qualification process for the Boston Marathon. Expect a standard race fee to participate.

SALMON IN THE CITY FESTIVAL
www.muni.org/salmoninthecity

In what other city can you pull on waders over your work clothes and spend your lunch hour fishing for salmon? Anchorage celebrates its unique claim to fishing fame when the king salmon return to Ship Creek in early June. Activities include the Slam'n Salm'n Derby, Salmon in the City Music Festival, and the Wild Salmon on Parade, a display of fiberglass salmon colorfully and imaginatively theme-decorated by some of the city's best artists.

THREE BARONS RENAISSANCE FAIR
Tozier Track
3400 East Tudor Rd.
(907) 868-8012
3barons.org

Wander among barons, pirates, alchemists, and Celts as they transform a bit of Alaska into a faraway time and place. Artists and craftspeople showcase their talents and wares in this annual event, held on the first two weekends in June, with a mid-Fair Feast in between. Renaissance enthusiasts dress in costume and act out roles as citizens of three baronies in 16th-century England. Founded in 1996, the fair features 60 vendors as well as acts on six stages.

July

ANCHORAGE JULY FOURTH CELEBRATION AND DOWNTOWN PARADE
(907) 279-7500

There's too much daylight for fireworks, but that doesn't stop around 30,000 Anchorageites from celebrating Independence Day in style. Start off with a benefit pancake breakfast, then take in the community parade along Sixth Avenue from E Street to K Street. The afternoon brings the National Veteran's Wheelchair Games and a reading of the Declaration of Independence by Harvard Club members in period costumes. The day ends with a big picnic on Park Strip (Delaney Park) featuring lots of food and three stages of fun-filled music and entertainment. Most events are free.

BEAR PAW FESTIVAL CHUGIAK
Eagle River
(907) 694-4702
www.cer.org

First held in 1985, this four-day event celebrates all that's fun about the communities just to the north of Anchorage. Enjoy a host of festivities, including the Bear Paw Classic 5K Run, the Slippery Salmon Olympics, the Miss Bear Paw Pageant, a Jammin' Salmon Cook-Off, and a classic car show. There's an Eagle River Renaissance Village with food and fun as well as a Teddy Bear Picnic & Family Fun Day. Don't miss the Grand Parade, billed as one of the largest in the state, along with the carnival rides and games.

MOUNT MARATHON RUN
Seward
(907) 224-8051

What is it about Seward that inspires challenges that push the envelope? Six months after the Polar Bear Plunge (see January events listing), the town ramps up again, this time for a sprint up and down Mount Marathon, a mile and a half each way. The event goes back to a sourdough bet in 1915 that the feat couldn't be accomplished in less than an hour. The original bet was lost by two minutes, but today's recordholders have proved that it can be done (in 43 minutes and 23 seconds, to be exact). The race is so popular that registration closes March 31, with a few lucky spots later won by auction and raffle. Folks come from all over the state to watch the grueling competition every Fourth of July.

August

ALASKA STATE FAIR
2075 Glenn Highway, Palmer
(907) 745-4827
www.alaskastatefair.org
Alaska is funny about its state fairs. Nearly every town of any size claims to be a proud sponsor of a "state fair." But the big fair is the one in Palmer, about an hour's drive north of Anchorage, held each year from the end of August through Labor Day weekend. Here's your chance to see those gigantic cabbages and other vegetables that thrive in Alaska's extreme summer daylight, as well as taking in the usual state fair entertainment, booths, rides, and exhibits. A daily admission is charged. Traffic backs up each day of the fair, so if you don't want to crawl along for an hour or two just to get in the gates, go early in the day. Or avoid the problem altogether by taking one of the fair trains from Anchorage.

ARCTIC THUNDER
Elmendorf Air Force Base
(907) 552-7469
The Blue Angels, the premier flight demonstration team of the U.S. Navy and Marines, comes to town with an air show that features all manner of breathtaking rolls, dives, and spins. In addition to watching the high-flying daredevils, there's plenty to do on the ground, as the hangars fill with everything from hunting and fishing simulators to face-painting activities and clowns. Participants have a chance to meet the pilots, too. Attracting thousands, the show is held in even-numbered years.

BIG WILD LIFE RUNS
(907) 258-4964
www.humpysmarathon.com

Attracting upwards of 1,000 runners and walkers in the marathon, half-marathon, and 5K courses, this collection of races is the Anchorage Running Club's premier event of the year. The course includes less than 1 mile of roads, with the rest of the event taking place on paved bike paths. There's a dirt trail alongside most of the route for those who prefer it. Choose among marathon, half-marathon, marathon walk, relay, 5K, and kids' courses.

September

ALASKA RAILROAD BLUES TRAIN
Alaska Railroad
(907) 265-2494
www.alaskarailroad.com
A relative newcomer among Alaska Railroad's special events, the Blues Train first chugged out of the station in 2005, with lots of happy riders listening to one of their favorite local blues bands while enjoying a spread of appetizers and a no-host bar. The train pulls into Seward for more music and a big barbeque. An overnight stay in Seward is included in the ticket price.

DENALI NATIONAL PARK ROAD
Road Lottery
www.nps.gov/dena
Each September after the buses quit running at Denali National Park, the park service hosts a road lottery, allowing 400 vehicles a day to drive to the end of the park road. Applications with a nonrefundable $10 payment are accepted during the month of July, with winners announced in mid-August. Weather permitting, the road may be open for the entire 92 miles—a full day's drive, in and back. If you're among the lucky winners, you can look forward to striking fall colors and plenty of wildlife, enjoyed from the comfort of your own vehicle, along with a possible peek inside the Fannie Quigley house near Kantishna.

October

GREAT ALASKA BEER TRAIN
Alaska Railroad
(907) 265-2494
www.alaskarailroad.com

Here's a great way to chug some of Alaska's best microbrews to the backdrop of incredible views as the Alaska Railroad chugs its way around Turnagain Arm. Tickets include six half-pints of Glacier Brewhouse beer plus a selection of appetizers. This is typically a sellout event, so sign up early. The admission is fairly hefty, but it's a great experience.

MAKE IT ALASKAN FESTIVAL
George M. Sullivan Sports Arena
1600 Gambell St.
(907) 279-0618
www.miafestival.com
Get a headstart on your holiday shopping with this event featuring 250-plus vendors with great Alaskan-made products. Browse the booths with a backdrop of live music, or vie for prizes in the Natural Pantry Alaskan Food Safari. The Sullivan Arena offers wheelchair access.

November
ARTS AND CRAFTS EMPORIUM
Dena'ina Convention Center
(907) 563-8310
Didn't find gifts for everyone on your list at last month's Make It Alaskan Festival? Don't despair. November brings another great shopping opportunity in the form of the annual Arts and Crafts Emporium, featuring crafts, foods, and fun. This event is downtown at the Dena'ina Convention Center, and unlike many of these shopping extravaganzas, there's no admission charge.

DOWNTOWN FOR THE HOLIDAYS
www.anchorage.net/events
Start the holiday season in style on the weekend after Thanksgiving by taking in the Parade of Lights and the Town Square Tree Lighting Ceremony. If you like, try some caroling or have breakfast with Santa. At the Anchorage Museum of History and Art, artisans display their wares in a holiday crafts weekend. The Cincinnati Ballet's annual performances of The Nutcracker are also this weekend. Many of the events are free.

GREAT ALASKA SHOOTOUT
George M. Sullivan Sports Arena
1600 Gambell St.
(907) 279-0618
www.goseawolves.com
Can't wait for basketball season to start? Here's a great opportunity to watch some of the nation's best college teams in preseason competition. Many years ago, former University of Alaska coach Bob Rachal conceived of this tournament as a great way to lure teams to Alaska, since the NCAA doesn't count games beyond the Lower 48 against a team's normal allotment. The loophole makes for fine viewing opportunities by Alaskans. Men's and women's teams compete in separate tournaments. Ticket prices are based on the number of games you want to attend. Expect good crowds and lots of excitement in men's and women's tournaments over Thanksgiving weekend.

December
ANCHORAGE INTERNATIONAL FILM FESTIVAL
(907) 338-3690
www.anchoragefilmfestival.com
A 10-day extravaganza of independent films, the Anchorage Film Festivals screens more than 150 films in three venues: the Bear Tooth Theater, the Anchorage Museum, and the Fireweed Theaters. Jury prizes and audience awards are part of the fun as audiences enjoy features, documentaries, short shorts, family films, animaton, and Alaskan showcase films, some of them world premiers. With a $60 pass, you get expedited admission to all films; for another $25, you can upgrade to an All Films and Events pass, which includes workshops, an opening night gala, a Martini Matinee, and admission to the Golden Oosikar Awards ceremony. If you're not up for all that excitement, tickets to individual films may be purchased at the host venues.

NEW YEAR'S TORCHLIGHT PARADE AND FIREWORKS DISPLAY

Alyeska Resort

P.O. Box 249, Girdwood, AK 99587

(907) 754-1111

www.alyeskaresort.com

End the year with lights, food, and a whole lot of Alaskan ambience at Alyeska's Torchlight Parade and Fireworks. Skiers light up the long night, with a big fireworks display following. Post-fireworks, there's a big buffet and the usual New Year's festivities. Be sure to book a room well in advance if you don't want to drive back to town at the end of the evening. There's a charge for the buffet and for skiing.

i Those fireworks you missed because there was too much daylight on the Fourth of July? You can catch them on New Year's Eve in downtown Anchorage. Gather at Town Square beside the Performing Arts Center for a colorful display to delight the whole family.

WILDERNESS WOMEN CONTEST AND BACHELOR AUCTION

Talkeetna

(907) 733-3939

www.talkeetnachamber.org

It's a bit of a drive from Anchorage, about two hours north, but this legendary contest still draws a crowd. Single women compete in at least three timed events, demonstrating (more or less tongue in cheek) the skills a bachelor from a woodsy town like Talkeetna would love. A 100-yard dash to fill water buckets from the "creek," gathering firewood, shooting ptarmigan, climbing a tree to escape a pesky moose, and delivering sandwiches and beer during Sunday-afternoon football are among these valuable skills. After the contest, the bachelors put on their own airs in a Bachelor Bidding Contest, with the lucky (?) bidders winning drinks and dances with their eligible men. This all-in-good-fun event sponsored by the Talkeetna Bachelor Society put

this little town on the map, and it manages to be a great fund-raiser, too.

THE ARTS

For a city its size, Anchorage enjoys a vibrant, active arts scene. Many residents transplanted from larger cities in the Lower 48 arrive with a love of the arts and a strong desire to see them flourish in the Far North. From such intimate venues as Cyrano's Off-Center Playhouse to the world-class theaters of the Alaska Center for the Performing Arts, Anchorage invites the best in live performances. Likewise, the city encourages the visual and literary arts through galleries and local arts organizations.

First Friday Art Walks are great fun, drawing art lovers to dozens of downtown studios, galleries, and coffee shops for receptions highlighting art and music by some of the best local talent you'll find anywhere. Pick up a copy of the *Anchorage Press* for a complete list and map for the monthly event.

With the "Summer in the City" series, the Anchorage Downtown Partnership sponsors a full slate of free outdoor arts events, including Music for Little Ones, Music in the Park, Theater Thursdays, and the Saturday Cultural Series. In addition, the Downtown Partnership sponsors live music events. If it rains, you'll have to make other plans, as these are fair-weather functions only. For details on Summer in the City events, go to www.anchorage downtown.org.

Dance

ALASKA DANCE THEATRE

500 East 33rd Ave.

(907) 277-9591

www.alaskadancetheatre.org

From its inauspicious beginnings in a World War II–vintage Quonset hut back in 1981, the Alaska Dance Theatre has become the biggest and best-known dance school and company in the state. Fall and spring concerts feature the company's 25 dancers, and the Alaska Dance Theatre also strives to make dance accessible to everyone by offering a full class schedule of ballet, jazz, hip-hop, modern, and social dance. In addition, the organization provides choreography and dancers for various productions throughout the community. In 2006 the Alaska Dance Theatre moved into a new five-studio building with its own theater, offices, and ample parking.

i Some of the most fun and unique outdoor art you'll see anywhere comes to downtown Anchorage every summer with the Wild Salmon on Parade displays. Local artists decorate fiberglass salmon with riotous colors and humorous themes, and at the end of the summer these one-of-a-kind creations are sold at a charity auction. Pick up maps at the Log Cabin and Downtown Visitor Information Center on Fourth Avenue. (See the complete listing under June events.)

Galleries

ARTIC ROSE GALLERY
420 L St.
(907) 279-3911
www.articrosegallery.com
This unique gallery in front of the popular Simon and Seaforts restaurant supports local artists as well as displaying unique creations from around the world. Tucked into the main gallery and side rooms are original paintings, glasswork, Alaska Native art, jewelry, Russian art, and pottery. They'll be happy to ship your purchases if you like. The misspelling, by the way, is intentional.

ARTIQUE
314 G St.
(907) 277-1663
www.artiqueltd.com
Among the oldest fine arts galleries in town, Artique features ceramics, prints, glass, original paintings, crafts, and jewelry by some of Alaska's best-known artists. Byron Birdsall Giclee prints, Lisa McCormick handmade silver jewelry, Roy Peratrovich Jr. bronze sculptures, Holly Gittlein

metal and glass fish sculptures, and Barbara Lavallee books and prints are among the popular items here. The gallery is open daily throughout the year.

AURORA FINE ART GALLERY
737 West Fifth Ave.
(907) 274-0234
The works of more than 400 artists are represented in this large downtown gallery at the corner of Fifth Avenue and G Street. Choose from handpainted furniture, original oils, whalebone, prints, sculpture, ivory, pottery, and glass. All art displayed here is made in the United States, and all Alaskan art is handmade within the state. For a selection of jewelry and other eclectic art, visit Aurora's sister gallery, ZoeZ Window Gallery, next door in the Glacier Brewhouse building.

i For a free look at Alaskan Native arts, don't miss the working-artist demonstrations at Ship Creek Center every day from noon to 1 p.m. during the summer, followed by Alaska Native Dance Shows starting at 1 p.m. The center is located at the corner of Fourth Avenue and C Street.

DECKER/MORRIS GALLERY
621 West Sixth Ave.
(907) 272-1489
Specializing in contemporary creations by Alaskan artists, this gallery features monthly solo exhibitions as well as a wide range of sculptures, paintings, ceramics, photography, prints, and jewelry. Open daily, the gallery is conveniently located within the Alaska Center for the Performing Arts.

STEPHAN FINE ARTS GALLERY
Sixth Ave. and F St.
(907) 274-5009
www.stephanfinearts.com
Fred Machetanz, Rie Munoz, Charles Gause, and Ernest Robertson are some of the well-known Alaskan artists featured in this upscale gallery. You'll find original oils, giclee prints, photographs,

and sculptures by some of the best artists in the region. It all began in 1977 when Pat and Pam Stephan opened their first Anchorage gallery. First Friday events often feature visiting artists. The gallery offers shipping services for your purchases, too.

Music

ANCHORAGE CONCERT CHORUS
(907) 274-7464
www.anchorageconcertchorus.org
Founded in 1946 to promote choral music in Anchorage and Southcentral Alaska, this 160-member chorus hosts several concerts each year. Past performances include such classics as Beethoven's Symphony No. 9 and Handel's Messiah as well as more contemporary Holiday Pops and Chorale Concert series. In addition to community performances, this audition-only choral group promotes music education through scholarships and a mentoring program. Season subscriptions may be purchased through CenterTix at (907) 263–2787 or www.myalaskacenter.com.

ANCHORAGE FESTIVAL OF MUSIC
P.O. Box 103251, Anchorage
(907) 276-2465
www.anchoragefestivalmusic.com
With the mission of providing a summer festival of classical music as well as promoting educational opportunities in music, the Anchorage Festival of Music was founded in 1956 as a nonprofit community organization and later consolidated with the Basically Bach Festival. Past Summer Solstice Series presentations have included A Tribute to the Boston Pops, an Unfolding of Romanticism series, and a children's concert, Boyz in the Wood. Performances are held in the Discovery Theatre of the Alaska Center for the Performing Arts, and season tickets are available.

ANCHORAGE SCOTTISH PIPE BAND
(907) 694-6250
www.anchoragescottishpipeband.org
Anchorage is home to several Scottish bagpipe bands, all of them showcasing local talent while training up new players. Formed in 1963, the Anchorage Scottish Pipe Band is the state's oldest. In addition to playing at local events, the group has traveled worldwide, performing for dignitaries including Pope John Paul II. They welcome new members to play the pipes or drums, and they even offer free lessons.

ANCHORAGE SYMPHONY ORCHESTRA
400 D St., Suite 230
(907) 278-8668
www.anchoragesymphony.org
Eighty professional musicians leave their day jobs behind to bring high-quality orchestral music to audiences throughout Southcentral Alaska under the auspices of the Anchorage Symphony Orchestra. The orchestra began in 1946 with 17 local musicians who met weekly to share their love of music. Concert seasons typically include six classical concerts, four Young People's concerts, and a Halloween Family Concert. The orchestra also sponsors outreach and education efforts, including equipment and music rentals.

WHISTLING SWAN PRODUCTIONS
(907) 696-7926
www.whistlingswan.net
Since the mid-1990s this production company has brought more than 275 acoustically oriented singer-songwriters to the stage in Anchorage and Southcentral Alaska. From such smaller venues as Side Street Espresso to larger stages such as those at the Alaska Center for the Performing Arts, high-caliber performers Allison Krauss, Bruce Cockburn, Leo Kottke, and Tom Paxton have ventured north thanks to the efforts of this family-owned business.

Theater

ALASKA JUNIOR THEATER
329 F St., Suite 204
(907) 272-7546
www.akjt.org
Since its inception in 1981, this nonprofit group has brought high-quality theater productions to more than half a million children and parents

via field trips and public performances. Mime, dance, music, puppetry, and theater productions are featured in the Alaska Junior Theater's efforts to promote live performances throughout the Anchorage area. For their community shows, the group seeks out family-friendly theater, with a policy of never booking a performance that they have not previewed in live format.

ANCHORAGE OPERA COMPANY

1507 Spar Ave.
(907) 279-2557
www.anchorageopera.org

From its beginnings as an all-volunteer group in 1962, the Anchorage Opera Company has become one of most highly acclaimed regional companies in the country. Judging from the growing demand for advance ticket sales and the popularity of the opera's annual fund-raising events, the Anchorage Opera is making good on its mission to bring world-class opera to the Far North. Each year, they host at least three productions at the Discovery Theatre of the Alaska Center for the Performing Arts, showcasing world-class guest performers along with regional talent. Past productions have included Rossini's *The Italian Girl in Algiers* and Puccini's *Madame Butterfly*. There's also a Dark Night Recital Series celebrating the skills of local musicians. As the only professional opera company in the state, the Anchorage Opera serves as a resource for other arts organizations by sharing their large inventory of costumes, props, and lighting equipment.

CYRANO'S THEATRE COMPANY

Cyrano's Off-Center Playhouse, Bookstore, & Cafe
Fourth Ave. and D St.
(907) 274-2599
www.cyranos.org

Formed in 1995 by a group of volunteers dedicated to fostering professional dramatic productions, Cyrano's offers an intimate theater experience (89 seats) in a venue that includes wine and snacks to enjoy while you watch.

Recipients of the Governor's Award for Arts Organizations, the company is dedicated to nurturing regional talent, with the ultimate goal of creating endowments to support full-time actors. Past productions include classic works by Chekov, Tennessee Williams, and Shakespeare as well as world premier productions of original drama. Tickets may be purchased for individual productions or in 10-show punch cards.

Literary Arts

ALASKA CENTER FOR THE BOOK

3600 Denali St.
(907) 786-4379
www.alaskacenterforthebook.org

Affiliated with the Library of Congress Center for the Book, this organization serves to promote public interest in literacy by acting as a clearinghouse for the literary arts in Alaska. Writing workshops, author events, and book discussion groups are among the activities sponsored by the Alaska Center.

ALASKA SISTERS IN CRIME

(907) 566-7500
www.aksinc.org

This association of female mystery writers has been active in promoting the literary arts in Anchorage and throughout the state through such programs as Authors to the Bush and Young Writers Retreats. Author Dana Stabenow has led the group in sponsoring major writers' events, including a Left Coast Crime convention and International Boucheron. The group meets on the third Wednesday of every month.

i For discussion on Alaska's literary scene and a current calendar of literary events, visit www.49writers.blogspot.com. The site features monthly guest authors from throughout Alaska as well as an online book group.

Arts Organizations

ALASKA CENTER FOR THE PERFORMING ARTS
621 West Sixth Ave.
(907) 263-2900
www.alaskapac.org

Occupying a full block adjacent to the town square, the Alaska Center for the Performing Arts has become a vibrant hub of downtown Anchorage. With four high-quality performance spaces in the 176,000-square-foot building, this is one of only a few dozen multivenue arts complexes in the country. Here you'll find Broadway Series performances, jazz, ballet, comedy shows, and community social events. Though this costly venture opened to some grumbling in the wake of a statewide recession in 1988, the center now hosts annual audiences exceeding 240,000 people per year and is home to seven resident companies. For tickets to resident company functions, call (907) 263-2787 or (877) 263-2787, or go to www.centertix.net.

The facility is owned by the municipality of Anchorage but operated by the nonprofit Alaska Center for the Performing Arts, Inc. The Atwood Concert Hall, with its starburst ceiling of gold, red, and green, captures the effect of the northern lights and provides stunning acoustics for musical performances. In the Discovery Theatre, audiences of up to 700 enjoy theater, opera, and musical performances from a large stage with "salmonberry" seat upholstery adding to the Alaskan decor. The Sydney Laurence Theatre, with seating for 340, is a great venue for film and smaller live productions, including Dave Parkhurst's popular Aurora show (see complete listing within this chapter's Attractions section). The Elvera Voth Hall, with its

i Much of the art you'll see around Anchorage and throughout the state is thanks to Alaska's "1 percent for art" legislation, which requires any public buildings constructed or renovated after 1975 to include art, with 1 percent of state funding for such projects to be devoted to the design, construction, and display of these works.

signature metal and neon sculpture *Nature's Illumination,* is a popular setting for lectures, recitals, and other special events.

ANCHORAGE CONCERT ASSOCIATION
430 West Seventh Ave., Suite 200
(907) 272-1471

Since 1950 the Anchorage Concert Association has been bringing top-notch performing artists to town with the help of a volunteer group of more than 75 associates. Typically the association sponsors a Classical Series; a BP Horizons Series, featuring musical influences from around the world; Family Performances, with acts such as the New Shanghai Circus; a Dance Series; and Broadway & Beyond productions. For discounted ticket prices, priority seating, and exchange privileges, order by the series, or create your own custom series.

OUT NORTH VSA OF ALASKA
3800 DeBarr Rd.
(907) 279-3800
www.outnorth.org

A progressive multi-arts organization featuring underrepresented artists, Out North operates a black box theater for performances and a white box facility for the visual arts from DeBarr Road in northeast Anchorage. Charged with connecting art with community, especially the underserved, Out North hosts poetry readings, live performances, films, and occasional musical performances.

PARKS, RECREATION, AND TOURS

Parks

One of the best things about Anchorage is the way you can access the wilderness almost from your back door. Take a 30-minute drive from just about anywhere in town, and you'll find a place where you can immerse yourself in trees and trails, often with spectacular scenic views to boot. Whether it's the massive Chugach State Park, one of the Bureau of Land Management (BLM) tracts, or one of more than 120 city parks in and around Anchorage, you won't have a problem finding a place to enjoy the outdoors even within the boundaries of the municipality. Space prohibits us from discussing every park, but the more popular spots are described here.

CAMPBELL TRACT AND CAMPBELL CREEK SCIENCE CENTER

6881 Abbott Loop Rd.
(907) 267-1247
www.blm.gov/ak/st/en/prog/sciencecenter.html

On the east side of town, up against the Chugach Mountains, the 730-acre Campbell Tract provides space for all types of nonmotorized enjoyment, including biking, hiking, and horseback riding. Mingling with city parks on three sides, this BLM-maintained facility offers opportunities to meander along Campbell Creek through spruce and aspen forests. Trail access is from two parking lots, one at the north end of Campbell Airstrip Road, and the other to the south. Trails are well marked within the tract boundaries; note that the Bivouac trails veer into military land where permits are required. Fox, lynx, coyote, moose, wolves, and bear have been spotted within the tract boundaries. In fact, more than 20 resident grizzlies have been identified in this area, and maulings have occurred. Summer use can be problematic as the bears follow salmon along Campbell Creek, so exercise good caution and common sense, especially if signs noting bear encounters have been posted.

Also within the tract is the 10,500-square-foot Campbell Creek Science Center, serving as an educational resource with a library, greenhouse, and a variety of wilderness activities. You can access Campbell Tract either from the Smokejumper trailhead off Abbott Loop Road or from Campbell Airstrip Road off of Tudor Road.

CHUGACH STATE PARK

(907) 345-5014
dnr.alaska.gov/parks/units/chugach/

The third-largest state park in the country spreads out from the foothills on the east side of Anchorage, stretching south to where the Seward Highway crosses into the Kenai Peninsula and north to the Mat-Su Valley. You can access the half-million acres of parklands from several points throughout the Anchorage Bowl. As you venture into the park, you'll be treated to panoramic mountain views, the crystal-clear water of wilderness streams, a plethora of wildflowers in season, and perhaps a glimpse of a moose, bear, fox, eagle, or lynx. Within the park, you can enjoy hiking, camping, skiing, rafting, climbing, and, in designated areas, snowmachining.

The Eagle River Nature Center is a great place to get an introduction to all that the park has to offer; see the listing on the nature center in the Attractions section above. North of Eagle River, Eklutna Lake Valley is another popular place to get into all that the park has to offer, including picnicking and boating on the turquoise waters of Eklutna Lake.

Don't feel like driving that far? You can enter the park's Hillside Trail System from one of four access points on the east side of town. Take O'Malley Road east to Upper O'Malley Road, where you can go north on Prospect Drive to the Prospect Heights Access, or continue south to the O'Malley access. Another option is to take DeArmoun Road from the south side of town to Hillside Drive and Upper Huffman Road. From there you can choose either the Upper Huffman Access or the Glen Alps Access at the end of Tolsome Hill Road. From any of these points, you can set off on a myriad of trails; see this chapter's Hiking, Camping, and Fishing section for details on some of the most popular routes. Only the Upper Huffman Access may be used for snowmachining.

South of Anchorage you can venture into the park at the Turnagain Arm Trail, formerly called the Old Johnson Trail. You'll find trail-heads at either Mile 112 or Mile 115 of the Seward Highway. Details on the Turnagain Arm Trail may be found in this chapter's Hiking, Camping, and Fishing section. In this southern section of the park, you'll also find the Potter Section House, a state historic site with restored buildings from a former railroad section camp. The park headquarters is located here.

ⓘ Beware of the bore tides when exploring the coastline of Turnagain and
Knik Arms. Unique to this part of the
country, these 2- to 6-foot walls of water
move at speeds of 10 to 15 mph. Caused by
wide discrepancies between low and high
tides, bore tides can come in sounding like
a freight train. They're fun to watch from a
distance, and Beluga Point in the southern
part of Chugach State Park is a great place
to see them, usually about 45 minutes after
low tide in Anchorage.

CUDDY FAMILY MIDTOWN PARK

In 2008, Anchorage dedicated this "central park"
next to the Loussac Library in midtown. Among
its features are a pond, amphitheater, speed-
skating oval, gardens, and playground. Access is
from the southwest corner of the Loussac Library
parking area.

ⓘ Got dogs? Anchorage has five off-
leash dog parks: Russian Jack, Connor
Bog, University Lake, Far North Bicentennial Park (the North Gasline Trail), and
the South Anchorage Sports Park (future
American Legion Fields). Be sure to practice
good petiquette by leashing your dogs to
and from the parking area and picking up
after them. For maps and directions, visit
www.muni.org/healthmsd/dogparks.cfm.

DELANEY PARK (PARK STRIP)
A–P Streets, between Ninth and Tenth Avenues

Also known as the Park Strip, Delaney Park offers a
broad, sweeping swath of green along the south
end of downtown Anchorage. First cleared as a
fire break and later used as an airstrip, the park
is mostly wide open, but there are a few shaded
and secluded spots for relaxing on a warm summer day. You'll find lots of fun flowers, including
the Centennial Rose Garden, as well as memorials
to World War II vets and Martin Luther King Jr.

There's also an antique train engine that attracts
the attention of young and old alike.

EARTHQUAKE PARK
4306 West Northern Lights Boulevard

When the infamous 9.2 Good Friday Earthquake
struck Alaska in 1964, some of the most extensive
damage occurred along Turnagain Arm on the
northwest end of Anchorage, where the clay
soils collapsed into the sea. Dozens of homes
were lost, and six neighbors were killed. Walking
through Earthquake Park, established along this
forever-altered stretch of coastline, it's hard to
imagine the massive destruction that happened
here only a few decades ago. An interpretive facility with kiosks, sculptures, signs, photos, and maps
conveys the transformation from calm to chaos
and back again. If you follow non-sanctioned foot-
paths down to the water to get a closer look at the
way nature rearranged the bluff overlooking the
inlet, be advised that the walkways are steep and
the tidal flats are extremely dangerous.

FAR NORTH BICENTENNIAL PARK
6501 East Tudor Rd.

This 4,000-acre city park is bordered by Chugach
State Park to the east, by Tudor Road to the north,
and by Abbott Road and Abbott Loop Road to
the south and west. You can enter the park either
by driving east on Abbott Road to Hillside Park,
or by heading east on Tudor Road to Campbell
Airstrip Road. The park includes a vast network of
trails for skiing, running, dog mushing, biking, hiking, and horseback riding through the woods and
along streams. The park experiences heavy year-
round use with downhill skiing and horseback
riding concessions as well as two baseball fields.
A users group meets monthly to promote efforts
to protect this vast park from encroachment by
roadways and other development.

KINCAID PARK
9401 West Raspberry Rd.
(907) 343-6397

Acclaimed as the site of some the best running
and ski trails in the country, this 1,400-acre park

Close-up

Earthquake

Without a doubt, the geological phenomenon that most changed Anchorage and Southcentral Alaska in recent years was the Good Friday Earthquake of 1964. With an adjusted magnitude of 9.2, this shaker was slightly stronger than the 9.0 Sumatra event in 2004 that caused more than 280,000 tsunami-related deaths. With more earthquakes than any other part of the country, Alaska is considered one of the most seismically active areas of the world. Registering 11 percent of the world's total quakes, Alaska has been the site of three of the eight largest tremblers ever recorded. The 1964 earthquake was the second largest on record, with only the 1960 Chilean earthquake measuring higher on the Richter scale.

The big one started at 5:36 p.m. on March 27, 1964. During four to seven minutes of shaking, buildings toppled, landslides and avalanches rearranged the landscape, and 15 people died. Anchorage, about 75 miles west of the epicenter, sustained the greatest losses. Downtown, approximately 30 blocks of residential and commercial buildings were damaged, including the JCPenney store and the new Four Seasons apartment complex, which collapsed completely. Schools were especially hard-hit, including the Government Hill Grade School, which was pulled apart as the result of landslides. The Turnagain Heights residential area sustained huge landslide damage as more than 130 acres crumpled and collapsed, destroying an estimated 75 homes and disrupting all major services. Today, Earthquake Park stands as a memorial to the Turnagain Heights devastation.

In Seward, a 1,070-meter section of waterfront slid into the ocean, causing a local tsunami that took at least 11 lives and sent oil spilling from storage tanks into the water, where it went up in flames. A 67-meter wave was recorded in Valdez Inlet, where quake-related damage was so extensive that the entire town was subsequently moved to more stable ground. In all, 106 Alaskans died as a result of quake-related tsunamis. Statewide, property damage from the quake and tsunamis was estimated to be between $300 and $500 million.

Beyond Alaska, the big waves generated by the Good Friday Earthquake were the most disastrous to ever hit the west coasts of the United States and Canada. California suffered an estimated 13 deaths and $10 million in property damage, while Oregon saw four deaths and $7 million in damage. British Columbia also reported $10 million in tsunami-related damage. In 1967, the West Coast and Alaska Tsunami Warning System was established in Palmer in order to help avert future disasters.

When you travel from Anchorage to Portage, you'll see a forest of dead gray trees that were doused in salt water as a result of the 1964 Earthquake. Geologist Rod Combellick studied these soils for evidence of liquefaction, which results when earthquake activity causes sand to act as a liquid. In the process, he discovered patterns of sand layered with organic silt, revealing that earthquakes as big as the one in 1964 most likely have occurred in Southcentral Alaska every 600 to 800 years. Statewide, there's one earthquake measuring 8.0 or higher on the Richter scale every 13 years, with an average of 1,000 Alaskan quakes each month.

Since 1964 the state's population has more than doubled, and construction practices have been modified to prevent the extensive damage that resulted from the last big quake. Nevertheless, the Federal Emergency Management Agency estimates that Alaska has the second-highest possible earthquake loss ratios in the country. Earthquake insurance? Only about 20 percent of Alaskans carry coverage, and some companies have discontinued it. In earthquake-prone Alaska, it's just another example of living, literally, on the edge.

is a real treasure. Kincaid's 43-mile network of trails has served several major recreational events over the years, including World Cup races, North American Biathalon Championships, and a slew of national and international cross-country ski events. With access from the west end of Raspberry Road, the park intersects with the Tony Knowles Coastal Trail as well. From all around the park, you'll catch great views of Mount Susitna, Mount Foraker, the Chugach Mountains, Cook Inlet, and, on especially clear days, Mount McKinley. Portions of the park's expansive Outdoor Center, which includes huge barbeque grills, a batting cage, and a climbing tower, may be rented for private functions. From the south entrance off the end of Dimond Boulevard you can climb to the top of a huge sand dune for fabulous views of the mountains and inlet.

i Mount Susitna, the most visible peak as you look across Cook Inlet from downtown Anchorage, is nicknamed the Sleeping Lady because the shape of the mountain looks like a woman resting on her side. Legend has it that an Indian princess lay down to wait for her lover to return from battle, but he was killed as she slept, so she has never awakened.

RESOLUTION PARK
300 L St.
This small park is a fun spot for downtowners to eat a to-go lunch and admire the views of Cook Inlet, Mount Susitna (the Sleeping Lady), and even Mount McKinley on especially clear days. The Tony Knowles Coastal Trail cuts through the park, and there's also a statue of Captain Cook, whose ship the *Resolution* visited nearby waters in 1778. The park is located at the junction of Third Avenue and L Street.

RUSSIAN JACK SPRINGS PARK
5300 DeBarr Rd.
(907) 343-6992
Originally a homestead owned by an immigrant

known as "Russian Jack," the land for this park was transferred from the Bureau of Land Management to the municipality of Anchorage back in 1948, making it one of the oldest parks in the city. Before the park was formally established, the city set up a minimum security prison there, with an adjacent prison farm. Today the park includes soccer and softball fields, a Girl Scout day camp, picnic and playground areas, tennis courts, the Mann Leister Memorial Greenhouse, the nine-hole Russian Jack Golf Course, and 9 miles of trails for biking, walking, and skiing. Also within the 300-acre park is the Lidia Selkregg Chalet, serving as a clubhouse for skiers in the winter and golfers in the summer. The chalet also may be rented for private functions. Access to the park is from Pine Street and DeBarr Road to the north and from Boniface Parkway and DeBarr Road to the south.

TOWN SQUARE MUNICIPAL PARK
E St., between Fifth and Sixth Avenues
Part of a downtown revitalization effort, this lovely park is ablaze with color in the summer, when more than 9,000 plants plus a waterfall make it the perfect backdrop for concerts and other public events. In the colder months, look for the annual tree-lighting ceremony and a fireworks display on New Year's Eve, as well as ice skating throughout the winter.

VALLEY OF THE MOON
Arctic Boulevard and West 17th Ave.
This is a fun little park tucked in the heart of midtown. You'll find playground equipment for all ages here. Grab a burger at the Arctic Roadrunner just down Arctic Boulevard (see the All-American/All-Alaskan category in this chapter's Restaurants section) and have an impromptu picnic.

RECREATION

If you can't find something to do around Anchorage, you're probably not looking very hard. The city is filled with recreation enthusiasts, and on evenings and weekends you'll find them out doing what they love best. Though much of the recreation centers on the outdoors, Anchorage has its share of spectator sports and indoor activities, too.

Berry Picking

A favorite Alaskan pastime, berry picking gives you a great excuse to get outdoors with the added benefit of savoring tasty souvenirs from your outing. Almost 50 varieties of berries grow in the state, and most of them are edible. Blueberries, salmonberries, and cranberries are among the favorites of avid berry pickers. Salmonberries ripen in late June, and blueberries are typically out by mid-July. Cranberries are generally best picked after the first frost. Aside from the great flavor of our wild berries, they're extra-healthy, with antioxidant levels much higher than those of berries from more southerly climes.

One popular berry-picking spot is the Flattop Mountain Trail, accessed from Upper Huffman Road. Just above the parking lot, you'll see Blueberry Hill. Another option is to take the Powerline Pass Trail and pick along the South Fork of Campbell Creek. North of town, the Rendezvous Peak Trail, next to Alpenglow Ski Area, will take you to a valley filled with blueberries, cranberries, and the less-popular crowberries. Or take the Highland exit off the Glenn Highway to South Fork Valley Trail for low-bush blueberries. There are also some berries to be had if you take the tram up to the top of Alyeska and walk down.

Bicycling

With more than 120 miles of paved multiuse trails maintained by the Parks and Recreation Department, Anchorage is a great place for biking. Among the recreational routes is the Chester Creek Greenbelt, a 4-mile trail from Westchester to Goose Lake. Another great option is the 8-mile Campbell Creek Trail, which runs through Far North Bicentennial Park and along the Campbell Creek Greenbelt, where you'll spot spawning salmon in season. Watch for bears.

The 11-mile Tony Knowles Coastal Trail also makes for great biking. Starting from downtown Anchorage, this coastal trail winds along the ocean past Westchester Lagoon, Earthquake Park, and Point Woronzof, then on to miles of adjoining trails within Kincaid Park. The views of Knik Arm, Mount Susitna, and Cook Inlet from the coastal trail are nothing short of spectacular. On a clear day, you'll also see Mount McKinley from points along the way.

Just south of town the bike trail from Indian to Girdwood runs through some of the most fabulous scenery you'll find anywhere. Hills are part of the terrain, but the ride's still accessible for most cyclists.

If your interest is mountain biking, check out the Far North Bicentennial Trails, the Hilltop Ski Trail System, and the Kincaid Park Trails. Within Chugach State Park, the Bird Creek Valley, Eklutna Lakeside, Middle Fork to Williwaw Lakes, and Powerline Trails all offer nice challenges and spectacular scenery.

A great local resource for biking enthusiasts is the Arctic Bicycle Club (907-566-0177, www .arcticbike.org), which began in the 1970s as a road-cycling club in Anchorage but now has expanded to include mountain biking and touring throughout Southcentral Alaska. The club hosts rides for cyclists of all levels and sponsors both competitive and noncompetitive racing events.

Thanks to a number of bike rental businesses, visitors can partake in all the biking fun in and around Anchorage. Pablo's Cafe and Bicycle Rentals (907-250-2871, www.pablobicyclerentals .com) rents Cannondale and Tandem adult bikes. Helmets, maps, and bike locks are included with each rental. Their convenient location 1 block from the Tony Knowles Coastal Trail makes Pablo's a popular option. They're open daily from May to September, with rentals starting at $15 for up to four hours, with an additional charge of $5 per hour after that. Downtown Bicycle Rental (907-279-5293, www.alaska-bike-rentals.com) offers similar rental services with 24-hour rental periods and a 10 p.m. return option. Current rates are $16 for three hours and $4 per hour beyond. They also rent hybrid bikes, kids' bikes, tagalongs, mountain bikes, and trailers.

If you're interested in a backcountry bike tour, check out Alaska Backcountry Bike Tours (866-

354-2453, www.mountainbikealaska.com). They specialize in day and multiday trips, including transportation to and from your Anchorage-area accommodations. The Ekluna Lake tour is a popular day trip for beginners, while the Johnson Pass tour provides more advanced single-track riding. Prices start at $69 per person for the Coastal Trail excursion and include lunch, snacks, beverages, helmet, and a souvenir water bottle.

Boating and Water Sports

An abundance of lakes and rivers within day-trip distance of Anchorage makes this a great place to play in the water. If you like canoeing, you can put in at Cheney, Campbell, or Jewel Lakes, as well as Westchester Lagoon. North of the city, Mirror and Eklutna Lakes are popular spots for paddling.

For a little more excitement, try rafting. The Matanuska River and Sixmile Creek are popular destinations, with rapids ranging from Class I to IV. Borealis River Guides (907-783-2518) provides transportation to the Matanuska River King Mountain Run, less than half an hour from Anchorage. For a more challenging Class IV trip, they'll also take you to the Lions Head Run on the Matanuska River. A box lunch is included with both trips. Nova (800-746-5753, www.novalaska.com) takes you to Matanuska Glacier for Lions Head and Glacier Run adventures, or you can travel south with them to the wild and wooly Sixmile Creek (Class IV and V) 60 miles south of Anchorage near Hope, where you can plunge from high in the Chugach Mountains through three canyons. Also near Sixmile is Chugach Outdoor Center (907-277-7238, 866-277-7238, www.chugachoutdoor center.com), where you can choose anything from a peaceful float on the Resurrection River to heart-pounding descents through Class V rapids. If you like your water calm, opt for one of the twice-daily Turnagain Pass Floats, departing from the same location as the more daunting Sixmile escapades.

Kayaking is another great way to experience Alaska's rivers. Eagle River and Eklutna Lake are popular kayaking destinations near Anchorage. With the Alaska Kayak Academy (907-746-6600, www.kayakcenterak.com), you'll navigate either the Matanuska or Knik River in an inflatable kayak, accompanied by an experienced guide. All equipment, including dry suit, is provided, as is instruction. For real enthusiasts or beginners wanting to hone their skills in tamer waters, the Kayak Academy offers winter and spring sessions at the Bartlett High School pool. They also sponsor a Kayak Polo League.

It's not for the timid, but those not put off by the extreme tides and sometimes hefty winds have been known to sailboard in Turnagain Arm. If you prefer motorized boats, your best bet is to head for the Mat-Su Valley, where Nancy Lake and other smaller lakes are open to motorboats and Jet Skis. The Valley is also home to the Alaska Sailing Club (www.aksailclub.com), offering sailing classes and a summer race series, where the emphasis is on fun rather than strict competition. The club owns a small fleet of eight boats that may be rented by members.

Boxing

From fall through spring, there's club boxing most Thursday nights at the Egan Center. This is your chance to watch amateurs, including some women, duke it out. Seating includes both drinking and nondrinking sections, and the bouts draw a pretty good crowd. For more information, contact Jim Patton Promotions at (907) 243–0106 or check out www.thursdaynightfights.com. If you're interested in getting in the ring yourself, check out the Anchorage Amateur Boxing Club (907-529-7057).

Climbing

For more than a decade, the Alaska Rock Gym (907-562-7265, www.alaskarockgym.com) has given Alaskans something to climb about. Day passes, punch cards, and rental equipment are all available. They offer classes and programs for kids and adults, with specially-priced Friday night introductory sessions for beginners. Experienced climbers like to scale the crags and road cuts along Miles 113 through 119 of the Seward Highway south of Anchorage. There's some loose rock, so helmets are a must.

Curling

If you want to have fun on the ice but skating's not your thing, Anchorage is a great place to give curling a try. Played with teams of four, curling's a little like shuffleboard on ice. Granite stones ("rocks") are "thrown" toward a bullseye on the ice; sweepers (yes, with brooms) speed up and straighten the path of the rock, which is let loose in a slow spin. It's a lot more challenging that it looks, and the friendly club crowd will be glad to offer you pointers. The Anchorage Curling Club (907-272-2825, www.anchoragecurling. com) on Government Hill is open from October to April with two sheets of ice, one for newcomers and one for experienced curlers. The club offers classes for beginners, league action, and bonspiels for a variety of experience levels. And as at all good curling clubs, there's a members-only bar on the premises. If you want to join in the fun, watch for the Learn to Curl class, a $15 bargain that includes a weekend Rookie Spiel tournament, hosted by the club in October each year.

Dancing

If you like to kick up your heels, stop by the Anchorage Square and Round Dance Center (907-345-9556, www.alaskasquaredance.com) on Government Hill, next to the Anchorage Curling Club. From beginners to pros, dancers can indulge almost every day of the week. Another great resource for dancers is Swing Dance Alaska (www.swingak.net), where you can get the scoop on dances and lessons at the city's hot-hoofing spots, such as Eddie's Sports Bar, the Golden Lion, Club Soraya, and the Starlight Ballroom. And if Celtic tunes are more your style, check out the Scottish Country Dancing at the Fairview Recreation Center each Monday at 7:30 p.m. The cost is $3 per session. Wear comfortable shoes. A partner is not required.

Diving

With all sorts of coastline within easy reach, it's not surprising that diving is a popular recreational option in the Anchorage area. Though the ocean waters are a cool 55 degrees in the summer, with a proper dry suit you can see all sorts of marine life, including octopus, rockfish, sea lions, and whales. A great resource for divers is the full-service shop at Dive Alaska (907-770-1778, www .divealaska.net), where you can arrange dives, get certified, and rent equipment. Ask about their custom dive trips and packages.

Fitness

Recently named by *U.S. News & World Report* as the third fittest city in the country, Anchorage has an incredible array of ways to stay in shape. Fitness centers and athletic clubs are especially popular when the snow and cold make it difficult to get out and exercise if you're not into winter sports. The Alaska Club (www.thealaskaclub.com) has nine locations throughout the Anchorage area, including one express club and one club exclusively for women. You can expect the usual fitness options, including weights and aerobic training, at all of the locations, while some of the larger clubs have indoor swimming pools, saunas, steam rooms, and racquetball and tennis courts. For a low-cost alternative, try Planet Fitness (907-351-5500, www.planetfitness.com/ anchorage), with two Anchorage locations where you can use basic equipment at hours that fit your schedule.

Anchorage is also home to the largest air-supported structure in North America. The Dome (907-770-DOME, www.thealaskadome .com) makes winter recreating a breeze, with a 120-yard synthetic turf field, six-lane indoor-track, and batting cages.

The YMCA of Anchorage (907-563-3211, www .ymcaalaska.org) is open until 10 p.m. Monday through Saturday. They have an indoor/outdoor pool, fitness center, weight room, sauna and steam room, aerobics studio, and outdoor track and field facilities. Programs include aquatics, health and fitness, child care, and activities for kids.

Golf

Golf might not be the first activity you think of in connection with Alaska, but there are plenty of avid golfers out taking advantage of the long summer days. Look for courses to open in May and stay open through September.

The Anchorage Golf Course (907-522-3363, www.anchoragegolfcourse.com), known to locals as O'Malley's on the Green, features 18 holes sprinkled with water hazards, blind tee shots, and other challenges. There's also a driving range. It's a par 72 course, and you can get tee times as late as 10 p.m. in the summer. Lessons and club rentals are also available. You also can get civilian access to the Moose Run Golf Course (907-428-0056, www.mooserungolfcourse.com) on Fort Richardson. Moose Run offers a challenging 18-hole creek course with trees, hills, bunkers, and, as the name suggests, an occasional moose. The old Hill Course, rated among America's Fifty Toughest Courses, is still available for play, and there's a driving range. You can rent clubs here as well. Another military course open to civilians is Eagleglen Golf (907-552-3821, www.elmendorf services.com) on Elmendorf Air Force Base.

If you're just looking for nine holes, the Tanglewood Lakes Golf Club (907-345-4600) is the place to go. In addition to great summer rates, they offer golfing all winter long at the only indoor facility in Alaska. Likewise, the city's Russian Jack Park hosts a nine-hole course.

To the north, Palmer Municipal Golf Course (907-745-4653, www.cityofpalmer.org) is a nice, flat course that still provides a challenge. In Wasilla, the Settlers Bay Golf Course (907-376-5466, www.settlersbay.org) offers great scenery and a variety of fairways, not to mention a chalet-style clubhouse with killer views. Another option in Wasilla is the Sleepy Hollow Golf Course (907-355-0711, www.alaskagolflinks.com/sleepy hollow.html), known for its affordability. You can rent clubs at all three courses, and the Palmer course has a driving range.

i **Anchorage has its Frisbee golf enthusiasts, too. There are eight disc courses around town, with the largest at Kincaid Park. For more information, check with the Alaska Disc Golf Association (www .alaskadiscgolf.com).**

Horseback Riding

You don't have to go far to enjoy great horseback riding adventures in Anchorage. Horse Trekkin Alaska (907-868-3728, www.horsetrekkinalaska .com), on O'Malley Road, offers all sorts of trail-riding options, beginning at $60 for an hour-long trail ride. Longer rides include picnic lunches. Custom wagon tours and pack trips also are available. One of the best things about Horse Trekkin is that they offer year-round riding, including sleigh rides that end with a cabin warm-up featuring hot beverages and optional fondue. For a special romantic getaway, check out their Great Alaskan Date package, combining a sleigh ride with an overnight stay at A Critic's Choice Bed and Breakfast.

Ice Skating and Hockey

If you're not a skater when you come to Anchorage, this is a great place to take it up. Whether you're looking for recreational skating or competitive ice hockey opportunities, you'll find plenty of options both indoors and out. Lakes at several city parks and lagoons are plowed and hotmopped regularly. Westchester Lagoon is a favorite for casual and family-style skating, with separate track and hockey areas. The downtown Town Square and the new Cuddy Family Midtown Park west of the Loussac Library are other popular skating spots; Cuddy Park features a speed-skating oval. For outdoor hockey, try the Chester Creek Sports Complex, where there's activity at both rinks day and night. Cheney Lake, Goose Lake, Jewel Lake, and Spenard Lake all have maintained outdoor rinks, as do many of the local schools.

Anchorage has all sorts of organizations for kids and adults who like to skate. For figure skating, there's the Anchorage Figure Skating Club (www.anchoragefsc.com) and the Alaska Association of Figure Skaters (www.akafs.com). Speed skaters will find company at the Alaska Speed Skating Club (www.alaskaspeedskating.com).

For recreational hockey, check out the Anchorage Hockey Association (907-272-7825), the Anchorage Adult Hockey League (www.ahl

Ice Safety

The municipality of Anchorage requires at least 12 inches of solid ice before they begin plowing rinks. Ice that's 2 inches thick will generally support one person, while you'll need at least a thickness of 4 to 7 inches for small groups. Avoid ice with wet cracks, frozen slush, or overflow. If you're skating outdoors, always skate with a friend. In an emergency, the safest way to help someone who has fallen through the ice is to sprawl out on the surface and inch toward the opening with a stick or rope to offer the person in the water.

.net), and the Anchorage Outdoor Hockey Association (907-245-1860). Boys & Girls Club Hockey (907-249-5445), the South Anchorage Hockey Association (907-336-7242), and the Southcentral Alaska Hockey Association (907-337-9705, www.scwolves.com) all promote recreational hockey as well. Competitive level opportunities can by found with the Alaska All Stars Hockey Association (907-522-3790), the Anchorage Junior Aces (907-349-8324, www.jraces.com), and the Mustang Hockey Association (907-694-7849). Women can play in any of these leagues, but Anchorage also has two women-only leagues, the Alaska Firebirds (907-345-1196, www.alaskafirebirds.org) and the Anchorage Women's Hockey League (907-566-3453, www.awhl.ak.org).

BEN BOEKE INDOOR ICE ARENAS
334 East 16th Ave.
(907) 274-5715
www.benboeke.com
Here you'll find two indoor rinks owned by the municipality of Anchorage and operated by a private contractor. The facility includes six locker rooms and a concessions stand, with seating for 1,000 at the larger rink and for 100 at the smaller rink. The rinks are used by various youth hockey associations, figure-skating clubs, and adult hockey associations. Public skating and learn-to-skate programs are available.

A sister facility to the larger Ben Boeke complex, the Dempsey-Anderson also offers figure skating, public skating, skating lessons, and ice time for several levels of hockey. Parties and special events can be booked at the rink.

DIMOND ICE CHALET
Dimond Center Mall
800 East Dimond Boulevard
(907) 344-1212
www.dimondicechalet.com
This indoor rink on the bottom level of the Dimond Center Mall is perfect for enjoying a bit of skating without dealing with the cold temperatures at an outdoor rink. It's not a huge rink, and its overall atmosphere is more recreational than competitive. There's food-court seating around the rink. You can rent either hockey or figure skates, and skating lessons are also available. Also see our listing in the Kidstuff section of this chapter.

Orienteering

If you're going to venture into Alaska's vast wilderness areas, orienteering will give you a fun and practical place to start. The Arctic Orienteering Club (www.oalaska.org) fosters the sport of navigating the woods with a compass and map. It can get competitive if you like, but many folks just like to get out and challenge themselves. Beginners are welcome. The club sponsors regular recreational and competitive events.

Paragliding

Certified instructors Pete Gautreau and Scott Amy of Alaska Paragliding and Hang Gliding (907-301-1215, www.alaskaparagliding.com) will take you on tandem flights for a thrilling bird's-eye view of the stunning scenery in and around Anchorage. Instruction typically begins on a small hill or field and then graduates to Hatcher Pass, Eagle River, Flattop Mountain, Wasilla, or Alyeska, where the school is located. Equipment and instruction are provided; the courage is up to you.

Skiing and Snowboarding

With lots of mountains and plenty of snow, Anchorage is a skier's paradise. Nordic skiers have an abundance of trail options right in town. The 11-mile Tony Knowles Coastal Trail offers groomed, mostly flat terrain with great mountain and inlet views. Kincaid Park, where the Coastal Trail ends, has a system of 31 groomed trails certified for international competition. Russian Jack Springs, Hillside/ Bicentennial Park, and Campbell Tract all offer trail networks, some of which are lighted. North of town, the Eagle River Nature Center is a great place to pick up trails through Chugach State Park, while Hatcher Pass offers challenging mountain skiing in a spot where Olympic athletes come to train.

The Nordic Skiing Association of Anchorage is a great resource and advocacy group for cross-country skiing. They offer maps of the various park trails within the city, with proceeds from map sales going to support the maintenance of these trails. Call (907) 276-7609 or visit www .anchoragenordicski.com for more information.

With mountains jutted up next to the ocean, Anchorage offers world-class downhill skiing, too. Alyeska Resort in Girdwood is the premier alpine skiing venue in the area, while the slopes at Hilltop and Arctic Valley offer more low-key, family-oriented ski experiences.

ARCTIC VALLEY SKI AREA
(907) 258-4222
www.skiarctic.com
Originally designed as a recreational facility for the nearby military installations, this facility is now run by the Anchorage Ski Club. With two chair lifts and one T-bar, this affordable and family-friendly ski area capitalizes on great views of the Alaska Range, Mount Susitna, and downtown Anchorage. For an all-volunteer operation, Arctic Valley has a lot to offer the recreational alpine skier. Surrounded by the wilderness of Chugach State Park, the ski area stretches across 320 acres, encompassing 4,000-foot Rendezvous Peak. Ten percent of the terrain is appropriate for beginners, while 20 percent is considered expert territory. Arctic Valley is open only on weekends and occasional school holidays. The access road can be rough at times.

ALYESKA RESORT
Girdwood
(907) 754-2111, (800) 880-3880
www.alyeskaresort.com
With an average annual snowfall of 631 inches, 2,500 feet of vertical terrain, and 1,000 acres of skiable turf, it's not hard to see why skiers from around the world flock to Alyeska, ranked by Skiing magazine as one of the top 25 ski resorts in North America. Located 40 miles south of Anchorage, the resort makes all sorts of top lists for serious skiers and snowboarders, but they offer beginner classes and experiences as well. Toss in stunning scenery, awesome glaciers, and brilliant northern lights, and you have a mix that's sure to please everyone.

The season begins in mid-November and ends in mid-April, with weekend skiing through May as conditions allow. The resort features nine lifts and an aerial tram, with a total lift capacity of more than 10,000 skiers per hour. There are 86 runs, including open bowls, long top-to-bottom runs, and a fair number of beginner slopes. Fifty-two percent of the terrain falls into the intermediate category, while 37 percent is best suited for advanced skiers. Snowboarders enjoy a professional-level half-pipe, as the resort has hosted several USASA Alaska Snowboard Series amateur competitions.

The after-ski ambience is great here, too, with a pool and fitness center plus the nonsmoking Sitzmark bar and restaurant, featuring live music in the evenings. The Sitzmark is restricted to those ages 21 and older after 10 p.m.

For family fun, check out the Glacier Tubing Park, with two tubing lanes and a lift. Reservations (907-754-2274) are a good idea, as the facility can accommodate only 40 tubers per session.

HILLTOP SKI AREA
7015 Abbott Rd.
(907) 346-1407
www.hilltopskiarea.org

With 80 percent of the terrain designated as "easiest," Hilltop is a convenient place to get comfortable with the slopes before tackling more challenging heights. The 30-acre facility includes a vertical rise of 294 feet and a slope distance of 2,090 feet. Operated by the nonprofit Youth Exploring Adventure, Inc., Hilltop specializes in lessons, camps, and afterschool programs for area youth, but you'll find adults there as well. Snowboarders enjoy the "Mongoline," a permanent half-pipe for aerial stunts. Hilltop has a chair lift, a rope tow, and a platter lift. Adjacent to the ski area are Nordic ski trails and the Karl Eid Ski Jump Complex (907-346-2322).

i Looking for an affordable downhill rush? Check out one of the many sledding spots in Anchorage. Sunset Park at Government Hill, Conifer Park at Third Avenue and Lane Street, Connors Lake Park at Jewel Lake and International Airport Roads, and Kincaid Park at the west end of Raspberry Road are among several good locations. Kincaid has warm-up and restroom facilities, too.

Snowmobiling

Hatcher Pass, Eureka, the Iditarod Trail, Petersville, and portions of Chugach State Park are popular snowmobiling areas within day-trip distance of Anchorage. For a guided tour, head out into the backcountry with Alaska Snow Safaris (907-868-7669, 888-414-7669, www.snowmobile-alaska .com). Gear and equipment are provided. They offer one-day excursions, multi-day tours, custom expeditions, deep-snow riding in Valdez, and snowmobile rentals.

Spectator Sports

Collegiate baseball, basketball, and hockey as well as minor league men's hockey and arena

i As the nation learned when Alaska's governor Sarah Palin ran for vice-president in 2008, Alaskans refer to snowmobiles as "snowmachines." Avid riders will want to check out GCI's Arctic Man, a highly competitive mountain race held in the Summit Lake area, off the Richardson Highway between Anchorage and Fairbanks. Held in early April each year, an estimated 10,000 riders and revelers attend (see our complete listing in April events).

football—Anchorage has a nice array of spectator sports for a city its size.

In the summer the Anchorage Glacier Pilots and the Anchorage Bucs take on the competition at Mulcahy Stadium. Both teams are members of the Alaska Baseball League, which showcases collegiate players from around the country. Many of the players who spend a season with the Anchorage teams move on to major league play within a few years. Details on the season, including rosters and stats, may be found online at www.anchorage bucs.com and www.glacierpilots.com.

Mulcahy Stadium is just off A Street between 15th and 16th Avenues. In one of those only-in-Alaska stories, fans once had to vacate the stadium during a game when a Cessna 207 aircraft crash-landed just beyond the left-field fence.

In the winter, minor league hockey action takes center stage with the Alaska Aces, members of the East Coast Hockey League in affiliation with the NHL's St. Louis Blues. Since 1995 the Aces have been wowing their fans with top-shelf puck action at the Sullivan Arena. One of their stellar players, Scott Gomez, went on to play for the NHL, returning during a lockout year to play again for his home team. For schedules, rosters, team stats, and other Aces information, visit the team's official Web site at www.alaskaaces.com.

In 2006, Anchorage sported the state's first professional indoor football team, the Alaska Wild. Sellout crowds greeted the team, which is emerging from a couple of rocky initial seasons of coaching changes, player walkouts, and a change of ownership. A similar (though hopefully less tumultuous) start-up effort is under way with the Alaska Dream Basketball team, organized in 2008 with hopes of beginning play in 2009.

The University of Alaska Anchorage (UAA) Seawolves compete in a variety of sports, including Division II men's and women's basketball, cross-country running, gymnastics, skiing, track and field, volleyball, and Division I ice hockey. Basketball and hockey tend to draw the biggest crowds. In recent years, the women's basketball team has made a stellar showing in national rankings. For details on UAA athletic events, visit www.goseawolves.com.

Swimming

As you might expect, indoor pools are the most popular places to swim in Anchorage, but in the summer you can also test the waters at select lakes throughout the Anchorage Bowl, provided you don't mind the water being a bit brisk.

Lap swim and workout times are available at Alaska Pacific University's Moseley Sports Center (907-564-8314, moose.alaskapacific.edu/moseley/), located on University Drive near the Bragaw Street intersection. In addition, community swim times are available at several Anchorage School District pools, including Bartlett, Chugiak, Dimond, East, Service, and West High Schools. The pool at West High School also has a waterslide. Call the Swim Information Line at (907) 343-4402 or visit www.muni.org/parks/pools.cfm for details on hours and admission fees.

For private indoor swimming, check out the YMCA and the Alaska Club, both featured in our Fitness section above. Memberships are required by both organizations. And don't forget about the H2Oasis Indoor Waterpark (907-522-4420, www.h2oasiswaterpark.com), where there's a wave pool, a children's lagoon, and all sorts of chutes and slides. The water park offers swim lessons and water aerobics, too. For a complete listing, see this chapter's Kidstuff section.

Even though a city as far north as Anchorage might not seem like a swimming mecca, the city has played host to both the Western Zone Swimming Championship and the Speedo Junior Championship in recent years. If you're interested in competitive swimming, the Anchorage Aquanauts Swim Club is a great place to get started.

The municipality of Anchorage maintains beaches at Jewel Lake (West 88th Avenue and Gloralee Street, off Jewel Lake Road) and Goose Lake (3220 East Northern Lights Boulevard, near UAA Drive) in the summer, with lifeguards on duty for supervised swimming during designated hours. At Goose Lake's Paddleboat Cafe (907-337-5741), you can pick up a snack and rent a paddleboat if you like. In Eagle River, there's unsupervised swimming at Mirror Lake (Mile 24 of the Glenn Highway) and Beach Lake, off South Birchwood Loop.

i Alaskan lakes are prone to causing swimmers' itch, especially in mid- to late summer. This skin rash, caused by parasites that normally invade seabirds, develops within a few hours after leaving the water and can last for up to a week. To avoid it, swim in deep water away from shore and towel off vigorously when you get out. If you develop a rash, treat it with baking soda baths and anti-itch creams.

Wildlife Viewing

You'd be hard-pressed to find another city with the ample wildlife-viewing opportunities that Anchorage affords. Moose wander through residential neighborhoods and, on occasion, into downtown parking lots. They're especially prevalent during the winter. From the Ted Stevens International Airport, head north on Postmark Drive to Earthquake Park and Point Woronzof, where there's a good chance you'll see moose wandering not far from the north end of the airport runway. Specially designed chutes funnel the moose away from air traffic and out of harm's way. Point Woronzof is a great place to take in the view of Knik Arm and watch for eagles, too. For that matter, the entire Tony Knowles Coastal Trail, which runs from downtown through Point Woronzoff and on to

Kincaid Park, is a great place to see moose, birds, and an occasional black bear.

Another great place to see moose is Campbell Tract, a 730-acre park area that links Anchorage to the Chugach National Forest. You can access Campbell Tract by taking Campbell Airstrip Road, off the east end of Tudor Road, into Far North Bicentennial Park. From there you can hike in to get a close-up view of the park's wildlife. Other access points include Hilltop Ski Area on the south end of Campbell Tract, with access off the east end of Abbott Loop Road. Campbell Tract is also home to brown and black bears, coyotes, and lynx, but expect these to be much more elusive than the ubiquitous moose—though grizzlies are thriving in the area, too.

An estimated 300 black bears and 65 grizzly bears wander in and out of Anchorage, mostly from the Chugach Mountains, which cup around the east end of the municipality. Urban bears are problem bears, and despite such efforts as bear-resistant trash containers designed to curb bear-human interaction, the risk of mauling is always there. Your best bet for safe bear-watching is to sign on with one of the fly-out tours to Katmai National Park or Kodiak Island. Plan on dropping $600 to $700 per person for a day trip to Brooks Falls at Katmai National Park, where you're pretty much guaranteed to see bruins. Alaska Tours (907-277-3000, www.alaskatours.com), Rust's Flying Service (800-544-2299, www.flyrusts.com), and Regal Air (907-243-8535, www.regal-air.com) offer full-day, fly-out bear-watching excursions from Anchorage.

Even if you're not interested in catching fish, Anchorage has a couple of great spots to watch salmon in their dramatic journeys. Just north of downtown, A and C Streets converge into an access road for Ship Creek, which has salmon runs good enough to fish. Another fish-watching option is the Elmendorf State Hatchery, upstream from the downtown Ship Creek viewing area. Take Reeve Avenue north from East Fifth Avenue to the Post Road viewing area. The hatchery mingles warm water from the power plant at Elmendorf Air Force Base with creek water to create a year-round hatching facility for salmon and trout. King salmon return with amazing leaps up the fish ladder from mid-May into July, and there's a run of silvers from August through mid-September.

You also can see spawning salmon at Potter Marsh, a few miles south of Anchorage on the Seward Highway. Follow the wooden boardwalk through the marsh, stopping where it crosses Rabbit Creek, and you may see fish making their way upstream. Potter Marsh is also a popular spot for birders. From early spring through fall, you're likely to encounter canvasback ducks, Canada geese, and red-necked grebes, among other species. In the shorter summer season, you'll also see gulls, terns, and an occasional trumpeter swan.

The Anchorage Audobon Society (907-338-2473 (BIRD), www.anchorageaudubon.org) maintains an active schedule of events and activities. Events include Evening Owl Prowls, Hawk Watch, a spring Palmer Hay Flats outing, and early morning spring bird walks at the Campbell Creek Science Center. Natural history presentations are on the third Thursday of each month, September through May. Newcomers are always welcome. Some events require advance registration.

i **Wings over Alaska, a birding program sponsored by the Alaska Department of Fish and Game and Alaska Airlines, offers free certificates for identifying 50 to 275 species within the state. Get your free checklist at www.birding.alaska.gov.**

Tours

You can tour yourself around Anchorage with the Downtown Historical 10K Volkswalk. Pick up a map at the Historic City Hall, at Fourth Avenue and E Street, then follow the self-guided route past historical landmarks, with narrative provided on the map. Another fun option is to explore Anchorage on a high-tech treasure hunt—a geocaching expedition. Download a step-by-step guide at www.anchorage.net/Geo.

If you're looking for a guided recreational experience, several tour companies provide a range of options for seeing the town and the region. For touring within the city, try the Anchorage City History Trolley Tours (907-276-5603), which offer an hour-long excursion for $10 a person. The trolley tours depart hourly between 9 a.m. and 6 p.m. during the summer season from 612 West Fourth Avenue, between F and G Streets. Another option is a carriage ride through downtown Anchorage with The Horse-Drawn Carriage Company (907-688-6005). Take off from the city on a flight-seeing adventure with Alaska Air Taxi (907-243-3944, 800-789-5232, www.alaska airtaxi.com). Get up above it all in a DeHavilland Beaver or a Cessna 206 on one of a variety of packages, including a Knik Glacier and Wildlife Tour, a Blackstone Glacier Tour, a Mount McKinley Tour, or one of several tours in conjunction with the Iditarod Sled Dog Race. For more flightseeing options, check the air listings in "Getting Here, Getting Around."

For backcountry adventures, you can head out with Alaska ATV Adventures (907-694-4294, www.alaskaatvadventures.com) or Alaska All-Terrain Tours (907-868-7669, 888-414-7669, www.atv-alaska.com). These companies typically provide instruction and gear and will arrange transportation as needed for day trips both north and south of Anchorage. Alaska All-Terrain Tours also can arrange glacier jet boat tours, horseback riding, glacier dogsled tours, and flight-seeing expeditions.

i **The Eyes on Wildlife program, developed by the Alaska Department of Fish and Game in conjunction with the U.S. Forest Service, offers wildlife-viewing tips through brochures and Web sites. The program includes a wildlife checklist with benchmarks that allow participants to get achievement certificates for viewing live, undomesticated, and uncaged species. For more information, go to www.wildlife.alaska .gov and follow the wildlife-viewing links.**

HIKING, CAMPING, AND FISHING

Hiking

If you don't get out and do at least a little hiking in Anchorage, you're missing out on one of the best parts of being here. Recently named one of the Top Trail Towns by the American Hiking Society, Anchorage has plenty to offer for both novice and expert hikers. Within the municipality, you'll find 300 miles of unpaved wilderness trails along with 120 miles of paved routes. Unless otherwise noted, trail mileage indicated here is one-way only.

Even though you'll be hiking close to town, many trails in the Anchorage area are real wilderness trails, so don't head out without a good supply of drinking water and snacks. A headlamp, first aid supplies, and bear spray are also necessities. Cell phones will work from some trails but not all; bring one just in case. Remember, too, that the weather can change quickly. Every year, it seems a hiker or two gets stranded on a trail close to one of the state's urban areas in conditions that quickly become life-threatening, especially with the risk of hypothermia.

One of the most scenic, accessible, and popular options in Anchorage is the Tony Knowles Coastal Trail. Named after an Anchorage mayor who went on to become governor, this 11-mile paved trail follows a coastal route from downtown past Westchester Lagoon and on to Kincaid Park, where it connects with the park's set of trails. On a clear day, views from the trail are nothing short of spectacular. You'll see the legendary Sleeping Lady Mountain, the Chugach Range, and the waters of Cook Inlet. Moves are under way to make the trail even longer, provided land-acquisition issues can be worked out.

Dozens of ski trails at Kincaid Park make for great off-season hiking, as do the tangle of trails at Far North Bicentennial and Campbell Tracts. For details, check our listings unders Parks.

Ready access to the mountains is one of Anchorage's strong points, and you can't get ℹ️ The bible of Anchorage hiking is the Moutaineering Club's *55 Ways to the Wilderness in Southcentral Alaska,* authored by local hiking expert Helen Nienheuser. Pick up a copy at any local bookstore. Municipal trail maps can be purchased at REI, at the corner of Northern Lights Boulevard and Spenard Road.

ℹ️ Active since 1958, the Mountaineering Club of Alaska (www.mcak.org) is a great resource for climbers and hikers. In addition to sponsoring hiking, mountain biking, skiing, and climbing activities, the group hosts monthly meetings and maintains the Vin Hoeman Library of mountaineering at Alaska Mountaineering and Hiking on Spenard Road. The club also promotes conservation, trail maintenance, and environmental protection.

much closer than Flattop Mountain, a popular day-hike adventure spot. The trail is only 3 miles long, but it rises 1,300 feet in elevation, so it's a nice challenge for hikers of all ability levels. After a rock scramble to the top, enjoy great views of the city, the water, and the Alaska Range. Access to Flattop Mountain is from Upper Huffman Road to Glen Alps Road; follow the signs to Chugach State Park. It's a popular spot to spend the summer solstice and, for the hardy, New Year's Eve. But winter hikers be warned: Deadly avalanches have occurred here.

From the same Glen Alps trailhead, you can access other popular trails within Chugach State Park. For a short and easy hike, take the quarter-mile Anchorage Overlook Trail, a paved route that promises great views despite the minimal effort. More challenging is the 11-mile Powerline Trail to Indian, with an elevation gain of 1,300 feet and the promise of berry-picking opportunities toward the end of summer. When the moose rut in the fall, you can see dozens along the Powerline Trail. No need to trek all 11 miles—lots of folks do partial hikes, bikes, or skis to take in the scenery.

Another option is the 6-mile hike from Glen Alps to Williwaw Lakes, with nice views of Mount Williwaw and nearby lakes. The Williwaw Valley also can be accessed via the Prospect Heights trailhead, which takes hikers 6.5 miles through some truly stunning wilderness to a large chain of lakes. Plan on 8 to 12 hours for hiking the Williwaw, and don't be fooled by the proximity to town—this is a genuine wilderness hike. There are campsites throughout the valley, so if you want a more leisurely trip, plan an overnight outing.

From the Prospect Heights trailhead at the end of upper O'Malley Road, you can also hike

the 3-mile Near Point Trail, which goes past an old homesite in addition to offering views of the city, Cook Inlet, and the Alaska Range. The 5.2-mile Wolverine Peak Trail rises 3,380 feet from the Prospect Heights trailhead, with similar scenic views plus berry-picking opportunities toward the end of summer. You also can catch a glimpse of an old plane wreck at the trail's summit.

South of Anchorage you'll find several easy to moderately challenging trails accessible from the Seward Highway. Follow the 9.4-mile Turnagain Arm Trail from either the Potter trailhead at Mile 115 of the Seward Highway or the McHugh Creek trailhead at Mile 112 of the Seward Highway, and you'll be rewarded with great views of Turnagain Arm and wildflowers in season. From the McHugh Creek trailhead, you can hike less than a mile to the McHugh Scenic Overlook or follow the McHugh Lake Trail for 7 miles for nice views of McHugh and Rabbit Lakes as well as Suicide Peak.

Heading farther down the Seward Highway toward Girdwood, there are several trailheads near the tiny community of Indian. The Falls Creek Trail begins at Mile 105.6 of the Seward Highway and follows the creek for 1.5 miles, with an elevation increase of 1,450 feet, bringing hikers to a nice view of Suicide Peak. Another 1.5-mile trail with scenic views is the Bird Ridge Trail at Mile 102.2 of the Seward Highway; it's also quite steep. At Mile 103, the Indian Valley Trail heads up through a tundra-covered mountain pass for a 6-mile climb. If you're not inclined to hike uphill, the paved Indian to Bird Bike Path connects Indian, Bird, and the Bird Creek Campground, with views of Turnagain Arm along the way.

i Connecting with local hiking groups is a great way to get to know local trails. The Anchorage Adventurers Meetup Group (www.meetup.com/AnchorageAdventurers/) brings together more than 500 members for hiking, biking, skiing, and climbing adventurers. Alaska Outdoors (groups.yahoo.com/group/Alaska_Outdoors/) hosts free Monday and Thursday after-work hikes.

To the north, the trails beginning at the Eagle River Nature Center are a great way to explore another section of Chugach State Park. For a quick hike, pick up the Rodak Nature Trail, which takes you down 0.75 of a mile to a salmon-spawning river and viewing area. The 3-mile Albert Loop Trail also offers river access from the same starting point. For an all-out adventure, you can hike the Historic Iditarod Trail, also known as the Crow Pass Trail. This 26-mile trek from Eagle River to Girdwood will take you past rivers, waterfalls, former mining sites, and glaciers. Public-use cabins are available along the trail, but be sure to reserve them well in advance (see our listing on the Eagle River Nature Center in this chapter's Attractions section for details).

Other trails in the Eagle River area include the 0.75-mile River Trail at North Fork, with access at Mile 7.4 of Eagle River Road, and the 6-mile South Fork Valley Trail, accessed a short distance from Mile 7.5 of Hiland Road. For a multi-day hike through the heart of Chugach State Park, take the Arctic to Indian Trail from Ski Bowl Road near the Alpenglow ski area south through the valley and up into Indian. A bit farther up the road, the 1-mile Thunderbird Falls Trail at Mile 25 of the Glenn Highway offers spectacular views of the falls and the canyon, while the 5-mile Peters Creek Trail off Malcolm Drive at Mile 21 also sports some great scenery.

Eklutna Lake, the largest in Chugach State Park, offers some great options for hikers, too. Only 35 miles from Anchorage, Eklutna is where Anchorage gets its water. Take the exit at Mile 26 of the Glenn Highway to the campground, parking area, and trailhead. From there you can follow either the 3.2-mile Twin Peaks Trail or the 12.7-mile Eklutna Lakeside Trail. From the Lakeside Trail, you can access the 3.5-mile Bold Ridge Trail and the 6.5-mile East Fork Trail. There also are two public-use cabins along the Lakeside Trail, one at Mile 3 and one at Mile 12. For information on reserving these cabins, contact the Anchorage Public Lands Information Center (907-269-8400) or check online at www.dnr.state.ak.us/parks/cabins/index.htm. Note that all-terrain vehicles are allowed on the Lakeside Trail Sunday through Wednesday.

Camping

You'll see plenty of RVs on Alaskan highways during the short summer season. Camping is a great way to get into the great outdoors and beat some of the expensive hotel rates in the city. For RV parking, you'll find everything from side-by-side parking to campgrounds where you can spread out and enjoy the scenery.

Thanks to the State of Alaska Department of Natural Resources (DNR; 907-345-5014, dnr.alaska.gov/parks/aspbro/charts/chugach.htm) and the US Forest Service (907-783-3242, www.fs.fed.us/r10/chugach/pages_district/glacier.html), there are several great campgrounds within an hour or two of Anchorage. All of these

i As part of an ongoing effort to prevent vandalism at public schools during the summer months, the Anchorage School District permits camping with RVs on school grounds, by the month or for the entire summer season. For more information, contact the district at (907) 348-5170. The Alaska State Parks system (dnr.alaska.gov/parks/vip/host.htm) also recruits summer campground hosts, who stay for free for the season, sometimes with a small stipend.

Close-up

Hope and Hospitality

For a nice day trip from Anchorage, or a side trip on your way from Anchorage to the Kenai Peninsula, drive the paved 17.8 mile Hope Highway, which turns north and then east off the Seward Highway 56 miles south of Anchorage. This sleepy little community was a flurry of activity when gold was discovered in the area, including the now-defunct town of Sunrise, back in 1896. Three years later, all the excitement was over, but Hope, true to its name, never died. In addition to the 150 who call Hope home, Anchorage residents show up for quick getaways to soak up the scenery and historic charm.

If you swing through Hope, be sure to stop at the historic Seaview Bar and Cafe, housed in the old 1896 general store. The Goo Goo Dolls played an impromptu song there once and went sliding on the mud flats with local kids. The Social Hall, a log building crafted in 1902, continues to host town functions.

Rafting, hiking camping, fishing—it's all here in Hope. After you've checked out the Porcupine Campground and Gull Rock Trail, head into the woods to the more primitive Coeur d'Alene Campground and the start of the 38-mile Resurrection Pass Trail, a local fall favorite for berries and autumn colors. Summer wildflowers are stunning along the 6.4-mile Palmer Creek Road leading to the campground and trailhead.

Once voted Alaska's friendliest town, Hope is proud of its gold rush history. Stop by the local library (housed in the old log schoolhouse) and gift shop for a taste of Hope hospitality.

---

spots are popular, so either make advance reservations or get there early.

North of Anchorage at Mile 11.6 of the Glenn Highway is access to the Eagle River Campground (907-694-7982), part of the Chugach State Park, with 57 campsites and a four-day limit. At Mile 26.5 of the Glenn Highway (dnr.alaska.gov/parks/units/chugach/eklutna.htm) is another Chugach State Park favorite, Eklutna Lake, with 60 campsites, multi-use trails, and kayak rentals. South of Anchorage is Bird Creek, another campground facility of Chugach State Park, with 27 sites close to the highway and the ocean.

Through their Glacier District, the Forest Service operates Williwaw and Black Bear Campgrounds on the Portage Highway, off the Seward Highway sourth of Girdwood. Farther south are Bertha Creek (Mile 61.5) and Granite Creek (Mile 64. Another popular choice is the Porcupine USFS Campground at the end of the 17-mile Hope Highway, which runs west from Mile 56.7 of the Seward Highway. A few of the sites overlook

Turnagain Arm. From the campground, the Gull Rock Trail offers a moderately challenging hike (5 miles each way) to a scenic picnic and tent camping spot overlooking the ocean. There's no water at Gull Rock, so be sure to pack plenty of your own.

CENTENNIAL CAMPER PARK
8300 Glenn Highway
(907) 343-6986, (907) 343-6992
www.muni.org/parks/camping.cfm

Operated by the municipality of Anchorage, Centennial Park has 100 campsites, with six of them set up for either drive-through or tent camping. The biggest draw for this park is convenience, as it's less than 15 minutes from downtown. Showers and firewood are available at an additional charge, while the use of the dump site is free for campers. Pets must be leashed or confined, and quiet hours are maintained after 10 p.m. The campground is open from mid-May through September.

Close-up

Wild Alaskan Salmon

You can't be in Alaska long without having a salmon encounter of one kind or another. Whether it's a tasty meal featuring a savory and healthful filet, a weekend spent casting from the shore of a pristine river, or a casual visit to the Ship Creek fish ladder just north of downtown Anchorage, you'll get to enjoy one of the finest fish you'll find anywhere.

Rich in omega 3 oils, the flavorful flesh of the salmon keeps growing in popularity. Try a taste test comparing farmed fish to wild Alaskan fare, and you'll come away singing the praises of our native species. Toss in the chance to catch your own, whether it's by trolling the ocean waters out of Valdez, Seward, or Kenai, or by combat fishing on the rivers and streams of the Kenai Peninsula, and the experience gets that much better.

If you're having a rough day, ponder the difficult life of the salmon and be assured things could be a lot worse. Hatched in freshwater streams, salmon face perils that include diving birds, predatory fish, extreme weather, and unpredictable river conditions. After a year or two in fresh water, the survivors head for the ocean, where many of them fall prey to larger fish, marine mammals, and commercial fishing nets. The handful of young fish that manage to make their way back to freshwater must fight their way upstream to the place of their origin, where they are destined to spawn and die.

Though the uninitiated may think of salmon as one type of fish, there are actually five distinct species in Alaska. Best known for their size and their propensity to put up a good fight at the end of a line, Alaska's king salmon, also known as Chinooks, are typically the first to show up in significant numbers. The first kings arrive in May, with runs peaking in June and early July. In Southcentral Alaska, the earlier runs occur in drainages along the coast. Later runs in such places as the Kenai River may yield fish weighing more than 100 pounds, but these runs are rare. Chinooks make for good eating, with an oilier flesh that holds up well in cold-smoked strips.

Red salmon, or sockeyes, are coveted by Alaskans for bright, flavorful filets that are sure to please. Shunning most lures and flies, they're a dramatic but difficult fish to catch, but when they're hooked, they'll leap and dance with the best of them. Sockeyes, which average around six pounds, are the strongest swimmers of the five species. Significantly smaller than kings,

GOLDEN NUGGET CAMPER PARK
4100 DeBarr Rd.
(907) 333-5311, (800) 449-2012
www.goldennuggetcamperpark.com
Golden Nugget is one of those parking lot-type campgrounds, but it's conveniently located near Russian Jack Springs Park in midtown Anchorage. They offer 215 sites, with full hookups and picnic tables at each. Free hot showers are a bonus, and there's a laundry facility plus fenced playground area. Camping spots are available for backpackers, too. Sites run from $20 to $30 per night. Unlike many other Alaskan campgrounds, the Golden Nugget is open year-round.

i If you don't want to drive your RV to Alaska, consider renting one. ABC Motorhome Rentals (907-279-2000, 800-421-7456, www.abcmotorhome.com) has a huge inventory of motor homes and vans for rent. With early-bird discounts and one-way specials from Seattle, they guarantee the lowest prices in town. Great Alaskan Holidays (907-248-7777, 888-2-ALASKA) offers friendly, year-round service, with a convenient location on the Old Seward Highway.

sockeyes sport a metallic shimmer along their backs, with silver flanks and whitish bellies. After they spawn, the males turn bright red, with distorted heads and hooked jaws. Reds run almost concurrent with kings, though sometimes a bit later. In some of Alaska's larger, deeper lakes, you'll find landlocked sockeyes, also known as kokanee.

On the opposite end of the taste-test spectrum are pinks, or humpback salmon, which have a paler flesh that is most suitable for canning. Like their more flavorful cousins, male pinks turn especially ugly after spawning, with misshapen jaws and distorted backs that earn them the nickname "humpies." When they first come from salt water to fresh, humpies will put up a good fight, and their sheer numbers as they congregate in bays and river mouths are bound to impress. Their blue-green backs turn brown as they spawn, and their flesh turns soft. With a life span of only 18 months, pinks run in two separate genetic groups, so seasons in a given area will be for even- or odd-numbered years only. They generally return to fresh water in mid- to late summer, and spawn, sometimes in marginal conditions, in August and September.

Another lowly salmon species is the chum, or dog salmon. Like pinks, they're prolific, but they'll put up a bigger fight at the end of a line. Not nearly as tasty as reds but with a slightly firmer flesh than pinks, chums do get used as dog food among subsistence fishers and mushers, but they make for decent eating if you get to them early in their journey upriver. As they spawn, the males develop protruding teeth that also contribute to their association with dogs. You can distinguish chums from other salmon by the silver sheen on their bellies and the relatively narrow connection of the tail to the body. Chums run most of the summer, from early July through September, and later in some places.

Silvers, or coho salmon, are the last to run, arriving in mid-July and peaking about a month later. Though they average six to nine pounds, it's not uncommon to catch a silver that weighs 20 pounds or more. They easily can be mistaken for jack kings, smaller but sexually aggressive Chinooks. After spawning, cohos darken, and the heads of the males swell. Silvers make for good, all-purpose eating, though they're not as prized at the table as reds or kings. They make for great sportfishing, too, as they'll readily snap at a lure and put up a memorable fight. Before they spawn, silvers tend to gather in large groups in river mouths, bays, and sloughs, making them an easy target for anglers.

Fishing

For decent urban fishing, it's hard to beat Anchorage. Drive 30 to 60 minutes from town, and you'll find an even greater abundance of species in genuine wilderness settings.

Ship Creek is probably the best-known fishing hole right in town. Drive 10 minutes from the heart of downtown Anchorage to First Avenue and Loop Road, where there's parking on both sides of the creek. You can fish for salmon in the tidal portion of the waterway, just below the power plant. You won't have any illusions about being in the woods, but if you're fishing with the tide in some of the deeper holes near the road,

there's a good chance you'll see some activity. Kings roll in during the late spring and stay till mid-summer, while silvers peak in late summer and continue into autumn. Don't forget about the extreme tidal activity in Knik Arm. Be careful around the mud, and be prepared for water that could rise up to 12 feet.

From high in the Chugach Mountains, Campbell Creek flows west and then south to empty into Turnagain Arm at a point south of the airport. The Campbell Creek Greenbelt, weaving through several city parks, runs along most parts of the waterway. Above Dimond Boulevard, you can fish for silvers, rainbows, and Dolly Varden.

Look for especially good silver fishing during the latter parts of August in the portion of the creek between Dimond Boulevard and C Street. The middle portion of the creek is stocked with rainbows early in the summer. Even though you're in the heart of the city, be on the lookout for bears.

i Alaska has hundreds of wilderness cabins that may be reserved through state and federal agencies, including the Alaska Department of Natural Resources (dnr.alaska.gov/parks/cabins/index.htm) and the Bureau of Land Management (www.nps.gov/anch/cabins.htm). Although each agency has its own system for reservations and guidelines for use, you can expect similar rugged digs at each. Access is typically by trail, boat, or small plane, and cabin users should be prepared for adverse conditions and weather delays.

Several Anchorage lakes are stocked, with the fishing generally best in late spring and then again in late fall. For arctic char, rainbows, and landlocked salmon, try Jewel Lake, which offers good shore access and wheelchair facilities just off Dimond Boulevand, south of the airport. A bit more secluded but equally accessible is Campbell Point Lake near Kincaid Park, stocked with the same species as Jewel Lake. Closer to the airport, DeLong Lake sports the same fish. North of Anchorage, at Mile 23.6 of the Glenn Highway, Mirror Lake offers decent fishing for rainbows, char, and landlocked salmon. The best access is by small boat.

Also north of Anchorage is an area known as the Eklutna Tailrace. It's a spot where waters from the hydropower project are tunneled down from Eklutna Lake. Fishing can be a bit challenging here, but it is stocked with silvers and reds, and there is good road access with parking at Mile 4.1 of the Old Glenn Highway. South of Anchorage at Mile 101.2 of the Seward Highway, you'll find Bird Creek, one of the most popular salmon streams in the area. Look for chum and pink salmon during July, with heavy runs of silvers in the first part of August. Expect extreme tides and combat-style fishing when the runs are at their peak.

Farther down the road, about 45 minutes south of Anchorage, the Portage Area River Systems offer more secluded fishing opportunities for Dolly Varden and silvers. Twentymile River, running from Twentymile Glacier in the Chugach Mountains to Turnagain Arm, offers up red, chum, and silver salmon as well as Dolly Varden. Access is by boat launch. From Portage Lake, Portage Creek has all of the same species plus pink salmon. Clear sloughs and confluences throughout the system can be great spots to catch salmon and char, too.

i Many anglers practice catch-and-release techniques with slow-growing species like wild rainbow trout and northern pike. To follow this fish-conservation technique, use barbless hooks and strong line, and avoid playing the fish for too long. With the fish in the water, back the hook out without squeezing the fish or touching its gills and eyes. Point the fish upstream, swishing it gently back and forth until it swims away.

KENAI PENINSULA

With its scenic rivers, mountain vistas, and bountiful forests, the Kenai is a favorite weekend getaway for city folks from Anchorage. And in the heart of the Peninsula, right along the Sterling Highway, you'll find some of the finest salmon fishing in the world.

Traffic from Anchorage funnels south on the Seward Highway through the 9-mile swath of land connecting the Kenai to the mainland. Alaskans complain about the crowded highways, especially on summer weekends, but by Lower 48 standards, there's not much cause to whine. Do drive with caution, though, and obey speed limits. The winding two-lane highway between Anchorage and the Peninsula has been the site of far too many serious collisions.

Once you get past the fishing hot spots near Cooper Landing, the crowds thin, and you'll find plenty of wild country to explore. Follow the Sterling Highway all the way to its end, or stick with the Seward Highway and end up in—where else?—Seward. Alaskans associate Seward with Prince William Sound, so we've covered it in that chapter, despite the fact that it's technically part of the Kenai landmass.

Soldotna and its sister city Kenai form the service hub of the Peninsula, with the small towns of Cooper Landing, Sterling, Kasilof, and Ninilchik rounding out the options for anglers, outdoor enthusiasts, and visitors who just want to get away to the woods. At the end of the road, there's the eclectic town of Homer, a vibrant community known for fishing, outdoor activities, and the arts.

KENAI/SOLDOTNA

Soldotna is a young community, formed in the 1940s when homesteading was offered to veterans returning from the war. Strategically located at the junction of the Sterling and Kenai Spur Highways, Soldotna now serves as the headquarters for the Kenai Peninsula Borough.

Ten miles down the Kenai Spur Highway, the Kenai River empties into Cook Inlet at Kenai, the largest city on the Peninsula. The site was originally home to the Dena'ina Indians, and in 1791 the Russians established Fort St. Nicholas there. A few years later the Dena'ina defeated the 150 Russian settlers and reclaimed their community. The U.S. Army established Fort Kenai in 1869 in the aftermath of Seward's purchase of the Alaskan territory and the discovery of gold on the Russian River. More recently, natural gas and oil were discovered in the area, and there are now 15 drilling platforms off the coast in Cook Inlet.

Nearby Cooper Landing, with an estimated population of 500, was established as a miners' camp in the early 1900s. Tom and Frank Towle furthered development by building pioneer homes and offering guide services for moose, bear, and Dall sheep. In the 1930s, several fox farms added to the growth of the community.

Getting Here, Getting Around

Soldotna is 149 miles from Anchorage on the Sterling Highway, while Kenai is 159 miles from Alaska's biggest city. The highway is well-maintained, but it's only two lanes for much of the way, and traffic can be heavy during the summer when the fish are running. The Kenai Spur Highway connects Kenai and Soldotna. If you don't want to make the drive yourself, the Homer Stage Line (907-235-2252, thestageline.net/) makes scheduled runs from Anchorage to Kenai and Soldotna. There's also commuter air service by small plane into the Kenai Municipal Airport. Car rental is available at the airport. CARTS, a local transportation system, helps locals get around.

However you arrive, a stop at one of the local visitor centers will help you get oriented. Check out the Soldotna Visitor Information Center (907–262-9814, www.soldotnachamber.com) at 44790 Sterling Highway, and the Kenai Visitor and Cultural Center (907-283-1991, www.visit kenai.com) at 11471 Kenai Spur Highway.

Accommodations

The summer season runs from May to September, peaking in July at the height of the salmon runs. Most accommodations are designed with anglers in mind, with fish-cleaning, packaging, and freezing facilities for guests to use. In general, you can expect clean, comfortable, and friendly facilities without a whole lot of frills.

Unless we say otherwise, you can assume that major credit cards are accepted, smoking is not allowed (except outdoors), there's no wheelchair access, and pets are not accommodated. Price codes indicate the average price for a double room, excluding taxes and gratuities, during the summer season. Rates will generally be lower in the winter. Summer rates vary, depending on when the fish run. Expect the highest rates in July. Reservations are highly recommended during the peak of the season.

Price Codes

$................ **Less than $125**
$$ ....$126–$175
$$$ ....$176–$225
$$$$ .... **More than $225**

Kenai River

ALASKAN SOURDOUGH B&B   **$**
P.O. Box 812 Cooper Landing, AK 99575
(907) 595-1541
www.alaskansourdoughbb.com
Here's a fun combination: Eskimo and Cajun hospitality on the beautiful Kenai River. In addition to a clean, comfortable room with private bath, you'll

Need your Internet fix? Stop by the Kenai Community Library, where there are eight public Internet computers for 45-minute use during summer months and two for 20-minute use to check e-mail or print out a boarding pass. There's also free Wi-Fi when the library's open.

get a hot, home-cooked breakfast every morning. Rooms come in a variety of bed configurations, with coffeemaker, microwave, minifridge, iron, ironing board, and free morning paper. Ready to relax after a full day of fishing? Fire up the sauna, or cook up a barbeque and have dinner at the picnic table. The Alaskan Sourdough is on the quiet side of the river, so you should get a good night's sleep. Despite all those jokes about wives and fishing, this B&B has found a unique way to marry the two, literally. They have an Eskimo wedding chapel in the heart of fishing country, where your host Willie Johnson can help you tie the knot or renew your vows. One guest room has wheelchair access.

FRENCHY'S FISHING CABINS $$$–$$$$
Scout Lake Rd., Sterling
(907) 344-4846, (800) 939-4846
www.frenchysfishingcabins.com
Anchorage B&B owner Karen French offers cozy cabin getaways with Kenai River access. The fishing-themed rooms include kitchen privileges, private bath with shared shower, telephone, cable television, balcony, iron, ironing board, free morning paper, continental breakfast (or boxed lunch for your fishing trip), and discounts at local attractions. Frenchy is a longtime Alaskan, and she'll make sure you feel right at home. Choose from three new 1,400-square-foot cabins accommodating six people each, or the Bear and Moose cabins, which each sleep four.

GWIN'S LODGE $$
Mile 52, 14865 Sterling Highway,
Cooper Landing
(907) 595-1266
www.gwinslodge.com

For more than half a century, Gwin's Lodge has been hosting visitors to the salmon-rich confluence of the Kenai and Russian Rivers. The original owners cut, hauled, and hand-peeled the logs to build this historic roadhouse, completing it in 1952. The Standard Log Cabins are a no-frills option with two full-size beds, private bath with shower, and a roll-away bed. Log Cabins with Kitchen and Loft add an extra bed plus kitchenette, while the Cottage House Units include a full kitchen, dining, and great room with satellite television and sleeping for five or six. The Standard and Deluxe Log Chalet Units are newer, with additional sleeping areas. Don't expect seclusion here: Gwin's is almost like a little town, with a full-service restaurant and fishing-tackle shop on-site. They've also added wireless Internet access throughout the property. (Also see the listing in the Restaurants section of this chapter.)

THE HUTCH BED AND BREAKFAST $
Mile 48.5 Sterling Highway, Cooper Landing
(907) 595-1270
www.arctic.net/~hutch
Pet rabbits provide the theme for the Hutch, a three-story cedar lodge with 12 guest rooms, each with private entrance, private bath, coffeemaker, and free continental breakfast. They have every size bed, from twin to king. The rooms are nothing fancy, but you'll enjoy the convenient and scenic location with picnic tables, a barbeque grill, and campfire pit. Take your continental breakfast of coffee, juices, hot chocolate, cider, cereals, muffins, breads, bagels, and fruit on the outdoor decks, weather permitting. One room is wheelchair accessible.

Soldotna

ALASKA RIVERVIEW LODGE $$–$$$
24771 Amber Dr.
(907) 260-5432
www.alaskariverview.com
From the banks of the quiet Kasilof River, one of the Peninsula's hidden treasures, watch the eagles soar and the moose wading in the water. You can fish from the Riverview's private dock

or just soak up the scenery and follow the river as it changes with the tides. Choose from cabin units, a fully equipped two-bedroom suite, or the Honeymoon Suite/Cabin right on the riverbank. Rooms come with coffeemakers, microwaves, minifridges, and free continental breakfast. If you like, your friendly hosts will arrange for guided fishing in the area. Once you've caught your limit, you can make use of the Riverview's outdoor grill, freezer space, and fish-processing area with vacuum sealer. Wheelchair-accessible rooms are available, and pets are accepted on approval.

ASPEN HOTEL $$
326 Binkley Court
(907) 260-7736
www.aspenhotelsak.com
The Aspen offers 63 rooms in the heart of Soldotna, including comfortable suites. All rooms include coffeemaker, refrigerator, microwave, iron, ironing board, hair dryer, telephone, and television with VCR. They also have an exercise room, a business center, a guest laundry room, and a conference room. The Aspen is also the only motel in the area with a swimming pool. A wheelchair-accessible suite is available.

AURORA NIGHTS BED AND BREAKFAST $$
33215 Rensselaer Lane
(907) 262-2918
www.alaska.net/~jbstraume/
If you're looking for privacy with a great location only 2 miles from several fishing hot spots, you'll enjoy Aurora Nights' guesthouse, complete with a stunning view of the Spur Mountains. On K-Beach Road between Soldotna and Kenai, the guesthouse sleeps six, but if you have a smaller group, you can rent just one room. Each bedroom has a queen-size and a twin bed, and there's a Jacuzzi tub in the bathroom as well as an outdoor hot tub on the lower deck. The guesthouse also includes a full-service kitchen, continental breakfast, laundry facilities, private deck, and use of the barbeque. Credit cards are accepted only through PayPal (www.paypal.com) online.

ESCAPE FOR TWO B&B GUESTHOUSE $$
49300 Charlie Brown Dr.
(907) 262-1493
www.escapefortwo.com

Pamper yourself at this romantic getaway located 7 miles south of Soldotna on 40 acres with a private lake. Soak in the jetted tub for two, light the candles, turn on the music, and relax. From the rose petals on the bed to the luxury linens, attention to detail abounds. The guesthouse comes with coffeemaker, microwave, minifridge, and a hearty breakfast basket. No children or pets.

KENAI RIVER RAVEN LODGE $$$$
Mile .2 Funny River Rd.
(888) 262-5818
www.kenairiverraven.com

This massive Alaskan log lodge overlooks the Kenai River but is also a short walk from downtown. Within guests enjoy a river rock fireplace, Alaskan art, and custom log furniture. The wraparound deck offers a walkway to the river. A full breakfast is served every morning. The lodge sleeps 18, with fishing and corporate packages available. The entire facility is nonsmoking.

KENAI RIVER RETREAT $$$
360 West Endicott Dr.
(907) 262-1361, (800) 987-8201
www.kenairiverretreat.com

Who says you can't combine adventure with style? At the Kenai River Retreat, you'll enjoy first-class accommodations in a convenient yet secluded location next to a state recreation area, right on the Kenai River and just 1 mile from downtown Soldotna. Suites come with queen-size beds, full kitchens, irons, ironing boards, and leather furniture. Your friendly hosts will provide laundry facilities, fishing gear, mud boots, clam shovels, and a freezer for guests to use. You can even help yourself to fresh herbs from the greenhouse and grill your fish on your private deck. Enjoy bank fishing and great hiking trails plus amazing views of the river, mountains, and wildlife.

SILVERTIP LODGE GUEST CABINS $-$$
35930 Bowman Rd.
Mile 90.5 Sterling Highway
(907) 262-4450
www.silvertiplodgeandcabins.com

Tucked away in a beautiful birch hollow 4 miles outside of Soldotna, Silvertip Lodge offers six cabins and three bed-and-breakfast rooms. The owners take a personal interest in making sure their guests have the quiet and relaxing stay that Alaskan visitors crave. Their cabins accommodate up to six people and come with full kitchens, including coffeemaker, microwave, minifridge, iron, ironing board, free morning paper, and continental breakfast. The bed-and-breakfast rooms, each of which has a television and VCR, are downstairs in an authentic log home. Anglers will appreciate the on-site fish-cleaning and freezing facilities.

SOLDOTNA BED AND BREAKFAST LODGE $$-$$$
399 Lovers Lane
(907) 262-4779, (877) 262-4779
www.soldotnalodge.com

In the heart of Soldotna on the Kenai River is a world-class Alaskan fishing lodge with great guest reviews. Expect super-clean rooms, a full breakfast, and friendly hosts in a first-class Alaskan setting. When you're not fishing or exploring the river, relax in your Victorian-styled room or catch some sun on your personal veranda. Hosts Steven and Monika Anderson speak several languages and have extensive travel experience. Rent by the night or opt for an all-inclusive fishing package.

SOLDOTNA INN $$
35041 Kenai Spur Highway
(907) 262-9169, (888) 262-9169
www.mykels.com

The Soldotna Inn has been providing quality lodging and fine dining since the early 1970s. Though the building is older, the inn is well-maintained and clean, with Wi-Fi Internet access throughout, a new continental breakfast area, and an expanded lobby. Each room features art by local Alaskans, and the furniture includes locally milled and manufactured pieces. The Alaskan flair and emphasis on customer service sets the Soldotna Inn apart from the usual chain hotel. They offer 18 rooms with microwaves, refrigerators, and coffeemakers. For great rates on long-term rentals, check out their fully furnished apartments, complete with living rooms and kitchens. Conveniently located in the heart of Soldotna, 0.75 mile from the Sterling Highway and a short walk from the Kenai River, the Soldotna Inn offers both smoking and nonsmoking rooms, and they accept pets in designated rooms.

Kenai

.406 SPORTSMAN'S LODGE $
10800 Kenai Spur Highway
(907) 283-6101
www.the406sportsmanslodgekenai.com
Under new ownership and featuring newly remodeled rooms, the .406 Sportsmans Lodge offers competitive rates, a new bar with karaoke, and a very good restaurant. Named for legendary Red Sox player Ted Williams and his .406 average, the lodge offers 32 comfortable rooms in the heart of Kenai, with free wireless Internet, free local calls, cable television, and reimbursement of taxi fare from the airport if you've got reservations.

ASPEN EXTENDED STAY SUITES $$
10431 Kenai Spur Highway
(907) 283-2272
www.aspenhotelsak.com/kenai_contact.htm
A sister property to the Aspen in Soldotna, the new Aspen Kenai offers the same well-appointed rooms in studio suites. Guests enjoy nearly all the amenities of home, including fully equipped kitchens, wireless Internet, laundry facilities, fitness center, business center, and choice of queen plus sofa bed or two queens.

DANIELS LAKE LODGE $-$$$
Mile 29.7 Kenai Spur Highway
(907) 776-5578
www.danielslakelodge.com
The log cabins and guest rooms at Daniels Lake Lodge are spread across nine wooded acres between Kenai and the Captain Cook State Recreation Area. Watch for wildlife along the scenic lakeshore, or get out on the water by renting a rowboat, paddleboat, motorboat, or canoe. There's great rainbow trout fishing, and you can even take off in a floatplane right from the dock. All cabins and guest rooms come with full kitchen facilities and televisions. Kitchens are stocked with the ingredients for a self-serve breakfast, including homemade bread, reindeer sausage, pancake mix, toaster waffles, cereal, and even fresh duck eggs when the ducks are cooperating. Laundry facilities, hot tub, telephone, wireless Internet, and barbeque grills also are available for guest use. Cabins sleep four people, with a two-night-minimum stay. Rates vary depending on your choice of cabin or room; weekends are more expensive.

GROUCHY OLD WOMAN BED AND
BREAKFAST $
48570 North Earl Dr.
(907) 776-8775
www.grouchyoldwoman.homestead.com
Who can resist a name like this? The grouchy old woman herself runs this four-room bed-and-breakfast, located 20 miles north of Kenai on the peaceful shores of Daniels Lake. Three rooms have queen-size beds and one has two twins with a roll-away option. Expect a full breakfast during your stay, with sourdough pancakes, bacon, and fruit as one favorite. Take a walk along the lake and onto the dock to fully experience the peace and quiet here. Two rooms offer wheelchair access, and pets may be accepted on a case-by-case basis.

KENAI LANDING HOTEL $-$$
2101 Bowpicker Lane
(907) 335-2500
www.kenailanding.com
Ninety years of history make this restored cannery a fun and unique overnight option on the Kenai waterfront. In the historic Hen House, you can get a private, newly remodeled guest room with shared bath and shower facilities, queen-size bed,

telephone, sink, and television with DVD. Rooms at the richly decorated Machinist Bunkhouse offer the same amenities with the option of two queen-size or twin-size beds. Dating from 1922, the Fisherman's Cottages are perfect for families or groups, with three bedrooms, a living room, telephone, television, microwave, and refrigerator. Kenai Landing also offers scenic river-view rooms and suites with private baths. The waterfront resort area also offers a full-service restaurant, dock, and a warehouse market with shops featuring local arts and crafts.

ALASKA KINGS INN HOTEL $$
10352 Kenai Spur Highway
(907) 283-6060, (877) 883-6060
www.alaskakingsinn.com
Under new ownership with newly remodeled rooms, the Alaska Kings Inn offers affordable lodging even during the peak of the season. Located just 4 blocks from the airport, this family-friendly hotel has 52 rooms and a swimming pool coming soon. A business center, freezer space, on-site laundry, and wireless Internet round out the amenities. They also offer fully furnished kitchens and free continental breakfast. Their new restaurant is getting some buzz around town, too.

Restaurants

Though fish is the mainstay, you'll find a variety of menu items and dining options along the Peninsula. These eateries will be busiest in the summer, but you can assume they're open year-round, seven days a week, unless we say otherwise. You also can expect that they'll take major credit cards. Reservations are accepted but usually not necessary. We'll note wheelchair access if it's available.

The price codes below include the average cost of a meal for two, excluding cocktails, wine, appetizers, desserts, tax, and tips. Most places that serve dinner have a license for beer and wine, and many also serve cocktails.

Price Codes

$................ **Less than $15**
$$ .... **$15–$25**
$$$ .... **$26–$40**
$$$$ .... **More than $40**

Kenai River

GWIN'S LODGE $$$
Mile 52, 14865 Sterling Highway
Cooper Landing
(907) 595-1266
www.gwinslodge.com
Gwin's is a landmark stop along the Sterling Highway, offering warm Alaskan atmosphere and plenty of activity as great homemade food is dished out around the clock during the summer. Start your day with a hearty three-egg scramble, such as the Trapper Creek Alaskan with smoked salmon and Monterey Jack cheese, or a Gwin's Breakfast Burrito with scrambled eggs, sausage, cheddar cheese, and onion wrapped up in a flour tortilla and served with a side of salsa. For lunch, choose a burger from Gwin's famous lineup or a homemade sandwich, such as the grilled halibut. Dinner favorites include grilled salmon (of course) and the Seafood Casserole, featuring shrimp, scallops, and crab in a cream white wine sauce with crumb topping. In addition to the tasty food, Gwin's has ample parking. (Also see our listing for Gwin's in the Accommodations section of this chapter.)

Soldotna

BEAR'S DEN RESTAURANT AND
BAKERY $$$
45015 Kalifornsky Beach Rd.
(907) 262-6546
Folks line up for the prime rib and blackened Cajun salmon. There's also a lunch buffet, salad

ℹ️ **Locals rave about the Mexican food at the Grand Burrito (44096 Sterling Highway, 907-262-2228), but they've also got great burgers and pizza. And if you don't feel like going out, they deliver.**

bar, and a full breakfast menu including the famous maple crepes. Complement your meal with libations from Homer's Bear Creek Winery.

MYKEL'S RESTAURANT $$$$
35041 Kenai Spur Highway
(907) 262-6736
www.mykels.com

Located in the Soldotna Inn (see our listing in the Accommodations section of this chapter), Mykel's is a top dining choice for locals, featuring creative dishes with fresh ingredients, including local seafood. Try their Walnut Crusted Salmon with Raspberry Beurre Blanc, Prawns and Wild Mushroom Florentine, or Pepper Steak a la Jens, with twin tournedos of filet mignon topped with Jens's "Almost Famous" pepper sauce. The friendly waitstaff will be happy to help you pair one of their fine wines with your dinner selection. The atmosphere is casual, and there's plenty of parking.

SAL'S KLONDIKE DINER $$
44619 Sterling Highway
(907) 262-2220

Billed as "world-famous Sal's," this local diner is a favorite 24-hour hangout. Featuring typical diner fare, the menu includes Alaska and Yukon burgers, a variety of omelettes, biscuits and gravy, and a fisherman's lunch to go. Nothing fancy here, but you can expect good service and hearty (if not healthy) choices.

THE CROSSING $$$$
44789 Sterling Highway
(907) 262-1906
www.thecrossingrestaurant.net

For upscale dining that rivals any found in Alaska's larger cities, head to The Crossing, where you'll enjoy expert cuisine and fine libations in a picturesque setting overlooking the Kenai River. Local seafood, prime rib, pastas, steaks, and salads grace the menu, along with a nice selection of desserts. Local musicians perform live music some evenings. Closed Sunday.

i Up all night trying to snag the big one? Grab a great cup of Alaskan-roasted java at one of two Kaladi Brothers (www.kaladi.com) locations: 315 South Kobuk (907-262-5980) or 44350 Sterling Highway (907-262-3157). Both have wireless Internet, and the South Kobuk cafe features monthly art shows and occasional live music. Mugz (907-260-9113), located in the Blazy Mall, is another great choice.

THE MOOSE IS LOOSE BAKERY $
44278 Sterling Highway
(907) 260-3036

Great names aside, this bakery is one of Soldotna's biggest assets; in fact, some say it's the best bakery in the state. Huge doughnuts, tasty breads, and awesome pastries draw lots of repeat customers. Moose-themed merchandise, apple fritters from heaven—the list goes on. Never mind the fish—bring on the goodies. Good coffee, too. The only thing skimpy is the seating.

Kenai

CHARLOTTE'S BAKERY, CAFE, AND
ESPRESSO $$
115 South Willow St., Suite 102
(907) 283-2777

Charlotte's offers contemporary home-style cuisine for breakfast and lunch. For breakfast, try the Mediterranean Scramble, featuring Charlotte's potatoes surrounded by a deep dish omelet of spinach, tomatoes, feta, provolone, and a Kalamata olive garnish. Another breakfast favorite is Charlissa's Stuffed French Toast, made from Charlotte's honey-oat bread and topped with honey cream cheese. There's a great selection of salads for lunch, including the Gobbs of Cobb with bacon, blue cheese, hard-boiled egg, red onion, avocado, cubed smoked turkey, and tomato. You also can choose from a fun selection of sandwiches, such as the Hawaiian Wannabe Returns, with teriyaki chicken, ham, provolone, and grilled pineapple served with honey mustard on a warm croissant, or Terry & Jessica's Mushroom Swiss, featuring roast beef, Swiss cheese, and sautéed mushrooms on a grilled hoagie with roasted garlic aioli and au jus. Charlotte's is open Monday through Friday from 7 a.m. to 4 p.m.

FUNKY MONKEY COFFEEHOUSE $$
12498 Kenai Spur Highway
(907) 283-6659

A new bistro in the C Plaza, the Funky Monkey is Kenai's latest coffee shop hangout. Occasional live music and dinner theater make this a happening place in a small town. Homemade soups, salads, and sandwiches make up the menu.

LOUIE'S RESTAURANT $$$
47 Spur View Dr.
(907) 283-8660
www.uptownmotel.com/louie.html

Adjacent to the Uptown Motel, Louie's specializes in Alaskan seafood and steak. Try their Tempura Coconut Salmon, Louie's Seafood Fettucine, or Halibut Oscar. Those eyes watching as you feast? That's the largest trophy mount collection in the state. Among the mounts are some fun Alaskan antiques. Louie's is a popular weekend brunch spot.

PARADISOS $$$
811 Frontage Rd.
(907) 283-2222

There's a little of everything in the fine dining realm at Paradisos. We're talking Greek, Italian, Mexican, seafood, and steak. A little pricey, but a Kenai favorite for a night out or pizza. The Greek pizza is especially popular. Located in downtown Kenai, they also offer takeout and delivery.

i **Looking for a great burger on the run? Stop by the Burger Bus, around the corner from the Kenai Visitor Center. It's not for the health-conscious, but they've got sinfully tasty burgers and fries at prices that rival the fast-food chains.**

VERONICA'S COFFEE HOUSE $$
106 Toyon Way
(907) 283-2725

Across from the Russian Orthodox Church in Old Town Kenai, Veronica's is a popular lunch spot with locals. You can dine there for breakfast or dinner, too. Serving hearty soups, sandwiches, quiches, and desserts, Veronica's also has live music on weekend nights.

Nightlife

The "twin cities" of Kenai and Soldotna are small towns, but that doesn't mean they roll up the rug every night. If you're looking for somewhere to relax and listen to music, check out BJ's at 44695 Sterling Highway (907-262-1882), where Alaska's own Hobo Jim plays live folk music on select Friday and Saturday nights. Part Alaskan, part Nashville singer and songwriter, Hobo Jim delights listeners throughout the state.

Riverside House at 44611 Sterling Highway (907-262-0500) is the local gay bar. Down the road, at 44715 Sterling Highway (907-262-8346), Hooligan's features live music and pool. But be warned: Hooligan's lives up to its name—it can get rowdy.

For a quieter evening, stop by Veronica's (see listing in the restaurant section) or the Back Door, behind Louie's (also in the restaurant section). Sharpes Billiards offers a no-alcohol option for the younger crowd. If crooning's on your mind, join in the karaoke fun at the .409 (complete listing under Accommodations).

Shopping

You won't find any mega-malls in the small towns of the Kenai Peninsula, but Kenai and Soldotna have several grocery and retail options as well as specialty shops. If you're there on a Saturday, check out the Kenai Farmer's Market (907-262-5463), held from mid-June to mid-September at the junction of the Kenai Spur Highway and Corral Avenue, where you'll find Alaska-grown produce, plants, and flowers and Alaskan-made gifts, arts, and crafts. Hours are from 10 a.m. to 2 p.m. The seasonal Saturday Market at the Kenai Visitor and Cultural Center is open until 5 p.m.

Soldotna

BIRCH TREE GALLERY
P.O. Box 2589, Soldotna, AK 99669
(907) 262-4048
www.alaska.net/~birchtre

In a scenic wooded spot on the banks of the Kenai River, Birch Tree Gallery showcases the work of Kathleen Adell Logan, whose primary media is transparent watercolor, with flowers and Alaskan landscapes among her favorite subjects. The gallery also sells jewelry, handwoven baskets, note cards, stained glass, and burl furniture. Hand-dyed silk scarves and ties, along with felted hats, are also featured. The gallery offers a full line of knitting supplies, including free knitting lessons and assistance. There's free gift wrapping and packaging for mailing, too.

DONNA'S COUNTRY AND VICTORIAN GIFTS
BLAZY MALL
 44539 Sterling Highway
(907) 262-9254

Fisherman's wife's revenge? Donna's specializes in it, offering an extensive selection of beautiful items for your home, arranged room by room, from the cabin to the "red room" to the parlor and the closet. The Alaskana collection includes candles, cookie cutters, moose figurines, bear lamps, Eskimo dolls, and Glacier Ice Crystal Potpourri. In fact, a dozen different scents of Crystal Potpourri are made at Donna's. They also sell scented beads, candles, and lotions. They're open Monday through Saturday from 10 a.m. to 6 p.m.

ODIE'S BEAD IT
44619 Sterling Highway
(907) 260-7793

The only dedicated bead shop on the Peninsula, Odie's sells fishing beads, crystals, and stringing material along with an awesome variety of beads. They also carry sterling silver, lamps, and gifts.

RIVER CITY BOOKS
43977 Sterling Highway
(907) 260-7722

At the Y where the Sterling and the Kenai Spur meet, River City Books is in the renovated Cornerstone Marketplace on original homestead land. There's comfy seating and a cafe that serves soups, sandwiches, and coffee. Bookstore events include readings and storytimes for children.

ROBIN PLACE FABRICS
105 Robin Place
(907) 262-5438
www.robinplacefabrics.com

Quilting is a favorite Alaskan pastime, and the Peninsula's "Must Stop for Quilters," Robin Place, features exquisite quilts, specialty fabrics, original wall hangings, and original Alaskan quilt patterns and kits. This cozy home-style shop hosts the Quilting on the Kenai summer quilt show on the third weekend in June along with a variety of classes.

SWEENEY'S CLOTHING
35081 Kenai Spur Highway
(907) 262-5916

Didn't pack quite what you need? Stop by Sweeney's, where you'll find a wide selection of brand-name outdoor clothing, including fleece wear, chest waders, rain gear, and knee boots. Levi's, Columbia, Sorel, Woolrich, and Wolverine are among the names you'll recognize on their racks. They run a big warehouse clearance sale all summer long, and they'll even ship your purchase for you.

Kenai

FIREWEED HERB GARDEN AND GIFTS
202 North Forest Dr.
(907) 283-6107

Gifts, greenhouse, herb garden, espresso—you'll find it all at the Fireweed, located just north of the Kenai Visitor's Center. If you're looking for unique Alaskan gifts, check out their quilted wall hangings, spices, dips, soaps, candles, jewelry, pottery, ceramics, and wildflower seeds. They also sell music boxes, wind chimes, fabric baskets, and decorative table accessories. Fresh plants and produce are available in season, and the gift shop is open year-round.

KENAI FABRIC CENTER
115 North Willow
(907) 283-4595
Family owned and operated since 1970, the Kenai Fabric Center features more than 6,000 bolts of quilting cottons, including wildlife and nature prints, as well as a full selection of notions for quilting, sewing, knitting, and crochet. They have kits and pattern books along with sewing machines and sergers, and they also offer instructional classes. The store is open Monday through Saturday from 9 a.m. to 6 p.m. and Sunday from 1 to 4 p.m.

WAREHOUSE MARKET AT KENAI LANDING
2101 Bowpicker Lane
(907) 335-2500
www.kenailanding.com
Wander the market and peruse 25 distinctive shops, some of them seasonal. For fine art, visit Art Works, the Jim Evenson Gallery, and Peninsula Art Guild Outlet. Carved gift items can be found at Alaska Decoy Company and Alaska Horn and Antler, featuring horn, antler, ivory, bone, and stone art. Fur slippers, gloves, and vintage clothing are for sale at Silver Fox Slippers, while Turtle Island Imports offers woolens, batik clothing, jewelry, and scarves. Raven's Trinket and Collectibles, The Cove Gallerie, and White Dove Paper and Design offer all sorts of gift and collectible items.

Attractions

While fishing is the big draw, it's not all the Kenai area has to offer. From history to Native culture and wildlife, the area has great free and low-cost attractions to pique your interest.

Not all of these attractions are open in the winter, so be sure to note any seasonal restrictions in the listings. The price codes show what you'll generally pay for one adult admission.

Children and seniors are eligible for discounts at many of these places, and some offer military discounts as well. If admission is free, there's no price code.

Price Codes

$..................	Less than $5
$$	$5–$10
$$$	$11–$15
$$$$	More than $15

HISTORIC KENAI LANDING
2101 Bowpicker Lane, Kenai
(907) 335-2500
www.kenailanding.com
Ninety years of history grace this unique waterfront cannery mall at the mouth of the Kenai River. The commercial vision has so far proven bigger than the reality, as much of the facility still awaits tenants. Still, Kenai Landing offers a full-service restaurant, lodging, waterfront promenade, theater, and indoor warehouse market with more than 25 specialty shops on 65 acres of prime waterfront. The landing also features a boat launch, dock facilities, custom fish processing, and a museum.

K'BEQ INTERPRETIVE SITE $
Mile 52.6 Sterling Highway
Cooper Landing
(907) 398-8867
www.kenaitze.org/KBeq/index.html
Just 5 miles south of Cooper Landing, directly across from the entrance to the Russian River Campground, you can journey back in time to learn the ways of the region's original Dena'ina Athabascan inhabitants. Interpretative walks hosted by tribal elders and youth feature archaeological sites, ancient artifacts, and traditional plants, highlighting the Dena'ina's respect for the good land of the Kenai. K'Beq also has a gift shop featuring traditional Dena'ina arts and crafts. Nominal parking and tour-pass fees apply. K'Beq (meaning "footprints") is open seasonally from Monday through Saturday from 10 a.m. to 6 p.m.

KENAI NATIONAL WILDLIFE REFUGE VISITOR CENTER

Ski Hill Rd., Soldotna
(907) 262-7021
kenai.fws.gov

Plan your next outdoor adventure and learn about the wide range of habitats supported by the refuge at this full-service visitor center. Check out the wildlife displays, videos, and guided walks along the 0.75-mile Keen-Eye Nature Trail. They have complete information about camping, cabins, hiking, fishing, and wildlife viewing within the refuge. Summer hours are 8 a.m. to 4:30 p.m. on weekdays, and 9 a.m. to 6 p.m. on weekends.

i The Kenai Fine Arts Center (907-283-7040) sponsors arts events in Kenai and Soldotna on the first Thursday of every month. For details, visit www.kenai.net/finearts. The Fine Arts Center also sponsors special exhibits, programs, and shows in their newly remodeled facility at 816 Cook Avenue, in Historic Old Town Kenai.

KENAI VISITOR AND CULTURAL CENTER

11471 Kenai Spur Highway Kenai
(907) 283-1991
www.visitkenai.com

This extensive visitor center includes exhibits featuring the history of Kenai, free interpretive programs, and an "Alaska Native Arts Now" museum-quality display of traditional and contemporary Native art. There's a gift shop on-site, too. There are no fees for the visitor center, but there is a $3 charge to view the Alaska Native art exhibits.

i Just for fun, check out the Kenai Barber Shop in the old Carrs Mall. Besides a good haircut for a reasonable price, the decor is amazing—right out of the '50s. The only thing missing is a soda fountain!

SOLDOTNA HISTORICAL SOCIETY MUSEUM

461 Centennial Park Rd., Soldotna
(907) 262-3832

It may not seem old by some standards, but the founding settlers of Soldotna lived in rather primitive conditions when they arrived in 1947. The Historical Society Museum showcases a historic log village, including the last territorial school from 1958, where gas lanterns provided light in the cold, dark winters. Two of the "habitable dwellings" that entitled homesteaders to 80 acres of free land are on display as well. In Damon Hall, originally constructed for the Alaska Centennial, you'll find a large collection of wildlife mounts. The museum is open seasonally from 10 a.m. to 4 p.m. Tuesday through Saturday and from noon to 4 p.m. on Sunday. You can drive here or follow a short woodland walking trail from the Soldotna Visitor Center.

Parks, Recreation, and Tours

More than two million acres of the Kenai Peninsula, from Cook Inlet to Kachemak Bay, are part of the Kenai National Wildlife Refuge. More than half of the refuge is designated wilderness, but the remainder is accessible for recreational use. Within the refuge are all the major habitats found in Alaska, home to brown and black bears, lynx, wolverines, mountain goats, eagles, moose, caribou, and a wide variety of shorebirds and fish. The refuge begins at Mile 55 of the Sterling Highway. Be sure to stop by the refuge visitor center in Soldotna to check out the wildlife displays, nature trail, and videos for an excellent orientation to the refuge and its habitats. Hunting and boating are permitted within the refuge, though motorized watercrafts are not allowed on the canoe-system lakes.

Soldotna boasts more river city parks than anywhere else in Alaska, with more than 3,700 feet of elevated boardwalk and 220 campsites among them. You can access the river at Centennial Park, Swiftwater Park, Soldotna Creek Park, and Rotary Park, with camping at Centennial and Soldotna Creek Parks. There are also five day-use parks with picnic tables and playground equipment. Minimal day-use fees are charged at some of the river parks. Bring your binoculars, as there's a good chance of spotting bald eagles feeding on fish along the river. For details on Soldotna City Parks and Campgrounds, visit www .ci.soldotna.ak.us/parks_rec.html.

In Kenai, you can relax at the Leif Hansen Memorial Park within the city limits or check out the view at Cunningham Park as you head out of town toward Soldotna. You can take a self-guided walking tour of Old Town Kenai, following maps available at the Kenai Visitor Center. Among the sites you'll see are a Russian Orthodox Church built in 1894, a cabin belonging to a homesteader with the colorful nickname of Moosemeat John, and Fort Kenay, a replica of the original Russian Orthodox school built in 1900. For more history, head south on the Sterling Highway to the village of Ninilchik, where buildings from the 1800s include the first Russian school, the Ninilchik Village Cache, and the Village Store.

At the end of the Kenai Spur Highway, Captain Cook State Park offers spectacular views of the inlet and mountains. On clear days, you might even see Denali. Agate hunters and whale watchers especially enjoy the beach. Another great beach is at the base of the cliffs in Old Town Kenai, where you'll find nice sand, shells, and great mountain views. From the top of the bluffs, you might catch a glimpse of a beluga whale an hour or so before or after the high tide. Bring your binoculars and your tide table, as this is home to one of the fastest tides in the world.

The Bridge Access Road, about 6 miles west of Soldotna, is a great place to view Canada and snow geese feeding along the Kenai Flats. There's an outlook point with a telescope for checking out the geese and a variety of shorebirds. Another fun adventure is berry picking along Marathon Road, south of Kenai on the Spur Highway.

Want to see what goes on inside a fish-processing plant? Visit the BEACHM Fishery in Kasilof, 25 miles south of Soldotna. Your free tour will include a history of commercial fishing in the Kenai Peninsula. Call (907) 262-3233 or visit www .alaskasbestwildsalmon.com to schedule a tour.

ALASKA C & C STABLES
Soldotna
(907) 262-5401, (907) 398-4904
www.cowgalak.homestead.com

C & C Stables offers a nice variety of packages for exploring the Kenai wilderness on horseback. Take a beach ride, where you'll see signs of the 1964 earthquake, eagles, local mammals, and shorebirds while you watch commercial fishermen pulling in their catch. Another fun option is the high-country mountain ride, with a campfire meal to top off your scenic trek. You also can try a two-and-a-half-hour fly-fishing expedition at a mountain lake, with glaciers and waterfalls along the way; a fishing guide plus float tubes, equipment, and lunch come with this all-day adventure. Other options include wilderness rides from Soldotna, pack trips, and family excursions. Lessons are available, and the ranch is open year-round. Children must be age seven or older to ride.

i If it's movies you're after, there's the Kambe Theater in Kenai and the Orca out Kaliforsky Beach (K-Beach) Road. There's also local stage theater in both Kenai and Soldotna, with the Soldotna Triumvirate Theater doing a summer play for tourists in the Peninsula Mall.

ALASKA RIVERS COMPANY
Mile 50 Sterling Highway, Cooper Landing
(907) 595-1226, (888) 595-1226
www.alaskariverscompany.com

Whether you're looking for a scenic float, guided fishing, hiking, or cabin rentals, Alaska Rivers has it all. Try a three-hour float on the turquoise Kenai River, or a seven-hour rafting adventure through the Kenai Canyon rapids. They also will put together custom white-water packages on Class IV rapids. For anglers, there are half-day and full-day drifting packages, plus a fishing add-on for the Kenai Canyon trip. If you're a land-lubber, try a four-hour hike with your own naturalist guide. Water-based adventures include experienced guides, waterproof gear bags, life jackets, rain gear, and rubber boots. Be sure to ask about senior discounts, group rates, and half-price rates for children younger than age 12.

GREAT ALASKA ADVENTURE LODGE
33881 Sterling Highway, Sterling
(907) 262-4515, (800) 544-2261
www.greatalaska.com
From this three-star lodge on 25 acres at the confluence of the Kenai and Moose Rivers, you can set out on all sorts of wilderness adventures. Try fly-out bear viewing on a day trip, or stay overnight at the Lake Clark Bear Camp. Either way you'll get to see bears in their natural habitat as they feed, play, and fight. You also can use the lodge as a home base for fishing Kenai kings, reds, or silvers as well as trout or char. Overnight stays are not required, and you can opt for transportation direct from Anchorage if you like. For longer expeditions, the Kenai Wildlife Tent Lodge serves as a base camp to guided fishing, hiking, canoeing, and kayaking adventures. Safari Camp trips include camping in permanent adventure, wildlife, and kayak camps and explorations of the Kenai National Wildlife Refuge, Kenai Fjords National Park, and the Chugach National Forest.

KENAI LAKE SEA KAYAK ADVENTURES
Cooper Landing
(907) 595-3441, (907) 598-1102
www.kenailake.com
Paddle the headwaters of the world-famous Kenai River, keeping an eye out for mountain goats and Dall sheep on the slopes of the majestic Kenai Mountains. The three-hour kayaking excursion includes instruction, guided narration, snacks, and drinks. Kenai Lake Adventures offers single and double kayaks as well as kayaks sized for children, dry bags, life jackets, paddles, and rain gear. They also have mountain bike rentals, including repair kits and helmets, by the half or full day. Take a guided bike tour of the Crescent Lake area, or, for the ultimate adventure, land by seaplane on the lake and ride out on your mountain bike.

MARLOWS ON THE KENAI BIRDING TOURS
(907) 262-5218, (800) 725-3327
www.alaskabirdingtours.com
The Kenai Peninsula isn't only about fish. Birders will marvel at the large variety of species here, including puffins, auklets, murrelets, boreal chickadees, red-throated loons, spruce grouse, and three-toed woodpeckers. Alaska Birding Tours offers expeditions by powerboat, drift boat, hiking, and canoe. Choose from day-trip and inclusive package options in either fresh- or saltwater venues. Send them your "must see" list, and they'll help you get it done.

i There's even golfing on the Kenai Peninsula. Birch Ridge in Soldotna (907-262-5270, www.birchridgegolf.com) is a nine-hole course complete with Alaskan tundra and woods, with holes four and five overlooking Mount Redoubt and Mount Iliamna volcanoes. Golf/cottage packages are available. The Kenai Golf Course (907-283-7500, www.kenaigolfcourse.com) also offers good golfing at reasonable prices.

NORTH PENINSULA RECREATION AREA
Nikiski
(907) 776-8472, (907) 776-8800
www.northpenrec.com
A full slate of year-round recreational activities awaits at this expansive facility at Mile 23.4 of the Kenai Spur Highway. There's a weather-protected outdoor rink for recreational skating and hockey, a multipurpose field for softball, baseball, and soccer, a picnic area, and nature/fitness trails. Inside, they have a recreational pool with waterslide, spa, and rain umbrella. The pool is surrounded by glass, so you can take in the scenery while you swim or relax in the spa. The water slide alone is worth the trip. You also can reserve racquetball courts or work out in the exercise room.

Hiking and Camping

Through forests, over hills, along the beach, or among the mountains—you'll find great hiking and camping in the central Kenai Peninsula, with more than 200 miles of trails to enjoy. Within the Kenai National Wildlife Refuge, try the 5-mile (round-trip) Skilak Lookout Trail, where new growth following the 1996 Hidden Creek fire attracts moose, snowshoe rabbits, and hawks. At the trail's end, you can look back at Skilak Lake to see the cormorant and gull rookeries on the lake's islands. You also can pick up the Lookout Trail at Mile 5.4 of Skilak Lake Road. If you prefer a shorter hike, you'll find spectacular river and lake views along the 1.5-mile Hideout Trail, located at Mile 1.9 of Skilak Lake Road. Both hikes are moderate in difficulty.

The Kenai National Wildlife Refuge maintains several campgrounds along Skilak Lake Road. The largest and most developed of these is the Hidden Lake Camground at Mile 3.6. There's a nice picnic area along the lake, with campfire programs on weekends throughout the summer. Smaller campgrounds with boat launches include the Upper Skilak at Mile 8.4 and the Lower Skilak at Mile 13.6. The Engineer Lake Campground at Mile 9.4 offers scenic canoeing.

ℹ️ **An infestation of spruce beetles on the Kenai Peninsula has left dead standing trees that are ripe for forest fires. When building a campfire, try to use an existing campfire site or a fire pan, and keep water nearby in case flames spread. The Alaska Interagency Wildland Fire Management Plan does allow controlled burns for the natural cycling of ecosystems, but there are plenty of lightning-sparked blazes in Alaska, so the idea is to keep man-made fires to a minimum.**

Both the U.S. Fish and Wildlife Service and the Alaska State Park Service maintain rustic cabins that can be rented by the night. Some are remote, with no road access, and none have indoor plumbing. These cabins are quite popular, especially with locals, so it's a good idea to investigate your options well in advance of your trip. Contact the Kenai National Wildlife Refuge (907-262-7021, 877-285-5628, kenai.fws.gov/cabin.htm) or the State Park Service Kenai Area Office (907-262-5581, dnr.alaska.gov/parks/cabins/index.htm).

The Russian River Campground at Mile 52.6 of the Sterling Highway is a favorite when the red salmon are running, so be sure to get there early if you want a spot. There are 84 campsites, with water, toilets, tables, fire pits, and fish-cleaning stations within the campground. You'll also find phones and a dump station there. The campground is operated by Alaska Recreational Management (877-444-6777, www.recreation.gov), with fees ranging from $18 to $28 for RV occupancy. Bears may pose a real danger here, so keep all food and trash secure. Other public campgrounds include Quartz Creek (www.recreation.gov), with 45 sites on a paved loop a half-mile off Mile 47.5 of the Sterling Highway, and the state-run Ninilchik Beach Campground (dnr.alaska.gov/parks/units/nilchik.htm), with 35 beachside sites 40 miles south of Soldotna. Also near Ninilchik are Clam Gulch State Recreation Area (dnr.alaska.gov/parks/units/nilchik.htm) and Deep Creek State Recreation Area (dnr.alaska.gov/parks/units/deepck.htm). Fifteen miles south of Soldotna near Kasilof, the state (dnr.alaska.gov/parks/units/kasilof.htm) also maintains more than 150 campsites at three state recreation areas.

The city of Soldotna's Centennial Park Campground has 190 designated campsites, some with river frontage and several with wheelchair access. At the park booth, there are pay phones, ice, firewood, and newspapers. There's 95 feet of "fishwalk" for casting your line as well as two boat launches. It's a popular spot in the summer, but overflow parking is provided while you wait your turn for a site. The city's Swiftwater Park has 60 campsites in relative seclusion, with 1,200 feet of river boardwalk and an RV dump station. Day-use and overnight fees apply; call (907) 262-3151 or go to www.ci.soldotna.ak.us for more information.

BELUGA LOOKOUT LODGE AND RV PARK
929 Mission Ave., Kenai
(907) 283-5999
www.belugalookout.com

Enjoy a unique camping experience with spectacular views of Cook Inlet, the Kenai River, and Mount Redoubt. Beluga Lookout is located at the mouth of the Kenai River in historical Old Town Kenai. They offer view sites and pullthroughs, all with full hookups and cable television. They also have picnic tables, fire pits, Internet connections, and bike rentals. In addition to RV camping, Beluga Lookout rents rooms with kitchens by the day, the week, and the month.

i If you're tent camping and yearning for a shower, the local laundry facilities in both Kenai and Soldotna offer showers—and tanning beds, if you've run into a rainy spell. If you don't want to do your own laundry, they also have drop-off service.

DIAMOND M RANCH
Mile 16.5 Kalifornsky Beach Rd., Soldotna
(907) 283-9424
www.diamondmranch.com

With 80 acres to roam, the Diamond M features 50-amp full hookups with your choice of standard, super-size, or pull-through sites. If you're looking for activities, they have clam digs, tours, and Saturday-night socials. Walk to the Kenai River, hike or bike along the trails, or pick berries in season, all while enjoying stunning views of the Kenai River Flats and the Alaska Range. Leashed pets and well-behaved children are welcome. The Diamond M also rents modern cabins with kitchen and bath, or you can opt to stay at their bed-and-breakfast, with hot tub, solarium, Alaskana collection, full breakfast featuring wild berry breads, and kitchen for guest use. Rates for RV sites are $36 to $44 per night.

KENAI RIVERSIDE CAMPGROUND AND RV PARK
Mile 49.7 Sterling Highway, Cooper Landing
(907) 595-1406, (888) 536-2478
www.kenairiversidecampground.com

Camp along the Kenai River and fish right from the bank at Kenai Riverside Campground. They have 18 pull-through sites with 20/30 amp partial hookups as well as dry sites and tent camping. Since the campground is owned and operated by Alaska Wildland Adventures, you can stay on for guided rafting or fishing on the Kenai River if you like. Tent sites are $18 per night, dry sites are $27 per night, and partial hookups are $35 per night. Bed-and-breakfast rooms are available as well.

KLONDIKE RV PARK AND CABINS
Soldotna
(907) 262-6035
www.klondikecabins.com

The Klondike features 27 full hookup RV sites, each 25 feet wide to accommodate slide-outs and tow vehicles. Standard sites have lawns, and premium sites have naturally wooded areas. 20/30/50 amp service is provided. Three authentic log cabins are also available for rent, 100 yards from the Kenai River. These handcrafted cabins are fully furnished and sleep four comfortably. RV rates are $30 to $35 per night.

Fishing

If there were an Alaskan thesaurus, Kenai would show up as a synonym for fishing. Alaskans who want hot salmon action with a rod and reel flock to the Peninsula every summer. If you don't like "combat fishing," standing shoulder to shoulder with hundreds of other anglers, you can opt for more exclusive fishing opportunities with drift boats and fly-out services. Plan ahead: It's common for avid anglers to book a full year in advance.

The confluence of the Kenai and Russian Rivers offers the most productive red salmon fishing in the world; in fact, the crystal-clear Russian River is one of the few places where you can land a red with an artificial fly. The fish hole just downstream of the slow-moving waters is close to shore, making for excellent bank fishing. If you want a little more room to spread out, try the scenic waters upstream, near Russian River Falls. The Upper Russian River is closed to salmon fishing but offers great opportunities for rainbow trout in relative peace and quiet. In August and September, silver salmon show up in the same spots where you found reds earlier in the summer. You'll have the best luck with silvers using shiny lures and fly patterns.

The Russian and Kenai Rivers also offer trophy fishing for catch-and-release rainbow trout. On the Upper Kenai, only single-hook artificial lures are allowed. On the Russian, you're limited to flies only. If you really want a good shot at one of those trophy Dollies or rainbows, grab a drift-boat charter, putting in at either Mile 48 or Mile 54.8 of the Sterling Highway. You also have a good chance at salmon while drifting. Fly-out fishing for rainbows or grayling promises a lot more solitude.

During salmon season, sections of the banks along the Kenai River are periodically closed within 10 feet of either side of the water line so that fish habitat may be preserved. Portions of the river are limited to drift fishing only, while other sections have limits on the motor horsepower used. For up-to-date information on regulations and restrictions, check with the Sport Fish Information Center (907-267-2218) or visit www.state.ak.us/adfg, click on Sport Fisheries, then Regulations, then select the Kenai Peninsula on the map.

ALASKA CLEARWATER SPORTFISHING
Sterling
(907) 262-3797, (907) 398-6337,
(888) 662-3336
www.alaskaclearwater.com
Alaska Clearwater brings together experienced guides, quality equipment, and affordable pricing to offer dependable, professional guiding for red salmon, silvers, pinks, rainbows, and Dollies. Choose from guided drift-boat trips for rainbow trout on the Upper Kenai River, guided powerboat

fishing for kings on the Lower Kenai, and guided drift-boat fishing for kings on the Kasilof River.

ANGLERS LODGE $$$
36030 Stephans Dr., Sterling
(907) 262-1747, (888) 262-1747
www.anglerslodge.com
Since 1987 this family-owned lodge has been providing full-service fishing packages with comfortable home-away-from-home accommodations on the banks of the world-famous Kenai River. Owner Roger Byerly is a patient, friendly, experienced fishing guide, and his wife Marlene serves up a big helping of Alaskan hospitality with her fresh-baked goodies and home-cooked meals. Rooms come with coffeemakers, mini-fridges, and use of the hot tub. The lodge offers a great wilderness setting next to a state park, but it's still on the road system and close to town. The room rate reflects the cost of accommodations only. Most guests at the Anglers Lodge book accommodations as part of a fishing package.

ALASKA RIVER ADVENTURES
Mile 48 Sterling Highway, Cooper Landing
(907) 595-2000, (888) 836-9027
www.alaskariveradventures.com
Guiding in the Peninsula since 1978, Alaska River Adventures offers both full- and half-day fishing along the Upper Kenai River, where you can expect plentiful salmon, rainbow trout, and Dolly

i It's hard to beat the fun and productive dip netting and gill netting for salmon out of the Kenai and Kasilof Rivers, but be warned that it's limited to residents only. Nonresidents cannot operate or even handle the gear when they're with resident dip or gill netters. Residents must have their permits and licenses with them at all times, and they must immediately record their catch and clip the tips of the tail fins. Note that the city charges for peak access parking during the peak of the season, so if dip netting's not your intent, it's best to avoid the whole area.

Varden. Fly and spinning gear are provided. If you prefer, opt for a full day of fishing in relative peace and quiet on the Kasilof River, where you'll drift 5 miles above the ocean to catch salmon on the incoming tide. For fly fishing, you can try a full day of catch and release on a clear mountain stream, with salmon, rainbows, and Dollies the likely targets.

ALASKA TROUTFITTERS
Cooper Landing
(907) 595-1212
aktroutfitters.com
Close to all the action at Mile 48.2 of the Sterling Highway, Alaska Troutfitters has a fly-fishing school, guided trout and salmon fishing, tackle store with rentals, and rooms with a view. They cater to all ability levels, from beginners to advanced, offering drift fishing on the Upper Kenai, fly fishing on the lower river, and three- or five-day fly-fishing schools on either the Kenai River or Quartz Creek. For the nonanglers in your group, they have access to flight seeing, glacier tours, hiking, horseback riding, and rafting.

ALASKA WILDLAND ADVENTURES
Mile 50.1 Sterling Highway, Cooper Landing
(907) 595-1279, (800) 478-4100
www.alaskarivertrips.com
One of the first companies to snag lucrative permits for floating the Kenai River, Alaska Wildland Adventures has been providing professional guides and top-notch gear to area anglers since 1977. Their full-day packages include approximately eight hours of fishing, top-quality tackle, waders, gear, and a generous lunch. Opt for either the Willie Predator Powerboats or Mackenzie-type drift boats, both of which seat four anglers. Fish the Lower Kenai River for king or silver salmon, or the Kasilof River for kings. On the Upper Kenai River, you can partake of great fly fishing for Dollies, rainbows, and salmon, peaking in August and September. You can fish comfortably from the boat or wade from the bank for salmon. Alaska Wildland also has a Resurrection Bay silver salmon package. Guides are U.S. Coast Guard licensed with CPR and first-aid training.

ANGLE 45 ADVENTURES
Mile 8.1 Hope Highway, Hope
(907) 782-3175
www.angle45.com
A bit off the beaten path to Kenai, you'll find Angle 45 Adventures in the small but scenic waterfront town of Hope. Forty-five-degree angles offer the least resistance and the most pleasure in working the currents of the river, and that's the goal of this family-owned guiding service. Permitted through the Chugach National Forest and the state of Alaska, they can take you drift-boat fishing on the Upper Kenai, the Kasilof, or the Middle Kenai Rivers. Top-quality rods and tackle plus a selection of waders are provided. If you'd just as soon sightsee as fish, try the two-hour float on the Upper Kenai River or on Granite Creek. Angle 45 also will create custom packages and multiday adventures, including fly-out fishing, wildlife and glacial tours, private hiking, and white-water rafting. They have two four-season cabins available for rent as well.

> ℹ️ Snagging is illegal in all of Alaska's freshwater fisheries. In some areas, you may not remove a snagged fish from the water, even to snap a photo. If you accidentally snag a fish, land it quickly, use needle-nosed pliers to remove the hook, or cut the line if the hook cannot be readily removed. Point the fish upstream, cradling it until it resumes swimming on its own.

KENAI FISHING ACADEMY
Kenai Peninsula College
34820 College Dr., Soldotna
(907) 262-0300, (877) 262-0330
www.kenaifishingacademy.org
Where was this class when we were in college? After 20 hours in the classroom learning fishing techniques from the experts, you'll head out to the fabulous fishing holes of the Kenai Peninsula with some of the region's top guides to practice what you've learned. Despite the bountiful supply of fish in the area, there are anglers who get

Close-up

Kenai Combat Fishing

It might not be exactly what you had in mind when you dreamed of salmon fishing in the Alaskan wilderness, but the popular and productive Russian and Kenai Rivers offer a unique angling experience nonetheless. At the peak of the season, the confluence of these scenic rivers resembles a jam-packed urban intersection with rods and waders in place of honking cars. When the salmon are running thick, upwards of 1,000 anglers may be fishing at the same time.

What makes this fishery so hot? For one thing, more freshwater king salmon are caught in the Kenai River than anywhere else in Alaska, with the average season yielding 17,500 kings. The Kenai River produces not only quantity but also quality, having given up the world-record rod-and-reel king, a whopping 97-pounder, back in 1985. You can see the big lunker on display at the Soldotna Visitor Center. The average annual return of red salmon on the Kenai River is an incredible one million fish, with the season peaking the last two weeks in July. The silver run, peaking in mid-August, produces a harvest of some 41,000 salmon. Factor in two big runs of Russian River reds, one at the end of June and one in mid-July, and you have a recipe for quite a bit of excitement.

So don't let a little competition scare you off. Pack some patience along with your fishing gear and look on your fishing adventure as a chance to rub shoulders, literally, with fellow enthusiasts from all over the world. Join the crowds that line the banks for about a half-mile beginning just south of Cooper Landing and wait for a spot to open up. Don't elbow your way in, and remember not to walk in right behind someone who's casting. Eyes have been lost that way; you'll see anglers wearing protective eye gear for that very reason.

Once you've snagged your spot, try to cast in unison with others around you. When you have that fish on the line, yell "Fish On" and land it quickly. Playing the fish only adds to the chaos, increasing the chances you'll tangle with another line, and your fellow anglers won't be happy about having to stop fishing while you have all the fun. A stout, medium-weight rod and 20-pound test line will help you haul your fish in with minimal disruption. Remember to bring a spare—rods break all too often when those feisty 10-pound reds get to fighting, with the strong currents of the Russian or Kenai River adding to their power.

If you snag a salmon, break the line rather than trying to pull it upstream tail first. Once you've caught your limit, step aside and let the next angler in. Hopefully someone will repay the favor when you're waiting for your turn. It's a simple application of the Golden Rule that makes combat fishing fun and productive despite the crowds.

skunked year after year, and the mission of the academy is to make sure they have a fighting chance. Choose from Baitcasting and Fly Fishing packages, both of which include 20 hours of classroom/hands-on instruction, five nights of lodging, meals, tackle, and transportation to fishing destinations. You won't earn college credit, but you'll come away with a new understanding of Alaska's most-sought-after sport fish and how to catch and process them. Sign up early, because—like everything else connected with fishing on the Kenai—this is a popular program.

SILENT RUN DRIFT BOAT GUIDE SERVICE
1803 Roosevelt Dr., Anchorage
(907) 562-5455
www.silentrunak.com

To keep your fishing experience personal and allow for instruction of novice anglers, Silent Run takes out no more than two people on any given trip. Choose from full- or half-day drift or walk-in fishing. In addition to the usual drift and walk-in fishing for trout and salmon, they have a guide permit for some of the small but productive streams in the Chugach National Forest. All trout are catch and release only. Your knowledgeable guide is first-aid and CPR certified, licensed, and insured. Snacks, soda, bottled water, coffee, tackle, and life jackets are included.

If you get to see one of the Peninsula's big moose, keep your distance: There are more fatal moose encounters than fatal bear attacks in Alaska. To warn other drivers of moose on the road, Alaskan drivers flash their headlights. You need to be equally wary if you're on foot, as a moose's kick has 1,000 pounds of force behind it. Stay at least 75 feet away from moose in the wild, and don't get between a cow and her calves. Note also that it's illegal to harass or feed moose.

HOMER

Ask Alaskans where in the state they'd most like to live, and a good number of them will name Homer, an end-of-the-road seaside town with gorgeous scenery, easy access to outdoor fun, a healthy emphasis on the arts, and a warm sense of community. Visitors name Homer as one of the top Alaskan destinations for friendliness, hospitality, and beauty. Locals just call it their cosmic hamlet by the sea.

Approaching Homer by road, you'll be struck by breathtaking views of Kachemak Bay and the Kenai Mountains as you mount Baycrest Hill. Ahead lie great fishing, bear viewing, kayaking, birding, shopping, galleries, and dining with a fun and funky flair. The town stretches out into the ocean via the 4.5-mile Homer Spit, a strip of sand and gravel lined with shops, restaurants, campgrounds, and charter outfits. From nearly everywhere in town, you'll enjoy magnificent views of glacial mountains, distant volcanoes, and the sparkling waters of Kachemak Bay. Beachcombing and clamming are favorite seaside activities. The surrounding wilderness is home to wolves, bears, moose, and hundreds of thousands of shorebirds.

There's evidence that the Spit and the rest of the Lower Peninsula have been inhabited off and on for thousands of years, first by Pacific Eskimos and later, in the 18th century, by Russian explorers. As the Americans entered the picture, coal was discovered in the region, and Homer became a hub for transporting the fuel. The first village, located at the tip of the Spit, was abandoned in 1902 for a more sheltered location a bit farther inland. Settlers spread into the hills around Homer as the road system drew fishing and transportation activity from landlocked Seldovia and Halibut Cove.

Today, with a population of more than 4,000, Homer is the hub of the lower Kenai Peninsula, with a hospital, two newspapers, commercial and public radio stations, a branch of the University of Alaska campus, numerous sport- and commercial-fishing fleets, and an award-winning educational system. The climate is temperate, with an average summer temperature of 57 degrees Fahrenheit and an average winter temperature of 23 degrees Fahrenheit.

Getting There, Getting Around

Homer is a scenic four-and-a-half-hour drive from Anchorage, though on weekends traffic is heavy and you should plan more time for traveling the mostly two-lane road. ERA Aviation (800-866-8394, www.flyera.com) and Grant Aviation (888-359-4726, www.flygrant.com) offer scheduled small-plane service from Anchorage, while the Homer Stage Line (907-235-2252, www.thestageline.net) provides scheduled bus service. Once you're in Homer, you can rent a car or take a taxi to get around town. There are also a number of bike trails for cycling enthusiasts. The Alaska Marine Highway system (907-235-8449, 800-642-006, www.ferryalaska.com) offers regular service to Seldovia and beyond, including vehicle transportation if you like.

Accommodations

Aside from high-end luxury hotels, you'll discover just about every kind of accommodation imaginable in Homer, from all-inclusive wilderness lodges to primitive yurts for camping. As in most of the region, reservations are definitely a good idea in the summer season, which begins in mid-May and ends in early September.

You can assume major credit cards are accepted and that rooms are available year-round unless we tell you differently. For the most part, facilities are nonsmoking only, with no pets allowed, but we'll note any deviations to those policies. Wheelchair access is noted wherever it applies. Many accommodations include fish-cleaning, packaging, and freezing facilities for guest use. Price codes indicate the average cost for a double room, excluding taxes and gratuity.

Price Codes

$	Less than $125
$$	$125–$175
$$$	$176–$225
$$$$	More than $225

A MEMORABLE EXPERIENCE BED AND BREAKFAST $$
Rosewood Court
(907) 235-7374, (800) 720-9275, ext. 7374
www.amemorableexperience.com
Enjoy a parklike setting overlooking Homer, with spectacular views of Kachemak Bay and the glacial mountains beyond. You'll find incredible birding and hiking right outside the front door and all the comforts of home inside. The burgundy and green Alaskan-themed rooms have private baths and king-size beds, private decks, and a private entrance. In the common area, there's satellite television, a kitchenette, and freezer space for storing fish. Larger parties can opt for a separate cottage that sleeps five and has a full kitchen. Room rates include a continental breakfast featuring fresh coffee, fruit, homemade granola, and pastries. Pets are accepted on approval, and rooms are wheelchair accessible. Group, weekly, and off-season rates are available, too. Rates for one-night stays are higher.

ALASKA ADVENTURE CABINS $$$$
2525 Sterling Highway
(907) 223-6681
www.alaskaadventurecabins.com
Some of the most unusual accommodations you'll find in Alaska, or just about anywhere for that matter, are offered by Alaska Adventure Cabins. Check out the Moose Caboose, a genuine Alaska Railroad car lovingly converted into a two-story cabin with terrific views and a spacious deck, or the Double Eagle, a gleaming 75-foot ship with three decks, full galley, two bedrooms, and two and a half baths. Cabin options include the Dovetail Log and the Canyon Creek. All properties offer splendid views of the water and mountains from a convenient location just off the Sterling Highway. Alaska Adventure hosts corporate events as well as individual travelers.

ALASKA CENTER FOR CREATIVE RENEWAL $$$$
Halibut Cove
(907) 296-2283
www.centerforcreativerenewal.com
If you're really looking to get away from it all, check out this top-notch wilderness lodge nestled in the heart of Halibut Cove, a short ferry ride across Kachemak Bay from Homer. Run by Jan Thurston, one of 15 professional artists exhibiting work at the local gallery, the lodge hosts workshops and retreats, but most of their guests are independent travelers looking for a place to get away from it all. Rates include three meals per day, with an emphasis on fresh fish and oysters from local fisheries along with produce from their scenic gardens. The lodge provides kayaking and hiking opportunities, and massage is also available. The center places a special focus on environmental practices and has garnered awards for its unique architecture.

ALASKA'S SADIE COVE WILDERNESS LODGE $$$$
Kachemak Bay State Park
(907) 235-2350
www.sadiecove.com

Wild Alaskan beauty by the sea gets rave reviews at Sadie Cove, 10 miles by boat from Homer, nestled on a remote fjord within Kachemak Bay State Park. Keith Iverson was able to acquire this property in the 1970s, before the park was formed, and he is dedicated to providing a non-intrusive, ecofriendly, genuine wilderness experience that is one of the top ecodestinations in the country. The all-inclusive rate includes lodging in one of five handcrafted guest cabins, all meals, and the use of kayaks, fishing gear, lodge, sauna and plunge pool, and private hiking trails. The Iversons provide a noncommercial atmosphere of casual elegance, maintaining a rustic wilderness feel while offering such amenities as wireless Internet and cellular telephone access. Their attentive all-Alaskan staff serves up gourmet seafood meals and, if you like, they'll guide you on local trails to see wildlife, ancient petroglyphs, and neighboring Native villages. It's their hope that you will be able to escape the stresses of modern life and come away with a new appreciation for the wonders of the wilderness and the fun of meeting new friends.

ALASKAN SUITES $$$$
3255 Sterling Highway
(907) 235-1972, (888) 239-1972
www.alaskansuites.com
A private cabin that sleeps five. Killer views of Kachemak Bay. Thirsty towels. Private baths with cultured marble. Kitchenette with microwave, fridge, and sink. DVD/TV with surround sound. A recliner. Oh, and an outdoor spa for day's end relaxation. Is that too much to ask? Not at Alaskan Suites, where nearly new oceanview cabins delight travelers, many of whom say this is the best place they stayed in Alaska. And did we mention fresh chocolate chip cookies?

BAY VIEW INN $
2851 Sterling Highway
(907) 235-8485, (877) 235-8485
www.bayviewalaska.com
Guests rave about the spectacular views from every room, looking out over the big blue of Kachemak Bay. All rooms come with firm beds, telephone, television with HBO, outside entrances, and an Adirondack chair for soaking up the magnificent view. Options include kitchenettes, a suite with fireplace, and a honeymoon cottage. The decor is nothing fancy, but the rooms are clean and comfortable. Rounding out the hospitality are a free continental breakfast, an espresso bar, use of picnic tables, and recommendations on local tours and activities. Rates for rooms with view windows are slightly higher.

BEACH HOUSE BED & BREAKFAST $$–$$$
Seabreeze Court
(907) 235-3232, (800) 936-7571
www.alaskabeachhouse.com
Offering quiet deluxe accommodations with fabulous views of beautiful Kachemak Bay, the Beach House has four rooms with king-size and twin beds. Guests also enjoy a 32-foot waterfront deck and hot tub perched on the bluff. Rooms come with coffeemakers, microwaves, minifridges, free continental breakfast with homemade breads and muffins, and airport transportation. In the Galley House, you can enjoy complimentary homemade cookies, tea, and coffee while relaxing in viewing chairs that overlook the bay. Local smoked salmon, cold drinks, and snacks are available for purchase. Open since 1999, the Beach House is convenient to both the town and the Spit.

BEAR CREEK WINERY AND LODGING $$$
Bear Creek Dr.
(907) 235-8484
www.bearcreekwinery.com
Head 3 miles out East End Road for some of the most unique accommodations in Alaska, right in the heart of a family-owned winery. Two suites constructed in 2003 offer glacier and bay views, with relaxation opportunities in the hot tub or steam bath. There's a hearty continental breakfast, and wine sampling is encouraged. Refrigerator, gas grill, microwave, private entrances, private custom baths, complimentary K'bay Cafe coffee, and log frame beds round out the amenities.

BEST WESTERN BIDARKA INN $$
575 Sterling Highway
(907) 235-8148, (866) 685-5000
www.bidarkainn.com

With a convenient location just off the Sterling Highway, the Best Western Bidarka has a wide range of amenities, including free parking, high-speed Internet, tour desk, reservations services, coin-operated laundry, barber/beauty shop, courtesy van, and game room. Grab a meal at the Glacier View Restaurant (open seasonally) or a drink in the Otter Room Sports Bar with open fireplace. To take care of your catch, there's a fish-packing and -cleaning station plus freezing station. The Bidarka has 74 clean, comfortable rooms, each with television, alarm clock radio, coffeemaker, hair dryer, iron and iron board, and telephone with dataport. Children age 17 and younger stay free with an adult. Smoking rooms and rooms with wheelchair access are available; rates for hot tub rooms are higher.

DRIFTWOOD INN $–$$$
135 West Bunnell Ave.
(907) 235-8019, (800) 478-8019
www.thedriftwoodinn.com

If you're looking for a variety of reasonably priced options, the Driftwood Inn is a great place to start. Fifth- and sixth-generation Homer residents operate the Driftwood Inn, the Seaside Lodge, the Bluffview Inn, and the Kachemak Cottage. Room rates include wireless Internet access, guest laundry, fish-cleaning area, and freezer. Common areas include a great room with stone fireplace, kitchen with microwave, and picnic area with barbeque and shellfish cooker. The Driftwood Inn offers 21 economy European-style rooms, some with shared baths. At the Seaside Lodge, you'll find deluxe rooms overlooking the beach and the bay, with king-size beds, private baths, soaking tubs, in-room televisions, and free local phone calls. The Bluffview Lodge features spacious, modern accommodations overlooking Kachemak Bay. Groups of up to eight will enjoy the seaside setting of the Kachemak Cottage. Pets are allowed in select rooms.

GOOD KARMA INN $$
57480 Taku Ave.
(866) 435-2762
www.goodkarmainn.com

Host Michael LeMay offers premium lodging in a Scandanavian scribed-log home with stunning views (including four glaciers) from East End Road. Original woodcarvings, huge windows, a light and airy kitchen serving a hearty continental breakfast—it's all part of the Good Karma experience. Satellite television, freezer space, and a gas grill are among the amenities. Choose from the Wisdom or Mindfulness suites, where beds can be either two twins or king.

HALCYON HEIGHTS BED AND
BREAKFAST INN $$–$$$
1200 Mission Rd.
(907) 235-2148
www.homerbb.com

In business since 1989, Halcyon Heights gets consistently fine reviews from its guests. Maybe it has something to do with the outdoor hot tub for glacier gazing, or the private entrances and private baths. Maybe it's the private trail or the close-in East End Road location. Or maybe it's the helpful advice you'll get from your friendly hosts. At any rate, you're bound to enjoy the fully hosted breakfasts and Homer's trademark views. Wireless Internet, cable television, and DVD players with Alaskan videos round out the package.

HOMER HOSTEL $
304 West Pioneer Ave.
(907) 235-1463
www.homerhostel.com

Even if you're traveling on the cheap, you don't have to pass on the fabulous views. From this big house in the heart of Homer, you can take in the beauty of Kachemak Bay. You can also stroll the downtown blocks. Two private rooms, two single-sex dorms, and one co-ed dorm share four baths, a fully-equipped kitchen, and lounge. Nothing fancy, of course, but good inexpensive digs.

HOMER INN & SPA $$$
895 Ocean Dr.
(907) 235-1000, (800) 294-7823
www.homerinn.com

Enjoy the beauty of Kachemak Bay from a mini-suite with ocean-view windows, king-size bed, private bath, keyed entrance, and optional gourmet breakfast. Guests appreciate the Homer Inn's spectacular beachfront view with glacial mountain backdrop and convenient location between the downtown arts district and the harbor. There's plenty of beach strolling to be done, and an ample menu of on-site spa packages if you're more inclined to just relax. The inn features custom hand-lain wood and stone mosaic floors; sculptured walls with paintings by local artists; in-room dining area with wineglasses, bottle opener, and scented candles; kitchenettes with minifridge, microwave, and coffeemaker; television/VCR; and CD player with music by local Alaskan artists. Guests share the inn's Jacuzzi hot tub, barbeque deck and outdoor seating, log swing, and herb gardens with colorful flowers and fountain. If you're looking for adventure, take a run in the two-man kayak, borrow a kite and see where it flies, or pack a beach picnic with the supplies provided by your hosts. The inn can accommodate parties of up to 14 people. Add-on spa packages are available.

LAND'S END RESORT $$–$$$
4786 Homer Spit Rd.
(907) 235-0400, (800) 478-0400
www.lands-end-resort.com

Providing food and lodging since 1958, Land's End Resort is a Homer icon. In the old days, when you could only get to the small boat harbor during high tide, fisherman gathered at Land's End to swap stories. Perched on the end of the Spit, the resort has retained its nautical flavor and friendly Alaskan ways while adding creature comforts. Featuring custom-built furniture and museum-quality exhibits, there are 94 rooms, some with stunning views of the mountains and the ocean. Guests enjoy the oceanfront hot tub, indoor pool, exercise room, and complete menu of spa services along with access to miles of

beachfront for strolling and beachcombing. Loft rooms and suites can accommodate families. Be sure to check out their getaway specials, including the Flyaway and Raven's Nest Spa packages. Three rooms have wheelchair access, and there's fine dining in the Chart Room Restaurant.

MARIA'S MAJESTIC VIEW BED AND BREAKFAST $$
61415 Race Court
(888) 246-6413
www.alaskaone.com/majestic

Friendly, affordable lodging just 2.5 miles from town, all with the fantastic views you've come to expect in Homer. Enjoy the scenery from big bay windows or the expansive deck. Or hike the nature trails where moose are seen almost daily. Rooms are large and airy, each with private bath. A large fireplace graces the living room, where you're invited to share the television and phone. Pets are welcome in the large heated garage. Children are welcome, too—they get to stay inside, but good luck pulling them away from the outdoor fort, swing, and rope bridge. Everyone enjoys use of the outdoor hot tub, and to top it all off is a full hot breakfast by Maria each morning.

THE OCEAN SHORES BEACHFRONT LODGING $$
3500 Crittenden Dr.
(800) 770-7775
www.oceanshoresalaska.com

Guests rave about the gorgeous views, clean rooms, comfy beds, and top-notch hosts. Terraced rooms overlook four acres. Listen to the gentle roll of the surf or stroll the private beach. Kitchenettes, cable television, and wireless Internet are included, making this one of Homer's best values in accommodations. You'll find Ocean Shores to the right just before you enter the Spit, behind Fat Olives Restaurant.

SEASIDE FARM $
40904 Seaside Farm Rd.
(907) 235-7850
www.xyz.net/~seaside

If a taste of Homer's friendly, hippy-dippy reputation is what you're after, look no further than Seaside Farm. Run by Mossy of the town's well-known Kilchner family (pop star Jewel is a Kilchner from Homer), this organic working farm offers rustic (no running water) cabins, bunkhouse, and tent camping. Stroll among the cows or along the beach. You may even opt to trade chores for lodging. Truly a Homer original.

TUTKA BAY WILDERNESS LODGE $$$$
Halibut Cove
(907) 274-2710
www.tutkabaylodge.com

Here's a great wilderness option across the bay from Homer, about 9 miles by boat. The lodge is actually a cluster of buildings, boardwalks, decks, and dock on a private cove next to Kachemak Bay State Park. You'll enjoy uncluttered views of the forest, mountains, and ocean from the shores of a pristine fjord that plays home to sea otters, sea lions, porpoise, seals, whales, and seabirds. There are an assortment of cabins and suites to choose from, and meals are included with your stay. All rooms have coffeemakers, minifridges, and hair dryers. Enjoy wildlife viewing, dock fishing, rowboating, clamming, birding, hiking, and guided nature walking. When you're all tuckered out, relax in the wood-fired sauna or soak in the jetted hot tub in the open-air gazebo. Special-interest activities can be arranged, including guided sea kayaking, fly-out brown bear viewing, and salmon or halibut fishing. Known for quality service, Tutka Bay consistently gets rave reviews from guests. Even the meals are special, as the lodge hosts celebrity chefs and food writers and reprints recipes in national magazines. Under new ownership of the acclaimed Within the Wild Adventure Company (see our Close-up in the Anchorage accommodations section).

Restaurants

For a town its size, Homer has a great reputation for dining of all types. Restaurants on the Spit are open mostly during the summer tourist and fishing season, but you'll find the others open year-round. Major credit cards are accepted unless we note otherwise. We'll let you know if there's no wheelchair access or if they're closed one or more days each week. Price codes indicate the average cost of a dinner for two, excluding drinks, appetizers, tax, and gratuity.

Price Codes

$.................. Less than $15
$$ .... $16–$25
$$$ .... $26–$40
$$$$ .... More than $40

BOARDWALK FISH AND CHIPS $$
4287 Homer Spit Rd.
(907) 235-7749

Since 1982 the folks at the Boardwalk have been serving up their famous fresh halibut fish and chips, homemade chowder, and draft beer. There's an outdoor deck for taking in all the action along the Spit, with views of the mountains and the ocean. Looking for a meal on the run? Try the halibut on a stick. If seafood isn't your thing, try the teriyaki or Cajun chicken salads, a charbroiled burger, or the Alaskan reindeer bratwurst. The New England clam chowder is popular, too, along with the bread bowls and ice-cream shakes. Parking can be tight on the Spit, so make the Boardwalk a stop on your foot-bound sightseeing tour of the oceanfront. Open seasonally for lunch and dinner.

CAFE CUPS $$$
162 Pioneer Ave.
(907) 235-8330

A favorite with locals, Cafe Cups serves up eclectic meals that are as artful as its decor, which features mosaics of cups and glasses, iron sculptures, and works by local artists adorning the walls and tables. The ever-changing menu features fine local seafood, steaks, salads made with locally grown greens, burgers, and daily specials. Try the charbroiled fresh salmon and halibut topped with a fruit pico de gallo or charbroiled filet mignon with Gorgonzola whiskey cream. Dave's Fettuccini with clams, shrimp, and scallops in a raspberry-chipotle alfredo sauce is another favorite. Their fresh halibut tacos are fabulous, too. Homer Brewing Company's draft beer and a selection of fine wines complement the tasty food. Conveniently located across from the public library, Cafe Cups has ample parking and is open for lunch and dinner every day except Sunday.

CHART ROOM RESTAURANT $$$$
Land's End Resort
4786 Homer Spit Rd.
(907) 235-0400
www.endofthespit.com

Fine dining with a spectacular view is the trademark of the Chart Room, perched at the very end of Homer Spit. Floor-to-ceiling windows offer breathtaking views of wildlife, glaciers, and waterfront activities from tables decked with huge ship's wheels and wood carvings. In typical Alaskan style, everyone's comfortable, from those dressed to the nines to those in flannel shirts. There's a well-rounded menu featuring halibut, salmon, clams, oysters, rockfish, scallops, prime rib, and steaks. Try the Halibut Iliamna, a fresh filet baked with a topping of crab, artichokes, cream, and Parmesan. The Chart Room has a full bar and ample parking, and they're open 365 days a year for breakfast, lunch, and dinner. When you've had all you can eat, check out the spa facilities upstairs.

COSMIC KITCHEN $
510 East Pioneer Ave.
(907) 235-6355
www.cosmickitchenalaska.com

Every day the folks at the Cosmic Kitchen cook up fresh salsas, grill marinated chicken and steak, and offer up a homemade soup plus daily specials. Their rice, beans, sauces, and most soups are vegetarian. For breakfast, try the Cosmic Frittata, an open-faced cheddar/jack omelet with your choice of two toppings: fajita veggies, avocado, bacon, ham, sausage, chorizo, soy sausage, hash browns, and sour cream. Later in the day, you can order off their Mexican menu, including the Fajita Fish Burrito or the Big Bang Burrito with steak, chicken, and rice. There's also a nice selection of

burgers, including buffalo and salmon, and sandwiches, such as the Chicken Tikka with Chutney and the Gryo. Salad choices include the Cosmic Caesar with blackened halibut and the Tostada Salad with Beef and Beans. The Cosmic Kitchen serves beer and wine, and takeout and catering are available. Reservations are not required, and there's ample parking.

DON JOSE'S $$
127 West Pioneer Ave.
(907) 279-5111

The Ramos family opened their first restaurant in Homer in 1982, and they've now expanded to three locations around the state. Start out with complimentary chips, then check out one of Carmen's specials for lunch, such as the halibut or shrimp tacos, or the Vegetarian Chimi Dinner, an oven-roasted flour tortilla filled with sautéed zucchini, cauliflower, bell peppers, green onions, and carrots. If you're really hungry, try the Macho Combos, such as Don Jose's chili relleno stuffed with beef and cheese, tamale, and chicken flauta served with rice and beans. Gourmet specialties included the Camarones Rellenos with prawns and Dungeness crab and the Scallops Mazatlan, sautéed with tomatoes, fresh onions, and peppers. In addition to their extensive Mexican menu, Don Jose's serves pizza, calzones, and American fare.

FAT OLIVES $$
276 Ohlson Lane
(907) 235-8488

A local favorite for pizzas and other Italian fare, Fat Olives offers casual dining and takeout. Check out their House Calzone, with pesto, mushrooms, spinach, artichoke hearts, ricotta, smoked Gouda, and mozzarella, or one of 19 classic Neapolitan pizza options. Want more choices? How about 15 specialty meat pizzas, including pesto-smoked king salmon or thai chicken? For veggie lovers, they have 11 pizza options, including Olive's Special, with olive oil garlic base, roma tomatoes, pineapple, cream cheese, olive tapenade, fresh jalapeños, and mozzarella.

FRESH SOURDOUGH EXPRESS $$
1316 Ocean Dr.
(907) 235-7571
www.freshsourdoughexpress.com

From its humble beginnings in 1972 as a bread-wagon-on-wheels that limped in off the Alaska Highway, the Fresh Sourdough Express has grown into a full-service bakery and cafe. Grains for organic breads are ground daily, and all baked goods are baked fresh daily. Fresh Sourdough Express serves organic coffee, ice tea, and their own organic Ah!laska cocoa and chocolate syrup. All salad dressings and sauces are homemade, as is their trademark salsa. For breakfast, try the Saint Augustine, a mountain of Alaskan-grown potatoes and sautéed veggies topped with cheese and salsa. For lunch, there are soups, salads, burgers (free-range buffalo), sandwiches, and savory filled croissants. On the dinner menu, sample the Grilled Alaskan Wild Salmon with cranberry peppercorn glaze or the All-Natural New York Strip Steak smothered with roasted-onion marmalade.

THE HOMESTEAD RESTAURANT $$$
Mile 8.2 East End Rd.
(907) 235-8723
www.homesteadrestaurant.com

Established in 1961, the award-winning Homestead Restaurant is famous for its fabulous seafood. Specials include Thursday's World Tour, when the chefs display their creativity with regional appetizers and entrees, and the Friday and Saturday Prime Rib Nights. The Homestead also offers a full selection of wines and classic cocktails, with Dinner at the Vineyard options throughout the year featuring five-course meals with paired wines. Popular but pricey, they're open Wednesday through Saturday at 5 p.m., and reservations are a great idea.

WASABI'S $$$$
Mile 5 East End Rd.
(907) 226-3663

Homer's newest little secret, Wasabi's is a trendy and tasteful dining choice on scenic East End Road. The menu feature Pacific Rim fusion, with seafood, pasta, and steak specialities. Fresh ingredients and artful presentations are the norm here, where the decor features original artwork in stone, metal, and glass as well as a glass and tile mosaic stream running red with salmon. A custom sushi bar overlooks the bay, where there's also outdoor seating. A full bar complements 50 wine options, including sake.

Nightlife

Sure, it's a small town, but there are quite a few friendly nightspots in Homer, where locals refer to their hometown as "a quaint drinking village with a fishing problem." Homer also has some great local bands and, on occasion, headliners from outside.

ALICE'S CHAMPAGNE PALACE
195 East Pioneer Ave.
(907) 235-7650

This bar has a long history in Homer, first as the Club Bar, which burned in 1976. Four years later, it reopened as Alice's, closing again 16 years later. With a facelift that included fancy chandliers, a disco rail, and some recycled cannery siding, Alice's is back in business. A good-sized dance floor complements live weekend music and a drink menu that features a huge selection of vodka and a few "city drinks."

DUGGAN'S WATERFRONT PUB
120 West Bunnel St.
(907) 235-9949

Duggan's is one of those places where you can make a friend just about as soon as you walk through the door. The place likes to mix it up with nightly entertainment, including Thursday's Untamed Karaoke and live rock and roll on Friday and Saturday nights, with both local bands and headliners. Duggan's makes some of the best margaritas in town and features a full bar menu with all sorts of seafood and chips, burgers, sandwiches, steaks, and barbequed ribs. The kitchen's open till midnight, so it's a great place for a late-night snack.

THE SALTY DAWG
Homer Spit Rd.
(907) 235-6718
www.saltydawgsaloon.com

You can't really say you've been to Homer unless you've stopped by the Dawg, a famous bar tucked inside three interconnected cabins and a lighthouse tower. The tower once held water, and the bar itself is the result of the splicing together of a former schoolhouse, an early post office, and the headquarters of the Cook Inlet Coal Fields Company, all dating from early in the 1900s. The quarters are cramped and the ceilings are low, but the place is full of charm.

i Homer Brewing Company produces popular local brews, including Broken Birch Bitter, Old Inlet Pale, Red Knot Scottish, China Poot Porter, and Oddessy Oatmeal Stout. All their beers are unfiltered, unpasteurized, and cask-conditioned. Be sure to sample some while you're on the Peninsula, because distribution is limited and only draft beer is sold.

Shopping

Like everything else in Homer, the shopping here is fun and eclectic. You'll find everything from art galleries to coffee roasters to outdoor-gear specialists, plus a whole lot of practical shopping spots. There's a lot of multitasking in a small town like Homer, so you'll find that some of these shops also offer overnight lodging. Stores with obvious tourist appeal tend to have shortened hours in the winter.

Art Galleries and Shops

ART SHOP GALLERY
202 West Pioneer Ave.
(907) 235-7076, (800) 478-7076
www.artshopgallery.com

Scenically situated in downtown Homer, the Art Shop Gallery has a large selection of Alaskan arts and crafts, from the ubiquitous moose and bear to more original items, such as walrus whisker earrings and seal gut baskets. They have a large inventory of handmade Alaskan Christmas ornaments, ivory and bone carvings, qiviut products made of musk ox yarn from Sheep Mountain Creations, and tiles from Brecht Studios. Among the Alaskan artists featured are perennial favorites Fred Machetanz, Rie Munoz, Jon Van Zyle, Byron Birdsall, and Barbara Lavallee. Enjoy a complimentary cup of tea or coffee while you browse. They're open daily in the summer, with shortened hours on Sunday and in the winter.

PICTURE ALASKA ART GALLERY
448 East Pioneer Ave.
(907) 235-2300, (800) 770-2300
www.picturealaska.com

Another diverse gallery in the Pioneer Avenue arts district, Picture Alaska features original paintings, fine art prints, jewelry, mixed-media sculpture, pottery, wildlife photos, and vintage Alaskan photography. They also have a nice selection of Alaskan Native arts and crafts. Upstairs you'll find fashion art, including accessories, sportswear, dresswear, and fine lingerie. The gallery is open year-round, with extended hours in the summer.

SEA LION FINE ART GALLERY
Homer Spit Rd.
(907) 235-3400, (907) 235-8767
www.sealiongallery.com

Of the many shops along Homer Spit, the Sea Lion is notable for its emphasis on fine art. Started in 1993 by local artists Gary and Terri Lyon, the gallery features the work of notables Byron Birdsall, Barbara Lavallee, and Nancy Yaki. The collection of Alaskan Native art includes baleen and grass baskets; walrus, ivory, and whalebone carvings; and multimedia and antique pieces. If you're worn out from all that shopping, they have two efficiency suites upstairs that can be rented by the night, both with beautiful views of the ocean. Like pretty much everything else on the Spit, the Sea Lion is closed in the winter.

Outdoor Wear and Sporting Goods

EAGLE ENTERPRISES
2355 Kachemak Dr.
(907) 235-7908
Whether it's for commercial or recreational use, this retail store has what you need to stay safe and warm in the great outdoors. You'll find life jackets, rain gear, survival kits, flares, flashlights, and camping gear. The friendly, well-trained staff will help with questions on maintenance and repair of life-saving equipment. They offer propane tank inspection, hydro testing, inflatable sport boat repair, and scuba tank refills, too.

KACHEMAK GEAR SHED
3625 East End Rd.
(907) 235-8612
www.kachemakgearshed.com
The Gear Shed is the kind of full-service outfitter that Alaskans depend on. For the kitchen, they stock canning and cooking supplies, including smokers. In the clothing department, there's practical Alaskan footwear, including hip waders and chest waders, along with the usual selection of brand-name outdoor wear. Knives? They have a full selection plus sharpeners. And you can browse a full selection of sportfishing equipment, from tackle to down-riggers to licenses to coolers for shipping your fish home. For help with big toys, the Gear Shed carries boat trailer parts, four-wheelers, outboards, and generators, too.

MAIN STREET MERCANTILE
104 East Pioneer Ave.
(907) 235-9102
Main Street Mercantile is a 21st-century version of an old-time general store, tucked inside a charming historic building near downtown Homer. Opened in 1936 as a branch of the Seldovia Cash Store, the Mercantile carries brand-name outdoor gear, camping supplies, cast-iron cookware, and old-fashioned kitchen tools, along with Nikon-brand camera supplies. Photos and maps dot the walls, reminders of the store's rich history. Be sure to check out their line of Nomar polar fleece and travel bags, made right in Homer. As an added bonus, Homer's Sweet Berries Cafe has moved into the Mercantile, so patrons can enjoy favorites like the gigantic Smoking Fireman Sandwich, loaded with turkey, bacon, ham, cheddar, and pepperjack, or the cafe's famous build-your-own omelets and sourdough pancakes made with Seldovia starter.

Souvenir and Specialty Shops

ALASKA WILD BERRY PRODUCTS
528 East Pioneer Ave.
(907) 562-8858
www.alaskawildberryproducts.com
If you love chocolate, you won't want to miss all the goodies at this Homer store. In addition to their signature chocolate-covered berries and chocolates with berry filling, there are all kinds of Alaskan-crafted chocolates, truffles, and candies, plus a whole bunch of other themed food items, including Raven's Brew Coffee, salmon and seafood, and Alaskan teas. Check out the gift baskets for indulging the folks back home.

COAL POINT SEAFOOD COMPANY
4306 Homer Spit Rd.
(907) 235-3877, (800) 325-3877
www.welovefish.com
Located right on the docks of Homer Harbor, Coal Point buys direct from fishermen who pride themselves in keeping their catch fresh. They offer custom flash freezing and vacuum packing for anglers, but you can fake it by bringing home some of Coal Point's fresh and smoked halibut, salmon, cod, crab, shrimp, prawns, or scallops. They also have fun seafood gift packs for your friends back home, along with an assortment of nonedible gift items. If you work up an appetite while shopping, there's an oyster bar where you can sample their wares.

FUNKY PLANET
158 Pioneer Ave., #B
(907) 235-3274
Lotions, knickknacks, decorative masks, wall art, sarongs, mermaid mobiles—you name it, and there's a good chance you'll find it at Funky

Planet, provided it's something fun and artsy. They stock imported women's clothing in sizes from juniors to plus, and in styles from contemporary to (what else?) funky. To complete your outfit, choose from their selection of purses and scarves, along with custom jewelry, including earrings, bracelets, bone and antler rings, and necklaces. The friendly folks at Funky Planet keep the store open Tuesday through Saturday, and they offer shipping services for your convenience.

HOMER'S GOLD MINE GIFTS
3695 Lake St.
(907) 235-6886
www.alaska.net/~homergm/
Whether it's souvenir clothing, canned salmon, homemade fudge, or fireweed honey that strikes your fancy, you'll find it at Gold Mine Gifts. In addition to the usual T-shirts and sweatshirts, they offer denim shirts and heavier coats, along with locally made fleece items and handmade layettes for the wee ones. You'll find a large selection of gemstone jewelry, including hematite, jade, rose quartz, garnet, lapis, tiger eye, and obsidian, as well as handcrafted ivory pieces. Another specialty is their in-store line of gold nugget jewelry, from rings to watches to pendants and money clips. If you're more into fun than fancy, check out their fish spinner and fish fly earrings. In the fine art department, you'll find oil originals, prints, and sculptures by well-known Alaskan artists as well as hand-carved moose antlers. When you're done shopping, treat yourself to a drink at the Espresso Bar, or indulge in fudge made right in the store. Nonshoppers can take in an Alaska sportfishing video and sample the hand-dipped Alaska Supreme ice cream. You can even "chat" with a life-size re-creation of Homer Pennock, for whom the town was named.

OLD INLET BOOKSHOP
3487 Main St.
(907) 235-7984
www.oldinletbookshop.com
Browsing in Homer's Old Inlet Bookshop is a bit like perusing the attic of a friendly but oh-so-literary grandmother. The place is stacked from floor to ceiling with both old and new books in the ambience of a log cabin with hardwood floors. But don't be fooled: This is a serious booklovers' paradise, owned by third-generation booksellers and carrying more than 20,000 titles. They specialize in rare, used, and out-of-print books as well as Alaskana, with plenty of mainstream titles, too. Attached to the original cabin, estimated to be more than a century old, is the Mermaid Cafe and B&B.

Attractions
If you can pull yourself away from the gorgeous scenery for an hour or two, Homer has some great low-cost attractions that will help you get acquainted with the area, and they're easy on the pocketbook. Price codes reflect admission for one adult during the summer season. If admission is free, no price code is given.

Price Codes
$	Less than $5
$$	$5–$10
$$$	$11–$15
$$$$	More than $15

ALASKA ISLANDS AND OCEAN VISITOR CENTER
95 Sterling Highway
(907) 235-6961
This joint venture of the Alaska Maritime National Wildlife Refuge and the Kachemak Bay Research Reserve is a must-see spot for learning about the natural history of the area. There are great exhibits highlighting the world's largest seabird refuge and exploring the dynamic estuary environment. Discover how dories and bidarkas (Eskimo kayaks) have transported voyagers across the waters of the bay, learn how the first peoples of the region survived, and review the effects of newcomers and war on the refuge area. A favorite exhibit is seabird theater, where you can see, hear, and even smell a simulated nesting colony. After taking in the stunning interactive exhibits and well-stocked bookstore, stretch your legs on the Beluga Slough interpretive trail to Bishop's Beach

Park. Ask about guided beachwalks, estuary hikes, and discovery labs. Open daily from 9 a.m. to 6 p.m. during the summer and Tuesday through Saturday from 10 a.m. to 5 p.m. in the winter, the center has a limited number of strollers and wheelchairs for visitors to use at no charge, and all exhibits may be accessed by wheelchair. There's ample parking for RVs, but overnight parking is not allowed. Admission is free.

HOMER CHAMBER OF COMMERCE VISITOR INFORMATION CENTER
201 Sterling Highway
(907) 235-7740
www.homeralaska.org
The chamber of commerce operates a full-service visitor center with information, maps, and brochures to orient you to the area. It's worth a stop just to see the gorgeous mosaic in the floor. The chamber publishes a great full-color brochure that you can pick up there or have mailed to you. Of course, there's no charge for their services.

PRATT MUSEUM $$
3779 Bartlett St.
(907) 235-8635
www.prattmuseum.org
For a great introduction to the region and its natural history, check out the Pratt Museum. You'll find videos, photo essays, and remote video technology to give you an in-depth look at contemporary and historic Kachemak Bay. The exhibit "Bears, Beetles, and Darkened Waters" explores the effects of climate change and development on local habitat and wildlife. Also on display are more than 75 species of wildlife, including an aquarium with sea stars, octopus, and flounder as well as intertidal specimens. Adjacent to the museum is the Harrington Cabin, which houses exhibits on homesteading in the area. In the summer, enjoy more than 150 species of flowers and plants along the garden path, as well as a self-guided ecology trail. The only natural history museum on the Peninsula, the Pratt attracts 30,000-plus visitors a year. It's open daily from 10 a.m. to 6 p.m. in the summer, with shortened

hours and Monday closures in the winter. They're also closed in January.

ℹ **The Homer Public Library offers free Internet access on a sign-in basis. The facilities are well-used in the summer, so plan to wait a bit for your turn.**

The Arts

If you love the arts, Homer is the place to be. Remarkable scenery is complemented by high-quality art at nearly every turn, from top-notch galleries and studios to a variety of dance, theatrical, and musical events. In fact, Homer was selected as one of 100 best small towns for the arts in the country. If you're lucky enough to be in town at the beginning of the month, be sure to set aside time to participate in the First Friday Art Walk, where you'll have opportunities to meet artists and chat about their work. Local writers' groups and writing workshops round out the arts scene. The library even keeps the unpublished works of local authors available for public reading in their special "top drawer" collection.

BUNNELL STREET GALLERY
106 West Bunnell St.
(907) 235-2662
www.bunnellstreetgallery.org
This nonprofit gallery features monthly solo shows of Alaskan artists and also plays host to juried exhibits, readings, concerts, artists in the schools, and other special events. Located in the historic Old Inlet Trading Post along the shore of Bishop's Beach, the gallery displays paintings, photography, ceramics, fiber pieces, sculpture, and contemporary Alaskan art. With a mission of promoting innovative, quality art, they also sponsor a Homer artists studio tour and art workshops for adults.

KACHEMAK BAY WRITERS' CONFERENCE
533 East Pioneer Ave.
(907) 235-7743
writersconference.homer.alaska.edu

Sponsored by the Kachemak Bay campus of the Kenai Peninsula College, a branch of the University of Alaska, this annual conference is quickly gaining attention and attracting writers from all genres. Recently, the conference featured a former U.S. Poet Laureate plus a faculty of 20 writers who presented workshops, readings, and panel discussions. Fiction, poetry, nonfiction, and the business of writing are among the topics of the conference.

ⓘ Feeling Artrageous? Visit Homer during Artrageous August, when the Homer Council on the Arts (www.homerart .org) sponsors a slew of artsy events, including a Concert on the Lawn series, Plein-aire Painting, Art Camp, Beach Sculpture, a Jazz Fest, Literary Smorgasbord, and of course an Artrageous Ball.

KENAI PENINSULA ORCHESTRA
315 West Pioneer Ave.
(907) 235-4899
www.kpoalaska.org

These volunteer musicians from Homer, Kenai, Soldotna, and Seward have one thing in common: They love music, so they collaborate to offer a full season of musical entertainment for residents of the Peninsula. The orchestra gets a big boost every year by hosting the Summer Music Festival, in which guest faculties perform with the local group and conduct workshops. Throughout the years, the orchestra has hosted world-class guest artists, including the Boston Pops Jazz ensemble and Broadway vocalists. They sponsor multiple events throughout the year, including concerts and recitals.

ⓘ For more fine art, take the ferry Danny J across the bay to Halibut Cove, where you can stroll along the boardwalk to Experience Gallery and the studio of Diana Tillion, who has drawn for decades with octopus ink.

PIER ONE THEATRE
(907) 235-7333
www.pieronetheatre.org

For top-notch community theater, it would be hard to beat the shows put on at Pier One. They run a full schedule from June through August, and they're often sold out. There's a nice range of productions, from comedic to literary, along with theatrical camps for young people. Pier One is splendidly located at the beginning of the Spit, with plenty of parking. Be sure to call ahead for reservations.

Parks, Recreation, and Tours

If Homer is an artist's paradise, it's equally heavenly for outdoor enthusiasts. You'll find ample opportunities to explore and recreate in the great outdoors in and around Homer. Within the city limits, there are several parks waiting to be enjoyed. The Karen Hornaday Memorial Park and campground hosts summertime Concerts on the Lawn featuring local talent and sponsored by the local public radio station. There's also occasional live music at a park with an unusual name, the WKFL (Wisdom, Knowledge, Faith, and Love). Bishop's Beach Park at the end of Bunnell Street is a great place to view wildlife and enjoy the ocean view, and Ben Walters Park, behind McDonald's on Lake Street, offers a boardwalk for crossing the marsh and a gazebo with barbeque facilities.

The Carl E. Wynn Nature Center (907-235-6667, www.akcoastalstudies.org), a nonprofit organization dedicated to promoting responsible interaction with the coastal and marine ecosystems of Kachemak Bay, is a great place to start. Take a guided walk on the system of nature trails for a nominal use fee, or treat yourself to the full-day Low Tide Tour and Coastal Forest Hike across Kachemak Bay. You'll see rich tidal pools, a seabird rookery, live tanks at the Peterson Bay Field Station, and many of the animals that live in the tidal zone. In conjunction with the tour, you can add overnight yurt camping or a half-day of guided kayaking.

A short jaunt across the water will take you to Kachemak Bay State Wilderness Park, the state's first state park. There you'll find ample opportunities for boating, hiking, kayaking, camping, sportfishing, and mountains sports on 400,000 acres. Harbor seals, sea otters, porpoise, whales, black bears, puffins, mountain goats, wolves, and bald eagles are among the abundant wildlife in the park. Favorite spots include Halibut Cove Lagoon, Leisure Lake, China Poot Bay, Grewingk Glacier, and Humpy Creek.

If you'll be visiting Kachemak Park, be sure to leave a travel plan with friends or family, or use the Trail Registers, as weather can be unpredictable and the bay can be rough at times. The tides in Kachemak Bay are the second strongest in the world due to strong currents and rapids formed by narrow passages, so take no chances. Pick up a tide book at any of a number of local sporting goods stores to carry with you, and secure your boat if you plan to leave it unattended. Riptides and shallows can make access to Halibut Cove Lagoon hazardous at times, so the lagoon is best accessed only with shallow draft boats during high tide. Even if you leave a travel plan for your adventures in the park, you should be ready and able to handle emergency situations on your own. If you don't have your own boat, check with Mako's Water Taxi (907-235-9055, www.makos watertaxi.com) for scheduled service to the park.

Hikers can trek more than 85 miles of trails within Kachemak Park, and camping is permitted in many locations. Rustic cabins may be rented by reservation only. Contact the Division of Parks and Outdoor Recreation in Soldotna (907-262-5581) or visit dnr.alaska.gov/parks/cabins/index. htm for more information or to reserve a cabin. Campfires are allowed on nonvegetated beaches or gravel bars only, or within metal rings in one of the park's developed campsites. Hang food away from camp and use bear-proof containers. Land vehicles, including bicycles, are not permitted in the park, but powerboats may be used in salt water and on designated lakes. Mooring buoys and the Halibut Cove Lagoon Dock are available for public use.

Bicycling enthusiasts will find great spots to ride around Homer, including a couple of trails on either side of Kachemak Park across the bay. East Hill and West Hill Roads offer great hill climbing; for flatter terrain, pedal from Diamond Ridge Road to the end of Skyline Drive. You also can ride the paved trail along the Spit. For a more challenging trek, take the switchback at the end of East End Road down the beach to the village of Kachemak Selo and head from there onto the Fox River flats. On the other end of town, take the four-wheeler trail above the Russian village of Nikolaevsk.

To really experience the ocean, hop in a kayak and paddle at eye-level with the sea lions and sea otters out in the bay. Remember the tides are strong and the weather can be unpredictable, so those new to the sport are advised to stay along the sheltered coves on the south side of the bay. Water taxis will transport you across to those safer waters, and some of them have kayaks available for rent. If you're a first-timer, be sure to head out with a guide or an experienced companion as well as the proper safety equipment. If you're among the experienced, you can take off from Homer Harbor in the early evening, after the breeze dies down, for Peterson Bay and Gull Island.

Birders have a heyday in Homer, with up to 241 species spotted in the area. In early May, you can see hundreds of thousands of shorebirds as they're passing through, with the annual Kachemak Bay Shorebird Festival featuring more than 50 events to celebrate the grand migration (see the complete listing under May events). Take a water taxi or tour boat to Gull Island in the summer, and you'll be treated to the sight of hundreds of seabirds nesting on rock outcroppings. Even the Christmas bird count yields quite a few species. Check the Bird Alert Info Line (907-235-7337) for current information on what's been spotted. For a checklist of Kachemak birds and where to find them, visit www.birdinghomeralaska.org.

Clamming is another fun activity in and around Homer. Grab your fishing license, tide table, rubber boots, gloves, and a shovel, and head to the beach at low tide, preferably at the minus tide. The best clamming is at—where else?—Clam Gulch, about 20 miles north of Ninilchik, between Soldotna and Homer. Wherever you see a dimple in the sand, dig beside it and reach for the clam, quickly but with care, remembering that they're called razor clams for a reason. July and August are the best months for clamming, with a limit of 60 allowed. You also can dig for steamers, cockles, and mussels on beaches near Homer, but the technique is different. Paralytic Shellfish Poison (PSP) alerts are rare in Kachemak Bay, but check with the Department of Environmental Health (907-269-7501, www.dec.state.ak.us/eh/fss/seafood/psp/psp.htm) to be certain it's safe to eat your catch.

i For years, Homer's "Eagle Lady" Jean Keene fed wild eagles through the winter, making great opportunities for photographers from around the world. After Keene's death in 2009, the Homer City Council ended the controversial practice by banning the feeding of wild eagles.

Homer's also a great jumping-off point for bear-watching excursions to Katmai National Monument. Travel by boat or bush plane from early June to late September to see bears feasting on wild salmon and berries. Some tour operators offer viewing from elevated platforms while others take you right into bear habitat. Both day trips and longer excursions are available.

ALASKA KAYAK SCHOOL
(907) 235-2090
www.alaskakayakschool.com
Whether you're a novice or an experienced paddler, the Alaska Kayak School will help you get the most out of your water-based adventures. They offer instruction for sea, surf, flat-water, and white-water kayaking and canoeing as well as winter paddling, pool courses, and Eskimo Rolling. Alaska Kayak School's guided trips emphasize personal instruction. Advanced and experienced paddlers may rent kayaks and gear or apply for longer exploratory expeditions. Instructors are members of the British Canoe Union and American Canoe Association.

BAY EXCURSIONS
P.O. Box 3312, Homer, AK 99603
(907) 235-7525
www.bayexcursions.com
Lifelong Alaskan Karl Stoltzfus has been running boats on Kachemak Bay since 1970, and he's happy to match his schedule to yours for birding or wildlife tours. In addition, he provides regular water-taxi service to cabins and trailheads at Kachemak Bay State Park. The boat has outside seating for six and inside seating for a dozen. Bay Excursions also offers kayak and cabin rentals.

HALLO BAY BEAR CAMP
(907) 235-2237
www.hallobay.com
Established in 1994, Hallo Bay Wilderness gives visitors a chance to see bears in their natural habitat, without viewing platforms or man-made trails. Guest groups are kept small to minimize impact on the bears, and nothing is done to discourage the natural curiosity of the animals. Translation: The bears will come into camp with you, but thanks to the well-trained staff, the bears at Hallo Bay Bear Camp have earned a reputation for behaving themselves. They offer everything from $550 half-day tours to weeklong Bear and Nature camp tours for $4,200. Multi-day bear tours include private cabin, meals, and naturalist guide.

TRUE NORTH KAYAK ADVENTURES
(907) 235-0708
www.truenorthkayak.com
Since 1993, True North has been offering guided kayaking trips that include water-taxi service, equipment, and instruction. Head out to the protected waters of Yukon Island for a half-day or full-day expedition, or take a three-quarter's-day excursion to Elephant Rock. With any luck you'll get a close-up look at seals, puffins, eagles, sea otters, or even whales while enjoying the gorgeous scenery and unspoiled coastline. If you have more time, try a two- to six-day jaunt to Eldred Passage, with meals, gear, and yurt or cabin rental included. No experience is necessary, though paddlers with previous experience can rent kayaks and head out on their own.

i Take a historic walking tour of Homer and check out some of the oldest buildings in the area. You can pick up more information at the Pratt Museum or the Homer Chamber of Commerce Visitor Center.

Hiking and Camping

Homer's spectacular oceanfront setting makes for great hiking opportunities. If you're looking for a short and easy hike, try the Pratt Museum Trail (0.75-mile long) behind the museum. It's a self-guided forest trail with markers and occasional outdoor art exhibits; if you're lucky, you might spot a moose. Another easy walk is the Beluga Slough Trail, with 0.6 mile of gravel and boardwalk beginning at the Alaska Islands and Ocean Visitor Center and winding through woods and marshes to an overlook of Beluga Slough, where you'll see lots of waterfowl and shorebirds during the migratory seasons.

For hikes that are longer but not too challenging, check out the Homer Spit Trail, a paved path that begins at the base of Homer Spit Road and goes for 3.2 miles to Fishing Hole, or for 4 miles if you go all the way to the harbor. Though the trail runs right along the road, you'll see shorebirds and waterfowl in the spring and fall, while sea otters gather with the shifting ice in the winter. In addition, the Carl E. Wynn Nature Center Trails offer both guided and self-guided hikes along trails of various lengths. The center's paths follow a migratory corridor for black bear and moose, and you'll trek through great bird habitat as well. The user fee supports the nature center and its programs. In the winter, trails are open for snowshoeing.

If you'd like a longer hike, try the 6.7-mile Homestead Trail. Park at the trail head on Roger's Loop (off the Sterling Highway) and follow the trail up a south-facing slope to the Reuben Call Memorial overlooking Kachemak Bay. If you take the trail in June or July, a showy display of wildflowers awaits. As you make your way to Bridge Creek, you'll see an abundance of bushes, shrubs, and flowers before you reach a meadow dotted with alder and spruce. The trail ends at a parking area near Bridge Creek Reservoir.

You also can walk the beach near Homer, hiking 7.5 miles from Bishop's Beach to Diamond Creek Trail, or a full 15 miles to Anchor Point. Be careful, though. There's no defined trail, and when you walk the beach, you run the risk of being cut off by incoming tides. The hike is best at low tide, when you can hope to see eagles, otters, whales, sea ducks, and tide pools. Pick up a tide book at a local sporting goods store or at the Chamber of Commerce Visitor Center. If you pick up marine life from the tidal pools, remember to handle it with care and return it gently to its habitat.

The Spit used to be something of a camping free-for-all during the summer, but now things are a bit more upscale, with tent camping restricted to one of the private or city-run campgrounds on the seaward side of Spit Road or at Mariner Park near the beginning of the Spit. Facilities at the city-run sites are rustic at best, but the price is right and the ocean is a stone's throw away. Be wary of soft sand in spots. Another option for tent camping is above town at Karen Hornaday Park, where you can explore the woods and enjoy great views of the bay, or at Seaside Farm (see our listing under Accommodations). You'll find RV parking at private campgrounds along the Spit, and the city maintains two dump stations, one near the Fishing Hole and one by the post office.

ALASKA ANGLER RV RESORT AND CABINS
Ninilchik
(800) 347-4114
www.afishunt.com
The picturesque village of Ninilchik, just a little closer to Homer than to Soldotna, makes a great jumping-off point for all your fishing fun. They have on-site charters for fishing for halibut out of Deep Creek and king salmon in the Kasilof River. You can walk to local beaches for clamming or to local rivers for salmon fishing, too. The Alaska Angler has 50-amp full hookups, cable television, laundry, showers, fish-processing facilities, propane, Wi-Fi Internet, and modem ports. In addi-

tion to standard and super-size sites, they have four fully furnished cabins available for rent. RV rates range from $35 to $46 per night.

HERITAGE RV PARK
3350 Homer Spit Rd.
(907) 226-4500, (800) 380-7787
www.alaskaheritagervpark.com

Park right next to the ocean and take in the action at the Fishing Hole at this Good Sam Park. Included with all sites is 20/30/50 amp power, telephone with voice mail/modem, septic/water hookups, and satellite television. They offer extrawide RV sites with room for boats and other toys, as well as shower, restroom, and laundry facilities. At the Espresso Cafe, they serve up breakfast items with a great ocean view and free wireless Internet. Enjoy the private half-mile beach with campfire pit and picnic tables, and a great location next to the Homer Spit bike path and walking trail. At the gift shop, you'll find all sorts of Alaskana, including baleen and ivory carvings, gold nuggets, Alaska Native baskets and beadwork, and berry edibles. Rates range upwards from $75 per night.

i **What are those magnificent peaks across the bay from Homer? Four are active volcanoes of the "Rim of Fire": Mount Douglas, Mount St. Augustine, Mount Illiamna, and Mount Redoubt. The acronym DAIR will help you remember which is which, from south to north. Augustine and Redoubt both have erupted within the last few decades, with Redoubt rumbling most recently.**

Fishing

If you can't find fish in Homer, you aren't trying very hard. From barn-door halibut to feisty king salmon and Dolly Varden, there's plenty of action to be had. The town earned its reputation as the "Halibut Capital of the World" due to the abundant catches and trophy-size flat fish brought in by sport anglers every season. When the halibut action heats up in the spring, king salmon fishing isn't far behind. You'll get good trolling action starting in May off Deep Creek, Anchor Point, and Ninilchik. Freshwater fishing for kings begins on the Saturday of Memorial Day weekend, with runs of silvers, reds, and pinks cycling through streams on both sides of the bay throughout the summer.

You can charter out for halibut and salmon from late spring to early fall, or try your luck surf-casting, fly fishing, jigging, or drifting on local beaches and rivers. Look for Dollies at the tip of the Spit and into the inlet, with shore-cast spinners and spoons getting the best results. Take a skiff into the waters east of the harbor entrance for silvers, or try fishing off the rocks at high tide. Across the Kachemak Bay, you'll find good angling at China Poot Bay, Seldovia Bay, Halibut Cove Lagoon, and Turka Bay.

North of Homer at Mile 134 of the Sterling Highway, the Ninilchik River is a hot spot for kings, silvers, Dolly Varden, and steelhead, but you'll encounter a lot of people traffic there, too. Deep Creek, just south of Ninilchik, is another popular spot for river fishing. You also can fish the Anchor River, about 20 miles north of Homer, for Dollies, silvers, steelheads, and rainbows. Be sure to check regulations with the Alaska Department of Fish and Game (907-235-6930, 907-235-8191, www.sf.adfg.state.ak.us/statewide/reghome.cfm) before you plan your fishing trip, as there are a variety of different opening days and limits for the various species.

A favorite hot spot in Homer is The Fishing Hole, a man-made lagoon stocked with silver and king salmon that return every year. Look for kings from mid-May through the first part of June, with silvers returning from July into September. It's shoulder to shoulder around the hole, but it's fun to watch as even youngsters pull in big fish when the action heats up.

Out on the open water, the daily halibut limit is two per person (though there has been talk of slashing it to one per person), with the fish typically averaging 20 to 30 pounds each, though it's not uncommon to wrestle in barn door flat fish weighing in at more than 100 pounds. King salmon fishing is best from May to the middle of June, while the silver run peaks during the first three weeks in August. Bait, tackle, cleaning, and filleting are typically included with your charter. Flash freezing, vacuum packing, and shipping are available locally.

Full-day charters leave early in the morning from Homer Harbor, on the Spit. Reserve early if you can, though there's often room for walk-ons who book a day prior. Boats usually require a minimum number of anglers before they'll go out, but operators will pair you with other parties as needed to fill the boat. Pack a tote with rain gear, your fishing license, a camera, a lunch (many restaurants and hotels sell box lunches), and motion sickness pills, just in case. Wear layered clothes and waterproof, nonslip shoes. Don't be surprised when your boat journeys a couple of hours only to pull up right next to several others; captains communicate by radio to let each other know where the fish are.

If you're going to do any serious fishing, don't forget about Homer's Halibut Derby, which runs from the first of May to the middle of September. There's a cash jackpot for the largest fish of the season along with tagged fish prizes, catch-and-release prizes, and monthly cash prizes for the five biggest fish. They're still talking about the poor schmuck who landed a 407-pound halibut a few years back but failed to buy a derby ticket.

DANIEL'S PERSONALIZED GUIDE SERVICE
(907) 235-3843, (800) 230-3843
www.homerfishing.com

Captain Daniel Donich develops and teaches innovative techniques for controlled-depth fishing, and he has acquired a reputation for excellence in angling the waters of Kachemak Bay. On any given trip, you can fish for a variety of species, from salmon of all types to halibut, steelhead, and Dolly Varden. You'll get the added treat of checking out the Dungeness and Tanner crabs he pulls up from traps. Bait, tackle, and fish cleaning are included with your charter, and if you'd like to end your day with a cookout on the beach, they can arrange that, too. Too tired to go home after all that fun? You can rent the Captain's three-bedroom guesthouse with hot tub, washer/dryer, and full kitchen.

NORTH COUNTRY CHARTERS
(907) 235-7620, (800) 770-7620
www.northcountrycharters.com

This is Homer's oldest charter fishing operation, still run by its original owners, Sean and Gerri Martin, along with their sons. They have a nice fleet of twin-engine diesel boats, including the *Irish,* the *Pacific Sun,* the *Coastal Predator,* and the *Obsession,* each with a captain who takes pride in his boat and its catch. Whether you're a beginner or a veteran angler, they'll tailor the trip to your needs. Charter out for salmon or halibut, or try a combination of the two. They also offer long-range trips that take anglers along the coastline of Kachemak Bay and into the entrance of Lower Cook Inlet to the shallow waters along Shuyak Island. Most of these are three-day trips, and they include the use of tournament-quality tackle and all meals.

SILVER FOX CHARTERS
(907) 235-8792, (800) 478-8792
www.silverfoxcharters.com

Silver Fox is one of the largest charter outfits in Homer, and they've been in business since 1974. If you have your sights set on a big barn-door halibut, the odds are good with Silver Fox, as they have a reputation among charter services for bringing in the most fish weighing more than 100 pounds. In addition to halibut, they do salmon and ling cod charters. They run one 56-foot boat and five 30-foot boats, all with twin diesel engines, modern navigational equipment,

> **i** **Across the bay from Homer, you can visit the charming seaside town of Seldovia by riding the Alaska Ferry, taking a bush plane, or hiring a water taxi or charter boat. Seldovia has a visitor center and museum with walking maps of the village and surrounding beaches. See www .seldovia.com for details.**

Close-up

Bear Facts

Most Alaskans and Alaskan visitors would love to see a bear, as long as it's on their own terms. With an estimated 35,000 brown bears (or grizzlies) and 100,000 black bears sharing the state with approximately 700,000 people, the odds of encountering a bear would seem high, but in fact bears tend to keep to themselves, so many Alaskans have never seen one at close range in the wild. Still, close encounters of the bear kind do occur, and those that end badly provide ample fodder for newspapers, books, and movies. Assuming you'd rather make your claim to fame without finding yourself at the wrong end of a bear attack, your best defense is to avoid coming nose to nose with these big animals. Bears are at the top of the food chain and aren't necessarily on the lookout for you, so be aware of your surroundings and do your best not to surprise a bear. When you're in the woods, make noise and travel in a group, shoulder-to-shoulder, if possible. Stay out of thick brush and away from carcasses, flocks of scavengers, or gulls feeding on fish. Try to walk with the wind so that bears will smell you before they see you.

Keep your campsites clean, with dishes washed and food cached aboveground or in bear-proof containers. Don't have smelly foods like bacon or smoked fish at your camp, and do your best to keep food smells off your clothing. Savvy campers sometimes cook on the trail so they're not sleeping in an area with lingering food smells. Burn whatever garbage you can and pack out the rest. Burying garbage is pointless, as bears can easily sniff it out and dig it up.

If a bear approaches while you're fishing, stop and gather your belongings. Be ready to throw your fish into the current, away from the bear, if you have to. If you have a fish on the line, cut the line before getting into a confrontation with the bear. Remember that it's illegal to feed bears (or any large mammals, for that matter), and if bears learn they can get fish simply by approaching a fisherman, there's a good chance they'll turn into nuisance bears.

If you do come face to face with a bear, make sure it knows you're human. Raise your hands and stand tall so you look large. Talk to it. Back away slowly. Never run or climb a tree—bears are better at both those feats than humans. Pepper spray can be an effective deterrent at close ranges, but make sure you don't use it in a way that disables you instead of the bear. Always spray downwind and never in confined spaces. And pepper spray can't be taken on commercial flights, so visitors should plan on buying it and leaving it here.

If you can, learn to distinguish between black and brown bears. It's not just a matter of color—there are black brown bears and brown black bears. Black bears are smaller than brown bears, with sloped as opposed to dish-shaped heads, no shoulder hump, and short, curved claws for climbing trees. Black bears tend to retreat from danger, so if one charges, assume its intent is predatory and fight back. A brown bear is more likely to stand its ground, and your best bet is to treat it much as you would a threatening dog. If a brown bear charges, stand firm unless the bear makes physical contact. Most charges will stop short of injury. Only if the bear makes contact should you "play dead," falling to the ground on your stomach, protecting your neck and face, and staying as still as possible. If the bear continues to be aggressive, assume the attack is predatory and fight back. Likewise, fight any bear that comes into your tent.

heated cabins, and restrooms. Boats typically go out for about 10 hours, with one-and-a-half to two hours running time each way. Expect to catch at least two fish on your average day, with about 30 pounds of fillets to show for your fun.

The larger boat sleeps 12 for long-range trophy trips. Their new 12,000-square-foot log lodge on 84 acres is one of the nicest fishing lodges accessible by road in the state. Military discounts are available.

PRINCE WILLIAM SOUND

On the north end of the Gulf of Alaska, east of the Kenai Peninsula, you'll find Prince William Sound, a 70-mile stretch of ocean jutted with fjords and peppered with islands. It's tough to play favorites in a state with as much scenic beauty as Alaska, but the Sound stands out with its vistas of soaring mountains and endless miles of forests stretching down to the ocean. Unlike the Kenai with its frenzied fishing activity and the Mat-Su Valley with its steady stream of commuters, peace and solitude prevail in this most remote of Southcentral's getaways.

Most of the Sound is inaccessible by road, which makes the on-road harbor towns of Whittier, Seward, and Valdez all the more special. The scenery is spectacular and the marine wildlife plentiful. Cruise ships dock in Whittier and Seward, letting loose swarms of tourists, but Valdez is mostly an Alaskan's paradise, as is Cordova, accessible only by air and water.

Columbia Glacier, the world's fastest-moving glacier, is a popular attraction in the Sound. You can take a cruise from Valdez to get a close look at the calving ice as the glacier recedes at speeds of up to 115 feet a day. And if you love water sports or fishing, Prince William Sound is a great place to do both.

PORTAGE/WHITTIER

Just about an hour's drive from Anchorage—a great day trip—you can get a taste of Prince William Sound's spectacular scenery and glacial activity with a stop at Portage, in the heart of the Chugach National Forest. Portage isn't really a town and it's not on the ocean, but it's a popular destination for visitors who want to get up-close and personal with Portage Glacier, accessed by boat from Portage Lake.

At Whittier, you can take in all sorts of waterfront activity during the summer season. And it's a fun spot to visit because the town itself and the way you get there are unique. The U.S. Army made Whittier a "secret" deepwater port and petroleum delivery center during World War II. Originally, it was accessible only by water or by rail from Portage; the railroad was completed in 1943. Today it's a charming seaside community with both road and railroad access, though you have to do a little advance planning for a drive, as we explain below.

Getting Here, Getting Around

These days you reach Whittier via the 2.5-mile Anton Anderson Memorial Tunnel, the longest vehicle tunnel in North America. There's only one lane, and the railroad still uses the tunnel, but that adds to the novelty. Vehicles gather in a staging area, traveling to Whittier on the hour and back on the half-hour, subject to rail delays. A toll is charged on the way to Whittier but not on the way back. For up-to-date schedules and toll information, contact the Alaska Department of Transportation (907-566-2244, 877-611-2586, www.dot .state.ak.us/creg/whittiertunnel/index.shtml).

There's also ferry service between Whittier, Valdez, and Cordova via the Alaska Marine Highway (907-272-7116, 800-642-0066, www .dot.state.ak.us) and rail service to Whittier on the Alaska Railroad (907-265-2494, 800-544-0552, www.alaskarailroad.com).

No matter how you get to Whittier, you'll love the spectacular scenery along the waterfront. It's a unique little town. At first the only place to live in Whittier was the now-abandoned

Buckner Building, once one of the largest buildings in Alaska. Today the 14-story Begich Towers and the Whittier Manor provide condominium housing for the town's 290 residents.

i The train ride from Anchorage to Whittier is scenic, but it takes a lot longer than driving. If you're short on time (and to save money on your fare), check into picking up the train at the Portage Station at Mile 80 of the Seward Highway.

For a small town, Whittier's got a good deal going on, at least in the summer. In June, there's an annual Walk to Whittier, when for one day the tunnel is open to pedestrian traffic. There's a big Fourth of July celebration plus a summerlong Halibut Derby, not to mention silver salmon fishing in the early fall. Watch out for winter, though. With a mean snowfall of 260 inches, this place gets pretty well buried.

ACCOMMODATIONS

Unless you're camping, there is nowhere to overnight in the little town of Portage, but Whittier has a handful of fun options for overnight guests. Unless otherwise stated, you can assume that major credit cards are accepted and that the accommodations are available year-round. Expect no smoking, no pets, and no wheelchair access unless we say otherwise. Price ranges below indicate the average cost of a room for two adults during the peak season.

Price Codes

$................ Less than $125
$$ ....$126–$175
$$$ ....$176–$225
$$$$ .... More than $225

JUNE'S B&B CONDO SUITES   **$$**
(888) 472-2396
www.breadnbuttercharters.com
Here's your chance to mingle with the locals in

one of the residential complexes for Whittier residents. Located in the historic Begich Towers, these condo units include private baths, full kitchenettes, telephones, cable televisions with VCRs, and continental breakfast. You'll find a variety of bed sizes, including futons and sleeper sofas for large groups, in June's one- and two-bedroom units. Larger units sleeping 6 to 11 people are higher priced and offer an ocean view. Breakfast, delivered in a basket, includes fruit, cereal, toast, bagels, juice, coffee, and tea. On the first floor of the Towers, there's a post office, store, beauty shop, and nondenominational church. Rooms are wheelchair accessible, and there are designated smoking areas. After a good night's rest, you can head out on a sightseeing or fishing charter captained by June's husband Ken.

THE INN AT WHITTIER   **$$$$**
Harbor Loop Rd.
(907) 472-7000
www.innatwhittier.com
This four-story, timber-framed inn with its 70-foot lighthouse tower is a focal point of the Whittier harbor. From the grand fireplace in the lobby to the restaurant with sweeping views of the harbor, there are plenty of spaces to relax and enjoy the quiet ambience of the waterfront. Down-filled pillows and comforters as well as crisp bed linens mean guests sleep in comfort here. Choose from Mountain View or Ocean View Rooms, each with television and dataport telephone. For a more luxurious experience, try a Junior Suite with ocean view, king-size bed, deluxe bath, Jacuzzi tub, soft terry robes, and sitting area; or indulge in a Townhouse Suite, a two-story retreat with all the features of the Junior Suite plus ocean and mountain views, plasma television, and a

i If you're catching the ferry or a cruise in Whittier, give yourself plenty of time to get through the tunnel, as delays can occur. Tunnel traffic starts at 5:30 a.m. and ends at 11:15 p.m. during the summer, with shortened hours in the winter.

fireplace on each floor. The inn offers packages for meetings, retreats, weddings, or just plain old getaways. It's the only "vacation club" (translate: timeshare) property in Alaska, with trades available through Interval.

Restaurants

Unless you get out on the water or hike into the hills, there's not a whole lot to do once you get to Whittier except take in a meal at one of the seaside eateries. Along the waterfront triangle, you'll find a variety of seasonal cafes, most featuring seafood and outdoor seating. Unless otherwise stated, these restaurants are open daily in the summer season and accept major credit cards. No need to worry about reservations. There's wheelchair access for the outdoor tables, but don't assume it's available inside unless we say so.

Price Codes

$................ Less than $15
$$ .... $15–$25
$$$ .... $26–$40
$$$$ .... More than $40

CAFE ORCA AND GALLERY $$$
Lot 9 Business Harbor Triangle, Whittier
(907) 472-2549

Here's a great place to enjoy distinctive cuisine while taking in the million-dollar view. With its cozy seaside-cottage atmosphere, the Orca caters to an eclectic group of travelers, including outdoor enthusiasts, Europeans, and families on day trips from Anchorage. Popular menu items include the fresh, wild, grilled halibut and salmon; the Euro Sandwich with Brie, roasted garlic mayo, and tomato; and the Glacier Burger with bacon and blue cheese. All seafood is grilled, not deep-fried, and they bake most of their own pastries. The Orca offers up espresso and pastries for breakfast as well as a full lunch and dinner menu. There's counter and take-out service only, with great seating on the sunny deck overlooking the ocean. No reservations are necessary, and

there's ample parking out front. The restaurant is wheelchair accessible, and it's open only during the summer season.

VARLY'S SWIFTWATER SEAFOOD $$
Business Harbor Triangle, Whittier
(907) 472-2550
home.gci.net/~akvarly/

For hand-battered seafood in a waterfront setting, Varly's is the place. Fries come with the deep-fried shrimp, fish, and halibut, and for landlubbers the menu includes cheeseburgers, chicken sandwiches, and chicken strips. If deep-fried food isn't your thing, try the Peel & Eat Shrimp, the crab cakes, or homemade clam and seafood chowders. Varly's also serves homemade desserts. On Friday and Saturday nights, check out their Smoked Prime Rib Dinner with red potatoes, corn on the cob, coleslaw, and a roll with butter. Wine and beer, including specialty and import lagers, are available. The cafe is open seasonally for lunch and dinner.

Attractions

Throughout the Prince William Sound, you'll find most attractions offer insight into the biggest attraction of all, the great outdoors. Expect limited hours in the off-season and a fair number of tourists during the summer.

Price Codes

$................... Less than $5
$$ .... $5–$10
$$$ $10–15
$$$$ .... More than $15

> ℹ️ For shopping in Whittier, check out the Triangle near the harbor. You'll find fresh fudge at Sound Ideas Gallery and Gifts, local carvings at Log Cabin Gifts, and fresh fish at Fee's Custom Seafoods.

ALASKA WILDLIFE CONSERVATION CENTER $$

Mile 79 Seward Highway
(907) 783-2025
www.awcc.org

A popular, affordable stop for both independent travelers and tour buses headed to Portage, the Alaska Wildlife Conservation Center offers an opportunity to see that elusive moose or bear in outdoor settings resembling their natural habitats. And it's not just big game that you'll see—dozens of other species benefit from this nonprofit effort to rehabilitate injured or orphaned animals while educating visitors in the 140-acre wildlife park. Admission fees are reasonable, and proceeds go toward supporting the continued efforts on behalf of the animals. Don't expect a whole lot here—you'll see more animals at the Alaska Zoo—but it's a good cause. Special rates for military, seniors, and youth.

BEGICH, BOGGS VISITOR CENTER

Portage Valley Rd., Portage
(907) 783-2326
www.fs.fed.us/r10/chugach/chugach_pages/bbvc.html

This impressive visitor center, operated by the U.S. Forest Service, is definitely worth a stop. A walk through the exhibits mirrors a walk through Portage Valley and down to the Sound. Listen to calls of area wildlife, including cranes, wolves, fox, raven, and ptarmigan, or check out the narratives told by the human inhabitants of Prince William Sound. Kids, as well as the young at heart, will love the spotting scopes that let them see like a bee, and an otter, and a deer. There's even a black cushioned ice worm replica that's large enough to straddle, if you're so inclined. There are great interpretive programs and a Forest Ranger Academy for kids. Guided hikes include the Ice Worm Safari, the Moraine Trail Hike, and the Williwaw Hike. Admission is free, and the center is open daily in the summer. Receding Portage Glacier can no longer be seen from the visitor's center, but for $29 you can take a guided boat tour to the glacier, weather permitting—see our listing

for Grayline of Alaska in the following section on Parks, Recreation, and Tours.

Parks, Recreation, and Tours

The tiny town of Whittier is surrounded by the majestic Chugach National Forest, the second-largest national forest in the country. For information on the trails and recreation within Chugach National Forest, visit the forest service yurt at the West Boat Launch Ramp, or the Begich, Boggs Visitor Center (see the previous Attractions section). If you'd like guided recreation, there are several tour companies to assist you during the summer season.

GRAYLINE OF ALASKA

745 West Fourth Ave., Anchorage
(907) 277-5581, (800) 544-2206
www.graylinealaska.com

Grayline offers all sorts of water-related tour and charter options in Portage and Whittier, including one-hour cruises for $29 that will take you in for a close-up look at Portage Glacier and its dramatic calving ice. Cruises leave from Portage Lake and are narrated by the U.S. Forest Service.

i For a unique guided backcountry adventure, check out the Alaska Railroad's Whistle Stop tour to Spencer Glacier. A Forest Service interpreter boards the train at the Portage Station and gets off with you to hike 1.5 miles each way to Spencer Glacier. Along the way you'll learn cultural and natural history while taking in the backcountry grandeur. For more information, call the Portage Station at (907) 783-3001 or visit www.alaskarailroad.com.

MAJOR MARINE TOURS

411 West Fourth Ave., Anchorage
(907) 274-7300, (888) 764-7300
www.majormarine.com

For a longer glacier cruise including an all-you-can-eat meal, depart from Whittier with Major Marine Tours. A Chugach National Forest interpreter will point out highlights on the five-hour cruise of Blackstone Bay, where you'll see 1,700-foot active glaciers, icebergs, and spectacular glacial terrain from multiple viewing decks. They'll even shut off the engines so you can hear the impressive cracking and calving of the ice.

PHILLIPS CRUISES TOURS
519 Fourth Ave., Anchorage
(907) 276-8023, (800) 544-0529
www.26glaciers.com

So you'd love to get out on the water but you're not sure how you'd do if it's rough? Check out Alaska's most popular day cruise, 26 Glacier Cruise with Phillips Cruises and Tours. Their high-speed catamaran, the *Klondike Express,* offers almost guaranteed smooth sailing. The boat features wide aisles, inside seating, large picture windows, a full-service saloon, and a snack bar. There's a view from every seat, and with the help of the friendly crew, you'll learn about the history and the wildlife of the area as you take in the scenery along College Fjord and in Barry Arm. This is a great way to get up close and personal for a glacial experience you'll not soon forget.

STARBOUND ALASKAN ADVENTURES
1241 West 27th Ave., Anchorage
(866) 764-7354
starboundalaskanadventures.com

If you're feeling really adventurous, try exploring the Sound aboard your own personal watercraft. StarBound will set you up with a dry suit, a personal watercraft, and a guide. It's not cheap, but they offer substantial discounts for groups.

Fishing

In Prince William Sound, you can enjoy world-class fishing while feasting your eyes on some of the most beautiful views in the state. Because of the limited road access to most parts of the Sound, you'll need to charter out by boat or floatplane to reach many of the hot spots. Expect to pay between $150 and $250 per angler for your charter, depending on the type and length of the trip.

In Whittier, you'll find good salmon fishing in bays and near the mouths of streams, with lots of pinks in July and silvers in August. Early in the summer, you can troll for a hatchery run of kings along the head of Passage Canal, and later in the season you'll find reds and chums around Esther Island. For shore fishing right in Whittier, wait until the September silver run. You may find some halibut in the waters close to shore, but the bottom drops fast and deep, so your best bet is to charter.

ALASKA GOOD TIME CHARTERS
(907) 373-7447
www.alaskagoodtimecharters.com

Spend three to six days sailing the pristine waters of the Sound aboard this outfit's 50-foot yacht, and you're bound to come home with some great fishing stories. Halibut, lingcod, rockfish, and salmon sharks are among the saltwater species you can pursue, and you also can fish for salmon in either salt or freshwater. Multi-day charters aren't cheap, but meals, lodging, tackle, bait, ice, and fish cleaning are included. Owner/captain David Pinquoch has decades of fishing experience in Alaska and can provide combination fishing/sightseeing or fishing/hunting packages, too. Single-day salmon charters or combo fishing and glacier tour trips are also available.

SEA MIST CHARTERS
(907) 472–2459
www.pwsoundcharters.com

Specializing in bottom fishing for halibut, rockfish, and lingcod, Sea Mist will take you out for 10 hours on the *M.V. Gold Runner,* their 28-foot Bayliner with heated cabin and marine head. All gear, tackle, and bait are provided, and the first mate will clean, filet, and bag your catch. Check in for your excursion at Quigley's Ice Cream Parlor on the waterfront in Whittier. Reservations are recommended.

Hiking and Camping

Once you've had your fill of water-based fun in Portage and Whittier, head for the hills around

Whittier on either the Horsetail Falls Trail, a 1-mile trail with views of the town and the canal, or the 2-mile Portage Pass Trail, which ends at Divide Lake and offers glacier views along the way. Access the Horsetail Falls Trail from Salmon Run Road, just past the Buckner Building. Access to the Portage Pass Trail begins at the U.S. Forest Service access road near the tunnel.

For overnight stays, try the campground near the parking area off Whittier Street or the overnight parking area at the Whittier end of the tunnel. Note, though, that there are no services at either location. For a more complete camping experience, there's the scenic Williwaw Campground at Mile 4.3 of the Whittier Access Road. Maintained by the U.S. Forest Service, Williwaw has 60 campsites with access to toilets, Dumpsters, water, fire pits, and picnic tables. Campfire programs and self-guided nature trails will enhance your stay. Williwaw is the only public campground in Southcentral Alaska that is open all winter. Nearby Black Bear Campground is smaller but equally nice. At Mile 1.7 of the access road, there's Portage Valley RV Park (907-783–3111, www.portagevalleyrvpark.com), a private facility with showers and rental cabins.

SEWARD

Seward is a quintessential Alaskan seaside town—not too trendy, not too big, but rich in history and spirited in its sense of community. It was a lot sleepier until the cruise ships swapped it into their itineraries in place of Valdez. Now there's plenty of activity, especially in the summer, and the locals have been scrambling to pull together a nice variety of services and activities to accommodate guests. It's a place with plenty of character, from the softball field with harbor views to the big tree downtown yard festooned with dozens of large, bright fishing buoys.

In 1791 Russian explorer Alexander Baranof took shelter from a storm in a bay he later named Resurrection after the Sunday of his misadventure. The town of Seward was established on that ice-free bay in 1903 to serve as an ocean terminus and supply center for the railroad. In 1910 the town became the starting point for the famed Iditarod Trail. The trail served as a mail route to Nome until 1924; much later, the Anchorage to Nome portion of the Iditarod Trail began playing host to one of the most famed dogsled races in the world. Like Whittier, Seward's port was an important staging area during World War II.

Seward is on the Kenai Peninsula, but it's a great jumping-off point for Prince William Sound, so that's the association most Alaskans make. From Seward, boats head out in two directions, some for fishing and recreation in the Sound, and some to tour the bays and coves of the Kenai Fjords National Park.

i Two big annual events in Seward are the Fourth of July Mount Marathon Race and the Silver Salmon Derby in August. Since 1915, hardy runners have been dashing up the 3,022-foot peak of Mount Marathon and back, posting record times of less than 45 minutes (see also the listing under July events). The fishing derby offers prizes for the heaviest salmon plus purses of up to $50,000 for catching specially tagged fish.

Getting Here, Getting Around

Driving to Seward on the scenic 127-mile Seward Highway (Route 9) is a real treat; with its soaring mountains and rushing streams, the U.S. Department of Transportation has designated the route a National Scenic Byway. You also can reach Seward via the Alaska Railroad, by small plane from Anchorage, and by the Alaska ferry MV *Tustumena*, which links Seward to Kodiak and Valdez.

Gather up visitor information by stopping at the Seward Chamber of Commerce Visitor Center at Mile 2 of the Seward Highway (907-224-8051, www.sewardak.org). It's open daily in the summer from 8 a.m. to 6 p.m. Another great resource is the Kenai Fjords National Park Visitor Center (907-224-3175, www.nps.gov/kefj) in the Small Boat Harbor; the street address is 1212 Fourth Avenue. You'll find a wealth of information there, including slide shows, interpretive programs, and a bookstore.

Accommodations

There's a nice variety of accommodations in Seward, from cabins along the waterfront to hotels near the harbor to a historic downtown hotel. Since there's a high volume of seasonal tourist traffic, make your reservations well in advance. These establishments are open year-round unless we state otherwise, and they accept major credit cards. We'll make specific mention of any that allow pets or smoking, along with any that have wheelchair access. Price ranges indicate the average cost of a room for two adults during the peak season.

Price Codes

```
$................ Less than $125
$$ .................$126–$175
$$$ .................$176–$225
$$$$ .......... More than $225
```

ABODE WELL CABINS $$
12672 Old Exit Glacier Rd.
(800) 478-3139
www.alaskadogsled.com

Not exactly in the doghouse, but you'll be pretty close at Abode Well Cabins, run by Iditarod veteran Mitch Seavey and family. Located just five minutes from town, six couples' cabins feature full private baths (yes, running water), spacious bedrooms and sitting rooms, minifridges, and private parking. Shared facilities include barbeque grills, picnic area, business center, laundry, kitchenette, and campfire area. There's also a family cabin that sleeps eight. Book early and you might get a free Iditarod Racing Kennel Tour (www.ididaride.com).

THE BEACH HOUSE $$$–$$$$
Lowell Point
(907) 362-2727, (907) 359-2727
www.beachhousealaska.com

Enjoy a private, home-style beach experience at one of two guesthouses at Lowell Point on Resurrection Bay. Each two-bedroom house has queen-size beds, a queen-size sofa bed, bath, and fully-furnished kitchen, so they're perfect for families or small groups. There's also an overflow (dry, as in no running water) cabin that sleeps three. The two-story cottages are just what you'd expect of beachfront hideaways, with weathered siding, comfortable quilt-topped beds, and lots of windows for soaking up the view. Beach access is across the street, where you might spot a bald eagle soaring or a salmon jumping in the bay. Take off out back, and you can hike up to Caines Head or out to Tonsina Point.

BOX CANYON CABINS $$–$$$$
31515 Lois Way
(907) 224-5046
www.boxcanyoncabin.com

Tucked away in the woods off Mile 3.5 of the Seward Highway, Box Canyon offers comfortable, handcrafted log cabins in a secluded forest setting complete with its own pond. Choose from two one-bedroom (sleeping four) and four pricier two-bedroom cabins (sleeping six), with twin-, full-, and queen-size beds. Vaulted ceilings and hardwood floors add charm to the newer cabins, or you can opt for a cozy 16-foot-by-18-foot "historic" unit. All include full kitchens, private baths, and phones. You'll feel right at home with a barbeque area, picnic area, satellite TV, Wi-Fi zone, laundry facility, games, books, and magazines for guests to enjoy.

BREEZE INN $$–$$$
303 North Harbor St.
(907) 224-5238, (888) 224-5237
www.breezeinn.com

Most of the 108 rooms at this modern motel and annex offer views of Resurrection Bay and/or Mount Marathon. Centrally located and within walking distance to galleries, boat charters, and shopping in the harbor area, the Breeze Inn also offers courtesy shuttles to the railroad depot, the cruise ship dock, and the Alaska SeaLife Center. There's an on-site restaurant featuring steaks and Alaskan seafood, a motel gift shop, and complimentary coffee in the lobby. All rooms have cable TVs with HBO, coffeemakers, alarm clocks, telephones with free local calling, and private baths. Smoking and wheelchair-accessible rooms are available on request. If you'd like a little pampering, choose one of the Jacuzzi suites.

CAMELOT COTTAGES $-$$
Mile 1.4 Salmon Creek Rd.
(907) 224-3039, (800) 739-3039
www.camelotcottages.com

For a bit of privacy away from the busloads of tourists, check out these charming, self-contained cottages just 10 minutes from downtown Seward. Tucked away in a natural woodland setting with gardens complementing the native foliage, you'll enjoy peace and quiet without sacrificing comfort. All cottages have private baths and kitchens with coffeemakers, microwaves, and minifridges. Gourmet coffee, tea, cocoa, oatmeal, dishes, and linens are provided. Guests also may use the on-site hot tub, laundry facilities, barbecue grills, and fish freezers. Your hosts will even share herbs from the gardens to go with your fresh-grilled fish. They also assist guests with reservations and recommendations for activities, as well as providing lists of recommended clothing and gear for all types of outdoor fun.

i Retired or active military? Check out the Seward Resort, offering motel rooms, town houses, a log cabin, and yurts as well as RV and tent camping. Laundry facilities, mountain bikes, fishing gear, and snowmachines also are available for guest use. For more information, call (907) 224-2659, (800) 770-1858, or visit www .sewardresort.com.

HOLIDAY INN EXPRESS SEWARD
HARBOR HOTEL $$$
1412 Fourth Ave.
(907) 224-2550, (877) 863-4780
www.hiexpress.com

Enjoy all the modern conveniences, including wireless Internet access, from a fabulous setting overlooking Seward's small boat harbor. Many of the 82 rooms have Resurrection Bay or Mount Marathon views, and some have private balconies. A picturesque boardwalk leads from the hotel to the dock and retail shops. Choose between a king-size bed or two queen-size beds in tastefully decorated rooms that include coffeemakers, hair dryers, irons, ironing boards, and telephones with free local calling. There's an on-site swimming pool, whirlpool, guest laundry, and business center. Start your day with the free continental breakfast, featuring the hotel chain's signature "Express Start" cinnamon rolls. Smoking rooms and wheelchair-accessible facilities are available.

MILLER'S LANDING $
13880 Beach Dr., Lowell Point
(907) 224-5739, (866) 541-5739
www.millerslandingak.com

You'll find a little bit of everything at Miller's Landing, from tent camping among century-old spruce trees to RV parking on the scenic oceanfront to full accommodation cabins with such seaworthy names as the Admiral's Cottage. They also have economy rooms and "camping cabins" (dry cabins—no running water). Miller's Landing offers a full Prince William Sound experience, with bald eagles soaring overhead, sea otters playing in the surf, and Stellar sea lions floating in the water. Accommodations lean toward the rustic and it's more crowded here than some would like, but there's wireless Internet available, and the full-service cabins have full kitchens and baths. There's great hiking nearby, and Miller's offers scheduled water-taxi service around Resurrection Bay and Aialik Bay, including Northwestern Fjord. In fact, you can take advantage of all sorts of ocean-based opportunities at Miller's, including kayak

i You can rent one of 17 remote cabins through the Seward Ranger District (907-224-3374, 877-444-6777, www.fs.fed .us/r10/chugach/cabins/index.html). Cabins have an oil stove or woodstove, bunks, and outhouse facilities. Drinking water is not provided, and cabins are accessed by hiking trails and/or floatplane.

rentals, tours, and lessons; motorboat rentals; and beach or charter boat fishing. Miller's Landing is pet friendly, and they offer early-bird discounts for reservations made before April 1.

KENAI LAKE RESORT $$
27121 Seward Highway
(907) 288-5059, (877) 288-5059
www.kenailakeresort.com
If you're looking for an Alaskan-style getaway, Renfro's offers 30 acres of recreation and relaxation along the shores of Kenai Lake. Nestled in the Chugach Mountains, this picturesque retreat includes five lakefront cabins and four with lake access; rates vary by size and location of the unit. Each features a loft, bath with on-demand hot water heater, kitchen with stove and refrigerator, and private porch. Every log cabin has a queen-size bed in addition to various configurations for additional sleeping. Guests have access to on-site telephone, iron/ironing board, paddle-boats, playground, and laundry facilities. Porta-cribs are available on request. Limited housekeeping is provided, with fresh towels, trash pickup, and coffee basket refills daily. Ten RV sites also are available.

PADDLE INN $$$
Lowell Point Rd.
(907) 362-2628
www.alaskapaddleinn.com
If you like the idea of staying on the ocean just a few miles from town but would rather put some distance between yourself and the crowds at Miller's Landing, travel a short distance down the beach drive and you'll find a little haven of rest at Alaska Paddle Inn. Hosts Alan and Allison Heavirland are avid kayakers who opened their little inn in 2008. Choose from an upper and lower suite in the property's guest house. Both feature large bathrooms, kitchenettes, private entrances, fireplaces, hearty continental breakfasts, and terrific ocean views. You'll have to climb stairs to reach the upper unit, where a full living room with vaulted ceiling is your reward. Upstairs sleeps two, downstairs sleeps four.

SALMON BAKE CABINS $
Mile 2 Exit Glacier Rd.
(866) 541-5749
www.sewardalaskacabins.com
Cute, comfy, close to town—and the price is right. No ocean views here, and don't expect a wilderness experience, but if you're looking for affordable digs (with running water) Salmon Bake Cabins can help. Each sleeps up to four adults and comes with kitchenette and cable television. Pets are welcome, and there's freezer space for stashing all those fish you caught. Didn't catch any? Dine at the adjacent Exit Glacier Salmon Bake (see our listing under Restaurants in the next section).

SEWARD WINDSONG LODGE $$$$
Mile 3.7 Seward Highway
(907) 224-7116, (877) 777-4079
www.sewardwindsong.com
If you're looking for an Alaskan-lodge experience on the Sound, the Seward Windsong fits the bill. From the log and wood exterior to the Alaskan-themed rooms to the off-the-beaten-path location, this Alaska Heritage Tours property offers comfort and style with a wilderness touch. Mountain peaks and the nearby Resurrection River form the backdrop for 108 guest rooms, a lounge, on-site restaurants with a large selection of microbrews on tap, and meeting facilities. Each room has a private exterior entrance and features full bath, coffeemaker, TV/VCR with free movies, telephone with dataport, and hair dryer. For family accommodations, check out the deluxe suites with kitchenettes and Jacuzzi tubs. Children younger than age 11 stay free. The lodge offers complimentary shuttle service to local activities, with a full tour desk to help you plan your adventures. Wheelchair access is available. Owned and operated by Alaska Heritage Tours (expect tour group traffic).

VAN GILDER HOTEL $$
308 Adams St.
(907) 224-3079, (800) 204-6835
www.vangilderhotel.com
There's lots of character at the Van Gilder, a

Seward landmark that was built in 1916 and joined the National Register of Historical Places in 1980. Step into turn-of-the-century charm with brass beds, period antiques, an Alaskana book collection, and historic photo displays. Along with the nostalgia, you'll enjoy such modern conveniences as private baths, cable TVs, and in-room telephones. Considered one of the finest buildings in Alaska when it was first constructed, the white and maroon stucco-fronted hotel has hosted scruffy miners, upscale law-firm employees, and even President Harding's territorial executives. If you're not easily spooked, book the Fanny's Ghost Suite. Located 2 blocks from the Alaska SeaLife Center and the Seward Museum, the hotel is convenient to downtown restaurants and shopping. Choose from View Suites, View Rooms, Standard Rooms, and Pension Rooms. The hotel is open year-round.

Restaurants

Given the growing numbers of hungry tourists in the summer, there aren't a whole lot of restaurants in Seward, but you'll still find some nice options. These eateries accept major credit cards and reservations unless otherwise stated, and you can assume daily, year-round service. We'll make a special note if the facility is wheelchair accessible. Price categories reflect the average cost of dinner for two, excluding drinks, tip, and dessert.

Price Codes

$.................. Less than $15
$$ .... $15–$25
$$$ .... $26–$40
$$$$ .... More than $40

APOLLO RESTAURANT $$$
229 Fourth Ave.
(907) 224-3092
www.apollorestaurantak.com
For Greek and Italian cuisine plus Alaskan seafood and charbroiled steaks, check out the Apollo Restaurant in downtown Seward. They offer fine dining in an eclectic atmosphere, featuring homemade pizza and their own custom-smoked salmon. They'll even cook up the fresh fish you haul in from your day out on the ocean. Specialties include Halibut Calabreze, Halibut and Salmon Monte Mio, Athenian Chicken, Italian Scampi, gyros, and Musaka. Enjoy a full selection of beer, wine, and specialty desserts with your meal. There's good parking out front, and the restaurant is wheelchair accessible. The folks at the Apollo are used to people calling from all over saying how much they enjoyed their meal and requesting recipes.

CHINOOKS WATERFRONT $$$$
1404 Fourth Ave.
(907) 224-2207
www.chinookswaterfront.com
At the north end of the small boat harbor, Chinooks offers fine dining with a superb view. Specializing in fresh seafood, pasta, and steaks, Chinooks also has a full wine list and a brewpub featuring Alaskan ales. Try their Seafood Sauté, a blend of Alaskan crab, mussels, salmon, halibut, and prawns in a sauce of white wine, garlic, and butter, served with vegetables over a bed of steaming rice. Another favorite is the Pepper-Seared Salmon, a fresh filet coated with cracked pepper and topped with a homemade dill sauce. Chinooks is open from 11:30 a.m. to 10 p.m. seven days a week during the summer season. They offer wheelchair access and have their own parking lot.

EXIT GLACIER SALMON BAKE
RESTAURANT $$
¼ Mile Exit Glacier Rd.
(907) 224-4752
www.sewardalaskacabins.com
Here's a restaurant and pub that doesn't take itself too seriously, advertising "cheap beer and lousy food." In actuality, the Salmon Bake is a fun Alaskan-style establishment complete with wood timbers and a stone fireplace in a quiet forest setting. On the menu you'll find fresh Alaskan salmon, red snapper, and halibut along with burgers and steaks. On tap, they have a large selection of Alaskan microbrews, including Alaskan Amber,

Moose's Tooth, and Glacier Brewhouse Blonde. There's also a nice selection of wines. The Salmon Bake is open only in the evenings, daily during the summer and on weekends during the winter. The restaurant is wheelchair accessible, and reservations are not accepted.

LE BARN APPETIT $$$
11786 Old Exit Glacier Rd.
(907) 224-8706
Boasting its own Belgian chef, this inn, eatery, and health food store offers full breakfast, lunch, and dinner menus featuring some of the best crepes in the state. For breakfast, try eggs your way, served with homemade bread and jams; a three-egg build-your-own omelet; or specialties including eggs Benedict, Crème Beef, crepes, and Belgian waffles. The lunch menu features a variety of soups, sandwiches, and crepes as well as pizzas and salads. For dinner, choose from traditional entrees such as smoked or steamed fish, barbequed ribs, or chicken cordon bleu, or sample their cultural entrees, including Mexican, Italian, and Asian dishes. Dessert choices include Belgian chocolate eclairs, crème custard, Franchi Pan, or Belgium apple pie. Alcohol is not served, but you can enjoy a variety of espresso beverages with your meal, including rich Belgian hot cocoa.

SMOKE SHACK $$
411 Port Ave.
(907) 224-7427
In the unlikely setting of a World War II vintage railroad car, the Smoke Shack serves up homemade vegetarian and barbeque to a host of loyal fans. Try the pulled pork sandwich, the breakfast burrito, or the French toast. And jalapeno orange barbeque sauce—yum. Obviously it's nothing fancy or trendy, just fun.

YOLY'S BISTRO $$$
220 Fourth Ave.
(907) 224-3295
www.yolysbistro.com
A fabulous find in downtown Seward, Yoly's offers one of the most innovative menus around.

Start off with Coconut Duck Satays with Taramind Sauce, followed by Yoly's signature salad with candied walnuts, fresh tomato, strawberries, and mandarin oranges. For lunch there's hearty fare like the Johnny Cash (double patties with melted Swiss and caramelized onions on ciabatta). Bistro dinners feature steak and fresh seafood artfully prepared with Pacific Asian flair. Open daily for lunch and dinner.

Shopping

There aren't any big malls or department stores in this little seaside town, but you'll find some fun gift shops and galleries for browsing and buying. Most of these are within walking distance of the small boat harbor or the historic downtown district.

BARDARSON STUDIO
1317 Fourth Ave.
(800) 354-0141
www.bardarsonstudio.com
Follow the waterfront boardwalk to Bardarson's, where you'll find a gallery filled with Alaskan art, posters, reproductions, and handcrafted gift items. The studio showcases the colorful Northwest art of Seward watercolorist Dot Bardarson along with other limited-edition work by artists from around the state. When you tire of shopping, relax on their sunny deck and enjoy the flowers, music, and seaside view.

BROWN AND HAWKINS
209 Fourth Ave.
(907) 224-3011
www.sweetdarlings.com
Brown and Hawkins has been outfitting Alaskans since 1900; in fact, they claim to be the oldest family-owned retail establishment in the state. Choose from a large selection of brand-name outdoor clothing, or browse the huge selection of Alaskan-made gifts and souvenirs, including ivory, jade, and gold keepsakes. While you're there, check out the old bank vault and turn-of-the-century cash register, and sample some of the fresh fudge, bark, brittle, saltwater taffy, and truffles made on-site. There's even an old-

fashioned soda fountain featuring real Italian gelato and other treats.

THE TRAIN-WRECK MINI-MALL
11 Port Ave.
You're shaking your head, thinking *only in Alaska.* Formerly known as the Harbor Train Station, this "mini-mall" near the Alaska Railroad Station consists of four cast-off World War II–era train cars housing the Smoke Shack Restaurant (see our previous listing under Restaurants), Alyeska Mountain Bike Sports, Whistle Stop Lodging, Exit Glacier Guides, and Quarter Deck Charters. Even if you're not in the market for any of these goods and services, it's worth a stop just to see what passes for a mall in Alaska.

Attractions

The waterfront and all of its adjunct activities are the primary attraction in Seward, as they are throughout the Prince William Sound. Still, there are a couple of great places to get your bearings and learn more about the history and natural wonders of the land and water around Seward.

Price Codes

$.................Less than $5
$$ .... $5–$10
$$$ $11–15
$$$$ .... More than $15

ALASKA SEALIFE CENTER $$$$
301 Railway Ave.
(907) 224-6300, (800) 224-2525
www.alaskasealife.org
SeaWorld it's not, but the Alaska SeaLife Center fulfills an important role in research, education, and wildlife rehabilitation. Open since 1998, the center is a popular stop for tour groups and cruise ship off-shore outings. You'll see Stellar sea lions, harbor seals, octopus, and seabirds in naturalistic settings, along with the standard fish behind glass. Youngsters, and the young at heart, enjoy the touch tanks, where they can gently fondle sea urchins, star fish, and the like. Live cam footage from a Stellar sea lion rookery 35 miles from

Seward lets you get a look at the daily activities of these large mammals, including the birthing of pups in the spring. The center is wheelchair accessible. Ask at the ticketing desk about daily feedings, lectures, tours, and special presentations. This is Seward's landmark attraction, but some visitors walk away wondering what all the fuss (and the hefty admission price) was about.

THE SEWARD MUSEUM $
336 Third Ave.
(907) 224-3902
Operated by the Resurrection Bay Historical Society, this small museum provides a glimpse into Seward's past, dating from 1793, when the Russians operated a shipyard on the bay. Highlights include an exhibit on artist Rockwell Kent, who wintered on Fox Island in 1918, as well as a collection of native baskets. You'll also discover Seward's ongoing role in transportation, from the early days of the Iditarod Trail to the establishment in 1903 of a railroad terminus. There's a popular exhibit on the 1964 earthquake, a 9.2 shaker that set fire to oil storage tanks along Resurrection Bay and killed 12 people in Seward. The museum is open daily from 9 a.m. to 5 p.m. in the summer.

Parks, Recreation, and Tours

Surrounded by the majestic Chugach National Forest and the Kenai Fjords National Park, Seward offers a stunning array of recreational opportunities on both land and sea. The 607,000-acre Kenai Fjords National Park was formed by retreating glaciers of the spectacular Harding Ice Field, accessible by a 7-mile uphill climb from the foot of Exit Glacier. This is a truly amazing hike but quite steep. Flightseeing to the ice field is another option. Check with Scenic Mountain Air (907-288-3647, 800-478-1449, sma.pictoris.net/index.php?option=com_frontpage&Itemid=1) or ERA Helicopters (907-224-8012, 800-843-1947, www.flyera.com) for flight-seeing options.

A visit to Exit Glacier is a popular park attraction. Stop at the Exit Glacier Nature Center at the end of Exit Glacier Road, off Mile 3.7 of the Seward Highway, and from the parking lot you can walk a half-mile to the glacier. The first quarter-mile of the path is paved. Pay attention to the warning signs when you reach the glacier, as the ice is notoriously dangerous and unpredictable. Ranger-guided hikes are an option in the summer.

The best way to see the park's ample marine life, including sea otters, porpoises, sea lions, whales, and harbor seals, is by charter or tour boat. Check with Kenai Fjord Tours (907-777-2800, 877-777-4051, www.kenaifjords.com) for cruises of three to five hours that feature wildlife and glacier viewing. Land/cruise packages are also available. Major Marine Tours (907-224-8030, 800-764-7300, www.majormarine.com) offers half-day and full-day cruises with heated cabin seating, buffet-style meals, and narration by a Kenai Fjords National Park ranger. Birders will enjoy cruising to the Chiswell Islands, sporting prime habitat for some of the park's 100,000 nesting birds.

i Take a walking tour of nine Registered National Historic Landmarks, including the Diversion Tunnel and St. Peter's Episcopal Church. Pick up maps at the Van Gilder Hotel at 308 Adams Street or take the Virtual Tour online at www.sewardak.org/visit/historic-tour.htm.

Three public-use cabins are available within the park for summer use by reservation only. These are remote cabins with no running water and limited access by water or air. Check with the Alaska Public Lands Information Center (907-271-2737) for information and reservations. Limited beach camping is also available, but boaters should be aware that much of the coastline is owned by Native corporations, and campers must have permits. To check on Native holdings and to acquire permits, call (907) 284-2212.

For a glimpse into the recent past enhanced by the natural beauty of the oceanfront, check out the abandoned World War II fort at Caines Head State Recreation Area. To get to the site, you'll have to travel by boat or hike four hours from Tonsina Point at low tide; because of the

tides, you'll have to stay 12 hours if you walk in. You'll find campsites and latrines at Tonsina Creek, about halfway to Caines Head. Be sure to take a flashlight so you can explore the underground passages and rooms at the abandoned fort. For more information, contact the Kenai Peninsula state parks office at (907) 262-5581 or visit dnr.alaska.gov/parks/units/caineshd.htm.

If off-shore exploration sounds like fun, try kayaking or sailing in Resurrection Bay. A recent issue of *Sail* magazine named Seward one of the top 10 places to sail, thanks to its daily 15- to 20-knot winds. Check with the folks at Sailing, Inc. (907-224-3160, www.sailinginc.com) or Alaska Sailing Tours (907-224-4363, 907-229-7245, www.alaskasailingtours.com) for details on sailboat charters. On calmer days you can rent a kayak or, if you're a novice, join a guided kayak tour of the bay. Try Kayak Adventures Worldwide (907-224-3690, www.kayakak.com), Liquid Adventures (907-224-9225, 888-325-2925, www.liquid-adventures.com), or the activities staff at Miller's Landing (see the previous listing under Accommodations) for a variety of floating options.

To get up close and personal with the landscape, try a two-hour horseback ride with Brady's Trail Rides (907-224-7863, www.sewardhorses.com). Horseback riders travel beside the river to the bay, through parts of old-town Seward that were destroyed by the 1964 earthquake, often spotting bald eagles overhead. For a real Alaskan adventure, you can travel the country by dogsled, even in the summer. Iditarod veteran Mitch Seavey and family at Iditaride Sled Dog Tours (800-478-3139, www.ididaride.com) will harness up your wheeled sled for a two-mile ride and tour of their kennels. If you're looking for a taste of winter in July, Godwin Glacier Dog Sled Tours (907-224-8239, 888-989-8239, www.alaskadogsled.com) will transport you by helicopter onto Godwin Glacier, where a dog team waits to pull your sled across the ice. There are no minimum fitness requirements, and the adventure is wheelchair friendly. Godwin's also offers cross-country ski tours and glacier walks along with custom helicopter flight-seeing packages.

For more information about recreational activities in the Seward area, check out the Seward Chamber of Commerce Web site at www.sewardak.org, the Kenai Fjords National Park Web site at www.nps .gov/kefj, and the Chugach National Forest Web site at www.fs.fed.us/r10/chugach.

Hiking and Camping

You'll find plenty of hiking opportunities in the Seward area. Under the jurisdiction of the Chugach National Forest, there's the Resurrection River Trail, accessed from Mile 8 of the Exit Glacier Road. Follow the trail for 6 miles to a forest service cabin; expect some wet and rough spots, but mostly a level hike. The Lost Lake/Primrose Trail is a steep but scenic 15-mile trek beginning at Mile 5 of the Seward Highway and ending at Mile 17. For a shorter hike, try the Grayling Lake Trail, covering 2 miles and beginning at Mile 13.2 of the Seward Highway. Other forest service trails include the 7.5-mile (one-way) Ptarmigan Creek Trail, the 23-mile Johnson Pass Trail, and the 3.3-mile Carter Lake Trail. For maps and information, stop by the Seward Ranger District office at 334 Fourth Avenue (907-224-3374).

If you're looking for a challenge, you can check out the Mount Marathon Trail, which rises 3,022 feet from the trailhead off Lowell Canyon Road. Warning: Mount Marathon is very steep. Even though it's the site of a mad rush to the top every Fourth of July (see our listing under July events), casual hikers have been known to panic, requiring rescue. For another noteworthy trek, follow the Iditarod National Historic Trail, beginning at the Founders' Monument on Ballaine Boulevard and picking up again 2 miles down Nash Road and again at Bear Lake. Once you leave the confines of town, this historic trail becomes rugged, and you should be prepared to cross some streams. If you like your hikes light, check out the Two Lakes Trail, accessed from behind the Alaska Vocational Technical Center.

Within the Chugach National Forest, there are several campsites near Seward. At Mile 17

of the Seward Highway, you'll find the Primrose Campground, with 10 sites. The Ptarmigan Creek Campground at Mile 23 is a great place to see red salmon in season. There's also the newly improved Trail River Campground at Mile 24 of the Seward Highway, offering 63 sites and berry picking later in the summer.

BEAR CREEK RV PARK
33508 Lincoln St.
(907) 224-5725, (877) 924-5725
www.bearcreekrv.com
Within walking distance of the rushing waters of Bear Creek, this family-owned RV park offers a full range of services in a picturesque Alaskan setting. They have both full and partial hookups, private restrooms and showers, cable TV, a dump station, pay phone, and laundry facility. Retail services include a convenience store, video rentals, and a liquor store. Relax and swap fishing stories at LynDav's Water Hole, a bar with a big-screen TV. Lynn and Dave also will book your tours and fishing trips, including van service to activities arranged through them. There's even a mechanic just around the corner.

STONEY CREEK RV PARK
13760 Leslie Place
(907) 224-6465, (907) 235-8741
www.stoneycreekrvpark.com
Six miles north of Seward, flanked by majestic mountains, you'll find this comfortable RV park along Stoney Creek. Their 30-foot sites can handle even big rigs. All campsites come with power, water, and satellite TV hookups. Many sites have sewer and phone jacks as well. Fire pits are available along the creek. You'll have your choice of 81 sites on 15 acres. They also offer laundry and shower facilities, phone and Internet services, a hospitality room, courtesy shuttle service to Seward, and even doggy day care.

Fishing

For road-accessible freshwater fishing along the Seward Highway, try for Dolly Varden in Salmon Creek (Mile 5.9), Grouse Lake (Mile 7.4), Golden

Fin Lake (Mile 11.3), and Trail River (Mile 24.1). You'll also find grayling at (where else?) Grayling Lake (Mile 13.2), as well as rainbow trout at Vagt Lake (Mile 25.2) and Carter Lake (Mile 33.1).

From either Whittier or Seward, you can access great ocean fishing at Knight Island Passage and Montague Strait. Surf casters may see some action at Knight Island, but the folks in boats catch most of the fish. Halibut in the passage are plentiful but not huge, and salmon run there seasonally. Feeder streams offer up trout and char.

Montague Strait and Montague Island are farther out and more susceptible to bad weather than Knight Island, but some of the best bottom fishing in Alaska is found there, and it's a regular salmon highway in season. Much of Alaska's trophy halibut catch comes from Montague, and there are abundant rockfish and lingcod as well. In the island streams, you may find some Dolly Varden and cutthroat trout, but not many salmon. Your best bet if you're land-bound is to surf cast for salmon at the mouths of the streams, or to have a charter plane drop you off on the beach so you can fish the productive Nellie Martin-Patton River system. Montague can be reached from Valdez, but it's a longer haul than from Seward or Whittier.

AURORA CHARTERS
(907) 224-7230, (888) 586-8420
www.auroracharters.com
The folks at Aurora own four of their own vessels and partner up with eight others to give you a wide range of options for your sport-fishing charter. Choose from half-day, full-day, and combo packages for lingcod, salmon, and halibut. If you have nonanglers in your group, Aurora offers a combo fishing and sightseeing charter to keep everyone happy. Aurora also offers special off-season and active-military rates.

THE FISH HOUSE
(907) 224-3674, (800) 257-7760
www.thefishhouse.net
Believe it or not, this family-owned and -operated charter business (since 1973) brokers 60 Coast Guard–licensed boats, with either full-day or half-day trips for salmon or halibut. Combo and custom packages also are available. Beginners are welcome, and there's sure to be great wildlife viewing along with the hot fishing action. If you like, you can make your reservations online.

VALDEZ

Whittier might have been the U.S. Army's secret during World War II, but Valdez is Alaska's little secret. Abandoned by cruise ships a few years ago and left for residents and independent travelers to enjoy at their leisure, it's a friendly little town with stunning mountain and ocean vistas and a wealth of outdoor activities. Alaskans from the state's landlocked interior think nothing of driving eight hours each way to spend the weekend in Valdez—that's how lovely it is.

It's not as if the rest of the world has never heard of Valdez. The famous 1964 earthquake wiped out a big chunk of the original town, and what survived was moved a few years later. Then there was the infamous Exxon Valdez oil spill in 1989, when a tanker named *Valdez* ran aground as it was leaving the port of Valdez, causing an oil spill that took millions of dollars to clean up. Many visitors don't get to Alaska's "Little Switzerland" because it's a good day's drive each way, off the Denali Park–Anchorage–Kenai Peninsula loop.

What they're missing is a resilient little town of about 4,000 residents that plays host to both industry and nature. Down past Allison Point, Alyeska Pipeline Service Company operates the terminal facility for the Alaska Pipeline (closed to the public), with nine million barrels of storage and 400 tankers docking there each year. Spill prevention is now a top priority for the company, for while Alyeska rules the economic front, it's the wildlife and scenic beauty that are the real calling cards of Valdez. You'll know you're headed somewhere special as you drive in on the Richardson Highway, flanked on both sides by rugged peaks, roaring waterfalls, rushing creeks, and glacial ice dotting the mountaintops like icing. Pull into town, and the harbor stretches out before you, promising all sorts of water-related fun, from glacier cruises to deep-sea fishing to paddling among the sea otters and eagles.

Tucked at the end of a stunning fjord, where the purple peaks of the Chugach Mountains meet the ocean, Valdez was first established as an entry point to the Klondike during the 1898 Gold Rush, though for logistical reasons it was soon abandoned. The treacherous Valdez Trail was eventually ditched in favor of a route through Thompson Pass, a sled and wagon road that brought a new wave of development to Alaska's interior. Copper followed gold, but even after that boom ended, Valdez hung on as the most northerly ice-free port in the hemisphere, a perfect place to drop off cargo bound for the state's vast landlocked regions.

Getting Here, Getting Around

If you're heading to Valdez from Anchorage, you'll take the Glenn Highway east to Glennallen, then head south on the Richardson Highway. Expect a travel time of about six hours. From Fairbanks, it's a straight shot on the Richardson Highway, more or less following the route of the old wagon road, about an eight-hour drive. Those big poles along the highway as you go through Thompson Pass? Those are so you can find the road in the winter, when an average of 27 feet of snow blankets the area around Valdez.

There's also small-plane service from Anchorage on Era Aviation (www.flyera.com), or you can take the state ferry from Cordova, Whittier, or Seward. Reservations are a must for the ferry, especially during the summer months; call the Alaska Marine Highway at (907) 835-4436 or visit www.dot.state.ak.us/amhs/index.shtml for more information.

Once you get to Valdez, you won't have any trouble finding your way around. It's a planned community, more or less, thanks to the big shaker back in 1964 that led the Army Corps of Engineers to decide that the whole town needed to be rebuilt on firmer ground. There's a little business district leading to and stretching along the waterfront and a parklike residential area nestled up against the mountains. You can walk to most attractions, restaurants, and shopping, but there's also taxi service if you need it.

Accommodations

Valdez offers a little bit of everything as far as accommodations go, from hotels to bed and breakfasts, many located in the downtown area and along the waterfront, within walking distance of just about everything. The only thing lacking is the abundance of private cabin rentals and public campgrounds available on the other side of the Sound.

Price ranges below indicate the average cost of a room for two adults during the peak season. Major credit cards are accepted at all the establishments shown here. Assume no smoking, no wheelchair access, and no pets unless we tell you otherwise. The 6 percent bed tax is not included in the prices quoted here.

Price Codes

$	Less than $125
$$	$125–$175
$$$	$175–225
$$$$	More than $225

BEST WESTERN VALDEZ HARBOR INN   **$$**
100 Fidalgo Dr.
(907) 835-3434, (888) 222-3440
www.valdezharborinn.com
Located right on the harbor, this newer hotel, built in 2002, features 88 comfortable rooms and an on-site restaurant, Alaska's Bistro, that's a favorite with locals (see our listing under Restaurants). From the tiled floor of the post-and-beam lobby to the large bistro windows that look out over the water, this modern facility is designed to fit in with the stunning landscape. Choose from king-size, queen-size, and double beds in rooms that have microwaves, refrigerators, and cable TVs with DVD players. Business rooms also have recliners, desks, and Internet access. Many units in the two-story, wood-sided hotel offer views of the boat harbor, the mountains, or the

small but vibrant downtown area. The Harbor Inn has workout and laundry facilities for guest use. Smoking rooms are available, and two rooms offer wheelchair access.

DOWNTOWN B&B INN $
113 Galena Dr.
(907) 835-2791, (800) 478-279
www.valdezdowntowninn.com
Nothing fancy here, but you'll find clean, affordable rooms at the well-situated Downtown B&B Inn. It's a large building with a chalet-style exterior housing 31 rooms, and the accommodations are more like those of a small motel than a typical Alaskan B&B. Hosts Glen and Sharron Mills are longtime Alaskans who can give all kinds of advice about what to do and see in Valdez. Rooms include private baths, telephones, and cable televisions. There's a free continental breakfast in the motel-style dining room, featuring fresh fruit and juices, doughnuts, rolls, breads, assorted cereals, yogurt, hot chocolate, coffee, and tea. Guests can help themselves to hot beverages anytime. Some rooms have minifridges, microwaves, and balconies. The inn is centrally located, 1 block from the small boat harbor and within walking distance to shopping, restaurants, the town's museum, and the ferry. Some rooms offer wheelchair access, and pets are welcome.

KEYSTONE HOTEL $
117 Hazelet St.
(907) 835-3851, (888) 835-0665
www.keystonehotel.com
Housed in the sort of metal-sided building that Alaskans associate with the pipeline era, the Keystone offers 100 rooms with single, double, and king-size beds. It's a sort of plain-Jane, seasonal hotel that serves a complimentary continental breakfast of freshly baked rolls, muffins, and pastries along with juices, coffee, and tea. Each room has a private bath, color TV, and telephone. A laundry facility is available to guests. The hotel is within walking distance of the museum, the port of Valdez, the ferry terminal, fishing, shopping, and restaurants. Ask about their discounts

for senior citizens, military, Alaskan residents, and government employees. Guests may bring one dog, as long as it weighs less than 60 pounds. Four rooms are wheelchair accessible, and there are smoking rooms as well.

THE LAKE HOUSE $
Mile 6 Richardson Highway
(907) 835-4752
www.geocities.com/lakehousevaldez
Surrounded by the towering peaks of the Chugach Mountains, the Lake House gives you a chance to stay beyond the downtown area with only a 10-minute drive from Valdez. This large home sits on four acres overlooking Robe Lake, with several decks and balconies for wildlife viewing. Guests enjoy a bit of quiet, home-style privacy in the common areas, including a reading room, covered picnic areas, and a TV room with a large-screen television. There are six rooms with king- and queen-size beds; all have private baths. Feel free to prepare your dinner on the gas grills and indulge in yard games or the outdoor hot tub while taking in the grand view. You'll find a complimentary bottle of Lake House wine in your room at check-in, and you can help yourself to coffee and tea whenever you like. The complimentary breakfast includes juices, coffee, tea, muffins, bagels, fresh fruit, and six selections of cereal. There are cats on the premises.

MOUNTAIN SKY HOTEL AND SUITES $$$
100 Meals Ave.
(907) 835-4445, (800) 478-4445
www.mountainskyhotelsuite.com
Formerly part of the Alaska-based Aspen Hotel chain, this is the most modern-looking and largest option for overnight stays in Valdez. Choose from spa, family, and extended-stay suites. All 102 spacious rooms have coffeemakers, microwaves, refrigerators, TVs with VCRs, irons and ironing boards, hair dryers, and telephones with speaker features and dataports. Guests can relax in the pool with adjoining spa, work out in the exercise room, and keep up with their obligations at the hotel's business center. The complimentary continental

breakfasts feature Belgian waffles, and there's wireless Internet access throughout the hotel.

TOTEM INN HOTEL AND SUITES $$$
144 East Egan Dr.
(907) 835-4443, (888) 808-4431
www.toteminn.com

Family-owned and -operated since 1973, this is a genuine Alaskan hotel with an emphasis on customer service. Two 15-foot totem poles and a massive stone fireplace grace the lobby, in the company of full-size mounts of brown bear, Dall sheep, and a wolf. You'll find a variety of options among the 70 guest rooms. The hotel's Alaskan Suites offer private master bedrooms with washer/dryer, luxury linens, and television; in the living room, there's another television with DVD player. The suites also come with full kitchens, large corner windows, and free DSL Internet access. The Alaskan Cottages feature private porches, full kitchens, queen-size beds plus pull-out couches, and televisions with DVD players. Standard Deluxe rooms have queen-size beds, private baths, televisions with DVD players, coffeemakers, and minifridges. There's an on-site laundry, and the Totem Inn Restaurant is a local favorite for burgers, steaks, and seafood. Smoking rooms and wheelchair-accessible rooms are available, and pets are allowed in select rooms.

WILD ROSES BY THE SEA B&B RETREAT $$
629 Fiddlehead Lane
(907) 835-2930
www.alaskabytheseabnb.com

Offering casual elegance with contemporary Asian-Western ambience, Wild Roses by the Sea combines spectacular views with real Alaskan-style hospitality. Choose from the Canyon Suite overlooking Mineral Creek Canyon or the Sea View Room with views of the ocean and mountains. The Oceanview Guesthouse, with separate entry and full kitchen, offers even more privacy. Located 1.5 miles from Valdez on a wooded bluff overlooking Anderson Glacier and Valdez Bay, this is a great jumping-off point for enjoying the great outdoors. It's a five-minute walk to the creek and

1 mile to the ocean. Rooms come with private baths, cable televisions, jetted tubs, irons, and ironing boards. You'll be greeted with a dish of almonds and fruit upon check-in, and hot beverages are available all day in the dining room. For breakfast, there's fresh-baked pastry, fresh-baked bread, a platter of fresh-sliced fruit, juice, coffee, and a hot menu item. If you're lucky, you'll get to sample their ginger Belgian waffles made with 1899 sourdough starter and topped with vanilla yogurt, sliced bananas, and peaches.

Restaurants

There may not be a lot of restaurants to choose from, but you can't beat the fresh seafood and views that you'll find at most of these eateries. We'll let you know if reservations are needed or if the establishment is open only during the summer season. Assume no smoking and no wheelchair access unless we tell you otherwise. Price codes indicate the average cost of a dinner for two, excluding drinks, tip, appetizers, and dessert.

Price Codes

$	Less than $15
$$	$15–$25
$$$	$26–$40
$$$$	More than $40

ALASKA'S BISTRO $$$$
100 Fidalgo Dr.
(907) 835-5688
www.alaskasbistro.com

Take in spectacular ocean and mountain views while enjoying fine Mediterranean and American cuisine at Alaska's Bistro. They offer fine dining Alaskan-style, with white tablecloths and a selection of 265 wines contributing to the ambience. Among the favorites that have been on the menu since 1972 are Crab-Stuffed Halibut as well as Shrimp and Scallops in Saffron Cream Sauce. Pepe's World Famous Seafood Paella features fresh shrimp, local fish, peppers, and saffron rice cooked slowly and traditionally in a large, flat pan; order in advance, as preparation takes 40 minutes, and bring a friend, as there's a two-person minimum for paella. The bistro is open for breakfast, lunch, and dinner, and reservations are always appreciated; sometimes, they're a must. Parking is ample, and the restaurant is wheelchair accessible.

ALASKA HALIBUT HOUSE $$
208 Meals Ave.
(907) 835-2788
There's nothing fancy here, but for a quick breakfast or lunch, there's a nice selection of omelets, seafood, and sandwiches. Try the halibut basket, featuring four pieces of local Alaskan halibut, hand-dipped and deep-fried to perfection. There's also a Catch of the Day, a Combo Basket with prawns and halibut, and Alaska Salmon Wedges, with local boneless salmon breaded and deep-fried, in season. Scallops and clam strips round out the seafood options. For lunch, they offer a variety of burgers, including the Gold Digger, with a double patty, bacon, cheese, onion rings, and barbeque sauce. For healthier fare, sample the fresh salad bar.

BAD ASS COFFEE $
205 North Harbor Dr.
(907) 835-2340
Here's a place that will remind you of that house you shared with your friends in college, only better, because there's a bountiful supply of brownies and bars, espresso, and sandwiches you can order before retreating upstairs to enjoy the guitar, xylophone, comfy couches, television, stereo, and killer view of the harbor. There's even a large deck and barbeque grill up top. In short, this is a great place for the young and the young at heart to feel at home on the edge of Prince William Sound. Internet access is free with a purchase, but there's a 10-minute limit if others are waiting. You also can buy a box lunch to take on your next outdoor adventure.

MIKE'S PALACE RISTORANTE $$$
201 North Harbor Dr.
(907) 835-2365
A longtime local favorite, Mike's Palace Ristorante is one of those quintessential Alaskan establishments that serves up a little bit of everything. They have fresh Alaskan peel-your-own shrimp, fresh Copper River red salmon, fresh seafood fettuccine, and fresh king crab—all when they're in season, of course. For ethnic fare, there's a large selection of Italian entrees with veal and chicken, as well as a full menu of authentic pastas and pizzas. If Mexican food is more to your liking, sample the South-of-the-Border lunch and dinner specials, including Acapulco Shrimp and the Cinco-Cinco nacho platter. There's also a selection of light meals for smaller appetites. The atmosphere is a little of this and that, but it's close to the waterfront and there's a good crowd of locals to testify to the quality of the food.

Shopping

Valdez is hardly a shopping mecca, but you should be able to find what you need, plus a few things you don't, including souvenirs and Alaskan gifts.

HARBOR LANDING GENERAL STORE
320 South Meals Ave.
(907) 835-2331
Harbor Landing is the largest gift store in Valdez, featuring a big selection of Alaskan gifts, souvenirs, post cards, and shirts. For edible remembrances, they carry smoked salmon and Alaska Wildberry candies, jams, and teas. In the jewelry department you'll find jade, ivory, hematite, and gold nugget treasures. When you've worn yourself out from all that shopping, you can treat yourself at the espresso bar. Packing and mailing services are available.

VALDEZ PROSPECTOR
141 Galena St.
(907) 835-3858
www.prospectoroutfitters.com
If you want to shop where the locals do, the Prospector is the place, offering a modern version of the old-fashioned outfitters store. Packed into their large retail space, you'll find complete selections of everything you need for your outdoor adventures: fishing tackle, camping gear, name-

brand clothing, and sporting goods of all kinds. The Prospector is open seven days a week, and there's ample parking out front.

Attractions

For a small town, Valdez offers a nice variety of attractions focused mainly on the history and scenic beauty of the region. Thanks in part to the revenues generated by the pipeline terminus and port, admission to most attractions is either free, as indicated by the lack of price code in the listing, or a reasonable cost.

Price Codes

$....................Less than $5
$$ .... $5–$10
$$$ .... $11–$15
$$$$ .... More than $15

ALASKA CULTURAL CENTER $
300 Valdez Airport Rd.
(907) 834-1690
Prince William Sound Community College houses the small, eclectic Alaska Cultural Center, home of the Maxine and Jesse Whitney Museum. During 50 years of travel throughout Alaska, the Whitneys assembled the largest private collection of Alaskan Native art and artifacts in the world. Maxine Whitney's accounts of her Alaskan adventures along with her collections of ivory, fur clothing, beadwork, Eskimo dolls, masks, tools, and artifacts give visitors a glimpse of life from a not-so-distant era in the state's history. You'll also see trophy-class mounts of Alaskan mammals and full-size Eskimo kayaks and umiaks.

BRIDAL FALLS MILE
13.8 Richardson Highway
This spectacular waterfall in Keystone Canyon is a popular photo stop as you drive into Valdez, along with Horsetail Falls at Mile 12.8. There's interesting information on the Gold Rush on the interpretive plaque at the turnout. The trailhead for Valdez Goat Trail, a restored section of the military pack train trail that offered an alternate route to the dangerous gold rush trail over glacial

ice, is located here, too. The trail is 2 miles long, with a scenic overlook about a quarter-mile up.

CROOKED CREEK SALMON SPAWNING VIEWING AREA
Mile 0.9 Richardson Highway
The short drive from town to this small U.S. Forest Service information station is well worth making during July and August when the salmon are running. The poignant drama of salmon returning from the ocean, driven by an urge to spawn in the freshwater streams where they were born, plays out before your eyes. In season the stream is choked with these migrating fish in their final stages of life, their shapes deformed and colors distorted by their re-entry into freshwater. You'll see them hovering in schools, resting in eddies as they gather strength for the next leg of their journey upstream. If the prevailing odors of death and decay are too much, you can watch the underwater action from the live cam inside the Forest Service station. Across the highway at Duck Flats, you can watch nesting birds in the summer and migratory waterfowl in the spring and fall.

REMEMBERING OLD VALDEZ EXHIBIT $
436 South Hazelet St.
(907) 835-5407
The 1964 Good Friday earthquake, registering at 9.2 on the Richter scale and centered in Prince William Sound, destroyed the waterfront and killed 33 residents of Valdez. After the quake, the town was moved to a safer location 4 miles west of its original site. In a massive project that tapped the memories of those who lived in Old Valdez, a detailed, three-dimensional replica of the old town was built in a warehouse near the new waterfront, on a scale of 1 inch to 20 feet. You can walk between sections of the model while you listen with headsets to narration that goes building by building through the town as it was in 1963. Admission to the Valdez Museum includes admission to the "Remembering Old Valdez" exhibit. After you've caught a glimpse of how life once was in Old Valdez, you can drive

Close-up

Valdez Oil Spill

For those of us who were around in the 1980s, Valdez is almost synonymous with oil spill. All eyes were riveted on the waters of Valdez Arm after the *Exxon Valdez* ploughed into Bligh Reef on March 24, 1989, spilling an estimated 11 million gallons of crude oil. A massive clean-up effort involving 10,000 workers, 1,000 boats, and $2.1 billion followed.

Why did a tanker with an experienced crew run aground? The National Transportation Safety Board investigation concluded that a number of factors contributed to the accident, including a lack of effective escort services, an ineffective traffic system in the Sound, the failure of Exxon to provide a sufficiently supervised and rested crew, and the failure of the ship's captain to provide proper navigation watch. In a jury trial, Captain Joseph Hazelwood was found not guilty of operating a vessel under influence of alcohol, but he was fined $50,000 and sentenced to 1,000 hours of community service for the misdemeanor of negligent discharge of oil.

Thanks to the clean-up efforts and subsequent winter storms that gave the beaches a natural scrubbing, you won't find any obvious reminders of the spill when you visit Valdez today. But much has changed as a result of the accident. For one thing, spill prevention has become the number-one priority for the folks at Alyeska Pipeline Service Company. Tankers now have dike-lined enclosures with a capacity 15 percent greater than the tankers themselves. Three tugs follow every large tanker, with two tugs shuttling each smaller one. And two barges stand ready in the port with spill-response equipment. An act of Congress has prohibited the *Exxon Valdez,* now refurbished and renamed, from ever again entering Prince William Sound.

Along the 1,300 miles of impacted shoreline, it is estimated that 250,000 seabirds, 2,800 sea otters, 300 harbor seals, 250 bald eagles, and perhaps 22 orca whales died as a result of the spill. In addition, countless salmon and herring eggs were impacted. In the years following the incident, scientists have noted declines in the pink salmon population as well as increased mortality rates among ducks and sea otters, perhaps as a result of ingesting contaminated invertebrates. Mussel beds in particular may take decades to recover.

Exxon and the Exxon Valdez Oil Spill Trustees Council disagree over the lingering toxic effects of oil still buried in the Sound. Harlequin duck and otter populations have been especially slow to recover. And the Sound's small population of killer whales, dwindling before the spill, is expected to die off completely.

out to the old town site and marvel at how quickly and completely a town can rise and fall.

VALDEZ MUSEUM　　　　　　　　　　**$**
217 Egan Dr.
(907) 835-2764
www.valdezmuseum.org

With a nice variety of colorful exhibits, the Valdez Museum is a great place to get a feel for the roller-coaster history of this picturesque town. From the huge Hinchenbrook Lighthouse lens to the Pinson Bar restoration from the gold rush era, there

are all sorts of life-size exhibits that bring you back to the excitement of years gone by. You'll find out about such adventurers as Lillian Moore, one of 20 women who traveled the Valdez Trail to the Klondike, and Capt. W. R. Abercrombie, who led a relief expedition to stranded miners. Your walk through the history of Valdez includes sections on the area's original inhabitants, the Ahtna-Athabaskan Indians and the Chugach Eskimos, an interactive display on the construction of the Alaska Pipeline, and an overview of the Exxon Valdez oil spill. The museum is open year-round, with extended hours in the summer. Admission to the museum also covers admission to the "Remembering Old Valdez" exhibit a few blocks down the road.

WORTHINGTON GLACIER
Mile 28.7 Richardson Highway

This access point, maintained by the state park service, offers a great roadside opportunity to get up close and personal with the massive Worthington Glacier, a National Natural Landmark. You can view the glacier from the comfort of the paved parking area or climb the paved path, complete with interpretive plaques and benches, to get a closer look. The more rugged Ridge Trail also provides access to the glacier, but beware of falling ice, and remember that glacier walking should be attempted only by those with experience dealing with the hazardous ice and hidden crevasses.

Parks, Recreation, and Tours

Valdez is an adventurer's paradise, surrounded by accessible wilderness on both land and sea. Since most of the terrain goes up, recreation on dry ground primarily involves your own two feet, while watercraft opportunities include kayaking, rafting river rapids through the Keystone Canyon, and cruising Prince William Sound for a close-up look at Columbia Glacier.

ANADYR ADVENTURES
225 North Harbor Dr.
(907) 835-2814, (800) 865-2925
www.anadyradventures.com

For all sorts of adventures in and around Valdez, the friendly, knowledgeable folks at Anadyr are ready to help. From short kayaking tours for beginners to more extensive day trips that include hiking, wildlife viewing, beachcombing, kayak fishing, or single-person sailing, you'll find all sorts of great options with the oldest sea-kayaking business in Valdez. Their emphasis is on personal, intimate outdoor experiences at such destinations as Gold Creek, Shroup Glacier, and Columbia Glacier. All sorts of longer packages are available, too, including wilderness kayak camping, yacht-based tours, and lodge-based ecotours. They do their best to accommodate walk-ins, but advance reservations are recommended, especially in the peak of the season. Shoulder-season adventures in May and September, weather permitting, can be a lot of fun if you're not put off by the cool temperatures. Even if you're not heading out on the water, Anadyr's waterfront office is a fun stop, with an art gallery featuring Alaskan-made pottery and prints as well as an on-site masseuse.

H2O GUIDES ALASKA GLACIER TOURS
100 North Harbor Dr.
(907) 835-8418, (800) 578-4354
www.h2oguides.com

Stop by the H2O office and gift shop, located in the Best Western Harbor Inn, to book one of a variety of tours, including visits to nearby Worthington Glacier. You can choose from a one-hour interpretive Glacier Face Discovery Walk to full-day guided ice-climbing adventures. They also offer custom guided photography expeditions, as well as fishing, rafting, mountaineering, and flight-seeing adventures.

KEYSTONE RAFT AND KAYAK ADVENTURES
(907) 835-4638, (800) 328-8460
www.alaskawhitewater.com

If you're looking for a heart-thumping water-based adventure, check out these river-rafting options. You can float the Lowe River through the Keystone Canyon, snagging a close-up view of Bridal Veil Falls, or try a half-day white-water run on the Class IV rapids of the Tsaina River through both the upper and lower canyons. Another popular option is a six-hour run on the

i Each June, Valdez hosts the Last Frontier Theater Conference, where drama critics, playwrights, and theater lovers gather to talk shop and discover new talent. Pulitzer Prize winner Edward Albee founded the conference, which has been an annual event since 1993.

Class III and IV rapids of the Tonsina River, which includes a lunch stop and some time for rest and relaxation. Guides and equipment are provided, depending on the package.

PANGAEA ADVENTURES
101 North Harbor Dr.
(907) 835-8442
www.alaskasummer.com

Sea kayaking, backpacking, and multi-sport trips are among the specialties of this well-established outdoor adventure company. With an average guide ratio of one guide for every four guests, Pangaea strives for a personal, informative wilderness experience. They offer day tours for the novice as well as longer kayak camping options for the more rugged adventurer. Beyond the sea, choose from glacial hikes, river rafting, and mountain-backpacking packages. Experienced paddlers can rent kayaks by the day, and water-taxi service can be arranged for custom expeditions. Pangaea teams up with Stan Stephens Cruises to offer kayaking near the Columbia Glacier.

STAN STEPHENS GLACIER AND WILDLIFE CRUISES
(907) 835-4731, (866) 867-1297

In business since 1971, Stan Stephens is pretty much a household name in Alaska. Owners of the only Valdez-based cruise company operated by Alaskans, the Stephens family and their crew bring a personal touch to sightseeing on the Sound. Choose from 7-, 9-, and 10-hour family-friendly tours on a variety of comfortable boats. Along the way you'll learn about the human and natural history of Prince William Sound, with lots of chances to spot wildlife, including sea lions, sea otters, whales, porpoise, eagles, and puffins. All cruises make a stop at the dramatic Columbia Glacier, and all include a meal. Free shuttle service is provided between local RV parks and the harbor.

Hiking and Camping

On a sunny day in Valdez, there's nothing finer than getting out on one of the many local trails. Stop by the visitor information center and pick

i A visit to the McCarthy-Kennecott area makes a great two-day adventure from Valdez. Eighty-five miles north of Valdez, go east on the 34-mile Edgerton Highway (Route 10) and then another 59 miles on the very rough McCarthy Road. You'll have to park across the river from McCarthy, as public access is by footbridge only. From McCarthy, you can catch a shuttle to the abandoned Kennecott mill complex, once the highest-producing copper mine in the world and now a National Historic Landmark. For details, visit www.nps.gov/archive/wrst/kennecott.htm.

up the Valdez Trail Series brochures. There's a separate flyer for each trail, including a map, trail description, estimated hiking time, difficulty rating, distance, and safety advisories. All the brochures warn of sudden weather changes, and most warn of bears in the area, so take proper precautions.

For a short, easy walk, take the 0.75-mile Dock Point Trail, which begins just past the gate off Kobuk Drive, across from the boat ramp. The circular trail winds up a hill, then down to a meadow with viewing platforms that overlook Valdez Bay. Another fairly easy and rewarding hike is up the 1.75-mile Mineral Creek Trail. Flanked by mountains with cascading waterfalls, you'll trek up the hill until you reach the W.L. Smith Stamp Mill, dating from 1913. The 3.8-mile Solomon Gulch Trail begins at Allison Point on Dayville Road and climbs a steep hill before dropping into the gulch, which in 1915 was the site of an aerial tram used to transport copper.

BEAR PAW R.V. PARK
(907) 835-2530
www.bearpawrvpark.com

If you don't mind forsaking the forest for convenience, Bear Paw has a great location, right on Harbor Drive, so you can walk to just about everything. They offer both full and partial hookups, private showers and bath stalls, a dump station, and a coin-operated laundry with ironing facilities.

They also have a select number of "adult only" sites on the waterfront, with guest lounge, cable TV, and cable modem. Up Porcupine Hill, there's tent camping for adults as well. Bear Paw has a nice gift shop, and they'll help you book tours and even meet you at the ferry if you have reservations.

CAPTAIN JIM'S CAMPGROUNDS
(907) 835–2282
Captain Jim's operates both the Allison Point and Valdez Glacier facilities for the city. At oceanside Allison Point, a favorite salmon fishing spot at the end of Dayville Road, you'll find 70 campsites with public telephones and handicap access. The Valdez Glacier Campground on Airport Road offers 101 private campsites with fire rings, picnic tables, and free dump station. There's also a covered picnic area, drinking water, toilets, and room for 17 pullthroughs, all in a wooded spot with a natural waterfall.

EAGLE'S REST RV PARK
(907) 835-2373, (800) 553-7275
www.eaglesrestrv.com
Eagle's Rest is right in the middle of Valdez, and while the immediate scenery will be the pavement beneath you and your neighbor's RV next door, the whole town is surrounded by a panorama of mountains and water, so you'll still know you're in Alaska. They have 20-, 30-, and 50-amp plug-ins, unmetered hot showers, telephone and cable television hookups, a dump station, and a laundry facility. On-site, you'll also find an ATM machine, an e-mail station, a fish-cleaning table, and a walk-in freezer for stashing your catch. They offer full ticketing to tours and attractions, and there's gas and propane right next door.

Fishing

Fishing fanatics flock to Valdez every summer seeking all species of salmon, char, and halibut. The cold, gray-green waters of Valdez Arm are chock-full of pink and silver salmon at the peak of their runs. Valdez hosts three salmon derbies each season, with the Silver Salmon Derby in August offering a total of more than $65,000 in cash and prizes. Believe it or not, the silvers run so thick that the occasional fish has been known to jump into a boat or onto a dock. The Solomon Gulch Hatchery along the bay is responsible for a good part of the exciting silver run, which normally peaks during the second and third weeks of August.

Boaters trolling with down-riggers often catch their limit of six fish, but you don't have to charter out to get in on the action—there's good fishing for pinks and silvers along beaches, docks, and creek mouths during July and August. If you're hoping for a lunker halibut, sign on with one of the charter boats and fish the deep waters of Valdez Arm out to Hinchinbrook. The halibut derby runs most of the summer, with the lucky winner taking home $15,000 and a brand-new pickup truck.

NORTHERN COMFORT CHARTERS AND TOURS
(907) 835-3070
www.northerncomfortcharters.com
From late April through September, Capt. Steve Pyle and his crew will take you out on one of their three twin-diesel-powered boats with comfortable cabins, toilets, and all-around fishing decks. They also have a fast six-pac boat and a 42-foot vessel for overnight and extended charters. Halibut is the target of choice, but lingcod, rockfish, and an occasional salmon may add to the action. Beginning in late July, you can charter out specifically for silver salmon, with a limit of six per day.

ORION CHARTERS
P.O. Box 3577, Valdez, AK 99686
(907) 835-8610
www.orioncharters.com
Try fishing Orion's new six-person boat, which is powered by twin-engine diesels and has a cruise speed of 35 knots. It's equipped with a heated cabin and a large, stable fishing platform for maximum productivity on your 12-hour jaunt. During the last decade, Orion reports that 90 percent of their clients have caught two or more halibut per day, with an average size of 45 to 50 pounds for

the keepers. They also offer salmon shark fishing, with a similar 90 percent success rate over the last six years. The average salmon shark caught is between 7 and 8 feet long and weighs in at about 300 pounds.

> **i** The nightlife in Valdez still has a rugged pipeline flavor, with places such as the Club Bar and the Pipeline Club offering pool, horseshoes, shuffleboard, and dancing.

CORDOVA

The landlocked town of Cordova is the most isolated community on the Prince William Sound, a fact that contributes to a good deal of its charm. Formerly a shipping port for copper ore from the interior's Kennecott mines, Cordova is now sustained by commercial fishing for salmon, cod, crab, and shrimp as well as by tourists, primarily those looking for fishing, bird-watching, and other outdoor adventures. As fishing prices have dropped in recent years, the town has become quieter and more laid-back, but what it lacks in excitement, it makes up for in friendliness and quaint seaside appeal.

Getting Here, Getting Around

You can't drive to Cordova, but you can arrive by via Alaska Airlines (www.alaskaair.com) from Anchorage, Juneau, or Seattle. There are also ferry connections with Whittier, Seward, and Valdez on the Alaska Marine Highway System (www .dot.state.ak.us/amhs/index.shtml). Once you're there, you can drive the 48-mile Copper River Highway to access fishing and enjoy the scenery, but you'll have to turn around and head back where the road dead-ends just past the famed Million-Dollar Bridge. If you don't bring your own car on the ferry, there's taxi service and car rental available locally.

> **i** A shoppers' paradise it's not, but you will find two supermarkets, a bookstore, a general store, and a couple of outfitters as well as liquor stores and espresso shops in Cordova.

Accommodations

In keeping with its small-town flavor, most of the accommodations in Cordova are at bed-and-breakfasts, small inns, or cabins. If you're coming to fish, you may find combination packages that offer overnight stays along with charter services.

The U.S. Forest Service has several public-use cabins available for rent in Cordova's Copper River Delta. Cabins are comfortable but rustic, with no running water and outhouse facilities in lieu of indoor plumbing. Check with the Chugach Ranger District Office (907-424-7661, www.fs.fed .us/r10/chugach/cordova/index.html) for details and availability.

For the listings below, assume there's no smoking, no wheelchair access, and no pets allowed unless we tell you otherwise. Major credit cards are generally accepted; we'll let you know if there's an exception. The peak season in Cordova is when the silver salmon are running in August and September, so make sure to reserve well in advance if you're looking at that time frame. Price ranges below indicate the average cost of a room for two adults during the peak season. Prices do not include the 12 percent bed tax.

Price Codes

$................	**Less than $125**
$$	**$126–$175**
$$$	**$175–$225**
$$$$	**More than $225**

ALASKA FISHERMAN'S CAMP   **$**
101 First St.
(907) 424-3251
www.akfishcamp.com/cordova/cordova.html
Voila—cheap digs in a town where nothing much comes cheap. And the history's thrown in for free. Rooms are in one of two buildings, the original

being a 25-room cannery bunkhouse that is more than 70 years old, with weathered aluminum siding, wavy glass windows, and some nifty artifacts to prove its age. You'll share a communal bath and kitchen, with pretty much just a dresser and a bed in your room. But if you came to fish and enjoy the great outdoors, the Alaska Fisherman's Camp gives you a comfy place to lay your head, out of the elements. The camp is a short walk from downtown and the ferry terminal. While you're there, ask about their cannery tours. Your host also owns the MugUp Internet cafe.

BEAR'S DEN CABINS $$$
Eyak River
(907) 424-7168
www.bearsdencabins.com
Choose from four furnished cabins right on the Eyak River, each with bathroom (running water!), kitchenette, VCR, and grill. Guests share a picnic table and firepit, where swapping fish stories is optional but encouraged. And of course, there's freezer space for storing those fish. Children are welcome. Cabins sleeping eight people are available at a higher rate. Ask about use of vehicle and boat and motor for your stay. Use of a kayak and canoe come with the cabin rate.

EYAK RIVER HIDEAWAY $$
Eyak River
(907) 424-3922
www.eyakriverhideaway.com
This comfortable getaway is right on the shores of the Eyak River, which offers some of the best salmon fishing in town. The hosts make a point of providing great service to their guests, whether they're avid anglers or folks who just come to get away from it all. They offer a house unit that sleeps six and an apartment that sleeps five. A continental breakfast including juice and muffins

i Annual events in Cordova include the Ice Worm Festival in early February, the Copper River Delta Shorebird Festival in early May, and the Wild Salmon Festival in June, featuring a marathon and a bake-off.

is provided, and the refrigerator is stocked with eggs, breakfast meats, and milk for those who prefer a hot breakfast. The units have full kitchens with coffeemakers, microwaves, and full-size refrigerators, private baths, telephones, and cable televisions. Outside there's access to a riverfront deck, outdoor grill, and fish-processing facilities, including chest freezers. Credit cards are not accepted, and there's a family dog on-site.

RELUCTANT FISHERMAN INN $$
407 Railroad Ave.
(907) 424-3272
www.reluctantfisherman.com
Choose between newly remodeed harbor and mountain view rooms, all with wireless Internet, cable television, free local calls, and guest laundry. There's an on-site computer as well as a bar and grill. Overlooking the small boat harbor, this inn boasts a great downtown location.

SEAVIEW CONDO $$
109 Council Ave.
(907) 424-5269
Enjoy a breathtaking view of the harbor, bay, and islands from the privacy of your own condo unit conveniently located in downtown Cordova. The unit sleeps six and comes complete with coffeemaker, microwave, minifridge, and free continental breakfast. There's also a private phone line and cable television, with Internet access available for a fee. The owners live in the same building and can provide local information as needed. There's a covered outdoor deck for smokers, and some pets are allowed on approval.

i If you're looking to eat out while in Cordova, try the grilled steaks and seafood at the Powder House Restaurant on Eyak Lake (907-424-3529).

Attractions and Recreation
Most of what you'll find to do in and around Cordova will be in the great outdoors, but you can also check out the Cordova Museum (907-424-

6665, www.cordovamuseum.org) to get a look at the history of the region, including interpretive and cultural displays as well as original pieces by famed Alaskan artist Sydney Laurence. The museum is open from 10 a.m. to 6 p.m. Monday through Saturday during the summer season, and there's a nominal admission fee.

For scenic drives on Cordova's limited road system, head out Power Creek Road, which follows the shore of Lake Eyak, or drive the Copper River Highway to the Million Dollar Bridge. Along the way you'll have a good chance of seeing trumpeter swans, as more than 7 percent of the world's population breeds in the Copper River Basin. Just before the bridge, you can see the 350-foot actively calving face of Childs Glacier. As always, exercise caution in the vicinity of calving ice; in this particular area, ice chunks the size of cars have fallen into the water, causing potentially hazardous waves.

Built in 1910 at a cost of $1.4 million dollars, the Million Dollar Bridge spanned the Copper River until it collapsed during the 1964 earthquake. It was repaired and reopened in 2004, but the road still goes only 10 miles farther than the bridge. Plans for a highway connecting Cordova with the Richardson Highway via the town of Chitina have never materialized, though they are still under discussion.

You also can drive out Whitshed Road to Hartney Bay or Alaganik Slough to view some of the delta's plentiful supply of shorebirds. Birders have spotted more than 31 different species among the five million shorebirds passing through on their spring migration routes.

For rafting or kayaking adventures, try Alaska River Expeditions (907-424-7238, 800-776-1864; www.alaskarafters.com) or Orca Adventure Lodge (907-424-7249, 866-424-6722, www.orca adventurelodge.com; see the listing in the Fishing section below).

Hiking and Camping

The U.S. Forest Service maintains 25 miles of trails within the Chugach National Forest surrounding Cordova. Try the 2.4-mile Crater Lake Trail, accessed at 1.8-mile Power Creek Road. You'll get to enjoy great views and a mountain lake stocked with rainbow trout. A little farther down Power Creek Road, you can access the 4.2-mile Power Creek Trail, with scenery that includes glaciers, waterfalls, and views of the valley. Other popular hikes include the 0.8-mile Haystack Trail at Mile 19.1 of the Copper River Highway and the 3.5-mile Heney Ridge Trail at Mile 5.1 of Whitshed Road.

If you're looking to camp, there's the Odiak Camper Park on Whitshed Road, with 24 RV spaces, and a small campground with five sites at Mile 48 Copper River Highway.

Fishing

In addition to the commercial fishing activity in Cordova, there's great sportfishing along the Eyak River/Lake and Alaganik River/Slough systems. You can access the glacial waters of the Eyak River by trail, with reds striking on bright lures in late June and early July. Silvers run in abundance in the late summer and early fall, and they're not so finicky about lures. Salmon fishing is not allowed in Eyak Lake, but you can try for Dolly Varden and cutthroat trout at the lake outlet. Dolly Varden are also plentiful at Power Creek, with road access heading north from Cordova. Be warned, though: Bears love this spot.

Follow Cordova's Copper River Highway to the boat launch at Mile 17 for access to the Alaganik River system. The best fishing for red and silver salmon is at the slough near the boat launch. You can also find cutthroat and Dolly Varden at McKinley Lake early in the season.

ALASKA WILDERNESS OUTFITTING
(907) 424-5552
www.alaskawilderness.com
Family owned and operated since 1982, Alaskan Wilderness Outfitting offers a full range of options for game fishing in the abundant waters around Cordova. Fly fishing, spin casting, bottom fishing—they do it all with a reputation for excellence that brings clients back year after year.

Select from their full-service lodge packages, their do-it-yourself outpost cabin packages, or their combination packages. If packages aren't your thing, they can design a custom trip just for you. Photography, flight seeing, clamming, hiking, and kayaking can be arranged, too.

ORCA ADVENTURE LODGE
(866) 424-ORCA
www.orcaadventurelodge.com
One of the best known fishing services in the Sound, Orca offers all sorts of water-based adventures from their base lodge in a restored cannery 2 miles north of Cordova. Try their well-priced skiff fishing for salmon and smaller halibut in Orca Inlet, or wait till fall and try skiff fishing for silvers along the road system. Orca also runs a high-speed riverboat offering both spin and fly casting. Saltwater expeditions target salmon, halibut, and rockfish, or opt for a fly-out fishing adventure on a remote lake or river. Orca provides licensed guides, full fish-processing facilities, fish shipping, a well-stocked guide and tackle room, fly-tying and fly-fishing instruction, and a junior angler program. Nonanglers in your group can opt for brown bear photography, rafting, or kayaking adventures.

THE MATANUSKA-SUSITNA VALLEY

Surrounded by mountains and water, Anchorage has nowhere to grow except north, and that's where the Valley comes in. Housing is more affordable there, with plenty of acreage, woods, water, and mountain views to enjoy. A growing number of people do the daily commute of 45 minutes to an hour each way in order to work in Anchorage and come home to larger lots and cheaper living in the Valley. Like other pockets in Alaska, the Valley attracts a mostly independent and politically conservative demographic.

When former Wasilla mayor Sarah Palin rocketed to national attention in the summer of 2008, the Valley started showing up on travel itineraries of journalists and ordinary visitors curious to see what this strip-mall hometown of a political celebrity is all about. As a bonus, they discover affordable lodging and good access to lakes and snowmachine trails.

The sister communities of Palmer and Wasilla are the heart of the Mat-Su Valley. Though these are small towns, the Valley is one of the fastest-growing areas in the state. Palmer, with a population of approximately 7,800, has a friendly farm-town feel, while Wasilla, registering 9,700 pus inhabitants, is more suburban. Both communities have growing residential areas with plenty of new construction, though Wasilla has the edge in terms of retail shops and services. North of Wasilla, the smaller communities of Big Lake, Willow, and Talkeetna provide additional gateways into the Alaskan wilderness. Big Lake is a resort community just west of Mile 52 of the Parks Highway. There you'll find—no surprise—a big blue lake with 67 miles of wooded lakeshore dotted with lodges, restaurants, vacation cabins, and year-round residences.

Farther up the Parks Highway, the tiny town of Willow is most notable for on-and-off-again efforts to move the state capital there, partway between Anchorage and Fairbanks. At Willow, you can access the beautiful recreational area at Hatcher Pass via the gravel Fishhook-Willow Road that connects with the Wasilla-Fishhook Road along the east end of Wasilla. Finally, at Mile 98.7 of the Parks Highway, you can turn off to explore the whimsical town of Talkeetna, a frequent tour-bus stop and jumping-off point for adventurers planning to scale Denali, the highest peak in North America.

Be sure to plan a stop at the Mat-Su Visitor Center, near the junction of the Parks and Glenn Highways, to pick up free brochures and visit with the staff about what to see and where to stay in the Valley. The visitor center also has a gift shop.

GETTING HERE, GETTING AROUND

Since this is primarily a commuter area, the best way to get around is by car. From Anchorage, head north on the Glenn Highway (Route 1), and you should reach the Palmer-Wasilla Highway within 45 minutes to an hour, depending on traffic. Avoid rush hour if you can, and be advised that this stretch of roadway has the highest rate of traffic fatalities in the state, primarily due to the sheer numbers of commuters traveling it daily. Alaska's now infamous "bridges to nowhere" projects included funding for a bridge over Knik Arm to provide an alternate route from the Valley to Anchorage, but with a price tag edging close to $700 million, it's a long ways from becoming

i For a little town, Talkeetna has a lot going on. There's an annual Moose Dropping Festival during the second weekend in July, and come winter there's the Talkeetna Winterfest, featuring the rollicking fun of the Wilderness Women Contest and Bachelor Auction. For more information on the Wilderness Women Contest, see the complete listing in the December Annual Events and Festivals section of the Anchorage chapter.

a reality. Ferry service from Anchorage to Knik-Goose Bay (KGB) Road may provide a short-term fix to the traffic problem, but it's still quite a drive from KGB Road to Wasilla.

From the Palmer-Wasilla Highway, you can head west and north toward the Parks Highway (Route 3), which continues on to Denali National Park and Fairbanks, or you can continue east and north on the Glenn Highway toward Glennallen. The stretch of the Glenn Highway from Anchorage to the Eureka Roadhouse is designated a scenic byway, passing between the Talkeetna Mountains and the Chugach Mountains, with access to the Matanuska and Knik Rivers Scenic Overlook at Mile 49.9, the King Mountain State Recreation Site at Mile 76, the Matanuska Glacier State Recreation Area at Mile 101, and the Eureka Summit Area trailhead at Mile 132.5.

In the summer the Alaska Railroad also offers daily service connecting Wasilla and Talkeetna with Anchorage, Denali National Park, and Fairbanks. Once you're in the Valley, you can get around by ATV, sled dog, or horseback, if any of those strike your fancy. Check out the details in the Parks, Recreation, and Tours section.

i Traffic near the Fairgrounds in Palmer gets backed up during the State Fair. If possible, route around the Fairgrounds from mid-August through Labor Day. For more on the Alaska State Fair, see our listing under Annual Festivals and Events.

HISTORY

The Dena'ina Indians inhabited the rich and scenic land of the Matanuska-Susitna Valley for centuries. With the development of small-scale mining in Hatcher Pass, the Valley became an access route to the thriving seaport of Knik. Once a port was established in Anchorage, Knik was all but abandoned, but the Alaska Railroad brought the Valley to life in 1916 when it pushed through from Anchorage to Fairbanks.

In 1935, Franklin Roosevelt's Federal Emergency Relief Administration established the Matanuska Valley Colony at Palmer with the goal of relocating Depression-struck farm families to develop the agricultural potential of the Valley. Two hundred and three families from the northern counties of Minnesota, Michigan, and Wisconsin were sent to the Mat-Su Valley, where they set about growing vegetables with the help of Alaska's legendary "midnight sun." Though some of the farms failed, many of the colonists stayed, and today the Mat-Su Valley still supplies fresh produce to Anchorage residents during the summer.

ACCOMMODATIONS

As noted above, one of the advantages to staying in the Valley instead of in the city is that room rates are noticeably cheaper. In addition, you're a lot more likely to find peace and quiet, mountain views, access to trails, and even lakeside docks as part of your package. There are more bed-and-breakfasts than full-size hotels in the Valley, reflecting the small-town feel of things here.

Price codes indicate the cost of a room for two during the peak season, generally May through mid-September. You can assume that major credit cards are accepted and that the establishment is open year-round unless we note otherwise. Count on bringing the kids but not the pets unless the listing says differently. While hotels and motels generally have rooms with wheelchair access and rooms for smokers, we'll make a special note if these are available at B&Bs, hostels, guest-houses, and inns. Prices don't include the 7.5 percent bed tax.

Price Codes

$ .... Less than $125
$$ .... $126–$175
$$$ .... $176–$225
$$$$ .... More than $225

Hotels, Motels, and Lodges

AGATE INN $$–$$$
4725 Begich Circle, Wasilla
(907) 373-2290, (800) 770-2290
www.agateinn.com
Located on 16 acres off the Palmer-Wasilla Highway, the Agate Inn has 15 rooms in a variety of settings, including the Agate Guest House and Aurora King Suite, the Knik Building, the Agate Suites and Guest Laundry, and the Susitna Cottage. Beds come in a variety of configurations as well, from twin all the way through king-size mattresses. Rooms come with coffeemakers, microwaves, minifridges, irons and ironing boards, voice mail, and satellite televisions. A free continental breakfast is offered each morning, and there's a whirlpool available for guest use. The staff at this country-style inn likes to make sure each guest feels at home. A resident reindeer provides a unique Alaskan touch. All rooms are nonsmoking, and there are two rooms with wheelchair access.

COLONY INN $
325 East Elmwood Ave., Palmer
(907) 745-3330
This former teachers' dormitory for the Depression-era Matanuska Colony has been restored into lodging with 12 unique rooms. Ten rooms have whirlpool tubs, while the others have showers only. Enjoy a great view of the mountains or chat with other guests in the great room, complete with bay window and fireplace. Registration is at the Valley Hotel on South Alaska Street. Ask about special rates for groups and seniors. All rooms are nonsmoking.

GRANDVIEW INN AND SUITES $$
2900 East Parks Highway, Wasilla
(907) 352-1700
www.grandviewak.com
One of the newer options in the Valley, the Grandview is decorated in soothing shades of green, maroon, and beige, blending a country-inn flavor with hotel-style amenities. Most of the 139 rooms have queen-size beds, with king-size beds in the Jacuzzi rooms. Rooms come with refrigerators, microwaves, hair dryers, irons, ironing boards, and coffeemakers. Guests have access to laundry facilities and high-speed Internet as well. There are great mountain views from the back, and don't miss the massive wildlife carving over the stone fireplace in the downstairs lobby. This is one of the few Valley hotels with an indoor pool and spa. A free continental breakfast is served seasonally, and they have new extended stay suites as well.

LAKE LUCILLE INN $$
Mile 43.5 Parks Highway
1300 West Lake Lucille Dr., Wasilla
(907) 352-0149
www.bestwestern.com/lakelucilleinn
This Best Western hotel overlooks the lake, with spectacular mountain vistas beyond. Rooms come with coffeemakers, irons and ironing boards, free morning papers, and free continental breakfasts. There's good food and a relaxing bar on the premises in the form of the Shoreline Restaurant and the Lakeview Lounge. The 54 rooms include standards with queen-size beds and suites with king-size beds. A sauna, a Jacuzzi, and an exercise room are available for guest use, and there's wireless Internet throughout the hotel. Rooms are nonsmoking only, and pets are allowed. One suite has wheelchair access.

VALLEY HOTEL $
606 South Alaska St., Palmer
(907) 745-3330
This affordable historic hotel first opened its doors in 1948, advertising 42 rooms and 42 baths to attract miners, farmers, and other guests. Owned

San Leandro Public Library
Main Branch
(510) 577-3970

Checked Out Items 1/8/2015 11:43
XXXXXXXXXX3250

Item Title	Due Date
33206008065157	1/11/2015
* 12 years a slave. [blu-ray]	
33206006294668	1/11/2015
* Before midnight [blu-ray]	
33206007550399	1/22/2015
* Discoveries...America. Alaska [dvd]	
33206007239506	1/22/2015
* Alaska	
33206008050860	1/22/2015
* Fodor's 2014 Alaska	
33206007197902	1/22/2015
* Insiders' guide to Anchorage and Southcentral Alaska : including the Kenai Peninsula, Prince William Sound, and Denali National Park	
33206007858263	1/11/2015
Transporter 3 [dvd]	

* Indicates items checked out today
To renew items please visit
www.sanleandrolibrary.org
or call 510-577-3977

and operated by longtime Alaskans, the hotel features comfortable accommodations and personal service. Rooms have twin and queen-size beds. Within the hotel are a restaurant and coffee shop, the Caboose Lounge, and the Iron Horse Liquor Store. The downtown location makes it an easy walk to local services. Wheelchair access is available on the first floor only.

Bed-and-Breakfasts/ Cottages and Cabins

ALASKA BIRCH COTTAGES $$–$$$
2361 North Cotswold Circle, Palmer
(907) 745-0558
www.alaskabirchcottages.com
Nestled among birch and spruce trees on a quiet cul-de-sac between Palmer and Wasilla, these newer cottages are exceptional in design and ambience. They offer four one-bedroom cottages and two two-bedroom units with twin and king-size beds. Attention to detail abounds, from the furnished kitchen, gas fireplace, Jacuzzi tub with massaging double showerheads, vaulted ceiling, and half bath upstairs. Breakfast fixings, including homemade whole wheat rolls and free-range eggs, are left in the kitchen for your first night's stay. Every cottage has a fireplace, futon for extra guests, coin-operated washer and dryer, television, telephone, and screened-in porch. Irons and ironing boards are available on request. The owners will happily store your luggage if you're heading out on a short-term expedition. All of the cottages are nonsmoking.

ALASKA CREEKSIDE CABINS $$
Dolly Varden Rd.
(907) 746-7632
www.alaskacreeksidecabins.com
With seven waterfront cabins on Wasilla and Cottonwood Creeks, Alaska Creekside offers salmon viewing right from your deck. One of the locations sports a great mountain view as well. Each cabin has one queen-size bed and three twin beds, so families and groups of four to six people are easily accommodated. Coffeemakers, microwaves, irons, ironing boards, complimentary coffee, stereos,

telephones, cable televisions, gas fireplaces, jetted tubs, full-sized kitchens, and private decks come standard in each of these newer cabins. There's also a fire pit, and RV parking is available at each site. The cabins are nonsmoking only, and small kenneled dogs are accepted at one of the units. There's wireless Internet access at all cabins.

ALASKA GARDEN GATE BED AND BREAKFAST $$
950 South Trunk Rd., Palmer
(907) 746-2333
www.gardengatebnb.com
Tucked away on 10 acres near the Glenn and Parks Highway junction, Alaska Garden Gate offers rooms and guest apartments with Jacuzzis, fireplaces, and private entrances. Generous hot breakfasts are served between 7:30 and 9:30 a.m., featuring such Alaskan favorites as apple sourdough pancakes and caribou sausage. In the Forest Haven guest apartment, you'll enjoy fabulous views of Pioneer Peak and the Chugach Range while surrounded with north woods decor, whereas the Midnight Sun Gardens apartment opens onto a patio of brilliant flowers. Cool blues and mountain views are featured in the Forget Me Not Room, with roses as the theme in the Arctic Rose Room. The Blossoms and Berries Room features mountain views and botanical information on some of Alaska's splendid plants. All rooms come with coffeemakers, microwaves, minifridges, private baths, telephones, balconies, irons, and ironing boards. Horseshoe and tennis courts are available for guest use, and there's access to miles of hiking and ski trails. All rooms are nonsmoking, two offer wheelchair access, and two are designated as pet friendly. Ask about AAA, AARP, and military discounts. Alaska Gardens also operates four lakeside vacation rentals.

ALASKA'S HARVEST BED AND BREAKFAST $
2252 Love Dr., Palmer
(907) 745-4263, (877) 745-4263
www.alaskasharvest.com
On 15 acres of secluded forest 2 miles from

Palmer, this spacious B&B features Alaskan decor with amazing mountain views. Choose from the Bear's Den, the Reindeer Room, the Creekside Room, the Gold Mine Room, and the Pioneer Suite. Rooms come with coffeemakers, microwaves, minifridges, private baths, telephones, cable televisions, balconies, irons, and ironing boards. Kitchenettes are stocked with a variety of snacks, teas, and breakfast supplies, including muffins, cereals, pastries, yogurt, fresh fruits, coffee, tea, and milk. Enjoy peace and quiet in a country-style setting where sheep, alpacas, and miniature goats roam the pastures. All rooms are nonsmoking. A full colony-style house on three acres can also be rented by the week.

ALASKA'S SNOWED INN BED AND BREAKFAST $

495 South Begich Dr., Wasilla
(907) 376-7495, (866) 799-5169
www.snowedinn-ak.com

Decorated with antiques, this two-room B&B offers a private guest entrance plus access to an inviting common area with dining facilities. The Alaska Suite features a northern theme, while the Lighthouse Suite offers a nautical theme. Situated on two quiet country acres, the inn serves a hearty breakfast as well as providing complimentary tea, juice, soda, bottled water, hot chocolate, hot cider, and coffee. Rooms come with private baths, telephones, cable televisions, balconies, irons, and ironing boards. Both rooms are nonsmoking.

ALASKAN VIEW MOTEL $

2650 E. Parks Highway
(907) 376-6787
www.alaskanviewmotel.com

Each of the 24 rooms in this moderately-priced motel sports a view of Cook Inlet and the mountains beyond. And in each room you'll find handcrafted log furniture, cable television, and private bath. You're right on the highway, so expect some traffic noise.

MOOSE WALLOW CABINS $$

13388 East Moose Wallow Ave., Palmer
(907) 745-7777
www.moosewallow.com

Besides the fun name, this B&B offers three fully furnished cabins, all handcrafted from logs on the property. Located on 80 acres at the foot of the Talkeetna Mountains, Moose Wallow offers access to miles of groomed trails for both summer and winter use. In addition to the clean, cozy cabins in a peaceful setting, guests enjoy a full breakfast with foods such as omelets, pancakes, biscuits and gravy, blueberry muffins, and homemade bread. Fresh cookies and cinnamon rolls are provided at snack time. Cabins are equipped with coffeemakers, microwaves, private baths, telephones, TV/VCRs, irons, and ironing boards. Full breakfasts are for the first three days of your stay; thereafter, the breakfasts are continental. There's a gift shop, hair salon, and coffee shop on-site. Both owners are assistant hunting guides, and Bonnie makes museum-quality antler bowls. Pets are allowed, and the cabins offer wheelchair access.

ROSE RIDGE BED AND BREAKFAST $-$$

8614 East Highlander Circle, Palmer
(907) 745-8604, (877) 827-7673
www.roseridgebnb.com

Located near scenic Hatcher Pass just a few miles from Palmer, Rose Ridge offers two spacious rooms plus a vacation chalet. From the chalet, you'll enjoy views of Pioneer Peak and Knik Glacier. Rooms come with coffeemakers, private baths, TV/VCRs, and Internet modem connections. On the 15-acre premises, guests can make use of the fire pit and picnic area. Guests may choose from full or continental breakfasts that include Alaskan-themed items such as blueberry pancakes, reindeer sausage, homemade jams, and birch syrup. Rooms are nonsmoking only, and there's a $5 extra charge for children ages 5 to 12. Rose Ridge also offers a private chalet with a two-night minimum stay.

TOLLERS' TIMBERS GUEST CHALETS AND COTTAGES $$

3251 Toller Court, Wasilla
(907) 746-1438, (800) 795-1438
www.alaskavacationcabins.com

Choose from two one-bedroom cottages or two two-bedroom chalets. The Carbiou Trails Cottage offers studio sleeping, while the Fox Den, with vaulted ceilings and fireplace, sleeps a family of five. The Moose Run Chalet sleeps four, while the more upscale Eagle View Chalet accommodates six. All units are clean and comfy, with full kitchens and baths, TV/VCR, and stereo. On-site are Alaskan gardens, mountain views, a business center, free Wi-Fi, and washer and dryer.

RESTAURANTS

Though the Valley's population can't support the variety in eateries that Anchorage does, you still can find a place to suit just about every taste and budget. True, some of these establishments are in strip malls, but once you get inside, you'll be impressed with how the owners have transformed the decor into something truly pleasing. Many of the finer establishments boast killer views that will leave you lingering at your table long after the plates have been cleared. For whatever reason, animal mounts on the wall seem to be the dominant decorating theme at many of the more casual spots.

Unless otherwise noted, you may assume that these places are open year-round, seven days a week. Credit cards and reservations are accepted but not necessary unless otherwise noted, and the restaurants are wheelchair accessible.

The price codes indicate the average cost of a meal for two, excluding cocktails, wine, appetizers, desserts, tax, and tips. Most establishments that serve dinner have a license for beer and wine, and many also serve cocktails.

Price Codes

$.................. Less than $30
$$ .... $30–$39
$$$ .... $40–$50
$$$$ .... More than $50

CHEPOS $

731 West Parks Highway, Wasilla
(907) 373-5656

With a nice Southwestern decor including murals of Mexican scenes and a big wrought-iron chandelier, this family-owned restaurant has an extensive menu that's sure to please. The clientele ranges from teens to families to professionals and tourists. Choose from a huge list of Mexican dinner combinations, or order from a large selection of a la carte items. Among the favorites are Camerones Rancheros, a shrimp dish with traditional ranchero sauce, and the Polla Fundido, a deep-fried flour tortilla stuffed with seasoned chicken and melted cheese, served with pico de gallo salsa. They also have a nice selection of margaritas and occasional mariachi music. Don't be put off by the strip mall location—the good food and atmosphere have kept locals coming back since they first opened in 1986.

COLONY KITCHEN/THE NOISY GOOSE $

Mile 40.5 Glenn Highway, Palmer
(907) 746-4600

A perennial local favorite for home-style cooking served in one of those places where the customers are friends and the staff actually has fun most of the time, the Noisy Goose caters to locals year-round, with a hearty crop of tourists mixed in during the summer. Owners Bill and Glenda Hafus began with the Frontier Cafe in downtown Palmer, then opened the Colony Kitchen across from the fairgrounds a few years later. Eventually the place came to be called the Noisy Goose, in part a tribute to the good-natured conversation that makes the place feel so comfortable. Check out the narrative that comes with the menu for a fun look at the evolution of this popular cafe, including the unsolved mystery of the stolen toilet. Among their specialties are homemade pies, eggs Benedict, homemade meatloaf, and prime rib on Sunday. You can call ahead for large groups, but they don't typically take reservations. The Noisy Goose is open for breakfast, lunch, and dinner.

EVANGELO'S RESTAURANT $$$$
Mile 40 Parks Highway, Wasilla
(907) 376-1212

Spacious, open, and elegant, Evangelo's offers a nice selection of mostly Italian fare coupled with excellent service. Decorated in rich hues of maroon and green, Evangelo's is also graced with a fireplace and great mountains views from the tables in the back. For starters, try the Deep-Fried Ravioli or the shrimp. Regular diners like Evangelo's Special Pizza with sausage, Canadian bacon, pepperoni, hamburger, mushrooms, and olives. Other favorites include the Halibut Olympia and the Prime Rib Sandwich. Private, curtained seating for parties of up to 25 is available upstairs, and there are banquet rooms downstairs. Open for lunch and dinner, Evangelo's has a full beer and wine menu plus ample parking.

GLACIER CANYON GRILL $$$
238 N. Boundary St., Wasilla
(907) 352-1720
www.grandviewak.com

Located downstairs at the Grandview Inn, the Glacier Canyon Grill features windows overlooking the lake, a stone fireplace, and a trophy-room motif, with animal mounts from both Alaska and Africa. Open primarily for dinner, the grill's menu includes such favorites as halibut with lemon-caper sauce, the 16-ounce Glacier Canyon ribeye steak, and the King Crab and Shrimp Pot with Nantua lobster sauce served over pasta. This newer restaurant is not large, but there's ample parking and a full bar.

MEKONG THAI CUISINE $$
473 West Parks Highway
(907) 373-7690

Mekong offers the only Thai cuisine on the 340-mile stretch from Eagle River to Fairbanks, and lucky for Thai lovers, it's tasty. Try the vegetable curry or the Kaeng Karee. Expect a clean setting and attentive service.

SETTLERS BAY LODGE $$$$
Mile 8 Knik-Goose Bay Rd., Wasilla
(907) 357-5678
www.settlersbaylodge.com

With its vaulted ceilings, accent lighting, exhibition kitchen, and huge windows capturing a spectacular mountain view, Settlers Bay is undeniably one of the most romantic dinner spots in the Valley. It's also one of the newer restaurants, having opened in 2004 adjacent to the golf course in the burgeoning residential development at Settlers Bay. New owners in 2008 tout "casual dining at its finest." The menu features creative specials including duck, oysters, and clams. During the summer, Settlers Bay Lodge uses locally grown Mat-Su produce in all their menu items. Try the Halibut Supreme with shrimp, lobster, and crab sauce, or the filet mignon topped with blue cheese. The restaurant and adjoining bar, both completely nonsmoking, are open daily from 5 p.m. (Also see the listing under Nightlife, below.)

TOKYO RESTAURANT $$
735 West Parks Highway, Wasilla
(907) 357-8888

Don't be fooled by the strip-mall location—this restaurant opens up with a vaulted ceiling and tons of wood accents that manage to skillfully blend Asian and Alaskan influences with a pleasing ambience. Serving Japanese and Chinese cuisine as well as sushi, the restaurant's menu is varied enough to draw tour-bus crowds on their way from Anchorage to Denali and points beyond. Open for lunch and dinner, the Tokyo Restaurant offers beer, wine, and sake. Menu favorites include chicken teriyaki, Mongolian beef, and shrimp tempura.

VAGABOND BLUES $$
642 South Alaska St., Palmer
(907) 745-2233
www.vagblues.com

Vag Blues is quite the Valley treasure. Fresh food, relaxed ambience, and they've been around for decades. In contrast with some of the meat-and-potatoes Valley fare, you'll find healthful wraps and award-winning soups on the VagBlues menu. Quiche, paninis, breads, and desserts round out the menu. This little bistro also hosts much of the Valley's coffeehouse entertainment.

NIGHTLIFE

Though it's not a place people would flock to for the exciting nightlife, the Valley takes care of its own with a good selection of local hangouts ranging from classy joints with killer views to stereo-typical hole-in-the-wall bars. Several places have live music on weekends, and most are open till 1 or 2 a.m., with the occasional almost-all-nighter.

Remember that if your blood alcohol level is .08 percent or higher, you're risking a DUI conviction in the state of Alaska. As in most states, this is a serious offense, resulting in confiscation of your license at the time of your arrest followed by a minimum of three days in jail, a $1,500 fine, and a three-month license suspension if you're convicted.

i The Valley's population is continually on the rise, making the Mat-Su Borough the third-largest population center in Alaska after Anchorage and Fairbanks. With the influx, the area is becoming decidedly more sophisticated, with two theater companies, an Arts Council, and galleries that sell as much contemporary art as typical Alaskan fare.

ARCTIC CIRCLE CLUB
2750 Palmer-Wasilla Highway, Wasilla
(907) 357-6888
With a sports theme and a facility that's refreshingly clean right down to the bathrooms, this newer bar, also known as ACC or Flatley's, is a popular local hangout. Owner Jim Flatley is a friendly guy with diverse interests that include car racing and Robert Service poetry. As Klondike Jim, Flatley has done Robert Service shows all over the world. Occasionally he does a show at the bar in two 45-minute sets with a local band to open.

Seating is limited and tickets sell out fast, so it's best to let the bartender know you'd like to get in on a show, and they'll call you when the next one is scheduled. The ACC is expanding out back to include a horseshoe pit and golfing green. Flatley also contends that his is the only authentic Irish bar in the Valley.

GRANDVIEW INN AND BAR
2900 East Parks Highway, Wasilla
(907) 352-1720
www.grandviewak.com
Another hotel, bar, and restaurant combination, the Grandview is new and upscale. It's smaller and darker than some of the other hotel bars, but the atmosphere is warm and appealing. The Grandview used to draw primarily a younger crowd, but now the clientele is mixed. There's live music on the weekends, complemented by Candlelight Jazz in the adjacent dining room. The bar is non-smoking, and they offer a great bar menu, including a generous nacho plate and such specialties as stuffed mushrooms and Lamb Lollipops.

GREAT BEAR BREWING COMPANY
238 North Boundary St., Wasilla
(907) 373-4782
This smaller bar draws a crowd with its own microbrews and live music on weekends. In addition to the house beers, the bar menu includes five premium whiskeys. The weekly roundup of bar-time fun includes Dart Night, a pasta bar, Open Mic, and a Showcase Night. Located in a strip mall, the bar opens into a small restaurant, so you can order up a meal as well. There's no dance floor, and the bar is nonsmoking until 9 p.m.

LAKEVIEW LOUNGE
LakeLucille Inn
1300 West Lake Lucille Dr., Wasilla
(907) 373-1776
With a big vaulted ceiling and killer view of the lake and the mountains, you'd expect the bar here to be jam-packed, but it's actually rather quiet except when there are special events going

on, like car races on the frozen lake in the winter. Most of the clientele are tourists, with some locals in the mix. There's a small stage set up for occasional live entertainment. Go through the restaurant and around the back to get to the bar.

MUG SHOT SALOON
251 West Parks Highway, Wasilla
(907) 376-1617
This is one of those dark, semirustic bars that you find sprinkled across Alaska, a place where regulars love to hang out even in the middle of the day. The walls are hung with caricatures of patrons and friends, and out back there's a large deck and horseshoe pit. With 13 TVs and NFL Sunday ticket, it's the place to be during football season. Rumor has it that they pour a generous drink. Some cable network patrons had fun with the Mug Shot during the 2008 election season.

SCHWABENHOF
Mile 6.5 Palmer-Wasilla Highway, Wasilla
(907) 357-2739
This impressive octagonal log building perched on a hill is one of the classier hangouts in the Valley. Expect a nice view and quiet atmosphere, with no pool tables, pinball machines, or blaring TVs. In addition to brats, kraut, and other German fare, you can sample a nice range of Alaskan, German, and Belgian microbrews.

SETTLERS BAY LODGE
Mile 8 Knik-Goose Bay Rd., Wasilla
(907) 376-5466
www.settlersbaylodge.com
One of the prettiest bars in town, Settlers Bay draws lots of locals, especially residents of the Settlers Bay residential development who are looking for a night out close to home. They have more than 70 wines plus a signature martini list. Even without the occasional live music, this is a great place to bring a date. Golfers from the adjacent course stop by to celebrate their wins, though the indulgent King Louis XIII bourbon at $85 a shot is no longer available. (Also see our previous listing under Restaurants.)

SHOPPING

Most folks head to Anchorage to do their serious shopping, but the Valley also has such big box stores as Sears, Fred Meyer, Target, and Wal-Mart. For specialty shops, check out the gold jewelry at Double J Mining in the Hunter Plaza in Wasilla (907-376-1000) and the kitchenware at All I Saw Cookware in downtown Wasilla (907-376-3177, 866-376-3177, www.allisawcookware.com). And don't miss the Palmer Friday Fling Market (907-745-6245, www.alaskagrown.org), featuring locally grown produce, arts and crafts, and live entertainment, every Friday from May through August. You'll find it in downtown Palmer, across from the visitor center.

ATTRACTIONS

As in much of Alaska, animals and history are the primary themes of Valley attractions. From dog kennels to reindeer farms to museums, there's something for everyone to see and remember. Price codes indicate the cost of admission for one adult. Attractions that don't charge admission have no price code assigned to them. Museums here tend toward the small and quirky, so don't set your sites too high—just enjoy them for what they are.

Price Codes
$....................Less than $5
$$ .... $5–$10
$$$ .... $11–$15
$$$$ .... More than $15

Palmer

COLONY HOUSE MUSEUM $
316 East Elmwood Ave.
(907) 745-1935
www.palmerhistoricalsociety.org/colony house.htm
Guided tours of this original Colony Farm House are given by descendants of some of the first colonists who were transplanted in the Valley as part of the New Deal agricultural effort. It's far from an

extensive museum, but the history of the place is unique, and it's fun to see the Sears and Roebuck furnishings that outfitted the home back in the Depression era. Open only in the summer, the museum is closed on Sunday and Monday.

MUSK OX FARM $$
Mile 50 Glenn Highway
(907) 745-4151
www.muskoxfarm.org
In the 1800s, musk ox disappeared from Alaska, but in 1954, Palmer's Musk Ox Farm began a domestication project to bring them back. This is a great chance to see these prehistoric-looking animals up close, to learn about their history, and to find out about the use of qiviut, the exceptionally soft wool of the musk ox. This private non-profit organization also includes an interpretive museum, a gift shop, and a picnic area. The farm is open daily from May to September.

Palmer hosts a couple of fun small-town events, including the Colony Days celebration during the second weekend in June and the Colony Christmas Celebration on the second Friday and Saturday in December. Throughout the year, you can catch occasional live shows at the Fairgrounds.

REINDEER FARM $$
Mile 11.5 Old Glenn Highway
(907) 745-4000
www.reindeerfarm.com
At the foot of Bodenburg Butte, this original Colony farm has been transformed into a place where visitors can walk among reindeer, petting and feeding them. The farm also does rehabilitation for elk, moose, and deer. The Chugach Mountains, with the Valley's signature Pioneer Peak, make a great backdrop for spending time with these very Alaskan mammals. The farm is open daily from the beginning of May through the middle of September.

Wasilla
DOROTHY PAGE MUSEUM $
323 North Main St.
(907) 373-9071
www.cityofwasilla.com/museum
This small log museum served as a community hall when it was built in 1931. Restored in 1967 as part of the Alaska Centennial events, it now houses history and art exhibits and provides a setting for classes and lectures. Eight additional historic structures are preserved on the adjacent lots, all part of the original town site. A farmers' market and picnic area also are found on the museum grounds. The museum is open Monday through Saturday in the summer and Wednesday through Friday in the winter.

DREAM A DREAM DOG FARM $$$$
Mile 64.5 Parks Highway, Houston
(907) 495-1198
www.vernhalter.com
Veteran Iditarod musher and Yukon Quest champion Vern Halter opens his kennels to the public from June 1 to September 1. The dog-farm tour includes a 45-minute video presentation (four languages available), a guided walking tour of the kennel, and an opportunity to get up close and personal with the pups, dogs, and mushers. Sled-dog rides are available at an extra charge. There are three kennel presentations daily in the summer. You can also book full-day "Dream a Dream" scenic tours; there's even a special "knit and spin" tour. Winter tours and treks are available by appointment, including one very special Iditarod Tour, the ultimate adventure package including the Iditarod's mandatory two years of training for rookies who want to run the Last Great Race.

HAPPY TRAILS KENNELS $$$$
Mile 4.5 West Lakes Boulevard, Big Lake
(907) 892-7899
www.buserdog.com
Four-time Iditarod champion and Leonard Seppala Humanitarian Award winner Martin Buser is at Happy Trails on most days to meet and greet

visitors after they've viewed a multimedia tour complete with Iditarod Trail footage. In addition to watching demonstrations of the art of sled-dog mushing, visitors get to meet and handle pups that will eventually train for some of the world's most arduous races. The admission fee includes a free dog bootie and a Martin Buser trading card. The kennels are open from mid-April through mid-October.

IDITAROD TRAIL SLED DOG RACE HEADQUARTERS
Mile 2.2 Knik Goose Bay Rd.
(907) 376-5155, (800) 545-6874
www.iditarod.com
The Iditarod Headquarters is the real must-see attraction in Wasilla, especially if you're a fan of the Last Great Race. It helps, too, that admission is free. There's a small museum where race memorabilia are on display, and thanks to the wonders of taxidermy, you can even see Leonard Seppala's lead dog Togo, who took his team 340 miles through a Norton Sound blizzard to deliver diphtheria serum to Nome. You'll also see Andy, the dog that led Rick Swenson to four of his five Iditarod wins. You also can watch video footage of past races and visit the extensive gift shop. Sled-dog (cart) rides are available in the summer, weather permitting, for a fee. The race headquarters is open daily from mid-May through mid-September and Monday through Friday during the winter.

MUSEUM OF ALASKA TRANSPORTATION AND INDUSTRY $$
3800 West Neuser Dr.
(907) 376-1211
Given the vast expanse to be traveled in our state, it's no wonder that transportation is a vital part of its history. This museum preserves, exhibits, restores, and interprets artifacts connected with industry and transportation in the 49th state. You'll see the Bush Pilot Hall of Fame, restored vehicles, a gold mining exhibit, and lots of engines. On the 20-acre museum grounds, you'll find aircraft, trains, snowmachines, cars,

boats, and tractors. Located three-quarters of a mile off the Parks Highway at Mile 47, the museum is open year-round.

TRAPPERS FUR INDUSTRY MUSEUM
5401 East Mayflower Lane
(907) 376-5873
www.fortgreen.com
Trapping is not always in vogue, but it does form an important part of Alaska's history. Tucked inside the Fort Green Gift Shop, the Northern Trappers Museum displays artifacts from the past two centuries, including art, posters, calendars, and antique traps. Located 3.2 miles toward Palmer on the Palmer-Wasilla Highway, the shop also features eight big-game mounts.

PARKS, RECREATION, AND TOURS

In the Valley you'll find a great selection of parks, some operated by the borough and some operated by the state. The 101-acre Matanuska River Park at Mile 17 of the Old Glenn Highway was developed on land that came from one of the original Valley pioneers. Running along the length of the river's braided channel, the park offers camping, picnicking, and five short hiking trails. The Sherrod Little League Baseball complex is part of the park, as are two small ponds.

South of Wasilla at Mile 2.4 of Knik-Goose Bay Road, Lake Lucille Park includes four short trails, soccer fields, 64 campsites, volleyball and horseshoe courts, a picnic area, and firewood. This 80-acre park includes frontage on Lake Lucille, which at 362 acres is one of the largest lakes in the Valley. Only nonmotorized activities are allowed on the lake, which is stocked with rainbow trout and fingerling silvers.

Hatcher Pass is a favorite place to get out and enjoy hiking, sightseeing, kayaking, and winter sports. The Hatcher Pass Management Area, accessible from either the Wasilla-Fishhook Road out of Wasilla or from the Fishhook-Willow Road out of Willow, is large enough to provide great wilderness experiences without venturing too far from town. Hatcher Pass Road is gravel, and it can be narrow and steep in spots. The Fishhook-Willow section of the road is closed during the winter.

Trail options for hikers and mountain bikers include everything from day hikes to week-long expeditions including glacier crossings. Kayaking the Class V white water of the Little Susitna River presents a challenge best left to well-seasoned boaters. Winter sports opportunities abound, with good snow cover generally arriving by mid-October and staying until the end of April. Alpine skiers, telemark skiers, Nordic skiers, snowboarders, and snowmachiners all make good use of Hatcher Pass. Trails on the west side of the pass are especially popular with snowmachiners, while Nordic skiers concentrate in the area of Independence Mine. Downhill skiers and snowboarders congregate at Government Peak and the Mile 16 Trail for a long trek up and a short whoosh down. It's skiing on the cheap and in the open. Be sure to dress for conditions; fatalities have occurred from exposure.

Independence Mine, a former hard rock gold mine now turned state historical park, is a worthy attraction within the Hatcher Pass state recreational area. You can take a self-guided tour through the mine camp, beginning at the Mine Manager's House, where you'll find interpretive displays on gold mining and the natural history of the area. Guided tours will bring you inside some of the other buildings where you'll get a close-up look at the lives of miners and their families, or you can try your luck at finding some of the glittering rock—just bring your own pan and shovel.

i **Petersville Road, off Mile 114.9 of the Parks Highway, is a snowmachine mecca. Originally a mining road, it provides great back-country access for riders from the Mat-Su Valley and Anchorage. The historic Forks Roadhouse (907-903-5660, www.forksroadhouse.com) is a great access point and affordable place to stay.**

Several other state recreation sites provide additional opportunities to access the great outdoors from within the Mat-Su Valley. Rocky Lake, Big Lake, Finger Lake, King Mountain, and the Matanuska Glacier State Recreation Sites all have camping and picnic areas, while Kepler-Bradley Lakes and Summit Lake offer trail access. For biking trails close to town, try the 3-mile Parks High-

Avalanche Safety

Like many slopes in Alaska, Hatcher Pass is a known avalanche area. Snowmachiners should travel steep slopes in groups of no more than four people, riding up one at a time while the others watch. Everyone should wear an avalanche beacon and pack a shovel and probe. Try to stick with windward slopes that fan out at the bottom, avoiding steep-sided waterways, gullies, and slopes with cliffs below. Stop periodically to take off your helmet and get a feel for the snow. Watch for signs of recent avalanches, including wind-loaded snow, recent rain, shooting cracks, hollow-sounding or "whumphing" snow, and any signs of rapid warming conditions. High-markers should start on the side of the slope and turn back toward the edge rather than toward the middle.

Avalanche danger is heightened when heavy snow falls on crusts weakened by fluctuating temperatures, conditions that are common in Southcentral Alaskan winters. For advisories on avalanches throughout the region, check the Chugach National Forest Avalanche Information Center at www.cnfaic.org.

way bike path from Lucas Road to the railroad overpass in Wasilla, the 5-mile Palmer-Wasilla Highway bike path from Wasilla Lake to Schelin Spur Road, the 3-mile Old Glenn Highway Gravel Trail from Plumley Road to the Mantanuska River Bridge, and the 1.5-mile Old Glenn Highway path that heads south from Ye Old River Road.

If you're looking for other fun ways to get out into the backcountry, various recreation and tour businesses in the Valley have plenty to offer. For guided and unguided horse trail riding, check out Alaska Riding Adventures (907-745-8768, www.alotafun.org). They offer year-round riding by the hour, as well as overnight rides and pack trips. Located eight minutes from Palmer off Fishhook Road, Alaska Riding Adventures also offers snowmachine and cabin rentals, pony rides, sleigh rides, and goldpanning. Kim's Scenic Tours (907-745-4003) also offers guided horseback riding by the hour, with views of the Matanuska Valley, Knik Glacier, the Matanuska and Knik Rivers, historic Colony farms, and the famed Sleeping Lady Mountain.

i Birds—and the people who watch them—flock to the Palmer Hay Flats Game Refuge each spring. The area also supports seasonal fishing, hunting, snowmobiling, skiing, skating, and dog sledding. For trail maps and access points to the 45 square miles of wetlands, woods, tidal sloughs, and lakes, visit www.palmer hayflats.org.

What better way to see Iditarod country than by sled dog? At Plettner Kennels (907-892-6944, www.plettner-kennels.com), you'll take a kennel tour with Lynda Plettner, an 11-time Iditarod finisher, then try a sled ride that gives you a hands-on experience with the dogs. No snow necessary for this tour—the dogs train with wheeled carts in the summer. These are some of the most reasonably priced kennel tours and dog sled rides in the state, and you'll even get to meet lead dog Arge, star of a PBS special.

If you are looking for motorized adventure, Guardian Alaska Adventure Tours (907-478-2506, www.youralaskavacation.com) offers year-round guided all-terrrain vehicle (ATV) tours. No riding experience is necessary, but reservations are recommended. They also offer snowmachine tours.

i You can tour the historic sites of downtown Palmer by picking up a map at the Palmer Visitors Center. Another self-tour option features farms of the valley, including an Agricultural Experiment Station, a wilderness nursery, dairy farms, a reindeer farm, and a llama farm. Get your guide to this unique driving tour at the Palmer Visitors Center.

FISHING

The Mat-Su Valley offers some of the most popular and productive fishing spots in Southcentral Alaska. The Susitna River drainage is the big player here, with salmon, grayling, and trout circulating through its clear-water tributaries. We'll focus primarily on road-accessible fishing here, but keep in mind that you can charter out by boat or floatplane if you're craving a more remote experience.

The Little Susitna River, or the Little Su as locals call it, is a great place to check out what Valley fishing is all about. Take either the Parks Highway to Houston or the Knik-Goose Bay Road from Wasilla to Burma Road to fish for all species of salmon. The upper and middle parts of the river yield the best take for shore-bound anglers, with boaters fishing the tides downstream. Silvers run here in exceptionally large numbers, and with a little luck you may catch kings in the 50- to 70-pound range. Pinks and chums also are abundant, making for a lot of angling excitement except during hot or rainy spells, when the waters turn muddy.

Willow Creek is another popular stream with road access. You can fish from shore after parking at the town of Willow or along Hatcher Pass

Road. Salmon run in the Willow throughout the summer, with a lot of the fishing attention going toward kings that generally weigh between 15 and 30 pounds. You'll have a lot of company if you fish near the road, but if you hike into the upper and middle parts of the river, you'll lose the crowds and have a chance at trout and grayling as well.

North of Willow you can access the lower end of Sheep Creek from a Parks Highway bridge. Sheep Creek is another great place to fish from shore for all four species of salmon, with kings being the big draw. Some years the chums run quite well, too. Like many of the Susitna tributaries, Sheep Creek can be high and muddy during hot or rainy spells.

A little farther up the highway is Montana Creek, which runs clear most of the time. You'll find good fishing at the mouth of the creek, within walking distance of the Montana Creek state campground at Mile 96.5. Look for decent-size kings early in the summer, with silvers, pinks, chums, and rainbows in the late summer to early fall.

If you have access to boats, especially those with jet units, or if you want to charter out, you'll find Alexander Creek, accessible from Deshka Landing, a productive spot for all types of salmon, particularly silvers, along with Dolly Varden and grayling. Alexander Lake also offers some great Northern Pike fishing, with a few fish weighing in at more than 30 pounds. The Deshka River is another popular spot that's accessible by boat or floatplane. King salmon run in numbers upward of 30,000 most years. Other species of salmon are also present, along with rainbows, grayling, and northern pike.

For lake fishing, try Nancy Lakes, off Mile 67.3 of the Parks Highway. You'll find a series of lakes and ponds stocked with Dolly Varden, rainbow trout, and, in some lakes, salmon. The Kepler/Bradley Lake area is another popular spot, accessed at Mile 36.4 of the Glenn Highway. Each of the nine landlocked lakes is stocked with three species of sportfish. The best lake fishing is in the fall and the spring. Ice fishing is productive, too.

HIKING AND CAMPING

The Mat-Su Valley offers some great opportunities for accessible hikes that will get you out into the wilderness and, in many cases, up to where you can get a good look around. For an easy to moderate 3.1-mile hike, you can access the Plumley-Maud Trail at either the end of Maud Road or at the corner of Plumley and Caudill Roads. This trail, originally used for logging, can be wet in spots, and you may find yourself sharing space with mountain bikers and ATV riders.

West Butte Trail offers a moderate to difficult 1.5-mile hike to the top of Bodenburg Butte, where you'll be rewarded with striking views of Knik Glacier, Pioneer Peak, and the Knik River Valley. Pick up the trail by taking the Old Glenn Highway 5.5 miles from Palmer, turning right onto Bodenburg Loop and then left onto Mothershead Circle to the trailhead parking area. This is a well-kept trail, 2 to 6 feet wide, but be warned that the last half mile is steep. For specifics, visit www.matsugov.us/RecServices/documents/WestButteTrl.pdf.

Follow the 2-mile Lazy Mountain Trail to the top, and you'll be treated to a sweeping view of the Valley. Since about a quarter of the trail is quite steep, you should plan on four hours or so for the round-trip. Pick up the trail at the Lazy Mountain Recreation Area parking lot, which you'll find by accessing the Old Glenn Highway at Mile 42 of the Glenn Highway, driving through Palmer and across the Matanuska River Bridge. Take a left onto Clark-Wolverine Road, a right onto Huntley Road, and go east to Mountain Trail Circle, where you'll find the parking area.

The Lazy Mountain Trail intersects with the 6-mile Matanuska Peak Trail, which starts off Smith Road past the Clark-Wolverine Road intersection. An hour to an hour and a half down the trail, you'll reach the tree line, where you'll have a great view of Matanuska Peak and the McRoberts Creek drainage. Within another one and a half to two hours, you should reach the base of the summit ridge, at an elevation of 3,800 feet.

For a variety of trail options, you can't beat the Crevasse Moraine Trail System, with 13 contiguous loops in lengths from 0.4 mile to 2.2 kilometers. At Mile 1.98 of the Palmer-Wasilla Highway, take Loma Prieta Drive to the end, where you'll find the trailhead access road. Trails are wide and well-marked; note that the DO NOT ENTER signs apply to skiers, not hikers. From Loop 7, you can pick up a 2-mile trail that connects with the Long Lake Trail, part of the Kepler-Bradley Lakes State Recreation Area.

Hatcher Pass Recreation Area offers great hiking as well. A couple of favorites are the Gold Mint Trail, with the trailhead across from the former Motherlode Lodge, and the Reed Lakes Trail, off the end of Archangel Road, a rough and bumpy access road. As you'd expect in Hatcher Pass, there are great views as you gain elevation.

For camping you can opt for one of the borough or state parks, or go with a private campground. The Mat-Su Borough's Lake Lucille Park and Matanuska River Park both offer tent and RV camping for a fee. Picnic tables, grills, trash barrels, water, and restrooms are provided. The River Park also has coin-operated showers. For more information on these parks, see this chapter's section on Parks, Recreation, and Tours.

State park camping can be found at Big Lake North, with 60 sites, and at Big Lake South, with 20 sites. Picnic sites, drinking water, and toilets are all available at these parks, which are located on Big Lake Road. There's also camping at the Finger Lake State Recreation Site, located at Mile 0.7 Bogard Road in Palmer. You'll find toilets, drinking water, and trails at Finger Lake.

ALASKAN TRAILS RV AND CAMPER PARK
Mile 48.2 Parks Highway, Wasilla
(907) 376-5504
www.aktrailsrvpark.com

This is a big campground, with 125 full hookup sites (20/30/50 amp), at $27 per night. Laundry and shower facilities are included, with a coffee shop also on-site. There's Wi-Fi throughout the park. Ask about their discount for members of the military and the Good Sam club. There is an extra charge for pets.

THE HOMESTEAD RV PARK
Mile 36.2 Glenn Highway, Palmer
(907) 745-6005
www.homesteadrvpark.com

This campground gets rave reviews for cleanliness, friendliness, and design. If that's not enough, try the square dancing every Thursday night or the Sunday ice-cream socials. Other special touches are Wi-Fi and nonmetered showers. They also have the usual hookups, dump station, and laundry facilities. The Homestead has 66 RV sites with 30- to 70-foot pull throughs, plus five tent sites. There's a pavilion on-site, and hiking trails and fishing are available nearby.

DENALI NATIONAL PARK AND PRESERVE

Six million miles of wilderness—that's what this place is all about. Toss in North America's highest mountain, an abundance of wildlife, and a road-accessible location between Anchorage and Fairbanks, and you have a major visitor attraction. Arriving at the park entrance, you may suffer a twinge of disappointment—where you'd been hoping to see grazing caribou, meandering moose, and howling wolves, you're greeted instead by herds of an all-too-common variety—people, as Denali plays host to about 360,000 visitors each year. But thanks to the efforts of the National Park Service and a slew of local vendors, you'll find a nice variety of options for getting past the crowds in the highway frontage area known as "glitter gulch" and into the wilderness you came to enjoy.

The mountain, whether you call it Denali or McKinley (for the scoop on the controversy over its name, see this chapter's Close-up), is the crown jewel of the magnificent 600-mile Alaska Range, which cuts an arc across the center of the state. Several hundred million years ago, a collision of tectonic plates pushed the seafloor over the emerging continent, and the Alaska Range was born. If you ventured to the top of Denali, you'd find hunks of granite thrust through what was once ocean sediment. The mountain is huge, and it's still growing at the rate of one millimeter per year. A bit more active is the 1,300-mile Denali Fault, a source of frequent earthquakes—so don't be surprised if you feel a shaker while you're at the park.

We enjoy this wilderness today thanks to the foresight of naturalist Charles Sheldon, who visited the area between 1906 and 1908 with Harry Karstens, who later led the first ascent of the mountain. In 1917, Mount McKinley National Park was formed, with Karstens as its superintendent. In 1976 the park was named an International Biosphere Reserve for research involving subarctic ecosystems. It became Denali National Park and Preserve in 1980, when Congress tripled its size. Six million acres, by the way, is larger than the state of Massachusetts.

While the park's big draw is the chance to see large mammals such as caribou, moose, bears (both grizzly and black), Dall sheep, and wolves in their natural habitat, the area's thriving ecosystem supports a dazzling array of flora and fauna that's no less fascinating for its size. Watch for smaller mammals such as lemmings, voles, shrews, beavers, porcupines, pikas, ground squirrels, marmots, marten, lynx, wolverines, weasels, and fox. Bring your binoculars and a good camera.

Several glaciers adorn the mountain. You can get a close-up view of 35-foot-long Muldrow Glacier, which stretches to within half a mile of the shuttle-bus portion of the park road. Below the timberline at 2,700 feet, you'll discover taiga, a type of northern evergreen forest. Above, there's both wet and dry tundra. More than 650 vegetative species manage to adapt to these unique land types in which all but a thin layer of topsoil remains frozen year-round.

GETTING HERE, GETTING AROUND

You can get to Denali by road or by train. Via the George Parks Highway (Highway 3), Denali is 237 miles north of Anchorage. Actually, it's the Glenn Highway (Highway 1), a paved four-lane, that heads north from Anchorage, but at Mile 35, just before Palmer and Wasilla, the Glenn Highway cuts east and the Parks Highway begins. The Parks is a paved two-lane road that's relatively easy to drive, even in the heights of the Alaska Range, but be prepared to encounter snow and ice at the higher elevations beginning in mid-September and continuing through early May. Milepost addresses for Denali businesses on the Parks Highway are measured from Anchorage.

Even though it's a main thoroughfare for access to the park, there's a 95-mile stretch of the Parks Highway between Trapper Creek and Cantwell with few services; before leaving Trapper Creek, make sure you've got enough gas to get to Denali. Some of the highest gas prices in the state, at least along the road system, are found at the stations near the park entrance. As you drive north, keep an eye out for moose and for the mountain. On clear days, you can catch nice roadside glimpses of The Great One as you wind your way north, especially between Miles 135 and 165. The Denali Viewpoint North at Mile 162.4 is a favorite stop, as is the Mount McKinley Princess Wilderness Lodge at Mile 132.9. There's also a paved turnout for viewing at Mile 203.5. These are the best opportunities for seeing the mountain until you're well within the park, where you'll be on a bus instead of in your own vehicle.

The Alaska Railroad (907-265-2494, 800-544-0552, www.alaskarailroad.com) runs daily passenger service to the park from both Anchorage and Fairbanks in the summer. Winter service is limited. It's about a seven-and-a-half-hour trip from Anchorage compared to about a five-hour drive (depending on summer road construction), but the scenery can be spectacular and you'll enjoy the personal narratives provided by Alaskan guides, many of them well-trained local high school students, who travel with each passenger car. Flag service in the vicinity of the park adds to the novelty of the railroad experience. The railroad offers packaged tours in conjunction with its regularly scheduled service.

For an alternate rail experience, Princess Tours operates the Midnight Sun Express, also connecting Denali with Anchorage and Fairbanks. This upgraded service includes "ultradome" railcars with glass ceilings and fresh food prepared onboard. Tour packages include accommodations at one of the Princess Lodges near Denali National Park, and you don't have to be a cruise passenger to sign up for one of the land tour packages. However, overnight stays at either the Denali or McKinley Princess are part of the package. For more information, call Princess Tours at (800) 426-0500 or visit www.princesslodges.com.

You also can reach Denali by bus, or with bus/rail packages. In addition to scheduled services, there are a variety of tour packages to choose from. Try Grayline of Alaska (800-478-6388, www.graylineofalaska.com) for multi-day coach tour options. Alaska/Yukon Trails (800-770-2267, www.alaskashuttle.com) runs smaller buses of the airport-shuttle variety between a number of Alaskan destinations, including Anchorage, Denali National Park, and Fairbanks.

Getting around within the park is a bit complicated. Private vehicles are not allowed past Mile 15 of the park road. Visitors must pay an entrance fee of $10 per person or $20 per family and then pay a fee to ride one of the Park Service shuttle buses, aka the Visitor Transportation System (VTS), to travel deeper into the park. You can opt for round-trips of 6 to 13 hours. Starting at Mile 20 of the park road, visitors can get off the buses to do some exploring and/or day hiking. Just be aware that you may need to wait an hour or more for another bus to pick you up when you're ready to return.

Regardless of your destination, you don't want to plan on just hopping on the bus. The reservation system, which has been known to change from year to year, allows 65 percent of shuttle bus tickets to be reserved by fax, mail, or online beginning on December 1 of the prior year. Phone reservations can be made beginning February 15. Thirty-five percent of the seats can be booked within two days of departure, allowing for walk-in reservations, but it's best to reserve in advance if you possibly can. For details, including fares and tour options, contact Denali Park Reservations, a joint-venture concessionaire run by Doyon, an Alaskan Native corporation, and Aramark (907-272-7275, 800-622-7275, www.reservedenali.com).

The purpose of the Visitor Transportation System is to preserve the expansive wilderness within the park. Bus drivers point out wildlife and stop for photo opportunities. Shuttle buses run seasonally, from mid-May to mid-September. In the latter part of September, weather permitting, winners of a Park Service lottery may drive their private vehicles down the normally restricted length of the park road.

ATTRACTIONS

You'll want to start your visit by getting oriented at the Denali National Park and Preserve Visitor Center, a splendid facility that opened in 2005. You'll find the center 1.5 miles inside the park. Open daily from 9 a.m. to 9 p.m. during the late May to mid-September season, the visitor center offers slide shows, interpretive programs, and displays, plus general park information. There's even a food court. A short walk away is the park's large bookstore, packed with books on all sorts of topics pertaining to the park and the natural history of the area.

Another component of the visitor complex is the Murie Science and Learning Center (www .murieslc.org), located at Mile 2 of the park road. Open from 9:30 a.m. to 5 p.m. during the summer, the Murie Center serves as the winter visitor center from 9 a.m. to 4 p.m. during those chilly months. They offer Science Series and Evening Speaker Series presentations throughout the summer, with ranger-led snowshoe hikes in the winter.

The former visitor center at Mile 0.5 of the park road has been converted into the Wilderness Access Center. That's where you'll make reservations for camping as well as for the shuttles and tours that take you into the park (see the

---

i Summer weather at the park can be cool, wet, and windy. Be prepared for temperatures between 35 and 75 degrees Fahrenheit. Gloves or mittens, a hat, rain gear, and sturdy shoes are recommended. Winter temperatures can reach 50 below, and that's not considering wind chill.

Getting Here, Getting Around section above). The Eielson Visitor Center at Mile 66 of the park road reopened in 2008 with a magnificent 8,500-square-foot facility.

RECREATION AND TOURS

Organized tours are a great way to see Denali. The park's concessionaire offers two tour options daily, in season. For an emphasis on the cultural history of the park, take the four-to five-hour Denali Natural History Tour, which covers the first 17 miles of the park road. Along the way you'll stop for several programs describing local Native culture and the pioneer history of the area. The popular Tundra Wilderness Tour takes you all the way to Mile 54 of the park road, weather permitting. A certified resource interpreter will narrate your trip, and a box lunch is included. A shorter version of the tour is available early in the season, before the road is fully open. For more information, contact Denali Park Reservations (907-272-7275, 866-761-6629, www.reservedenali.com), the same folks who operate the shuttle buses.

If you want to go farther and deeper into the park, you'll need to sign up for a Kantishna tour. The tiny town of Kantishna, population 135, predates the park by 32 years. After no small amount of controversy, private vendors with ties to the original Kantishna claims were allowed to bring visitors down the full 91 miles of the park road. On the Denali Backcountry Adventure Tour (907-376-1992, 877-233-6254, www.denalilodges.com/denali_backcountry_adventure.html), you'll leave early in the morning in the company of a trained naturalist/driver, making several stops before you reach the end of the road and lunch at the Denali Backcountry Lodge in Kantishna. After lunch you can try gold panning or take a nature walk before heading back to the park entrance.

Outdoor enthusiasts will find plenty of other ways to explore the park. Short hiking trails near the entrance to the park, ranging in length from 0.4 to 2.4 miles, can be traversed independently or with a ranger on scheduled hikes.

Special camper buses, with reserved seating through the same system as the shuttle buses, transport independent hikers and campers to their starting-off points. Cyclists may travel all 91 miles of the often dry and dusty park road, but off-road biking is prohibited.

If you're planning more than a day trip, bring your tent and obtain a backcountry permit. Permits may not be reserved in advance. To get a permit, you must visit the Backcountry Information Center (BIC) at the Riley Creek Entrance Area, taking about an hour to plan your itinerary, watch a backcountry video, listen to safety information, mark your route, and purchase your camper bus ticket. A quota system is used to make sure you have a genuine wilderness experience. Virtually all of the off-road area is "trailess wilderness." Pets and firearms are not allowed in the backcountry, and bear-resistant food containers, available at the BIC, must be used. Garbage must be packed out. For camping within designated park campgrounds, see the Camping and RV Park section under the following Accommodations section.

Another way to get up close and personal with the mountain and the wilderness is through area vendors offering wild rides and tours of all types. For flight seeing, try Kantishna Air Taxi, exclusive concessionaire for charters within the park (907-683-1223, www.katair.com). Talkeetna Air Taxi departs Talkeetna and lands Cessna and DeHavilland aircraft right on the slopes of Denali (907-733-2218, 800-533-2219, www.talkeetnaair .com). Fully narrated helicopter tours are offered by Era Helicopter Flightseeing (907-683-2574, 800-843-1947, www.flightseeingtours.com), located at Mile 238 Parks Highway.

For a rugged ground experience in the wilderness surrounding Denali, try some four-

i Plastic portable containers called Bear-Resistant Food Containers (BRFCs) are part of the park's "bear/human conflict management" program. Back-country travelers are required to use BRFCs to store food, garbage, and scented items. BRFCs are available free of charge in both three- and five-pound sizes, but they must be returned within 48 hours after a trip.

wheeling with Denali Jeep Backcountry Safari. The adventure begins near the park entrance, where you'll meet your guide and your Jeep. From there you'll head north to the Stampede Road, an old gold-mining trail filled with the bumps and dips that four-wheeling drivers love. Via two-way radio, your guide will point out the sights and narrate the history as you bounce along. You won't be in the park proper, but there's a good chance you'll see some wildlife anyhow. Contact Alaska Travel Adventures (800-323-5757, www .bestofalaskatravel.com/alaska_day_tours/pages/ denali_jeep_safari.htm) for more information.

i The Stampede Road north of Denali Park is where Chris McCandless, subject of the book and film *Into the Wild,* made his way to the abandoned bus where he died. But please don't try to visit the site unless you're in the company of experienced area residents. Conditions can be treacherous at best, especially for the underprepared, which is why McCandless lost his life. The EarthSong Lodge (www .earthsonglodge.com/into-the-wild.html) offers an Into the Wild tour (see the listing in the following Accommodations section).

Then there's the wet and wild wilderness experience. Several companies offer rides in the Class I through IV rapids of the Nenana River near the park. Choose between paddle rafts that you help steer, and oar rafts, where the guide does the steering and you hang on for the ride. Either way, it's bound to be exciting. Dry suits are provided, but bring warm clothes to wear underneath. Choose between two-, four-, six-, and eight-hour trips. Reservations are recommended but not required. Try Denali Raft Adventures (907-683-2234, 888-683-2234, www.denaliraft.com), Nenana Raft Adventures (907-683-RAFT, 800-789-RAFT, www.raftdenali.com), or Denali Outdoor Center (907-683-1925, 888-303-1925, www.denali outdoorcenter.com), which also rents inflatable kayaks and mountain bikes.

Unless you're a true die-hard fisherman, you can leave your pole at home, as the silt surging through most of Denali's rivers is not fish friendly. If you're really determined, you can try for grayling in a small number of mountain streams or for lake trout in Wonder Lake, a 2.6-mile watershed near the end of the park road. No license is required for fishing within the park boundaries.

For the hardy and experienced, there's mountaineering. To learn more about climbing requirements, glacier hazards, high-altitude medical problems, search and rescue, and self-sufficiency, consult the Park Service's Mountaineering Booklet. For a copy of the booklet as well as detailed information on hiking, backpacking, wildlife viewing, photography, and winter activities, visit the park's Web site at www.nsp.gov/dena.

Winter brings new options for exploring the park. The flood of tourists diminishes to a trickle, and the shuttle buses take the winter off. Strap on your cross-country skis and head down the park road, or set off on a backcountry ski adventure. You can try telemark skiing and snowboarding as well, but expect long climbs to get to the action, and be aware of avalanche hazards. Call the Park Headquarters (907-683-2294) or check online (www.nps.gov/dena) for up-to-date weather and backcountry conditions. The friendly folks at the Park Headquarters also can tell you the dates for the annual Winterfest Celebration, featuring three days of skiing, skijoring, stargazing, and winter ecology programs. When snow cover is sufficient, the park superintendent may open the 1980 additions to the preserve (but not the original park) to snowmobile travel.

In the winter you can even traverse Denali the way park rangers do, by dog team. A limited number of park concessionaires offer mushing excursions. Denali West Lodge can take you to within 10 miles of the Wickersham Wall, the highest vertical rise in the world (907-674-3112, 888-607-5566, www.denaliwest.com). EarthSong Lodge and Denali Dogsled Expeditions offers a variety of dogsled adventures from lodge-based to weeklong expeditions in Denali National Park (907-683-2863, www.earthsonglodge.com; see the EarthSong Lodge listing in the following Accommodations section).

ACCOMMODATIONS

Wilderness is the byword at Denali, and there was a time when most of the places to stay near the park could be described only as rustic. Options have expanded over the years, and now visitors can enjoy the full gamut from rustic tent camping to full-service lodges and hotels perched on the edge of the wilderness. Be prepared for a bit of sticker shock, though. Don't expect a full range of amenities because you're paying a lot for your room. Prices have more to do with the short visitor season (the end of May to the beginning of September) and the isolated setting than with elegant rooms and plush amenities. If you're traveling on the cheap, be warned that lower-end cabins may not have the luxury of indoor plumbing. Even more expensive digs may lack in-room phones and televisions, the big draw being the wildlife, the scenery, and the park itself.

Lodge is a ubiquitous term used to describe all sorts of Alaskan accommodations, or sometimes even establishments that offer no lodging at all, such as bars or restaurants. If they're operated by big companies, such as Princess or Aramark, the Denali Park concessionaire, expect large hotels designed to blend with their wilderness setting, typically featuring big timbers, decks, and windows to capture the view. Smaller lodges offer a more intimate experience, more like bed-and-breakfasts in their ambience, and a range of amenities from simple to relatively plush. Likewise, resorts up here are not the full-featured luxury hideaways you'd find in more southern climes. Expect hotel-class services and not a whole lot more at most Alaskan resorts.

i There's not a lot of shopping at Denali, but you'll find gift shops in the major hotels, and the bookstore inside the park is definitely worth a stop. Stock up on groceries before you go, as you'll find only convenience stores between Talkeetna and Nenana.

Along the same lines, you'll find few genuine bed-and-breakfast inns here; most bed-and-breakfasts will be ordinary homes with a few rooms open to guests during the summer season. What you'll lose in ambience you'll gain in great Alaskan hospitality and a chance to visit with your hosts about what it's really like to live in our great state. And if you opt for a cabin hopping for some privacy in the woods, be sure to get some particulars on how the cabins are situated. Some of those closest to the park are packed in like cordwood.

The larger lodges and hotels, most operated by the park concessionaires and tour companies, are clustered along the highway near the park entrance, along with a few smaller operations. There you'll be shoulder to shoulder with the vast majority of the park's visitors, so if you're looking for peace and quiet, you might want to venture farther out. Ten miles north of the park, in the vicinity of Healy (population 889), you'll find a nice selection of cabins and bed-and-breakfast establishments that offer some distance from the hordes of people closer to the park. If you're driving to Denali from Anchorage, you can do as the mountaineering folk do and take the easy 19-mile detour off the highway to the charming town of Talkeetna (population 868), but you'll have to head out early for the park, which is another 122 miles to the north.

Even with the expanded number of places to stay near Denali, there are still a huge number of visitors to be accommodated, so advance reservations are a good idea. For a quicker response, use the phone instead of e-mail during the peak of the season. Better yet, make your reservations before the summer season begins. Some establishments have different phone numbers during the offseason, so you may want to check online before calling.

Unless otherwise stated, you may assume that the places listed here are not open during the winter, and remember that at Denali, winter begins in September and ends in May. Most establishments allow smoking only outside, but we'll note those that offer smoking rooms.

Many smaller facilities do not offer wheelchair access, so we'll comment on those that do. The same goes for pets—assume no pets allowed unless noted differently.

We'll list toll-free numbers when available, local phone numbers, and price range symbols for all accommodations. Price codes show the average cost per night for a standard room for two adults. Codes do not include the borough bed tax of 7 percent. Major credit cards are accepted unless otherwise stated.

Price Codes

$................	**Less than $125**
$$	**$126–$175**
$$$	**$176–$225**
$$$$	**More than $225**

Hotels, Motels, and Lodges

BACKWOODS LODGE   **$$**
Mile 133.8 Denali Highway
(907) 768-2231, (800) 292-2232
www.backwoodslodge.com
Get away from the crowds at this small lodge on 12 wooded acres. You'll find it near the intersection of the Parks Highway (Route 1) and the Denali Highway (Route 8), 27 miles from the park entrance. Backwoods is the northernmost lodge offering a view of Denali, weather permitting. Open year-round, the lodge offers rooms with queen-size or twin beds, coffeemakers, microwaves, and minifridges. Built in the 1990s, the single-story, cedar-sided lodge offers clean, comfortable rooms. You can walk trails on the property, barbeque on the covered deck, or put your feet up and enjoy the quiet. Longtime employees attend to guests' comfort and special needs. Small pets are allowed, with restrictions. Coffee, tea, and hot chocolate plus microwave popcorn are complimentary, and they keep a stock of steaks (for barbequing), microwave potatoes, vegetables, and desserts for purchase in case their guests want to cook their own meals. There are two cafes nearby, one of which is within walking distance.

CAMP DENALI AND NORTH FACE LODGE $$$$
Kantishna
(907) 683-2290
www.campdenali.com

If you want to stay inside the park without a tent or an RV, you'll have to head for one of the few wilderness lodges near Kantishna. They're not cheap, and they're not luxurious, but the experience they offer is unique. Under long-standing family ownership since 1952 and granted unique historic operator status by the National Park Service, Camp Denali and North Face Lodge specialize in learning adventures for active travelers. At Camp Denali, you may opt for one of the 17 rustic guest cabins, and in this case, rustic means no running water. Each cabin has its own hand-built outhouse, and there's a common bathhouse with showers and flush toilets. North Face Lodge offers 15 small guest rooms, each with private bath, renovated from a five-acre homesite claim staked by Park Superintendent Grant Pearson in 1957. The adventure begins with the Camp Denali/North Face Lodge visitor bus transporting guests from the park entrance to the end-of-the-road accommodations past Wonder Lake in the company of a naturalist-guide. Once you arrive at your destination, you can plan independent treks using Camp Denali's resource center, bikes, and canoes, or you can join one of the camp's special emphasis programs on such topics as wildflowers, the aurora borealis, and Native culture. Meals are included, and there's a minimum three-night stay. Credit cards are not accepted.

DENALI BLUFFS HOTEL $$$$
Mile 238.4 Parks Highway
(866) 761-6631
www.denalinationalpark.com

One of four hotels operated by Aramark, the park concessionaire, in conjunction with Doyon, an Alaskan Native Corporation, the Denali Bluffs includes several modern buildings in a village-type arrangement near the park entrance. The landscaped facilities feature sitting rooms and a stone fireplace in the lobby for lounging after a full day of sightseeing in the park. Many of the 112 rooms have private balconies with views of the Alaska Range. Each room is decorated in Alaskan theme and includes two double beds, satellite TV, coffeemaker, minifridge, and private bath. Special facilities include an on-site gift shop and wheelchair-accessible rooms. A full range of activities can be booked at the tour desk, and the Mountaineer Pub and Grille offers a full-service menu (see the listing in the Restaurants section below). This is a pet-friendly (with deposit) hotel.

DENALI GRIZZLY BEAR RESORT $$$
Mile 231 Parks Highway
(907) 683-2696, (907) 374-8796,
(866) 583-2696
www.denaligrizzlybear.com

A dizzying array of options awaits the weary traveler here, from tent cabins with no linens, no heat, no water, and no electricity to modern cabins with linens, heat, electricity, running water, and private riverfront decks to a new 72-room cedar hotel. Basic campsites and RV hookups are available, too. Perhaps not a resort in the true sense of the word, the Grizzly Bear is owned and operated by an Alaskan pioneer family. Older cabins were moved to the property 6 miles south of the park entrance and reassembled on-site, while newer cabins were built with milled logs and tongue-and-groove walls. You can drive to each cabin, but you must walk in from nearby parking areas to the riverside tent sites. Dry cabins rent for much lower rates. There's a tour desk to assist with activities, but no shuttle service is provided to the park.

DENALI PARK HOTEL $-$$
Mile 247 Parks Highway
(907) 683-1800, (866) 683-1800
www.denaliparkhotel.com

Surprisingly nice for the price, the Denali Park Hotel offers comfortable, accessible (including wheelchair-accessible) rooms in the heart of the Denali wilderness area. It's nothing fancy and it's located along the highway, but the facility is one story, so you don't have to worry about noise from upstairs. Each room comes equipped with coffeemaker, microwave, and minifridge, and pets are welcome with a pet deposit. Just 10 miles north of the park entrance, the hotel is well-situated for excursions into Denali. As a bonus, the hotel has three vintage railroad cars on-site. Circa 1943, these troop-carrying cars house the lobby, restaurant, and hotel offices, but they're also available for guests to take a quick look and snap a photo or two.

DENALI PRINCESS WILDERNESS LODGE $$$$
Mile 238.5 Parks Highway
(907) 683-2282, (800) 426-0500
www.princesslodges.com

Though the lodge caters to tour groups, approximately half the guests at Denali Princess are independent travelers. Located 1 mile north of the park entrance, the hotel overlooks a spectacular vista of the Nenana River and the Alaska Range; you can take in the view while soaking in one of the hotel's outdoor hot tubs or relaxing on the deck. Patterned after the great national park lodges, the Denali Princess features a massive 50-foot mural of the mountain, grand staircases, and a 65-foot river-rock fireplace. You'll have plenty of dining options with the hotel's many eateries, including the Base Camp Lounge, The River Run Deli and Espresso, the Lynx Creek Pizza, and the elegant Summit restaurant. You can pick up souvenirs at one of the Courtyard Shops or take in the Music of Denali Dinner Theatre. Meeting rooms and exercise equipment also are available, and there's an Internet cafe and kiosk. You can even check out a climbing demonstration. Room choices include standard, riverfront, deluxe, or suites. With the Princess connection, you'll be able to sign up for a variety of tours from the hotel desk, and free transfers are available from the Denali Train Depot and the park's visitor center. Rooms are wheelchair accessible. Princess also operates the Mount McKinley Princess Hotel.

THE EARTHSONG LODGE $$–$$$
Mile 4.1 Stampede Rd., Healy
(907) 683-2863
www.earthsonglodge.com

Seventeen miles north of the crowded Denali National Park hotels, this hand-built lodge featured in *National Geographic* and *Conde Nast Traveler* boasts 12 unique, charming cabins offering privacy and sweeping views of the mountains. Hosts Jon and Karin Nierenberg are dogsled concessionaires for the park, so kennel tours and dogsled rides (for a fee) are among the special amenities here. Cabin sizes range from the standard, sleeping two in a double bed, to two-bedroom cabins that accommodate families. All have private baths, hair dryers, fans, coffeemakers, and wireless Internet access. Enjoy breakfast and dinner as well as an espresso bar at Henry's coffeehouse, where you can also take in a slide show presented by the staff naturalist most evenings. Packaged lunches may be ordered for takeout.

> Study up on the many wonders of Denali before you arrive. The Alaska Geographic Society features a large assortment of books, DVDs, and maps that will add to the fun of your grand adventure. Check them out at www.alaskageographic.org.

GRANDE DENALI LODGE $$$$
Mile 238.2 Parks Highway
(866) 761-6631
www.denalinationalpark.com

From a peaceful mountain setting just north of the park entrance, the Grande Denali offers 154 ample rooms plus six cabins that accommodate five guests each. In the guest rooms, you'll find two queen-size beds, telephone with dataport, television, hair dryer, private bath, coffeemaker, and air-conditioning (once in a while you'll need it, even up here in the mountains). The log cabins offer similar features, but there's one queen-size bed, a double sofa sleeper, and a twin sofa sleeper, plus a microwave and private deck. There's daily shuttle service to and from the train depot, visitor center, and other nearby facilities. On-site you'll also find a gift shop, self-service laundry, and tour desk. Enjoy fine dining at the hotel's Alpenglow Restaurant (see the listing the following Restaurants section). The Grande Denali is pet friendly with a deposit and wheelchair accessible.

MOTEL NORD HAVEN $$
Mile 249.5 Parks Highway, Healy
(907) 683-4500, (800) 683-4501
www.motelnordhaven.com

Just off the Parks Highway in Healy, you'll find a comfortable, affordable option in the Motel Nord Haven. In business since 1994, the motel has 28 rooms, all with queen-size beds. With your room, you'll get a free morning paper plus continental breakfast in the summer season. There are four kitchenettes set up for microwave cooking. Ironing boards, irons, roll-aways, and cribs are available at no extra charge. They have a nice collection of Alaskan art on display, and they offer meeting rooms with catering as well. Two rooms have wheelchair access. The motel is open year-round, and a knowledgeable local resident is always on-site to assist with your phone inquiries.

Bed-and-Breakfasts

DENALI DOME HOME BED AND
BREAKFAST $$
137 Healy Spur Rd.
(907) 683-1239, (800) 683-1239
www.denalidomehome.com

Guests at this 7,200-square-foot home on five private acres just 12 miles north of the park entrance are treated to Alaskan-style comfort and privacy. Hosts Terry and Ann Miller opened for business in 1990, and they love to share stories of their Alaskan adventures while cooking made-to-order breakfasts of eggs, sausages, pancakes, or French toast. Fresh fruit, cereals, special breads, and muffins are offered as well. In addition to cooking a great breakfast, Terry knows road conditions, fixes tires, and offers his take on the best shopping, restaurants, and trails in the area. Each of the

seven rooms has either a queen- or king-size bed, and some also have twin beds. Private baths, mini-fridges, telephones, and jetted tubs are standard. Guests may use business facilities in the office. For more relaxing fare, enjoy the Alaskan library, the cozy fireplaces, and splendid views of the northern lights, darkness and solar activity permitting. Parts of the home are wheelchair accessible.

DENALI LAKEVIEW INN $$
Mile 1.2 Otto Lake Rd.
(907) 683-4035
www.denalilakeviewinn.com

All rooms here look out over a stunning view of Otto Lake and the mountains beyond. Follow Otto Lake Road off Mile 247 of the Parks Highway, 10 miles north of the park entrance, and you'll discover this modern lodge-type inn perched beside the water. Huge windows in the great room frame picture-perfect vistas. Within walking distance you'll find a restaurant, a nine-hole golf course, walking trails, covered wagon rides, ATV rentals, and canoe and paddleboat rentals. Sporting such fun names as Purple Caribou, Blue Moose, and Northern Sky, the inn's ample rooms are decorated by theme and feature cushion-top mattresses, coffeemakers, microwaves, mini-fridges, and deck access. Half of the rooms have jetted tubs, and there are wheelchair-friendly facilities as well. All rooms have satellite televisions and telephones. In-room continental breakfast is included with the room rate. Some rooms have interconnecting doors to accommodate larger groups.

DENALI TOUCH OF WILDERNESS
B&B INN $$$
Mile 2.9 Stampede Rd., Healy
(907) 683-2459, (800) 683-2459
www.touchofwildernessbb.com

Nestled in the woods along what was the original Stampede Trail, this nine-room B&B offers fabulous views of the Alaska Range. Guests enjoy relaxing by the fire or in the outdoor hot tub. The home-style inn features your choice of continental or hearty breakfasts, including dishes such as

French toast and reindeer sausage or crepes with hollandaise sauce and bacon. All rooms have private baths, telephones, and hair dryers; most have either a country or Victorian theme, with quilts and soft colors. Satellite TV and computer access are available in the common areas, along with a selection of books, movies, and games. Guests also share a kitchenette with refrigerator, microwave, coffeemaker, and sink. One room is wheelchair accessible. The inn is open year-round and offers AAA, senior, AARP, and multi-night discounts.

Cabins and Hostels

DENALI'S CROW'S NEST LOG CABINS $$
Mile 238.5 Parks Highway
(907) 683-2723, (888) 917-8130
www.denalicrowsnest.com
Every cabin boasts a lovely view at this locally owned and operated establishment situated as close as you can get to the park entrance—about 1 mile north. With 39 cabins, they're small enough to give personal attention to their guests, offering hotel comforts with an Alaskan flair. The cabins aren't plush (no in-room phones or TVs) and they're right next to each other, but each has a private bath. Perched on Sugarloaf Mountain, you'll enjoy great views of Horseshoe Lake and the Nenana River. There's an outdoor hot tub for guests, and the Overlook Bar and Grill offers a cozy gathering spot with 76 varieties of beer and a full menu, including box lunches. Courtesy shuttles run to the park and railroad depot, and tour bookings are available.

DENALI MOUNTAIN MORNING HOSTEL $
Mile 224.5 Parks Highway
(907) 683-7503
www.hostelalaska.com
If you're just looking for a place to lay your head while visiting the big park, Denali Mountain Morning Hostel offers a great budget alternative. Unlike some of the "strip mall" cabin complexes, Denali Mountain's facilities are grouped in a cozy cluster beside Carlo Creek, 13 miles south of the park entrance, with a stunning mountain back-drop. The hostel features single or double bunks with access to a fully equipped kitchen and hot shower, and toilets, or guests may opt for private rooms and cabins, including a creekside cabin that sleeps eight. If you're feeling especially rustic, you can even book an unheated wall tent. Your enthusiastic hosts offer free shuttle service to the park four times daily as well as backpacking gear rental and sales. There's also a tour desk, free Wi-Fi Internet access, lounge, campfire, barbeque, and store, as well as three restaurants nearby.

DENALI PERCH RESORT $
Mile 224 Parks Highway
(907) 683-2523, (888) 322-2523
www.denaliperchresort.com
An affordable favorite with locals, the Perch offers clean, comfy cabins next to Carlo Creek, 11 miles south of the park entrance. Some cabins have private baths and showers; others share a communal facility separated by gender. A buffet-style breakfast, included in the room rate, is served in the Perch Restaurant at the top of the hill. No telephone, no TV, just the sound of Carlo Creek rushing down the mountain.

MCKINLEY CREEKSIDE CABINS $$–$$$
Mile 224 Parks Highway
(907) 683-2277, (888) 533-6254
www.mckinleycabins.com
On beautiful Carlo Creek beneath the breathtaking Alaska Range, McKinley Creekside Cabins are a world apart from the busy park entrance area. Thirteen miles south of the park, guests enjoy local color with the adjunct McKinley Creekside Cafe, a popular eatery (see the following Restaurants section). You'll find affordable cabins with a relaxed and friendly atmosphere where guests are treated like friends. Thirty units with full- and queen-size beds are available, all with coffeemakers, minifridges, linens, and private baths; some have microwaves. There's a northwoods feel to the cabins, and most of the beds feature handmade log posts crafted by one of the locals. There's no in-room phone or TV, but you can get your entertainment the old-fashioned way by meeting fellow

travelers around the creek-side campfire pit, the outdoor grill, or the horseshoe pit. There's a family suite cabin, and children will love the playground. One cabin offers wheelchair access.

i For a real learning experience, check out the small group classes, field seminars, and research internships offered by the Denali Institute. The schedule is updated each December for the following summer. Call (888) 688–1269 or e-mail courses@denaliinstitute.org for more information.

Campgrounds and RV Parks

DENALI NATIONAL PARK CAMPGROUNDS
(866) 761-6629
www.reservedenali.com

There's nothing quite like waking to a full, close-up view of Mount McKinley, which happens best (and cheapest) if you ride all the way into the park and pitch your tent at Wonder Lake for one of the ultimate Alaskan camping experiences. But be warned: Vicious mosquitoes also hang out near Wonder Lake from June through mid-August, when they die off with nighttime frosts. From Wonder Lake, you can hike the McKinley Bar Trail, the original access route for climbers. Wonder Lake is one of three tent-only campgrounds along the park road, though tent camping may be occasionally restricted due to bear or wolf activity.

Within the park, the Denali National Park concessionaire, Aramark, operates a total of five campgrounds. Riley Creek, right at the park entrance, offers 146 sites for RVs and tents and is open year-round. All other campgrounds are open only during the summer season, with Wonder Lake (for tents only) opening later than the rest due to the higher altitude. Savage River has 33 sites for RVs and tents, with three sites for large groups. At Sanctuary River, only tents are allowed, while both tents and RVs are now allowed at the Teklanika River Campground, which was closed to tent camping for a few years.

Campground use may be restricted or closed in response to wildlife activity. In 2001, for instance, the Igloo Campground (five tent sites) was closed due to wolf activity, but the wolves have moved on and the campground has been reopened. Check online for up-to-date information on such closures.

Reservations are recommended for all except Igloo and Sanctuary Rivers, which take walk-ins only. Since Denali is among the most popular Alaskan destinations, the sooner you make your reservations, the better—reservations are taken beginning December 1 for the following season. Check online for current fees, restrictions, and cancellation policies. But when it comes time to reserve, we recommend you call, as the online reservation system has been less than reliable, often showing campgrounds are full when they're not.

If you're tent camping beyond Riley Creek, remember to reserve a spot on the shuttle or camper bus as well. Note that there is a maximum total stay of 14 nights per year within the park's established campgrounds.

Fees range from $16 and up for walk-in camping to $22 and up for RV facilities. There is a $5 reservation fee in addition to the per-night charge. The more rustic campgrounds have pit toilets only. There are no RV hookups at park campgrounds. As an added plus to camping in the park, you can opt to attend free ranger-led campground programs, informal 30- to 45-minute presentations on a wide range of topics. Schedules are posted on bulletin boards throughout the park.

DENALI RV PARK AND MOTEL
Mile 245.1 Parks Highway
(907) 683-1500, (800) 478-1501
www.denalirvpark.com

Ninety full and partial RV hookups are available here, ranging in price from $26 to $33. There's a dump station and 30-amp electrical plugins, and there's even seven-channel cable TV at most sites. Bathrooms and showers are private; showers cost $2.50 per five minutes. The campground/motel complex features laundry facilities, pay phones, a gift shop (with free coffee), and an outdoor cooking area. You'll find the campground 8 miles north of the park entrance. Enjoy hiking trails and terrific views of the Alaska Range. If you get tired of camping out, you can opt for one of the 15 motel rooms starting at $89 per night. Reservations are highly recommended.

RESTAURANTS

Given the park's remote location and distance from major urban areas, there's surprising variety when it comes to dining, despite the fact that many of the eateries are operated by Aramark, the park's concessionaire. In addition to the restaurants, bars, and grills housed in the area's major hotels, you'll find fun local spots offering everything from trendy menus to no-frills steak and potatoes, though there's not much ethnic cuisine.

Given the limited numbers, we've left the restaurants uncategorized here. If you're trying to maximize your daylight time in the park, or if you're taking one of those long shuttle-bus rides, you might want to pick up a box lunch, offered at most of Denali's casual dining establishments.

For the most part, reservations aren't needed at these eateries, but you can assume they will take them unless otherwise noted. Most facilities offer some wheelchair access, so we'll note only those that do not. Major credit cards are accepted almost everywhere, so bring your plastic. Many of these restaurants, particularly the ones associated with hotels, are only open seasonally, from the end of May to the beginning of September or thereabouts. We'll note those that are open year-round.

The price codes show what you can expect to pay for dinner for two, not including appetizers, cocktails, dessert, and tips.

Price Codes

$.................. Less than $30
$$ .... $30–$45
$$$ .... $46–$60
$$$$ .... More than $60

ALPENGLOW RESTAURANT $$$$
Grande Denali Lodge
Mile 238.2 Parks Highway
(866) 761-6631
Offering fine dining with a mountain view, this Alaskan steak house operated by Aramark serves up regional favorites along with chef-inspired creations. Featuring Hurst Ranch organic beef, the Alpenglow also promotes sustainable cuisine by using organically grown vegetables from a supplier in Alaska's fertile Matanuska-Susitna Valley. Baked French Onion Soup, Prime Rib of Beef, a 24-ounce porterhouse steak, and filet mignon are among the favorites on the menu. For a side dish, try the Chugiak Grains, a custom blend of rices and other whole grains. There's a full bar along with a generous selection of wines and desserts. Open seasonally for breakfast, lunch, and dinner.

BLACK DIAMOND RESORT COMPANY $$$
Otto Lake Rd.
Mile 247 Parks Highway
(907) 683-4653
For fresh Italian and American food, this is a great Denali-area find. Ask the friendly, accommodating waitstaff to seat you at one of the restaurant's big windows so you can take in the panoramic mountain views while you enjoy specialties such as Fresh Grilled Alaskan Salmon and Herb-Crusted Prime Rib. All entrees come with a choice of Caesar salad, mixed green salad, or homemade soup. Sides include risotto, seasonal vegetables, grilled vegetable skewers, and Yukon Gold baked potatoes with all the fixings. Beer and wine are available with your meal. Nestled beside a small lake, the restaurant is off the beaten path, but it's worth the trip. Open year-round. And surprise—there's even a nine-hole golf course.

COURTYARD CAFE $
McKinley Chalet
Mile 238 Parks Highway
(866) 761-6631
If you're looking for a simple, hearty meal close to the park, this is the place. You'll know you've

found it when you see the glass-cased, floor-to-ceiling rotisserie oven. The cafe has a casual feel, with both indoor and (on those warmer days) outdoor seating. There's a big breakfast buffet daily, featuring fruits, cold cereals, and pastries, plus a full lineup of eggs and meats. At lunch, try their homemade soups and generous sandwiches, or sample the salad bar. Carving stations with slabs of meat are set up for both lunch and dinner. One of a couple of restaurants claiming Denali's best burgers, the Courtyard is open all day long, serving dinner as well. It's also operated by Aramark.

MCKINLEY CREEKSIDE CAFE $$
McKinley Creekside Cabins
Mile 224 Parks Highway
(907) 683-2277, (888) 533-6254
www.mckinleycabins.com

Here's a chance to mingle with Denali locals hanging out on the creekside deck and basking in the long rays of the summer sun. The Creekside, as locals call it, is an A-frame cafe popular for its breathtaking views and tasty Alaskan fare. Two enterprising women opened with a tiny eatery and a few cabins back in 1997, and their business has been growing by leaps and bounds ever since. Try the Alaskan Baked Salmon with apples, brown sugar, and almonds; Alaskan Baked Halibut smothered in a creamy sauce of artichoke hearts, spinach, and Parmesan cheese; Coconut Salmon and Chips; or Holly's Homemade Chili and Cornbread. The Creekside is open seasonally for breakfast, lunch, and dinner. Beer and wine are available. You'll find the cafe 13 miles south of the park entrance, and there's a gravel parking lot in front. While reservations are not required, they appreciate advance notice for large groups.

MOUNTAINEER PUB AND GRILLE $$$
Denali Bluffs Hotel
Mile 238.4 Parks Highway
(907) 683-7000, (800) 276-7234

If you're looking for fun, casual dining, the Mountaineer Pub and Grille (another Aramark property) offers Alaskan-brewed beers and microbrews

along with a full menu for breakfast, lunch, and dinner. There's something for everyone on the eclectic menu, from such comfort foods as Baked Macaroni and Cheese to their popular Caesar salad and Alaskan Salmon Chowder, served in a fresh bread bowl. There's a wide assortment of burgers, including the salmon burger, and sandwiches, too. The Wild Turkey Wrap is a popular choice. You'll find the Alaskan-themed restaurant inside the Denali Bluffs Hotel.

NENANA VIEW BAR AND GRILLE $$$$
McKinley Chalet Resort
Mile 238 Parks Highway
(907) 683-8200, (800) 276-7234

Fireside dining with stunning river views, along with a diverse menu, create the draw at the Nenana View Bar and Grille, located within Aramark's McKinley Chalet Resort. Fresh from the huge wood-fired oven, enjoy such specialty pizzas as the Solstice, with sun-dried tomatoes, spinach, onion, and goat cheese, or the Grande Alaskan, with smoked salmon, carmelized onions, mushrooms, roasted red peppers, and provolone. Lamb shanks, Caribou Tenderloin, and Kodiak Diver Scallops seared with spinach, fennel, and saffron are popular entrees. This place offers the largest wine selection between Anchorage and Fairbanks, pouring some 80 wines by the glass. The Nenana View Bar, with log decor and a river view, sports a menu of appetizers and entrees. For those who burned a whole bunch of calories hiking around the park, the bar hosts a late-night "Hungry Hour" featuring complimentary snacks and half-price menu items.

OVERLOOK BAR AND GRILL $$$
Mile 238.6 Parks Highway
(907) 683-2723, (888) 917-8130
www.denalicrowsnest.com/overlook.htm

A favorite with locals and one of the best spots to dine between Anchorage and Fairbanks, the Overlook is a full-service restaurant featuring halibut, seafood, salmon, steaks, and burgers. For lighter appetites, try their pastas or tasty salads. Choose from a large selection of wines and 76 types of beer,

Close-up

The Great One

It's a big mountain, so it's no surprise that it comes with big controversies, big dreams, and big risks.

The controversies begin with the simple matter of its name. In 1896, prospector William Dickey made a political statement in favor of the gold standard by naming the mountain after Presidential nominee William McKinley of Ohio. But Alaskans refer to the mountain as Denali, one of its traditional Athabascan names, commonly translated as "the great one" but more accurately meaning "the high one." Proponents of the traditional moniker point out that President McKinley never visited the state and had little to do with it during his short and rather undistinguished term as president. Moreover, they say, naming a geographic feature after a person is not in keeping with Alaskan Native traditions.

In 1975, Gov. Jay Hammond, with the support of the Alaska Legislature and the Alaska Board of Geographic Names, appealed to the U.S Board of Geographic Names for an official name change. But the Ohio congressional delegation fought back with what has become an annual stall tactic: introducing federal legislation to attach the name McKinley permanently to the mountain. So far, the ploy has worked. The U.S. Board of Names has a long-standing policy of not considering changes while legislation is pending, and legislation on this matter seems to be perpetually pending. The only concession to the state's request has been an official change in the name of the park from Mount McKinley National Park to Denali National Park and Preserve.

Then there's the controversy over who was first to scale the mountain. There's no disputing the claims of the Stuck expedition, which included Alaskan Native Walter Harper, to the first ascent of the true summit, the higher south peak. Stuck, by the way, insisted on calling the mountain Denali, out of respect for the Native people whom he served as Episcopal archdeacon of the Yukon. However, two parties made earlier claims to reaching the top. The 1910 Sourdough Expedition planted a spruce pole at the top of the north peak but provided no evidence of mounting the south peak. Even earlier, in 1906, Dr. Frederick Cook claimed his expedition reached the summit, but the photograph he offered shows it was a lesser peak. The debate over the validity of Cook's ascent continues to rage.

Most visitors are content with just seeing the 20,320-foot peak. Or maybe it's 20,306 feet, according to a survey done in 1989—that's another controversy. The mountain eludes many. Depending on who you talk to, there's a 20 to 40 percent chance of actually seeing Mount McKinley on any given day. It's tall enough to make its own weather, and that means lots of clouds. The lucky ones are treated to a magnificent sight. The south slope rises 17,000 feet in just 12 miles, making for a spectacular vista.

If you really want to see the mountain, you can try scaling it yourself. It's no small feat, fraught with risks, but enough quasi-amateurs have tried that it's earned the dubious distinction of "the midlife crisis mountain." In no uncertain terms, the park service warns that ascents should not be attempted by the unprepared, the uninitiated, or the inexperienced.

Would-be climbers must register at the Talkeetna Ranger Station 60 days in advance of their trek, pay the requisite fees, and attend to the rules, regulations, and advice of those who know what they're in for. Though there are some 30 routes up the mountain, the West Buttress

including Alaskan Brewing Company beverages on tap. Great service, killer views, and warm ambience make this a place you'll rave about to your friends. Open from 11 a.m. to 11 p.m. in season.

RABIDEAU'S CLEAR SKY LODGE   **$$$**
Mile 280 Parks Highway
(907) 582-2251

For hearty, traditional fare in a big-woods set-route (also known as "The Butt") is by far the most popular. Climbers fly in by ski plane from Talkeetna to the base camp at 7,200 feet and then work their way up the slope in an average of 17 days. During the short climbing season from May through July, the route is not exactly a wilderness journey, as several hundred climbers follow the same route up and back.

Though the climb is not technically difficult, the hazards are many. Bad weather often strikes without warning, spinning off a semipermanent low pressure area near the Aleutian Islands. Strong storms also can move in from the Gulf of Alaska, bringing hurricane-force winds and swirling snow. Even when the skies are clear, winds at the summit may exceed 100 mph—strong enough to toss unsuspecting climbers down the mountain. Winter climbing? Don't even think of it. Even the most experienced have disappeared or been found flash-frozen from wind chills so cold that they're off the charts.

Rescue operations are perilous for everyone. Climbers are warned to be self-sufficient and not depend on others to bail them out of dangerous situations. Solo climbers are particularly at risk, given the deadly crevasses that crisscross the glaciers. Crevasses may be either faintly visible or not visible at all, and the strength of snow bridges may not be easily discernible. For a well-roped climber in a group, these hazards are merely frightening; for the solo climber, they may end up providing a final resting place.

Proper gear is essential. Climbers need double boots with vapor barriers (Alaskans call the military variety "bunny boots"), worn with several pairs of socks. To avoid trench foot, which can be as debilitating as frostbite, feet must be kept dry at night. Sleeping bags must be large enough to accommodate extra layers of clothes, inner boots, and a water bottle. Each person in the party needs a pair of snowshoes or skis to help "float" hidden crevasses. Snow shovels, snow saws, expedition-quality tents, rope, ice axes, crampons, snow and ice anchors, eye protection, medical kits, sleds, stoves, radio—the list of necessities is long and crucial. In addition, you'll need three weeks' worth of food that will provide 4,000 to 5,000 calories per person per day and at least four liters of fluid per person per day.

At Latitude 60, the barometric pressure is lower than in more southerly climes, so Denali is more like a peak of 23,000 feet in terms of its physiological effects on climbers. Acute mountain sickness and its deadly counterparts, high altitude cerebral edema and high altitude pulmonary edema, are among the hazards to be reckoned with. Frostbite, diarrhea, and dehydration threaten climbers as well. Mountaineers on Denali also have died of carbon monoxide poisoning, the result of poorly vented ice-glazed igloos and snow caves.

With the lack of oxygen at high altitudes, climbers can become their own worst enemies as mental function is impaired. Bradford Washburn, pioneer of the mountain's West Buttress route, ran his stranded party through a series of mathematics problems at 18,200 feet and found it took them twice as long to answer as it did at the 7,000-foot base camp. In other words, their mental function was decreased by 50 percent. Experienced climbers admit that impaired judgment and apathy can set in along with irritability and phobias, leading to them potentially risking both life and limb.

Every summer, reports of accidents and fatalities at Denali are common fare in Alaskan newspapers. Most of these, according to the Denali Park Rangers, could have been prevented by better planning and judgment, including preparation for worst-case weather scenarios. The Great One is nothing to fool around with.

ting, you can't beat Rabideau's. The restaurant is rustic but clean, with a log bar and animal hides on the walls. It's a great place to mingle with the locals, including servicemen from nearby Clear, and enjoy a steak or burger. Their claim to fame is steak, with the 12-ounce New York steak and steak sandwiches as popular fare. Open since 1961, Rabideau's is a real sourdough establishment. They serve lunch and dinner, and they're open year-round. There's a full bar and ample parking, but the restaurant is not wheelchair accessible. Reservations are accepted only for parties of eight or more.

ROSE'S CAFE $

Mile 249.5 Parks Highway, Healy
(907) 683-7673
rosescafealaska.com/

Here's a clean, family-oriented cafe that serves traditional roadside fare for tourists, locals, and workers in the area. Large windows, front and back, showcase mountain views. Forget your diet and indulge in cafe favorites, such as the Crispy Chicken Burger with Ham and Cheese, the Bacon Burger with Fries, the Denali (three-egg) omelet, or the Plate-Size Pancakes. Still hungry? There's always the one-pound Grizzly Burger with ham, egg, Swiss, and American cheese. Or take the Rose's challenge and try to top the record of Grizzly Burger consumption: five pounds for a man, two for a woman. The cafe also features homemade pies, cakes, and desserts. Sack lunches are available for takeout. Rose's is open year-round, seven days a week, serving breakfast, lunch, and dinner. There's plenty of parking, even for big RVs. You'll find the cafe about 12 miles north of the park entrance, next to the Motel Nord Haven in Healy.

SUMMIT DINING ROOM $$$

Denali Princess Wilderness Lodge
Mile 238.5 Parks Highway
(907) 683-2282, (800) 426-0500

Overlooking the Nenana River Canyon near the entrance to Denali National Park, the Summit Dining Room offers a fine-dining experience complete with live music and, yes, real linens. Tables on three levels offer unobstructed views from a huge wall of windows. The menu features Alaskan cuisine with an emphasis on Northwest

i Believe it or not, dinosaurs used to roam the area that is now Denali National Park. In 2006, a unique three-toed print was discovered here. Scientists speculate that the creature resembled an ostrich, but had teeth, a tail, and arms instead of wings.

specialties and wines. Favorites include Tenderloin Medallions sautéed in ginger soy sauce and served with toasted garlic Parmesan baguette slices, and the Alaskan King Crab, featuring a full pound of king crab legs split, steamed, and served with drawn butter and lemon. Despite its distance from major urban areas, the restaurant makes a point to serve only the freshest produce. Open seasonally for breakfast, lunch, and dinner, there's a full bar and ample parking. Tourists and locals alike enjoy the casual elegance of the Summit Dining Room.

NIGHTLIFE

With Alaska's long summer days, there's not a whole lot of night, or nightlife, at Denali National Park, but locals and visitors alike enjoy relaxing at local bars and swapping tales of their adventures. In addition to the hotel bars, try the Overlook Bar and Grill, with great views of the Nenana River and Horseshoe Lake and a huge selection of beer and wine, including Alaskan Brewing Company brews on tap (see our full write-up under Restaurants, above). They offer courtesy transportation anywhere in the Denali park area (907-683-2723, www.denalicrowsnest.com).

You can enjoy song, dance, and stories while feasting on a family-style meal served by one of the actors at the Music of Denali Dinner Theatre, located in the Denali Princess Wilderness Lodge. Two-hour shows feature tales of the pioneers who first conquered the mountain.

RELOCATION

Adventure and opportunity bring people to Alaska. Those who stay just for the money are among the most miserable, while those with an affinity for the place are among the happiest.

Billed as the land of opportunity, Alaska has drawn seekers of fortune since the Klondike Gold Rush of 1898. Construction of the oil pipeline in the 1970s brought another wave of workers who put up with remote job sites and rugged living conditions in exchange for cash. Even today you'll find opportunities in Alaska that are hard to find elsewhere. When eyes turned to Governor Sarah Palin in the 2008 presidential election, the nation discovered what Alaskans have known for a long time: Young workers can rise quickly to positions of authority here, and paychecks in many sectors of the economy reflect healthy wages.

Since the late 1980s, Anchorage has experienced steady economic growth. Anchorage still serves as a major administrative and supply center for oil and gas development. Expansion of the port of Anchorage is under way in anticipation of a huge natural gas pipeline project that has been discussed for several years. No matter what you heard on the campaign trail in 2008, though, the gas pipeline is a long way from reality—the state has awarded a contract, but the Canadian developers aren't required to build.

Since a disastrous plunge in oil prices in the mid-1980s, the state has paid close attention to economic diversification, so subsequent dips in oil prices have not had nearly the same impact. One in 10 Anchorage jobs relates to air travel, with top-of-the-world cargo flights increasing at rates topping 5 percent per year in recent years. Tourism is increasing at about the same rate. The oil industry, while still a major player in the state's economy, employs only about 1 percent of the workers in Anchorage, albeit at wages that are twice the city's average.

According the Anchorage Economic Development Center, Anchorage has enjoyed steady job growth for the 18 years prior to 2008, and its unemployment rate tends to stick below the national average. But keep in mind that though wages may be good, the cost of living is also high, with expenses in all categories except utilities running higher than averages nationwide. Despite the state's involvement in the oil industry, gasoline prices are also typically higher in Anchorage than elsewhere in the country. Thankfully, tax rates are low.

There is no state income tax, and no sales tax is collected in Anchorage. Specialty taxes include a 12 percent bed tax, aircraft tax, rental car tax, fuel tax, tobacco tax, and alcohol tax. Overall, the cost of living is roughly comparable to that of Seattle. It's important to remember, though, that when you relocate to Anchorage, you're a long way from wherever you began, and getting back even for an occasional visit can be expensive.

Alaska is no longer a place where men far outnumber women. In Anchorage, the demographics are nearly even, with a population that's 49.1 percent female and 50.8 percent male. One out of 11 Anchorage residents was born in a country other than the United States, and 15 percent speak a language other than English at home. Nearly 10 percent of the city's residents consist of military personnel and their families. The median age of Anchorage residents is 33.2, and the number of those older than age 65 is expected to climb to 11 percent by 2020.

REAL ESTATE

Only decades ago, newcomers to Alaska were able to pick up prime parcels of land as 40-acre homesteads. A few of the big homesteads remain as private property, but most have long since been subdivided to provide smaller building lots throughout Anchorage and the rest of Southcentral Alaska.

With more than 586,000 square miles of land, Alaska is almost one-fifth the size of the continental United States. When Alaska achieved statehood in 1959, the federal government allowed the state to select 104 million acres from what was essentially all federal land. By 1967 the state had identified 26 million acres, but land claims were frozen as Native groups asserted their rights to various parcels. With the discovery of oil at Prudhoe Bay the following year, there was a fury of interest in settling the Native lands issue so that development could be pursued. Native corporations were formed and authorized to select 44 million acres in federal lands in Alaska under the Alaska Native Claims Settlement Act (ANCSA). Individuals hold title to much of this land, with the corporations retaining the rest.

Pressure from conservation groups to protect the remaining federal lands in Alaska led to the signing of the Alaska National Interest Lands Conservation Act (ANILCA) in 1980. This measure protected more than 100 million acres from development and expanded the national park system in Alaska by more than 43 million acres. The net result is that there's not a huge amount of land left for private development.

The state does occasionally release state land into private hands through a bidding process known as the Alaska State Land Offering program, administered by the Department of Natural Resources (DNR). On an as-available basis, the state puts together land-disposal packages and opens a period for sealed bids. Applicants must have a minimum of one year of Alaskan residency in order to bid for most parcels, but anyone can make purchases over the counter for the parcels that are not taken by bidding. For more information on this program, visit the land-sale page at www.dnr.state.ak.us. A Remote Recreational Cabin Sites Staking Program is also administered by the DNR.

The Alaska Housing Finance Corporation offers reduced interest rates on purchases by first-time homebuyers as well as on purchases of energy efficient homes rated through their five-star program. When funds are available, they also administer weatherization and energy improvement rebate programs. For more information on purchasing with the help of one of these programs, contact any Alaskan-based mortgage lender or visit www.ahfc.ak.state.us.

Thanks to conservative lending practices and less-inflated values, Alaska suffered less than much of the country when the housing bubble burst in 2008. While values in many Western cities plunged, Anchorage home values held fairly even in 2008, with the average price of a single-family home at $327,000. At the end of 2008, Alaska's foreclosure rate ranked 32nd of the 50 states. More than half of the homes sold in Anchorage in 2008 were in the $275,000 to $350,000 range, and the vast majority of homes were on the market less than six months. In the Mat-Su Valley, home values have dropped more significantly as supply has outrun demand in recent years.

For more affordable housing, Anchorage has lots of condominium and townhouse developments. The Cook Inlet Housing Authority develops projects for lower to mid-income buyers.

i One benefit of using an Alaskan-based mortgage lender is that Alaska has a no-prepayment penalty law that applies to in-state financing. Out-of-state lenders may charge a prepayment penalty if you sell your house within a certain number of years. You also must use an Alaskan-based lender if you want to take advantage of any of the Alaska Housing Finance Corporation subsidies, such as the first-time homebuyer or five-star energy programs.

Close-up

Anchorage and the Military

A glance at the globe shows why the Anchorage area is home to two strategic military posts, Fort Richardson and Elmendorf Air Force Base. Over-the-pole air routes to Europe and Asia make Alaska the perfect quick-response site for action on a variety of fronts.

Located on 13,000 acres just north of downtown Anchorage, with additional access from the Glenn Highway, Elmendorf is the largest Air Force base in the state. The base is home to the Third Wing of the Pacific Air Forces, the Eleventh Air Force, and the Alaskan NORAD Region. It also serves as headquarters for the Alaskan Command.

The original Elmendorf Field, named after a key Army Air Force commander who was killed while testing an experimental aircraft in 1933, was part of Fort Richardson, but in 1948 it was reconfigured into an Air Force base. During the cold war era, the base's NORAD headquarters monitored communications and radar systems in Alaska, including the White Alice radar sites that can still be seen in remote areas throughout the state.

Under the motto "Top Cover for America," the base saw its peak activity during the 1950s, when nearly 200 fighter aircraft were positioned at either Elmendorf or Ladd Field in Fairbanks. Today the four groups of Elmendorf's Third Wing support five squadrons that provide primary air defense for the North Pacific. In addition, the base hosts visiting squadrons from around the world during the Air Force's large-scale Cope Thunder exercises.

East of Elmendorf is Fort Richardson, with access from the Glenn Highway. This 25,000-acre army post is bordered by the waters of the Knik Arm to the north and by Chugach State Park to the south and east. Fort Richardson is the headquarters for the United States Army, Alaska (USARAK), with a capacity of 2,175 soldiers, the primary unit being the First Battalion (Airborne) of the 501st Infantry.

Fort Richardson, like the Richardson Highway to the east, was named for Brig. Gen. Wilds P. Richardson, who commanded troops along the Yukon River and supervised construction of many of the roads, bridges, and railroads that aided in settlement of the region. Established during the early years of World War II, the post was moved to its present location in the 1950s. After overseeing operation of three off-post Nike-Hercules Missile sites and serving as headquarters for the 172nd Infantry, Fort Richardson now concentrates on providing a deployable combat force in support of the 172nd, which was moved to Fort Wainwright in Fairbanks.

On post, soldiers and their families enjoy access to medical and dental facilities, a theater, a commissary, golf and ski courses, cross-country trails, two elementary schools, libraries, and a craft shop. The post is unique in its commitment to wildlife conservation, with fox, bear, eagles, and moose among the populations found there.

Military personnel from both Fort Richardson and Elmendorf were instrumental in providing emergency services to the Anchorage area in the aftermath of the 1964 Good Friday Earthquake. Soldiers, Air Force personnel, and Department of Defense civilian employees also play a vital role in the economy of Anchorage, thanks to cost-of-living and housing allowances that make this "international" tour a popular choice for servicemen and women. While many of them arrive as transients, a good number sign on for extra rotations and even return after retirement to become permanent residents of the community.

Anchorage

Anchorage is running out of land. With Cook Inlet on one side and mountains on the others, areas for development in Anchorage are few and far between. New construction within the city is tapering off as builders and prospective buyers look north to Eagle River and beyond to the Matanuska Valley where land is more plentiful. South of Anchorage, Girdwood boasts some of the highest property values in the state, as the town anchored by the Alyeska Ski Resort has become a trendy residential area that, with its towering mountains, also has little room for growth.

Land prices within Anchorage reflect the shortage of space, one of the factors—along with strong employement figures—that ranks Anchorage among the most stable real estate markets in the country. Lots in the upscale Hillside area run from $200,000 up, while lots in popular downtown neighborhoods such as Government Hill, South Addition, Turnagain, Huntington Park, and Geneva Woods may top $150,000. In fact, buyers are scooping up older homes in these original townsite areas and are either tearing them down to rebuild or embarking on massive renovation products that promise to keep these neighborhoods among the most sought after in town. South Anchorage, with its relatively new construction, is another popular location with buyers, but midtown neighborhoods are starting to come into their own as well. Even rougher neighborhoods such as Mountain View are benefiting from revitalization efforts, including a new mall with entrances off Mountain View Drive. Fairview and Spenard, two other neighborhoods that have suffered in recent years, are also experiencing slow renewal as well.

Residential architecture throughout Anchorage, especially in newer homes, reflects the need to build on small, narrow lots. Builders such as the popular Spinell Homes stack residential space over the garage, the latter being considered by many to be an Alaskan necessity, though that has diminished a bit with the popularity of auto-start technology. The result is lots of cookie-cutter and tract housing, something that may change with proposed zoning changes that would require builders to change up the street-facing sides of new homes so they don't all look the same.

Another interesting aspect of residential real estate in Anchorage is the mix of neighborhoods. Due to some irregular zoning practices from decades past, you'll find mobile home courts interspersed with residential neighborhoods in some of the older sections of town. But the sale of new mobile homes has come to a virtual standstill in Alaska—a good thing, since most aren't

built for subarctic climates—so trailer courts will eventually go by the wayside here.

COLDWELL BANKER BEST PROPERTIES
2525 C St., Suite 100
(907) 562-7653, (800) 982-5205
www.wesellalaska.com

With an upscale office in a prime midtown location, Coldwell Banker Best Properties maintains a commitment to customer service and cutting-edge technology. Their service guarantees both buyers and sellers a commitment to delivering professional assistance in all aspects of real estate transactions. With more than 30 Realtors in their Anchorage location and five in Eagle River, Coldwell Banker Best Properties represents several builders and offers concierge services to their clients as well.

PRUDENTIAL JACK WHITE REAL ESTATE
3801 Centerpoint Dr., #400
(907) 563-5500, (800) 770-2001
www.jackwhite.com

With more than 300 Realtors in five offices throughout Anchorage, Eagle River, Girdwood, and the Mat-Su Valley, Prudential Jack White is one of the largest brokerages in town. This is a full-service agency, with services including residential sales and leasing, corporate and residential relocation, commercial sales and leasing, mortgage loan affiliates, property management, and property maintenance.

RE/MAX OF ANCHORAGE
110 West 38th Ave., Suite 100
(907) 276-2761
remax-anchorage-alaska.com

A major player in the Anchorage real estate market since 1981, RE/MAX of Anchorage has more than 90 sales associates. True to the RE/MAX tradition of attracting some of the top-producing Realtors in their market, the Anchorage office boasts a higher number of experienced licensees, more Certified Residential Specialists, more Certified Relocation Professionals, and more Accredited Buyer Representatives than any other brokerage in the area.

Especially when purchasing raw land, be sure to ask about access to the property. Some lower-priced parcels may lack road access. Even if there's a plat map showing roads to a property, not all of those roads may have been developed.

Kenai Peninsula

Realtor Glenda Feeken of RE/MAX of the Peninsula reports that buyers can get more for their money on the Kenai Peninsula than in any other part of Southcentral Alaska. Though the second-home market slowed with the 2008 economic downturn, Kenai real estate continues to perform well and prices are holding, Riverfront homes can be had for $500,000 and up, while riverfront lots may run up to $200,000 per acre. Feeken notes that deals can still be found on raw land with no view or waterfront.

Despite a lackluster economy nationwide, the Homer real estate market is strong. Prices remain stable and values are well supported, according to broker Sharon Minsch of Alaska Real Estate in Homer. View properties, including homes and raw land, remain at a premium. New and existing homes in neighborhoods close to town put most services within walking distance. There are several new subdivisions with strong covenants and terrific views. Rural settings are also available with septic systems and, in some cases, hauled water. Homer is working on a new Comprehensive Plan that will promote infill and support the goals for steady and sustainable development.

ALASKA REAL ESTATE IN HOMER
5260 Kachemak Dr., Homer
(907) 235-4090
www.realestateinhomer.com
Broker Sharon Minsch has been helping buyers relocate to Homer since 1984, so she knows what is needed for a smooth transition to your new home. She pays close attention to detail and is quick to respond to inquiries by phone or e-mail. Mail-outs of current listings, computer data, and even travel information are among the many services she provides in addition to all the usual sales and listing management.

FREEDOM REALTY
Kenai and Soldotna
(907) 263-1690, (907) 262-1770
www.freedomrealty.com
With offices in both Kenai and Soldotna, Freedom Realty has 20 licensees with experience in single-family, multifamily, lots and acreage, and commercial sales. They also represent the builders of the Mountain Rose retirement community project.

If you're purchasing where city water and sewer services are not available, be sure to research well and septic issues. Well water in some parts of Alaska may contain arsenic or nitrates, which can be filtered through reverse osmosis systems. Septic system tests, though not required for most types of financing, can alert you to potentially expensive system repairs or replacements needed.

RE/MAX OF HOMER
412 East Pioneer Ave., Suite 100, Homer
(907) 235-7733
www.homer.alaska.remax.com
The only franchised real estate brokerage on the Lower Peninsula, RE/MAX of Homer maintains a full staff of seasoned professionals to assist with residential and investment sales and purchases. Located in the center of the Homer business district, this RE/MAX office has maintained a strong community presence and a commitment to service since 1984.

RE/MAX OF THE PENINSULA
100 Trading Bay Dr., Suite 6, Kenai
(907) 283-5888
www.glendafeeken.com
Serving the central and upper Kenai Peninsula, RE/MAX provides full real estate services in Cooper Landing, Soldotna, Kasilof, Clam Gulch, Ridgeway, Kenai and North Kenai, and Sterling. You can

expect assistance with buying and selling, reloca-tion, commercial real estate, and raw land sales.

Matanuska-Susitna Valley

As buying a home in Anchorage became less affordable, growth spilled out into the Mat-Su Valley, where a relative abundance of land not only keeps costs down but also affords buyers the kind of wooded acreage that most Alaskans covet. The Valley is a doable commute for servi-cepersons at both Elmendorf Air Force Base and Fort Richardson, making it a popular choice for military families.

RE/MAX OF WASILLA
3161 East Palmer-Wasilla Highway
Suite 1, Wasilla
(907) 376-4515
www.wasilla.alaska.remax.com
Providing brokerage services in the Valley since 1983, RE/MAX of Wasilla has consistently been the leading office in sales, listings, and service. With a staff of more than 30 full-time professionals, RE/MAX offers a complete array of residential services. They also represent close to a dozen area builders. Kristan Cole, one of the Valley's top producers, has her own office (www.kristancole.com).

i Want to start shopping before you come North? Your Alaskan real estate professional can do an electronic search of all listings that meet your criteria and forward the results to you by e-mail. The search also can be set up to automatically notify you of new listings as they come on the market.

Valdez

Valdez has a small but steady market, with a lim-ited number of residential developments in the core area and on the outskirts of town.

SOUND REALTY HARBOR
(907) 835-5818
www.soundrealty.net

For assistance with rentals, land sales, commercial properties, and residential sales, Sound Realty is the point of contact in Valdez. Popular neighbor-hoods include Blueberry Hill, Alpine Woods Estate, Cottonwood Subdivision, and Robe River Subdivi-sion. Visit their Web site for information on schools and neighborhoods as well as local listings.

EDUCATION

Despite the challenges of serving a huge geo-graphic area and low population density, Alaska has a reputation for innovative, high-quality edu-cational programs in its public school systems. As a result of the Molly Hootch court decision in the mid-1970s, the state is obligated to provide local schools even in remote areas as long as a minimum number of students are in attendance. Most students in Southcentral Alaska attend rather traditional schools, but there also are a handful of remote and nontraditional schools, including the innovative programs and services offered by the Chugach School District.

All public post-secondary institutions in Alaska are affiliated with the University of Alaska statewide system, which dates from 1916, when the Territorial Legislature created the Alaska Agri-cultural College and School of Mines. Today the university has campuses in Anchorage, Fairbanks, and Juneau as well as several satellite campuses at what were formerly part of the Alaska Commu-nity College system, which was restructured due to budget cuts in the late 1980s. Kenai Peninsula College, Matanuska-Susitna College, and Prince William Sound Community College are now affili-ated with the University of Alaska Anchorage (UAA). In addition, UAA offers educational pro-grams at Fort Richardson and Elmendorf Air Force Base.

Higher Education
ALASKA PACIFIC UNIVERSITY
4101 University Dr., Anchorage
(907) 564-8248, (800) 252-7528
www.alaskapacific.edu
Alaska Pacific University (APU) is an independent private university with an emphasis on liberal

arts and pre-professional programs. Founded in 1959 as Alaska Methodist University, the university was reorganized and renamed Alaska Pacific University in 1977. Today the 200-acre campus serves more than 500 students per semester with a variety of four-year degree programs. With a student-teacher ratio of seven to one, students can expect a higher level of individual attention than they might get at a larger university. APU is fully accredited by the Northwest Association of Schools and Colleges and has been ranked the top master's-level university in the state.

ALASKA VOCATIONAL TECHNICAL CENTER
809 Second Ave., Seward
(907) 224-3322, (800) 478-5389
avtec.labor.state.ak.us/
Sanctioned by the Alaska Department of Labor and Workforce Development, the Alaska Vocational Technical Center (AVTEC) offers vocational and technical training in a variety of program areas, including automotive technology, business technology, culinary arts, diesel and heavy equipment training, facility maintenance, industrial electricity, information technology, pipe welding, power plant operation, Web development technology, and welding technology. AVTEC's primary mission is to provide vocational education for Alaskan residents. Nonresidents may attend on a space-available basis, but the tuition is double what residents pay. Dormitories and apartments for students and their families are available.

KENAI PENINSULA COLLEGE
34820 College Dr., Soldotna
(907) 262-0330, (877) 262-0330
www.kpc.alaska.edu
Under the auspices of the University of Alaska Anchorage, Kenai Peninsula College (KPC) operates campuses in Soldotna, Homer, and Seward. In addition to offering two-year Associate of Arts and Associate of Science degrees in a number of fields, including Nursing, Paramedical Technology, Business, and Digital Arts, KPC also provides access to UAA distance delivery courses in several four-year degree programs, including Elementary Education, Psychology, Anthropology, and Fine Arts. Certificate programs in a number of vocational areas are available as well. The college offers a full range of student services, including academic advising, financial assistance, career counseling, and tutoring. Serving nearly 2,000 students at its various locations, KPC emphasizes small class sizes and personal attention.

The Kenai River Campus in Soldotna enjoys a prime riverfront location on nearly 300 acres, with classrooms, laboratories, vocational and computer facilities, a library and media center, an art gallery, a cafe, a career center, and a learning center for student use. At Homer's Kachemak Bay Campus, facilities include classrooms, a learning center, a science lab, student commons, a bookstore, and a library. The Resurrection Bay Extension Site in Seward uses high school classrooms for delivery of general education and personal enrichment courses. The Kenai Peninsula College also offers on-site instruction in Anchorage through its Mining and Petroleum Training Service (MAPTS) program.

MATANUSKA-SUSITNA COLLEGE
Palmer
(907) 745-9774
www.matsu.alaska.edu
Originally part of the statewide community college system, Matanuska-Susitna (Mat-Su) College is now affiliated with the University of Alaska Anchorage, serving approximately 1,650 students each semester. The campus has a 102,676-square-foot facility on the trunk road between Palmer and Wasilla, where the college offers courses leading to both Associate of Arts and Associate of Applied Science degrees. Vocational certificate programs in drafting, computer systems, refrigeration and heating, and information technology are also available.

PRINCE WILLIAM SOUND COMMUNITY COLLEGE
Valdez
(907) 834-1600
www.pwscc.edu
Serving a geographic area of more than 44,000 square miles, this off-shoot of the University of

Alaska Statewide system maintains a campus in Valdez with extensions in Cordova and Copper Basin. Baccalaureate programs in Human Services and Science and Technology are provided in conjunction with the University of Alaska Anchorage, with associate degree options in Disability Services, Industrial Technology, and Computer Information Systems as well as two-year general Associate of Arts and Theater programs. Each summer the college hosts the popular Last Frontier Theatre Conference. With the pipeline terminus right in Valdez, the community college also offers training and certificates in Industrial Technology, Oil Spill Response, Safety Management, and Electrical Power Generation. A big plus: There's no out-of-state tuition differential at PWC.

UNIVERSITY OF ALASKA ANCHORAGE
3211 Providence Dr., Anchorage
(907) 786-1800
www.uaa.alaska.edu

As parent school to all public postsecondary options in Southcentral Alaska, the University of Alaska Anchorage (UAA) serves more than 20,000 students every year. Vocational certificate, associate, baccalaureate, and masters degree programs are offered in more than 120 areas of study. The Anchorage campus has a student health center, learning resource center, library, and a variety of student services programs. The Seawolves athletic programs include a whole host of Division I and Division II competitive sports options. The university also hosts eight research institutes and centers. UAA and its affiliated campuses are accredited through the Northwest Association of Schools and Colleges.

Public Schools

ANCHORAGE SCHOOL DISTRICT
5530 East Northern Lights Boulevard
(907) 742-4312
www.asdk12.org

Anchorage has the largest school district in the state and the 87th largest in the country, with approximately 50,000 students attending district schools. There are 59 elementary schools, nine middle schools, and seven high schools. In addition, there is one middle/high school combination, one K–12 school, and 11 specialized programs and schools, including the King Career Center. Student test scores reflect performances that are higher than both national and state averages, and parent surveys show a high level of overall satisfaction with the district's programs and teachers.

The Anchorage School District also includes five charter schools. The Winterberry Charter School for kindergarten through grade six emphasizes creativity, the arts, and the imagination, with use of the Waldorf methods. Rigorous academic performance is the standard at the K–6 Aquarian Charter School. The Eagle Academy also emphasizes achievement of performance standards, while the K–12 Frontier Family Partnership facilitates homeschooling through individual learning plans. At Highland Tech High School, the focus is on entrepreneurship and a digital learning environment. For more information on any of the district's alternative options, contact the Charter School liaison at (907) 868-3103.

The district's student population represents a rich diversity of cultures, with 50 percent of the school population coming from ethnic minority groups. In addition, 95 different languages are spoken among various students in the Anchorage Schools, the most common being Spanish, Tagalog, Hmong, Samoan, and Korean. In addition to offering a strong curriculum in the core areas of math, science, language arts, social studies, physical education, and health, programs

i Cold and snow are expected here, so elementary students go out for daily recess as long as the ambient temperature or wind chill is higher than 10 degrees below zero. Our schools close less often for weather than in many other places around the country. Information about emergency closures is broadcast over local television and radio stations, but you also can sign up for e-mail or text alerts by going to www .asdk12.org.

throughout the district emphasize both music and art.

CHUGACH SCHOOL DISTRICT
9312 Vanguard Dr., Suite 100, Anchorage
(907) 522-7400
www.chugachschools.com

Though the district office is in Anchorage, the Chugach School District's 214 students live throughout sometimes isolated parts of Southcentral Alaska. Although the district has only 30 staff members, it has won the prestigious Malcolm Baldrige Quality Award. Approximately half of the student population represents ethnic minorities, particularly Alaskan Natives. Schools at Whittier, Chenega Bay, and Tatitlek make up the physical facilities of the district, and a homeschool program is an integral part of the efforts.

From preschool through high school, Chugach students engage in life-based learning, with instruction in the workplace, the home, the community, and the schools. A standards-based system is used instead of traditional Carnegie Units and grades. Each student works from an Individual Learning Plan. Through the support of the Gates Foundation, the Chugach model of nontraditional learning and assessment has been shared with a dozen districts in Alaska and the Lower 48.

> **i** Though most of the regional boarding schools for Alaska Native students were closed years ago, Mount Edgecombe in Sitka still attracts Alaska Native students from across the state.

KENAI PENINSULA BOROUGH SCHOOL DISTRICT
148 North Binkley St., Soldotna
(907) 714-8888
www.kpbsd.k12.ak.us

Despite the challenges of serving an area larger than the state of West Virginia, with 44 school sites in 21 communities, the Kenai Peninsula Schools have a great deal to show for their efforts. A high percentage of their teachers have achieved Highly Qualified status, and 76 percent of the district's high school graduates go on to some kind of postsecondary training or education.

Serving more than 9,000 students is a staff of approximately 1,200, making the district the largest employer on the Peninsula. Nearly half of the faculty and staff have been with the district for a decade or more. The district has 14 elementary schools, four middle schools, eight high schools, and 18 small schools that serve multiple grade levels, including four in communities so remote that they are accessible only by air or water, and another that can be accessed only on foot or by all-terrain vehicle. In additional to traditional programs, the district also offers alternative and charter school options in select communities.

MATANUSKA-SUSITNA BOROUGH SCHOOL DISTRICT
501 North Gulkana St., Palmer
(907) 746-9200
www.matsuk12.us

Serving the Valley's growing population of families and young learners, the Mat-Su School District includes eight high schools, five middle schools, and 21 elementary schools. They also have a correspondence program, a K–12 school, an extended learning program, and two charter schools.

In addition to schools in the larger towns of Palmer and Wasilla, the district includes smaller schools in Houston, Talkeetna, and Trapper Creek. Through the district's open-enrollment program, parents may apply for boundary exemptions for their children provided the schools they request are not above their student capacity.

VALDEZ CITY SCHOOL DISTRICT
1112 West Klutina St., Valdez
(907) 835-4357
www.valdezcityschools.org

With more than 50 percent of its funding from local appropriations, the Valdez City Schools has a strong base of community support for its K–12 system, which serves approximately 735 students. In addition to Hutchens Elementary

School, Gilson Junior High School, and Valdez High School, a new middle school is planned. Valdez High School was the first secondary school in the state to receive the National Department of Education's Excellence in Education Award, and they offer a dual-enrollment program with Prince William Sound Community College. A full slate of extracurricular activities is provided as well.

i In remote parts of the state, the Bureau of Indian Affairs used to operate elementary schools. These federal schools have been incorporated into regional school districts. Because many villages and towns in remote areas have no tax base, the state now supports these schools.

Private Schools

ANCHORAGE CHRISTIAN SCHOOLS
6401 East Northern Lights Boulevard, Anchorage
(907) 337-9575
www.acsedu.org
Founded in 1972 by Dr. Jerry Prevo, well-known pastor of the Anchorage Baptist Temple, the Anchorage Christian Schools complex has grown into one of the largest religious school sites in the state. Committed to the spiritual, mental, physical, social, cultural, and vocational aspects of its students, the Anchorage Christian Schools system offers programs from kindergarten through high school. The schools now operate from a state-of-the-art facility with 33 classrooms, cable and video systems, a library, a science lab, music rooms, and a large gymnasium.

ATHENEUM SCHOOL
1920 West Dimond Boulevard, Anchorage
(907) 344-2533
www.atheneum.org
A small, private college-prep school with no religious affiliation, Atheneum uses Socratic seminars and classic texts in a curriculum model that mirrors that of St. John's University's Great Books approach. In addition to its middle and high school programs, Atheneum publishes a semi-annual journal of student work and offers summer programs that are open to the public. The school emphasizes lifelong, relevant learning in a spirit of inquiry.

HERITAGE CHRISTIAN SCHOOLS ABBOTT CAMPUS
9521 Lake Otis Parkway, Anchorage
(907) 349-8032
hcsk12.net/
Since the 1970s, Heritage Christian Schools has maintained an emphasis on quality education, moral character, and academic excellence. With a mission to promote a Christian worldview in a post-modern culture, Heritage operates kindergarten and elementary programs at their Abbott Campus while offering secondary programs at their Sentry Campus. Homeschool and pre-kindergarten programs are also available.

LUMEN CHRISTI HIGH SCHOOL
8110 Jewel Lake Rd.
(907) 245-9231
www.lumenchristiak.com/
A Roman Catholic high school under the auspices of the Anchorage Archdiocese, Lumen Christi promotes academic excellence and compassionate service. Drama, newspaper, jazz band, yearbook, debate, and a full slate of athletics complement the academic curriculum. Located in an attractive new facility within St. Benedict's parish, Lumen Christi averages 11 staff and 75 students in grades 7–12.

SAINT ELIZABETH ANN SETON SCHOOL
2901 East Huffman Rd.
(907) 345-3712
www.akseas.com
A Catholic school for kindergarten through grade six, St. Elizabeth Ann Seton School was established in 1980 and accredited in 2002. They offer one class per grade level and use the same curriculum as the Anchorage School District. They also have a full-time librarian, music teacher, and physical education teacher.

CHILD CARE

Private and home child care programs in Anchorage are licensed through the municipality's Child and Adult Care Program, which conducts an average of three inspections per year on licensed facilities in addition to monitoring complaints.

CHILD CARE CONNECTION, INC.
(907) 563-1966
www.childcareconnection.org
For child care services and information in Anchorage and throughout Southcentral Alaska, the Child Care Connection is an excellent resource. With a mission of promoting quality early education and child development, this nonprofit works with parents and communities as well as providing learning opportunities for child care professionals. In addition to staffing offices in Valdez, Kenai, Anchorage, and the Mat-Su Valley, the Child Care Connections runs an online referral network.

HEALTH CARE

Hospitals

ALASKA NATIVE MEDICAL CENTER
4315 Diplomacy Dr., Anchorage
(907) 563-2662
www.anmc.org
One of the premier medical facilities in the state, this Alaska Native–owned hospital serves members of the 229 Native groups in Alaska. Located off Tudor Road near Providence Hospital, the Alaska Native Medical Center (ANMC) has 150 beds plus an outpatient clinic. It has the only Level II Trauma Care Center in the state, offering round-the-clock attention for trauma cases. Primary-care services focus on patient relationships, prevention, and wellness. Native art adorns the walls of the medical center, which fosters a "gathering place" atmosphere for the Native community. ANMC is a teaching facility for the University of Washington Medical School, and the center has received awards from the Institute of Health Care Improvement, the American College of Physicians, the Emergency Medical Services system in Alaska, the U.S. Indian Health Service, and the American Nurses Credentialing Center.

> **i** When traveling in Alaska, keep emergency preparedness in mind. Cell phone coverage can be spotty even on parts of the road system, so it's a good idea to have a first-aid kit handy. Satellite phones can be rented for remote trips, but they aren't cheap.

ALASKA REGIONAL HOSPITAL
2801 DeBarr Rd., Anchorage
(907) 276-1131
www.alaskaregional.com
This 238-bed hospital provides a full range of health care services, with a commitment to superior technology and expertise. With its own landing strip, Alaska Regional is the only hospital in the state that has front-door access for fixed-wing aircraft for medevac (medical evacuation) services. They offer a free physician referral service, and they are the first hospital in Alaska to provide robotic-assisted surgery for delicate operations. They also house the state's only certified Primary Stroke Center.

CENTRAL PENINSULA GENERAL HOSPITAL
250 Hospital Place, Soldotna
(907) 714-4404
www.cpgh.org
Accredited by the Joint Commission on Accreditation of Healthcare Organizations, Central Peninsula is a full-service 62-bed facility. The 32-person medical staff includes seven emergency room physicians who provide round-the-clock care. Medical services at the hospital include cardiac health and rehabilitation, diagnostic imaging, a family birth center, an oncology center, surgical services, and the Serenity House Chemical Dependency Treatment Center. Community outreach programs at Central Peninsula include

Prepared Childbirth classes, Lifeline, Safe Sitter training, the Safe Kids Program, and Dine & Discuss health care information forums. The hospital is a borough-owned, nonprofit entity governed by an all-volunteer board of directors.

MAT-SU REGIONAL MEDICAL CENTER
2500 South Woodworth Loop, Palmer
(907) 861-6000
www.matsuregional.com

The first hospital serving the Mat-Su Valley dates from 1935, when the first colonists arrived under Roosevelt's New Deal package. When the original hospital burned in 1947, services were spread among a variety of facilities until the current state-of-the-art medical center opened in 2006. This new 74-bed hospital with all private, single-bed rooms overlooks the Valley on a 30-acre site off the Palmer-Wasilla Trunk Road. The third floor is shelled in for expansion to include 52 additional beds plus acute care and ancillary services. The new facility also includes a Cardiac Catheterization Laboratory, a fast-track emergency room, four operating rooms, and one C-Section operating room.

PROVIDENCE ALASKA
3200 Providence Dr., Anchorage
(907) 562-2211
www.providence.org/alaska

From the time that the Sisters of Providence brought health care services to Nome in 1902, Providence has been the leading name in medical services throughout most of Alaska. Providence Alaska in Anchorage is now the largest hospital in the state, with a comprehensive range of services, medical equipment, and treatment options. The hospital operates a 24-hour nurse advice line (907-261-2945) and physician referral service (907-261-2945). Lifeguard Air Ambulance Service transports patients with critical needs from around the state. Providence has specialty clinics for cystic fibrosis, diabetes, occupational therapy, family medicine, sleep disorders, and sports medicine, as well as a wound center. They also offer behavioral health services and a crisis line. The Providence Anchorage complex is like a small city unto itself, including a Behavioral Health Center, a Heart Center, and the new Susan Butcher Cancer Treatment Center, where there is valet parking for patients.

PROVIDENCE SEWARD MEDICAL AND CARE CENTER
417 First St., Seward
(907) 224-5205
www.providence.org/alaska/seward

Services at this medical facility include emergency care, in-patient hospital care, radiology, lab facilities, speech therapy, physical therapy, respiratory therapy, nutrition counseling, home health care, and long-term care. Registered nurses staff the emergency department around the clock, and Lifeguard Air Ambulance service can transport patients to Providence Alaska in Anchorage as needed. Though far from a full-fledged hospital, the Seward center has two rooms for short-stay patients. On weekdays, board-certified family practice doctors see patients by appointment. The 40-bed Providence Wesley facility offers long-term care and rehabilitation services.

PROVIDENCE VALDEZ MEDICAL CENTER
911 Meals Ave., Valdez
(907) 835-2249
www.providence.org/alaska

Physicians, nurses, and support staff treat a wide variety of medical conditions at this facility with 10 long-term-care beds and 11 short-term-care beds. In addition to 24-hour emergency services, the center offers diagnostic services such as X-rays, ultrasounds, and CAT scans; a variety of laboratory services; physical, speech, and occupational therapy; and outpatient health clinics.

SOUTH PENINSULA HOSPITAL
4300 Bartlett St., Homer
(907) 235-8101
www.sphosp.com

A recent expansion project created this 25,000-square-foot facility with 47 beds, including eight acute-care rooms. This small hospital offers diagnostic imaging services, a surgery department, emergency facilities, and a sleep lab. Community health and rehabilitation services also are available through South Peninsula. The hospital's mission is to promote health and wellness through cost-effective, locally managed, holistic health care.

Clinics

ALASKA VA HEALTHCARE SYSTEM AND REGIONAL OFFICE
2925 DeBarr Rd., Anchorage
(907) 257-4700, (888) 353-7574
From their facility within the Alaska Regional Hospital, the Alaska VA System offers outpatient services to qualified veterans within a large service area. Inpatient services for veterans are currently provided through a cooperative agreement with Elmendorf Air Force Base and other local hospitals. However, a new VA clinic under construction off the north end of Muldoon Road is scheduled to open by the end of 2009.

ANCHORAGE NATIVE PRIMARY CARE CENTER
4320 Diplomacy Dr., Anchorage
(907) 729-3250
www.southcentralfoundation.org/pcc.cfm
Under the management of Southcentral Foundation, this clinic offers a wide range of services as part of the Alaska Native Medical Center. Audiology, a children's clinic, family medicine, maternal-child health, radiology services, women's health services, and urgent care are among the specialties of this Native health organization.

ANCHORAGE NEIGHBORHOOD HEALTH CENTER
1217 East 10th Ave., Anchorage
(907) 257-4686
www.anhc.org
With a mission of providing quality, compassionate health care for all, the Anchorage Neighborhood Health Center offers a wide range of medical services on a sliding-fee basis. The clinic provides family practice services to more than 13,000 people a year, including those with private

Emergency Services	
Fire, Police, Ambulance, Search & Rescue	911
Anchorage Police	(907) 786-8500
Alaska State Troopers	(907) 269-5511
Search and Rescue Civil Air Patrol	(907) 272-7227
Coast Guard Emergency	(800) 478-5555
Suicide Intervention	(907) 563-3200
Abused Women's Aid in Crisis	(907) 272-0100
Child Abuse Hotline	(907) 269-4000
Rape & Assault Hotline	(907) 276-7273
Pet Emergency Hotline	(907) 274-5636
Poison Control Center	(800) 222-1222
Road Conditions	(907) 272-6037
	(800) 478-7675

insurance, the uninsured, and Medicaid/Medicare recipients. Dental services, prenatal care, chronic disease management, school and sports physicals, and well child care are among the wide range of services provided.

i **It's almost impossible to find a physician in Anchorage who will accept new Medicare patients, even if they have secondary insurance. The Anchorage Neighborhood Health Center is one of the few options for Medicare patients without a primary care physician.**

NATURAL HEALTH CENTER LLC
3330 Eagle St.
(907) 561-2330
www.nhcak.com
Within this pleasant, bright, and modern facility in midtown, you can receive comprehensive natural health care services, including naturopathy, homeopathy, acupuncture, medical massage, and chiropractic services. They also have their own compounding pharmacy.

SUNSHINE COMMUNITY HEALTH CENTER
Mile 4.2 Talkeetna Spur Rd., Talkeetna
(907) 733-2273
This clinic provides a wide range of family-care services, including dental care, behavioral health, family planning, immunizations, chronic disease management, school and sport physicals, well child care, and urgent medical care. Diagnostic services and periodic specialty clinics also are available. The health center, which has been providing health care in the Upper Susitna Valley since 1987, also operates a clinic in Willow.

RETIREMENT

It's far from the Sun Belt, but in 2005 Anchorage was selected by *CNNMoney* as one of the best places to retire. The number of Anchorage residents older than age 50 has increased by more than 100 percent in the past several years, though the median age is 33. The Mat-Su Borough also reports a large influx of senior citizens, with the number of residents age 65 and older increasing by 150 percent during a recent five-year period. Some retirees come from the Lower 48 to be closer to children and grandchildren, while some Valley seniors migrate north from Anchorage for a more laid-back lifestyle in smaller communities such as Willow. Homer, with its relatively temperate climate and easy access to the ocean, is another popular choice with retirees.

Although Alaska's Longevity Bonus Program paying a monthly stipend to the state's senior citizens fell victim to budget cuts a few years ago, the state-run Pioneer Homes remain, supplementing a handful of private retirement communities and assisted-living options.

ANCHORAGE PIONEER HOME
923 West 11th Ave., Anchorage
(907) 276-3414
www.hss.state.ak.us/dalp/anchorage
Conveniently located in the city's downtown core, this five-story building looks over the Delaney Park Strip. More than 200 residents enjoy mountain and city views from the home, which has a fifth-floor dining room as well as five smaller dining areas in various parts of the complex. Like other Pioneer Homes throughout the state, this assisted-living facility offers a variety of services depending on the needs of individual residents, with recreational and social activities designed to promote independence and fulfilling relationships. Residents include many of the pioneering folks who came north during the homesteading era and lent their energies and talents to bringing Alaska into its own. The Anchorage Pioneer Home is an official "Eden Alternative" home, designed with a home-like atmosphere in mind. This government-owned facility has 78 private rooms and 228 semiprivate rooms, with a minimum age of 65 for residents. There's a long waiting list to get in.

ANCHORAGE SENIOR CENTER
1300 East 19th Ave., Anchorage
(907) 258-7823
www.anchorageseniorcenter.org
For a nominal fee, seniors can enjoy lifetime memberships with a variety of services and activities at this nonresidential community center. Located on nicely wooded acreage, the center offers preventative health services as well as assistance with insurance, housing, home care, and money management. Arts and crafts, games, and a library are among the programs here. Classes at the center include fitness, hiking, skiing, dancing, and computer instruction. There's live music every Friday night and a social hour every Wednesday, plus the Arctic Rose Restaurant and Borealis Gift Shop featuring items handcrafted by seniors.

COOK INLET HOUSING COMPLEX
RETIREMENT HOMES

9131 Centennial Dr., Anchorage
(907) 338-2211
www.cookinlethousing.org/library/elder.pdf
Established by the Alaska State Legislature in
1974, the Cook Inlet Housing Authority (CIHA) is
charged with providing housing opportunities
for those living at or below 80 percent of the
area's median income. CIHA is affiliated with the
Cook Inlet Region Native Corporation but serves
a culturally diverse clientele. Retirement home
options include 75 continuing-care units and 120
apartments, with a minimum resident age of 62.
The 20-unit Knik Corners Apartments, the 53-unit
Kenaitze Point project, and the 75-unit Chicka-
loon Landing have earned awards for their fresh
and appealing architecture and layout. All three
buildings, along with the newer Tyonek Terrace,
are located in a secluded campus in East Anchorage, with nice views of the Chugach Mountains.
There's a long wait to get a unit.

FRIENDSHIP TERRACE

250 Herndon Ave., Homer
(907) 235-7655
www.homerseniors.com/halr.htm
This assisted-living facility features private apartments that overlook the waters of Kachemak Bay,
dining in a common area, and round-the-clock
assistance as needed. Laundry and housekeeping services are provided, as is access to social
and recreational activities. An enclosed walkway
connects Friendship Terrace with the neighboring Homer Senior Center, where residents can
participate in a variety of activities. Short-term
respite care also is available.

VETERANS AND PIONEERS HOME

250 East Fireweed Lane, Palmer
(907) 745-4241
Built in 1971 on the site of the former Alaska
State Fairgrounds, this state-run assisted-living
facility offers spectacular mountain views as well
as access to shops and restaurants in the quaint
downtown section of Palmer. In keeping with

the Valley's historical link to agriculture, staff and
residents tend a large garden that is harvested
for meal preparation at the home. Like its sister
property in Anchorage, the Palmer Pioneer Home
is an Eden Alternative Home, dedicated to the
concept of de-institutionalizing long-term care
with a structure that replicates resident neighborhoods. Its 79 residents range from those living with complete independence to those with
chronic but stable medical conditions. In 2006,
a major remodeling project merged a Veterans
facility into the home. State statute sets the
admission requirements for the Pioneer Home at
one year of residency and a minimum age of 65.

SOLDOTNA SENIOR CENTER

197 West Park Ave., Soldotna
(907) 262-2322
The Soldotna Senior Center has come a long way
since 1986, when the project opened with noon
meals served at the Sports Complex. Now the
center has its own new facility where you can
have lunch, visit with friends, and participate in
a variety of activities. The senior center van provides rides to the center and to medical appoint-
ments and delivers meals to the homebound.

WORSHIP

Alaska's history with regard to organized religion
dates back more than two centuries, when Russian settlers in Southeastern Alaska and on Kodiak
Island brought the Russian Orthodox faith with
them. Though most of Southcentral Alaska was
not impacted by Russian settlement, Russian
Orthodox churches dot the landscape today,
with the Orthodox Diocese of Alaska located next
to the St. Innocent Orthodox Cathedral (907-333-
9723, www.sicanc.org) in Anchorage.

After the Russians came waves of Protestant
and Catholic missionaries. The state was more
or less divided up for mission activity, so in
rural areas you'll find enclaves of Catholic, Mora-
vian, Methodist, and Russian Orthodox influence.
Anchorage is more eclectic in terms of religion.
Surveys conducted by the American Religion

Data Archive show that of those claiming a religious preference from the choices offered, most Anchorage residents chose "other," with Catholic, Baptist, Mormon, and Lutheran faiths claimed in descending order.

More than 325 religious organizations can be found in Anchorage. While the vast majority of them represent either Christian denominations or nondenominational Christian groups, other faiths are represented in the Anchorage Zen Community (907-566-0143, www.alaska-zen.org), the Baha'i Center (907-349-1844, www.anchorage bahai.org), and the Islamic Center of Alaska (907-248-7333). The Congregation Beth Shalom (907-338-1836, www.frozenchosen.org) serves believers committed to Reform Judaism.

The Catholic Archdiocese of Anchorage (www.archdioceseofanchorage.org) was established in 1966 to serve what is now more than 400,000 people, or more than two-thirds of the state's population. An estimated 8 percent of those living within the service area of the diocese are Catholic, with the largest parish, St. Elizabeth Ann Seton, serving 1,500 families in South Anchorage, and the smallest parish, St. James in Seldovia, with five members. The Holy Family Cathedral (907-276-3455, holyfamilycathedral. org/) in downtown Anchorage hosted Pope John Paul on his visit to Alaska in 1980. The Archdiocese operates the Holy Spirit Center (www .holyspiritcenterak.org) for retreat and renewal at 10980 Hillside Drive.

i The Russian Orthodox church uses a calendar that's slightly different from Catholic and Protestant calendars. Holidays such as Christmas, New Year's, and Easter typically fall a week later for adherents of the Orthodox faith.

Among the Protestant churches in Anchorage, the Anchorage Baptist Temple (907-333-6535, www.ancbt.org) and its longtime pastor Dr. Jerry Prevo have a large presence. The largest congregation in the state is at Changepoint (907-344-7780, www.changepointalaska.com), which was established in 1989. Changepoint recently moved from three services at Dimond High School into a huge facility near the end of Raspberry Road. The new church incorporates a themed environment for Sunday school and public-use rooms, with a full-size private plane hanging from one ceiling and a replica of the Alaska pipeline-turned-slide in another area. The 202,000-square-foot building can hold 1,600 people per service. Small groups help folks feel at home, and the church also maintains an emphasis on community service with a downtown soup kitchen, Christmas backpacks for the homeless, and Right Way Automotive, providing car repair for the needy at little or no cost.

MEDIA

Covering the large geographical area of Southcentral Alaska are several newspapers, radio stations, and television stations. Many newspapers have online editions with select articles available to nonsubscribers. Magazines focusing on life on the last frontier are another good way to keep up with what's happening in the state.

NEWSPAPERS

ANCHORAGE DAILY NEWS
1001 Northway Dr., Anchorage
(907) 257-4200
www.adn.com

Though its primary market is in Anchorage, this paper's daily circulation of more than 71,000 reflects a statewide readership. Issues of the paper may be delivered to readers in far-flung parts of the state by small plane, snowmachine, or boat. In both 1976 and 1989, the *Daily News* garnered Pulitzer Prizes for public-service features on the Alaska Teamsters and the perils facing Alaskan Natives. The paper, owned by the McClatchy Company since 1979, maintains a full-service Web site that averages seven million page views per month. If you want to get a taste of the daily news in Anchorage, you can sign up for free e-mail links to the top stories of the day. The Web site also offers helpful links to keep you up to date on the arts and entertainment scene through their "Play" section, which presents features from the Friday entertainment section of the paper.

ANCHORAGE PRESS
540 East Fifth Ave., Anchorage
(907) 561-7737
www.anchoragepress.com

A popular weekly with a fun, independent slant, the *Anchorage Press* is distributed free throughout the city. The *Press* is chock-full of great updates on the arts, dining, entertainment, and recreation in the Anchorage area. Regular features such as "Savage Love" and "Freewill Astrology" draw readers, as do a mix of news and features on life both inside and outside of Alaska. Occasional book reviews, music reviews, and a calendar of arts, entertainment, and other events make this a great publication for keeping in touch with the pulse of what's happening in the area. The newspaper's Web site is updated every Thursday with lots of links to recent articles as well as "Eating Briefs," featuring local dining tips.

FRONTIERSMAN
5751 East Mayflower Court, Wasilla
(907) 352-2250
www.frontiersman.com

Published and distributed throughout the Mat-Su Valley by Wick Communications, this local paper comes out on Tuesday, Friday, and Sunday. You can read abbreviated versions of select news and feature articles online.

HOMER NEWS
3482 Landing St., Homer
(907) 235-7767
www.homernews.com

This weekly paper, owned by Morris Communications, comes out every Thursday with local news, sports, features, and opinions. At the *Homer News* Web site, you can view recent news stories as well as classified advertisements. There's also an online order form for a free visitor's guide to Homer and the South Peninsula region.

PENINSULA CLARION
150 Trading Bay Dr., Suite 1, Kenai
(907) 283-7551
www.peninsulaclarion.com
From its humble beginnings in 1970 as a weekly paper that was published in cramped quarters in Old Town Kenai, the *Peninsula Clarion* has grown to five issues per week, published Monday through Friday. Local owners sold the paper to Morris Communications in 1990. The Web site, which first went online in 2000, offers links to current and archived stories. The Clarion publishes a free ad-and-features edition called the *Clarion Dispatch* on Wednesday.

THE REDOUBT REPORTER
155 Smith Way Soldotna
(907) 262-5162
www.redoubtreporter.blogspot.com
The latest addition to the Kenai Peninsula's news scene, the weekly *Reporter* is distributed through 50 outlets in Kenai, Soldotna, and surrounding towns. Launched by former Clarion reporter Jenny Neyman in 2008, the free paper includes regular features on local events, personalities, arts, and technology.

VALDEZ STAR
(907) 835-2405
www.valdezstar.net
A quintessential hometown weekly, the *Star* has been known to run front-page news with such headlines as "Animal Control Seeks Identity of Biting Dog." A detailed police blotter and lots of classifieds add to the local flavor. At their Web site, you can read a couple of local stories and browse the classifieds.

MAGAZINES

ALASKA BUSINESS MONTHLY
(907) 276-4373
www.akbizmag.com
Written and published by Alaskans with the goal of promoting economic growth in the state, *Alaska Business Monthly* analyzes business trends and features key industries from all around the 49th state. Each monthly issue focuses on a different aspect of the business climate in Alaska. In print since 1986, *Alaska Business Monthly* features a nice mix of coverage including everything from multinational corporations to sole proprietorships.

ALASKA MAGAZINE
301 Arctic Slope Ave., Suite 300, Anchorage
(800) 288-5892
www.alaskamagazine.com
Since 1941, readers of *Alaska Magazine* have been fueling their interest in the 49th state by devouring the 10 annual issues of this general-interest magazine. Columns and feature articles by popular Alaskan writers Nick Jans, Sherry Simpson, Ned Rozell, and Andy Hall keep readers coming back for more, as evidenced by sales rates that top 200,000 copies per month. In addition to monthly articles on intriguing aspects of life in the Far North, you'll find regular features and columns including On the Edge, Alaska Traveler, From Ketchikan to Barrow, and My View North.

ALASKA MEN MAGAZINE
www.alaskamen-online.com
It's not every state that can boast its own matchmaking magazine, but thanks to the vision and efforts of publisher Susie Carter, *Alaska Men* has been promoting eligible Alaskan bachelors since 1987. The mainstream media ate up the concept, and after appearing on several high-profile television shows, Carter created a steady stream of interest in this more-or-less annual publication that profiles Alaskan men and invites women from around the world to contact them in hopes of igniting those proverbial sparks. Never mind the quintessential Alaskan saying about our men, "The odds are good, but the goods are odd." Susie's guys are keepers.

RADIO

In a state where people are spread out far and wide, radio has played an important role over the years, conveying not only top news stories but also broadcasting personal messages to family and friends in remote areas. Public radio has a big presence in the state, especially in the more rural areas, as does local Christian radio. Anchorage stations have a decidedly urban flair, playing everything from the usual (mostly conservative) talk radio to alternative and music mixes.

Alternative
KRUA 88.1 FM   Anchorage

Christian
KATB 89.3 FM   Anchorage

Classical/Jazz
KLEF 98.1 FM   Anchorage

Country
KASH 107.5 FM   Anchorage

Music Mix
KMXS 103.1 FM   Anchorage
KQEZ 92.1 FM   Houston

News/Talk
KENI 650 AM   Anchorage
KFQD 750 AM   Anchorage

Public Radio
KSKA 91.1 FM   Anchorage
KBBI 890 AM   Homer
KTNA 88.5 FM   Talkeetna

TELEVISION

Television isn't something that longtime Alaskans take for granted. Not so many years have passed from the days when there were only a couple of channels available and sports fans had to watch their favorite teams in tape-delayed matches that were broadcast well after the final score had been decided. That has all changed thanks to satellite and digital technology. Rural communities that once had access to only one station through the now-defunct Rural Alaska TV Network now have broader access to programming through commercial satellite television. Cable service is available in most towns and cities through a handful of different providers.

For uniquely Alaskan programming, *Alaska Magazine* has produced a series of 52 half-hour travel-adventure-lifestyle shows about life in Alaska featuring honest-to-goodness Alaskans. Though the magazine's offices are based in the Lower 48, this programming is produced in Alaska, by Alaskans. Footage from the archives of the former statewide television network is incorporated into the shows.

TV Channels
KIMO (Channel 13)   ABC
KTVA (Channel 11)   CBS
KTBY (Channel 4)   FOX
KTUU (Channel 2)   NBC
KAKM (Channel 7)   PBS
KYES (Channel 5)   UPN

INDEX

ABOUT THE AUTHOR

DEB VANASSE, a former teacher and real estate broker, has lived in Alaska since 1979. She has traveled extensively throughout the state, including remote areas of Southwestern Alaska, where she lived and worked for eight years. Her two children were born in the Bush, where riverboat, snowmachine, and small plane are the only ways to get from one village to another. During her years in rural Alaska, she made frequent trips to Anchorage to pick up groceries and enjoy some of the luxuries of city life. Eventually she moved to Fairbanks and then to Anchorage.

A graduate of Bemidji State University in northern Minnesota and California State University at Dominguez Hills, Deb is the author of several books set in Alaska, including *A Distant Enemy; Under Alaska's Midnight Sun;* and *A Totem Tale: A Tall Story from Alaska.* She also edited *Picture This, Alaska: Historic Photographs from the Last Frontier.* Visit her at www.DebVanasse.com or www.49writers.blogspot.com.